John Carpen

ASYLUM

Created by
John Carpenter, Thomas Ian Griffith and
Sandy King

CITY OF ANGELS, HEARTS OF
DARKNESS
Volume one

Jones King Olsen Manco

A Storm King Comics Publication

STORM KING
COMICS

John Carpenter's

ASYLUM

Created By
John Carpenter
Thomas Ian Griffith and Sandy King

PROLOGUE:Written by Sandy King with Bruce Jones
Issues #1-3 Written by Bruce Jones
Issues #4-5 Written by Bruce Jones with Sandy King and Trent Olsen
Issue #6 Written by Sandy King and Trent Olsen

Art by Leonardo Manco

Colors by Kinsun Loh

Letter Artist Janice Chiang

Cover art by Leonardo Manco

Edited by Sandy King

Story and characters by Thomas Ian Griffith and Sandy King

Visual Consultant and Book Design David Redier-Linsk
Graphic Designer/Onboarding Sophie Gransard Davies
Office Co-Ordinator Sean Sobczak
Assistant Editor Trent Olsen
Convention Media Relations Ross Sauriol
Publicity by Sphinx Group—Elysabeth Galati

Previously published as issues #1-6 of the Storm King Comics series John Carpenter's Asylum

John Carpenter's Asylum "City of Angels, Hearts of Darkness" Volume One, October 2014.
Published by Storm King Comics, a division of Storm King Productions, Inc.

PRINTED IN CANADA

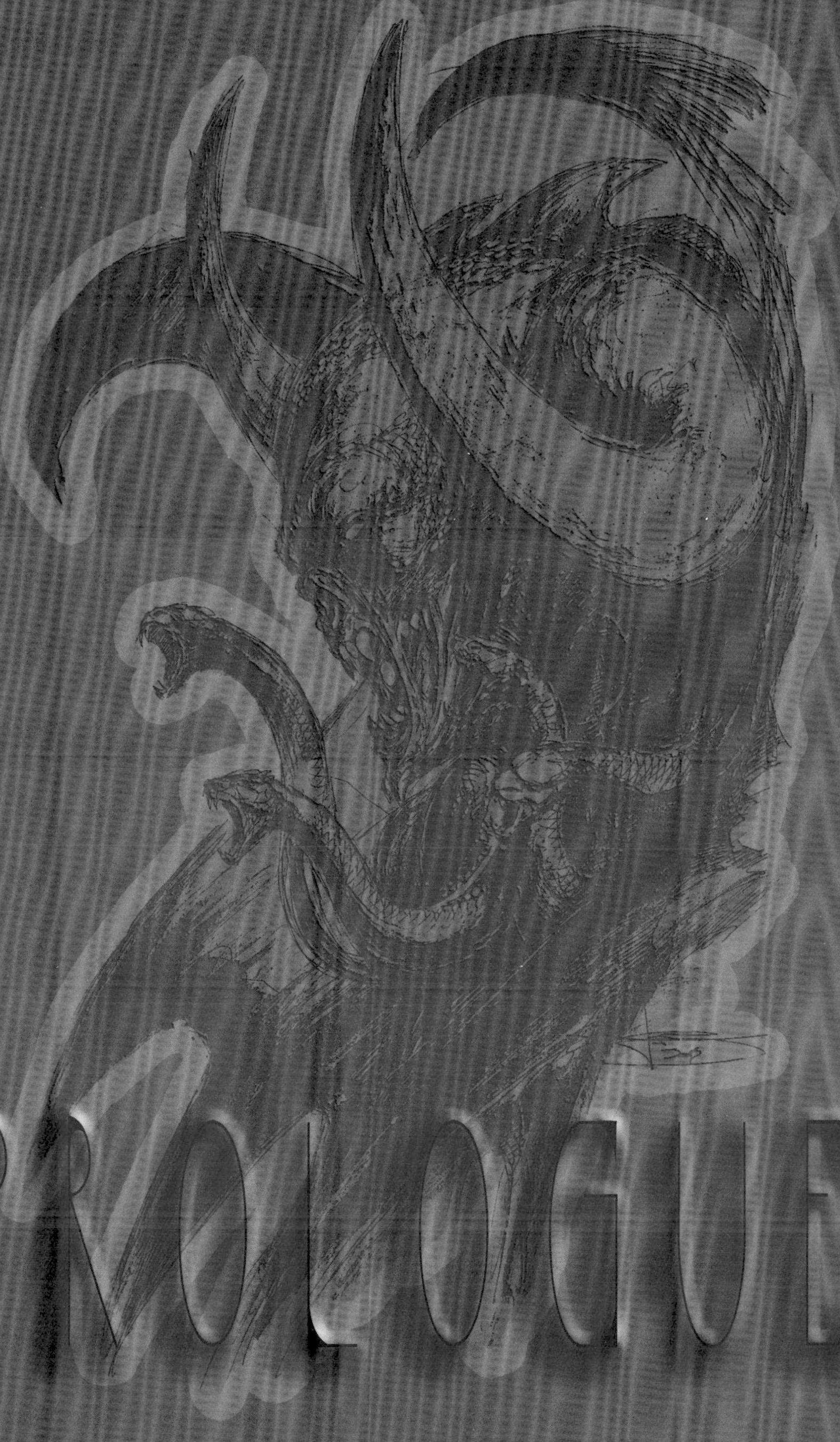

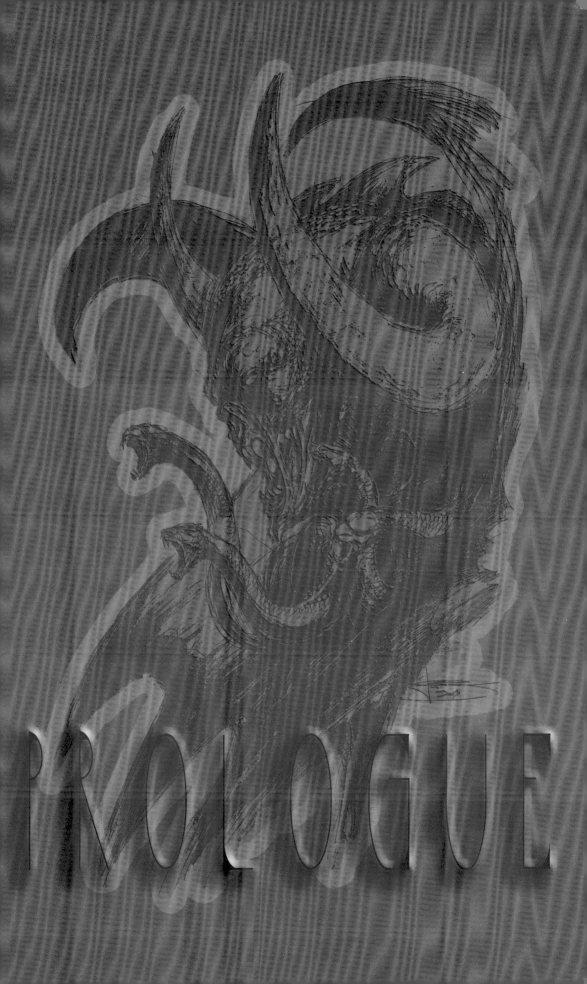

PROLOGUE

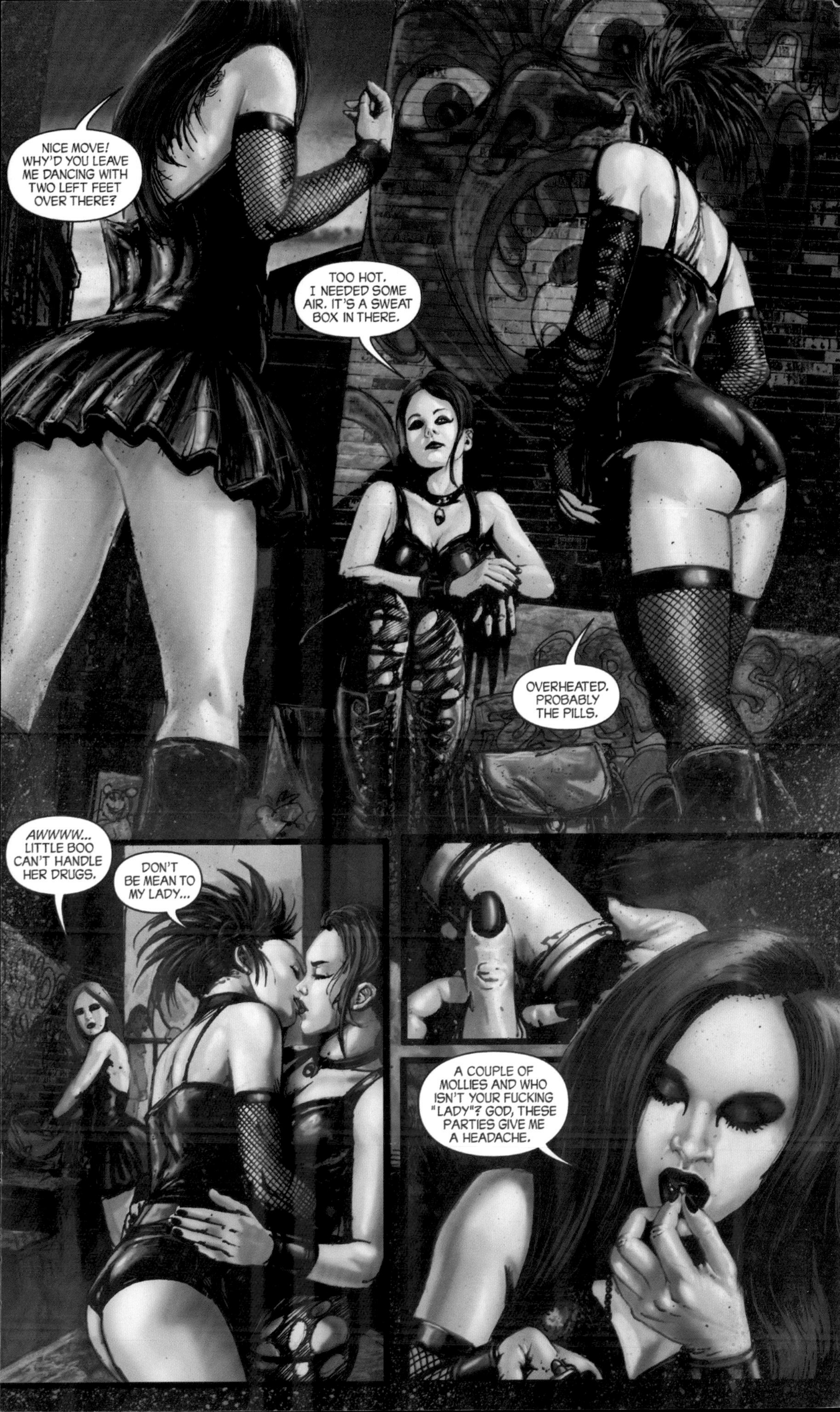
NICE MOVE! WHY'D YOU LEAVE ME DANCING WITH TWO LEFT FEET OVER THERE?
TOO HOT. I NEEDED SOME AIR. IT'S A SWEAT BOX IN THERE.
OVERHEATED. PROBABLY THE PILLS.
AWWWW... LITTLE BOO CAN'T HANDLE HER DRUGS.
DON'T BE MEAN TO MY LADY...
A COUPLE OF MOLLIES AND WHO ISN'T YOUR FUCKING "LADY"? GOD, THESE PARTIES GIVE ME A HEADACHE.

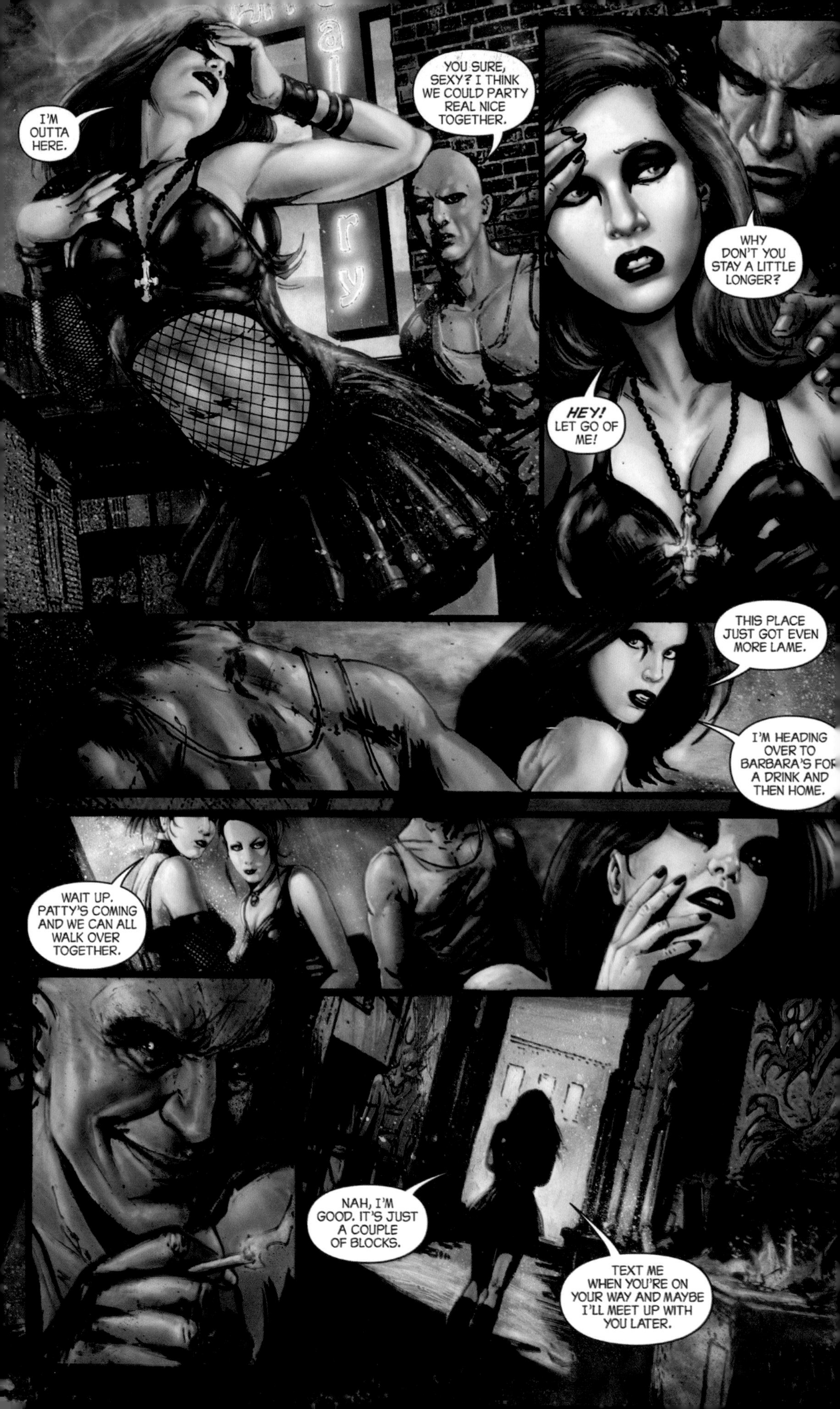
I'M OUTTA HERE.
YOU SURE, SEXY? I THINK WE COULD PARTY REAL NICE TOGETHER.
WHY DON'T YOU STAY A LITTLE LONGER?
HEY! LET GO OF ME!
THIS PLACE JUST GOT EVEN MORE LAME.
I'M HEADING OVER TO BARBARA'S FOR A DRINK AND THEN HOME.
WAIT UP. PATTY'S COMING AND WE CAN ALL WALK OVER TOGETHER.
NAH, I'M GOOD. IT'S JUST A COUPLE OF BLOCKS.
TEXT ME WHEN YOU'RE ON YOUR WAY AND MAYBE I'LL MEET UP WITH YOU LATER.

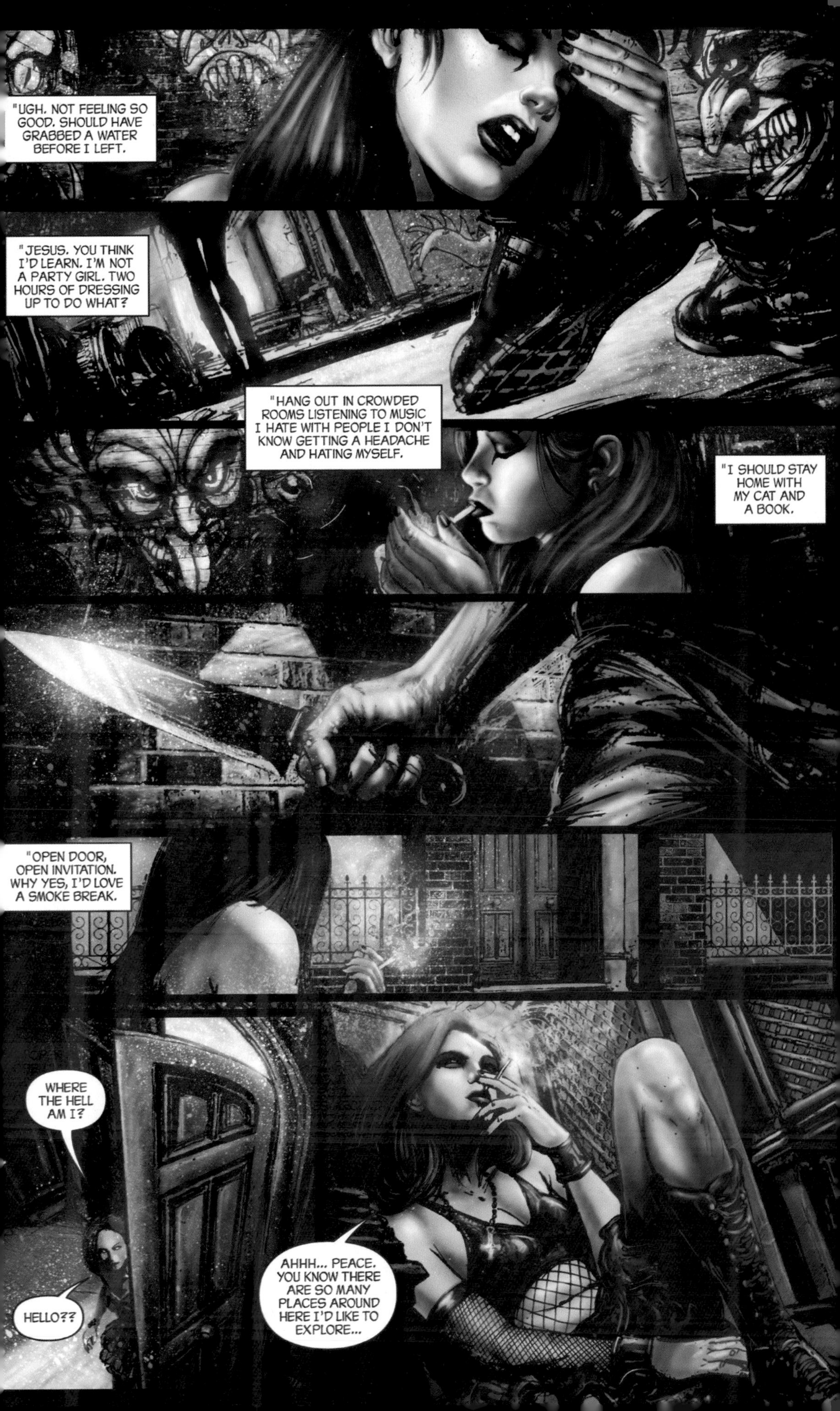
"UGH. NOT FEELING SO GOOD. SHOULD HAVE GRABBED A WATER BEFORE I LEFT.
"JESUS. YOU THINK I'D LEARN. I'M NOT A PARTY GIRL. TWO HOURS OF DRESSING UP TO DO WHAT?
"HANG OUT IN CROWDED ROOMS LISTENING TO MUSIC I HATE WITH PEOPLE I DON'T KNOW GETTING A HEADACHE AND HATING MYSELF.
"I SHOULD STAY HOME WITH MY CAT AND A BOOK.
"OPEN DOOR, OPEN INVITATION. WHY YES, I'D LOVE A SMOKE BREAK.
WHERE THE HELL AM I?
HELLO??
AHHH... PEACE. YOU KNOW THERE ARE SO MANY PLACES AROUND HERE I'D LIKE TO EXPLORE...

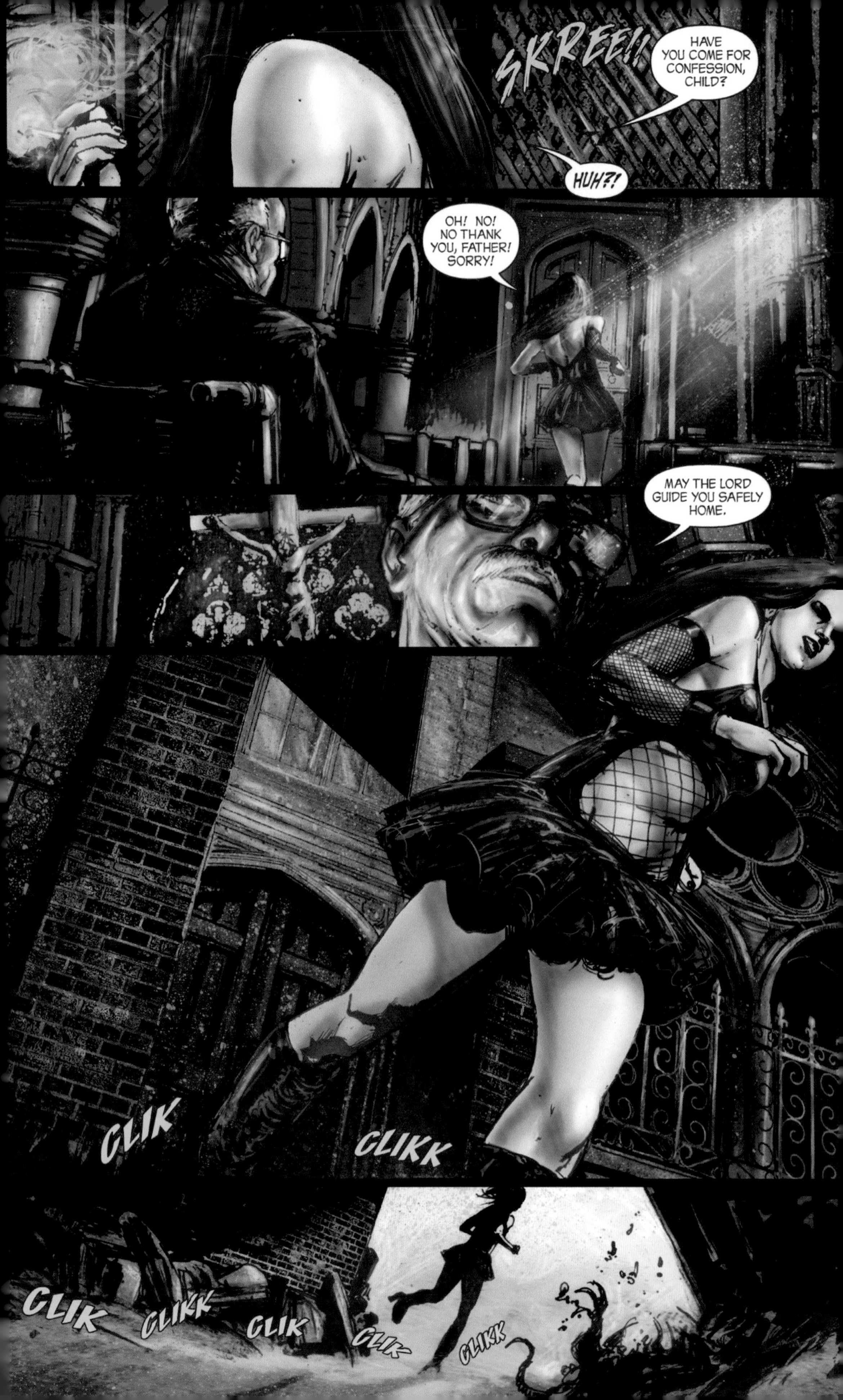
SKREE!!
HAVE YOU COME FOR CONFESSION, CHILD?
HUH?!
OH! NO! NO THANK YOU, FATHER! SORRY!
MAY THE LORD GUIDE YOU SAFELY HOME.
CLIK
CLIKK
CLIK
CLIKK
CLIK
CLIK
CLIKK

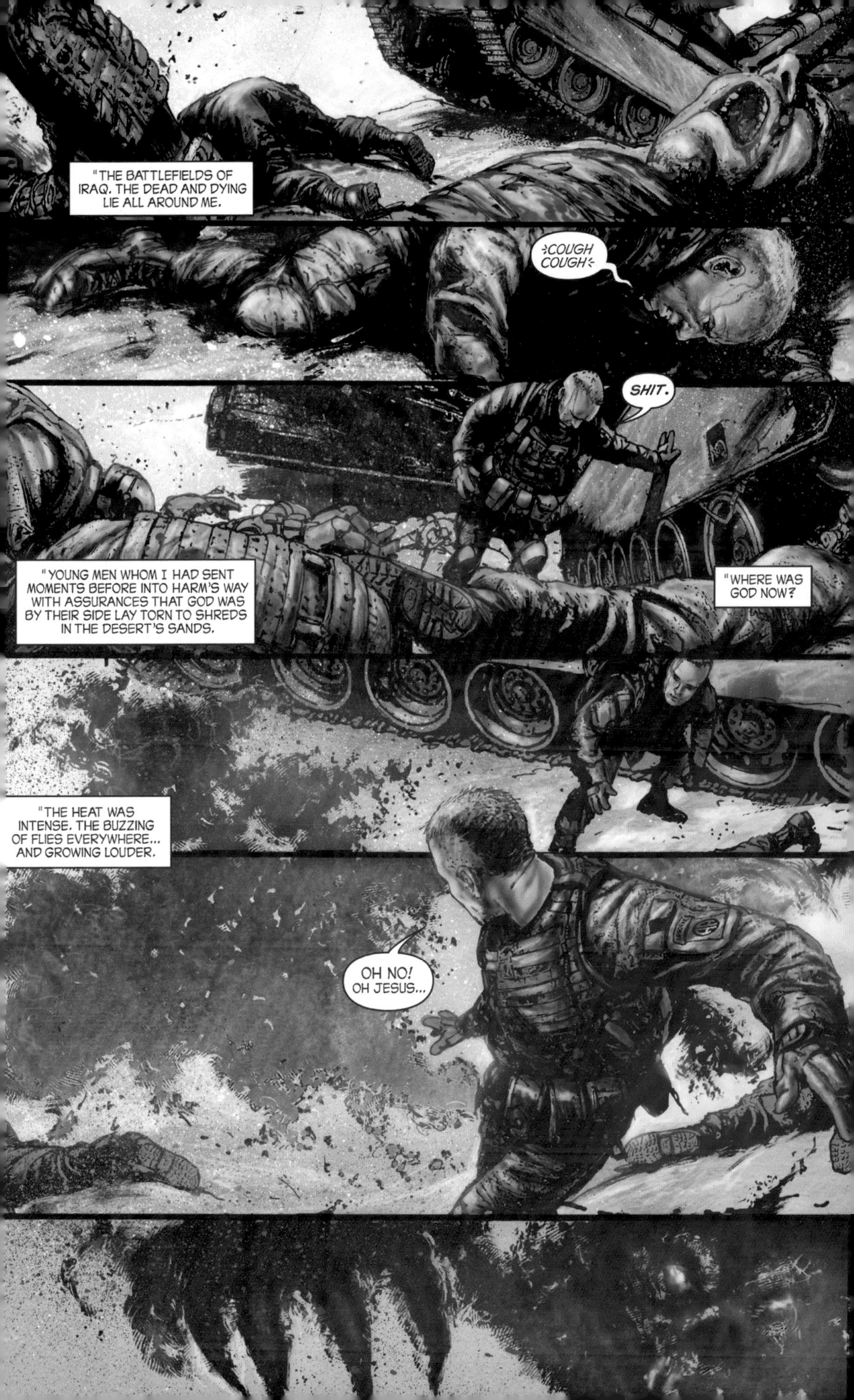
"THE BATTLEFIELDS OF IRAQ. THE DEAD AND DYING LIE ALL AROUND ME.
COUGH COUGH
SHIT.
"YOUNG MEN WHOM I HAD SENT MOMENTS BEFORE INTO HARM'S WAY WITH ASSURANCES THAT GOD WAS BY THEIR SIDE LAY TORN TO SHREDS IN THE DESERT'S SANDS.
"WHERE WAS GOD NOW?
"THE HEAT WAS INTENSE. THE BUZZING OF FLIES EVERYWHERE... AND GROWING LOUDER.
OH NO! OH JESUS...

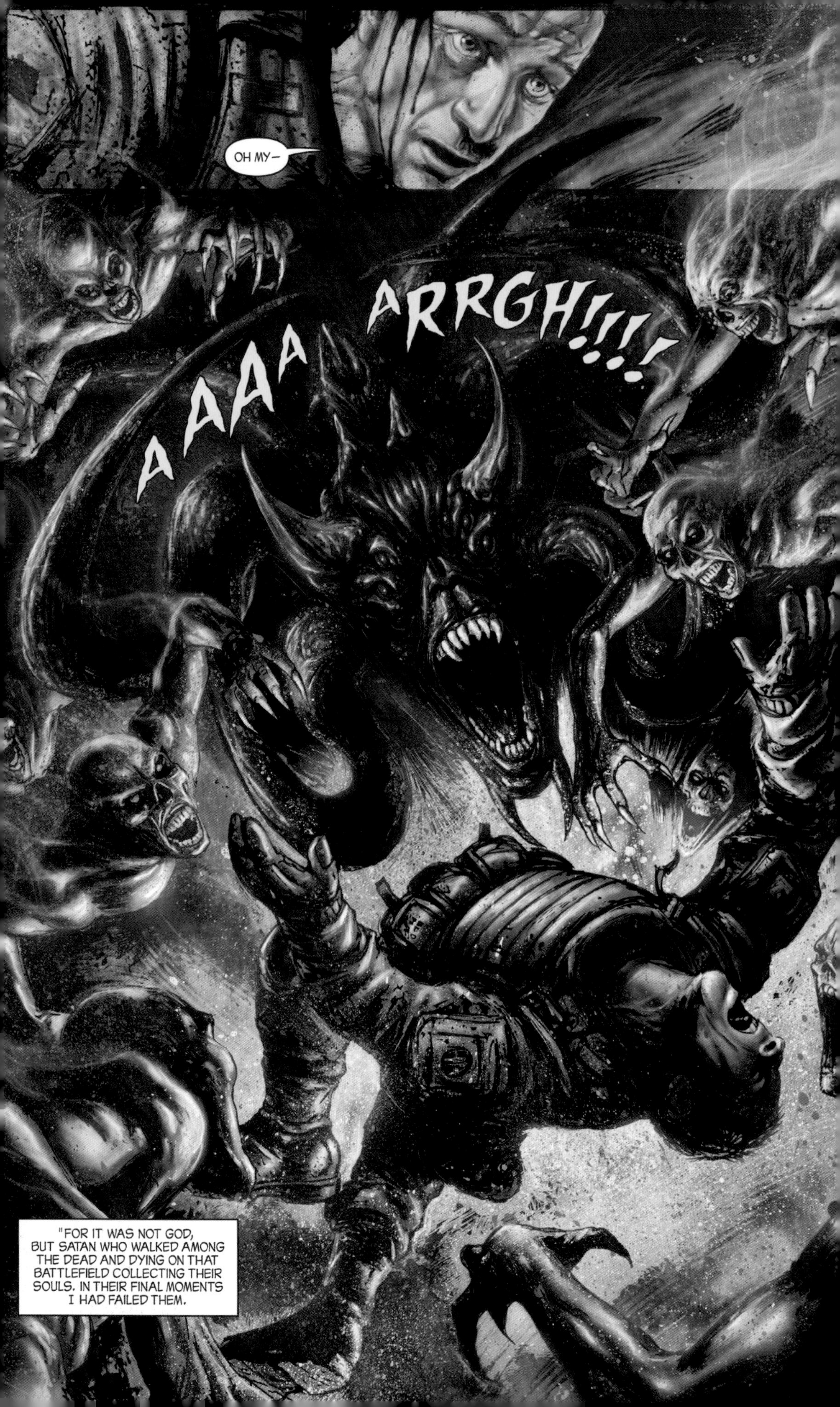
OH MY—
AAAAARRGH!!!!!
"FOR IT WAS NOT GOD, BUT SATAN WHO WALKED AMONG THE DEAD AND DYING ON THAT BATTLEFIELD COLLECTING THEIR SOULS. IN THEIR FINAL MOMENTS I HAD FAILED THEM.

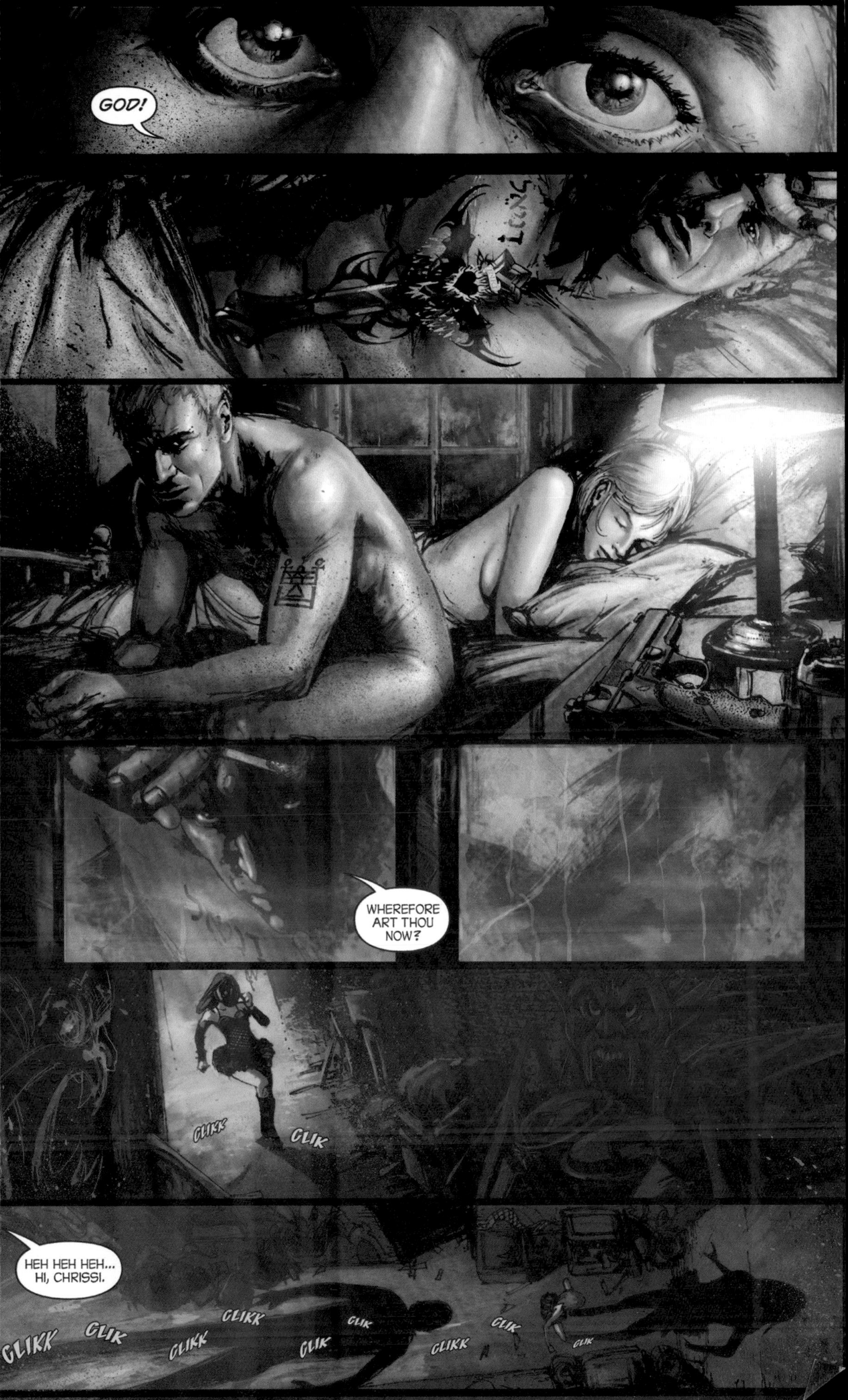
GOD!
WHEREFORE ART THOU NOW?
CLIKK
CLIK
HEH HEH HEH... HI, CHRISSI.
CLIKK
CLIK
CLIKK
CLIKK
CLIK
CLIK
CLIKK
CLIK
CLIK

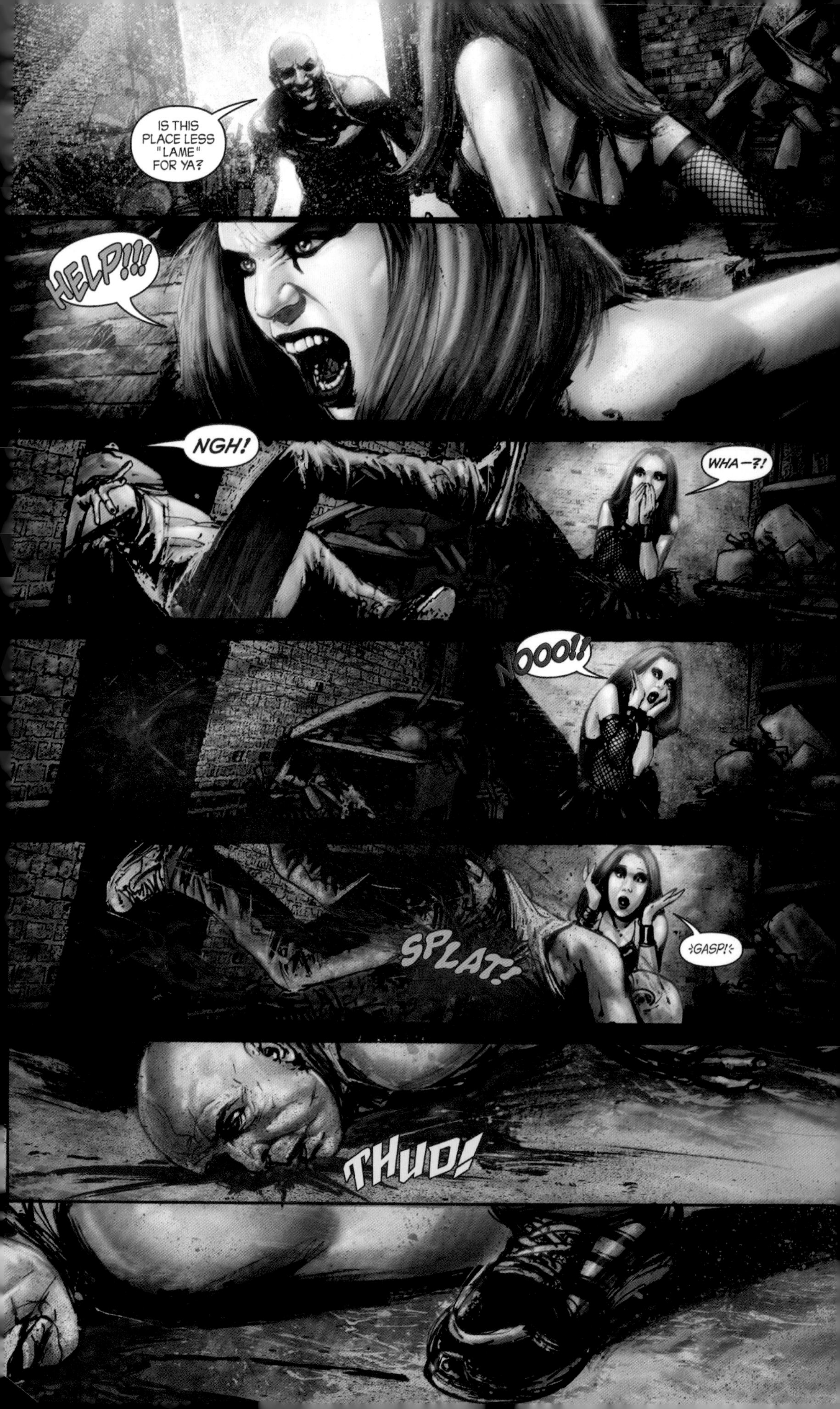
IS THIS PLACE LESS "LAME" FOR YA?
HELP!!!
NGH!
WHA—?!
NOOO!!
SPLAT!
GASP!
THUD!

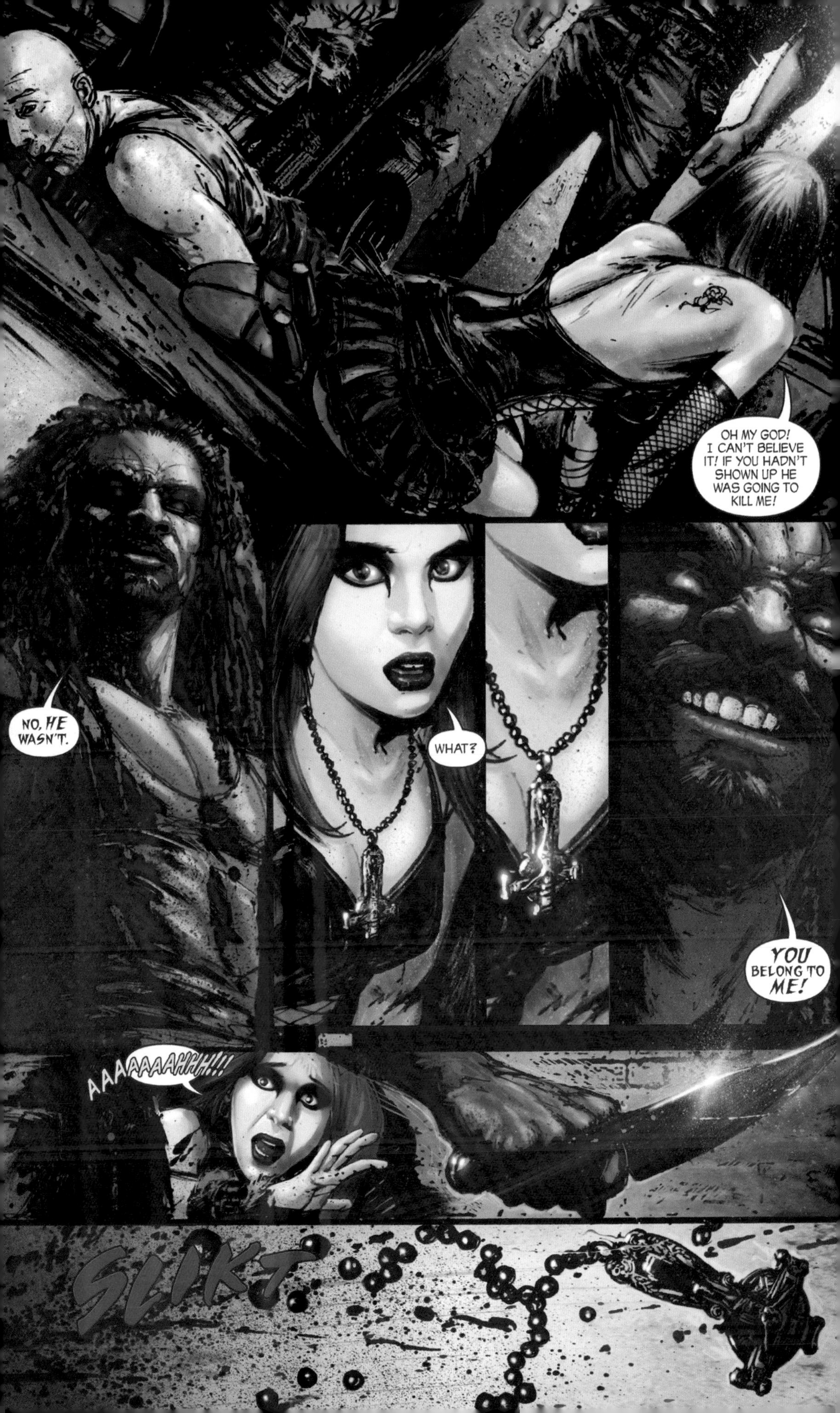
OH MY GOD! I CAN'T BELIEVE IT! IF YOU HADN'T SHOWN UP HE WAS GOING TO KILL ME!
NO, HE WASN'T.
WHAT?
YOU BELONG TO ME!
AAAAAAAHHH!!!
SLIKT

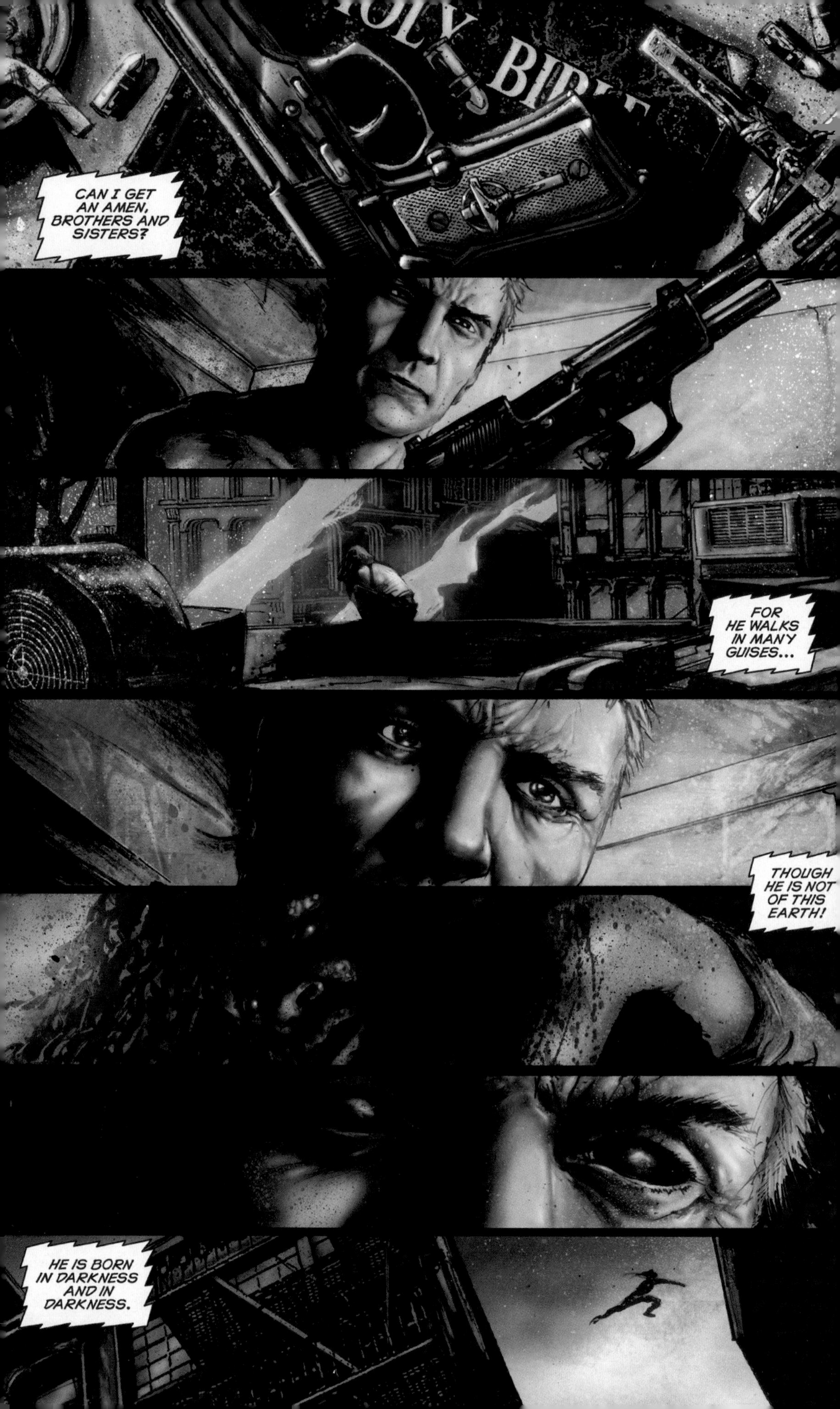
CAN I GET AN AMEN, BROTHERS AND SISTERS?
FOR HE WALKS IN MANY GUISES...
THOUGH HE IS NOT OF THIS EARTH!
HE IS BORN IN DARKNESS AND IN DARKNESS.

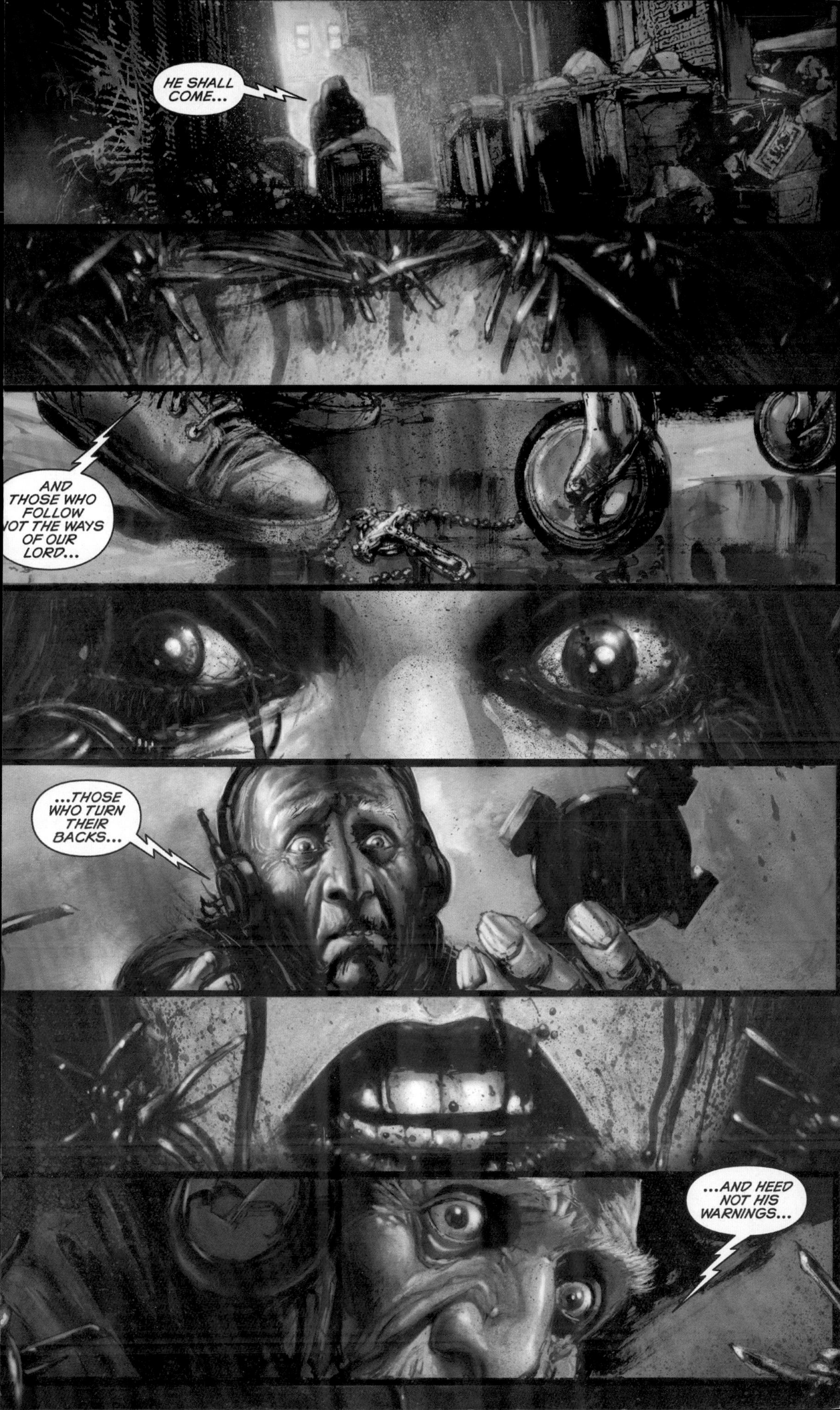
HE SHALL COME...
AND THOSE WHO FOLLOW NOT THE WAYS OF OUR LORD...
...THOSE WHO TURN THEIR BACKS...
...AND HEED NOT HIS WARNINGS...

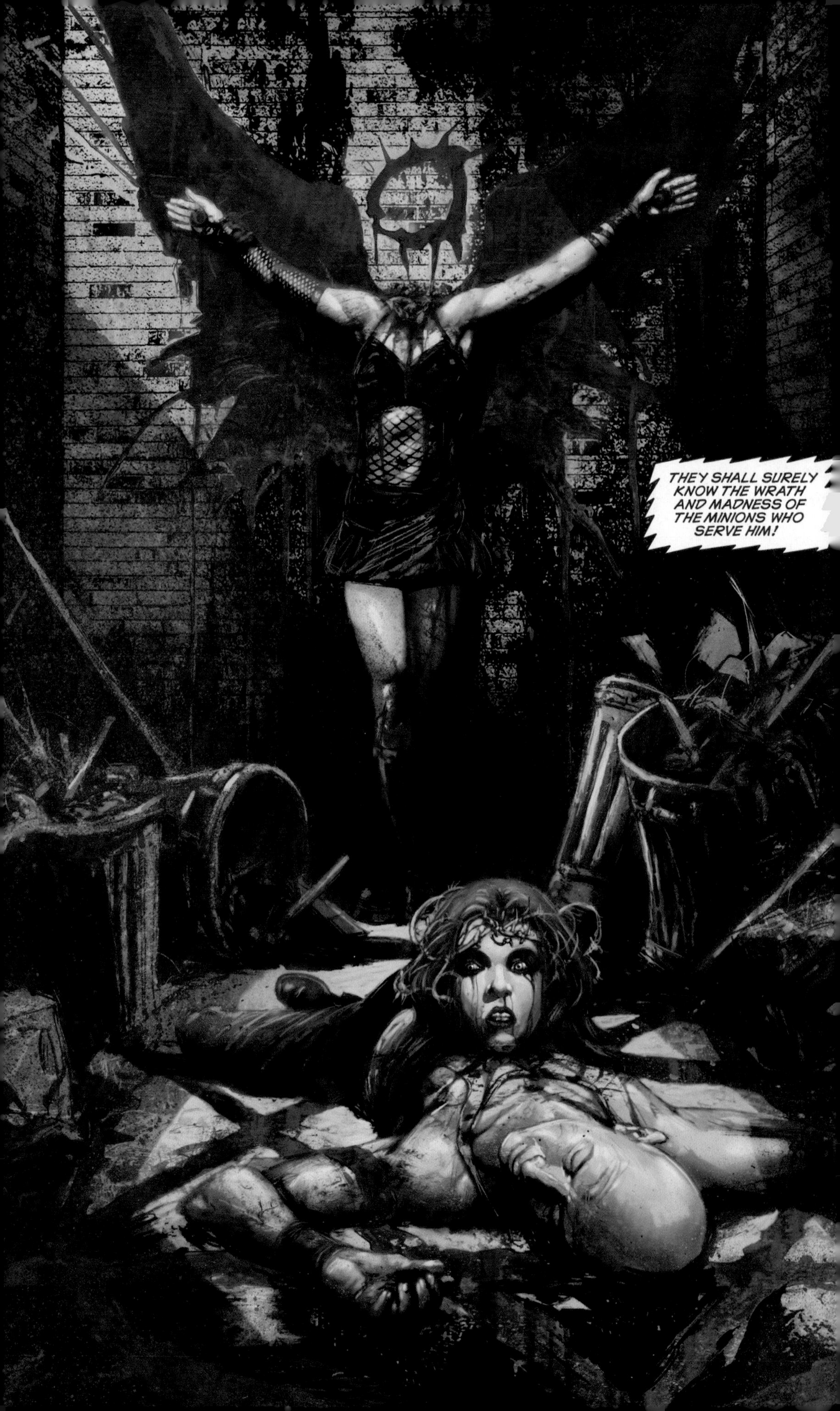
THEY SHALL SURELY KNOW THE WRATH AND MADNESS OF THE MINIONS WHO SERVE HIM!

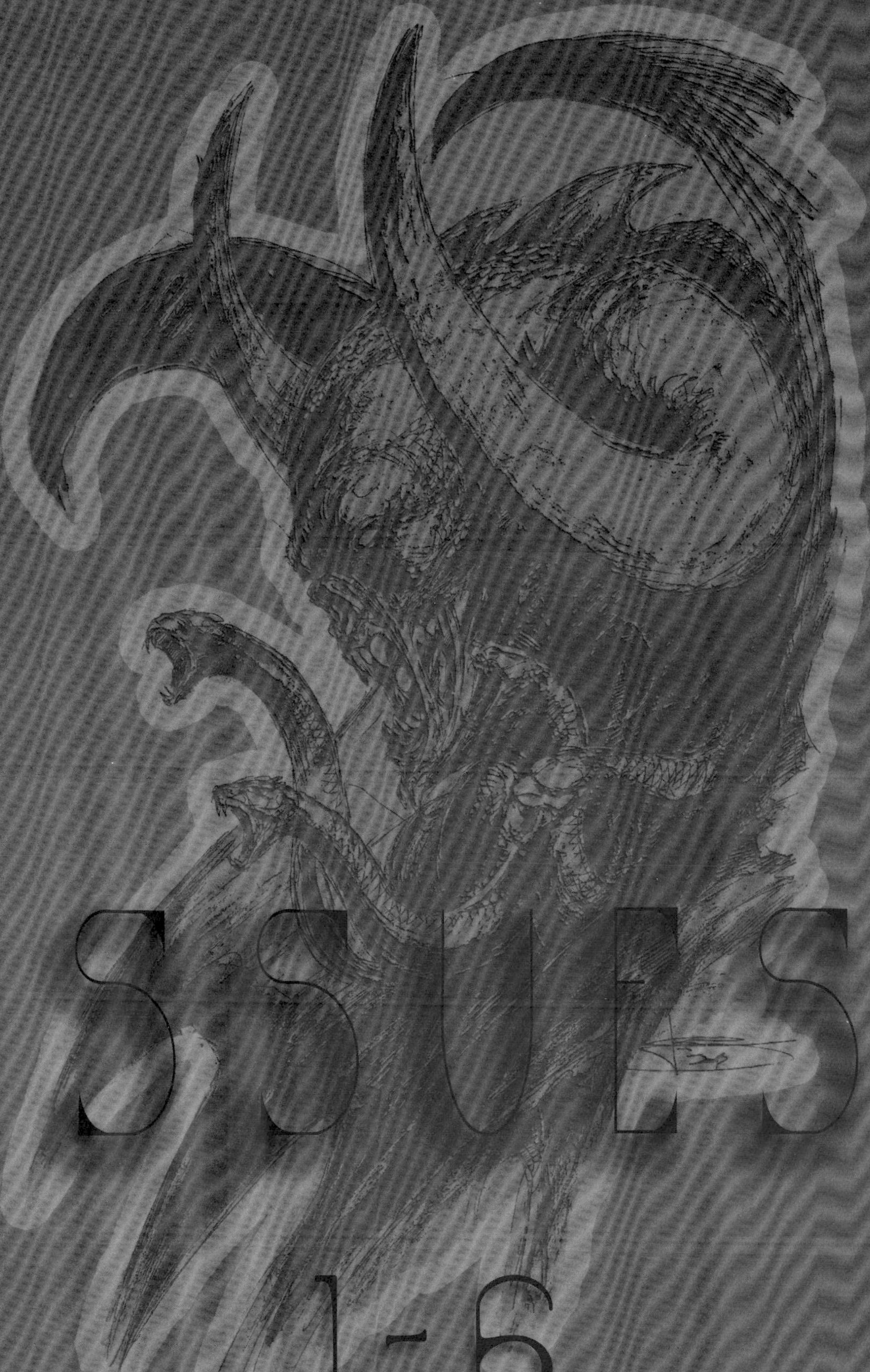

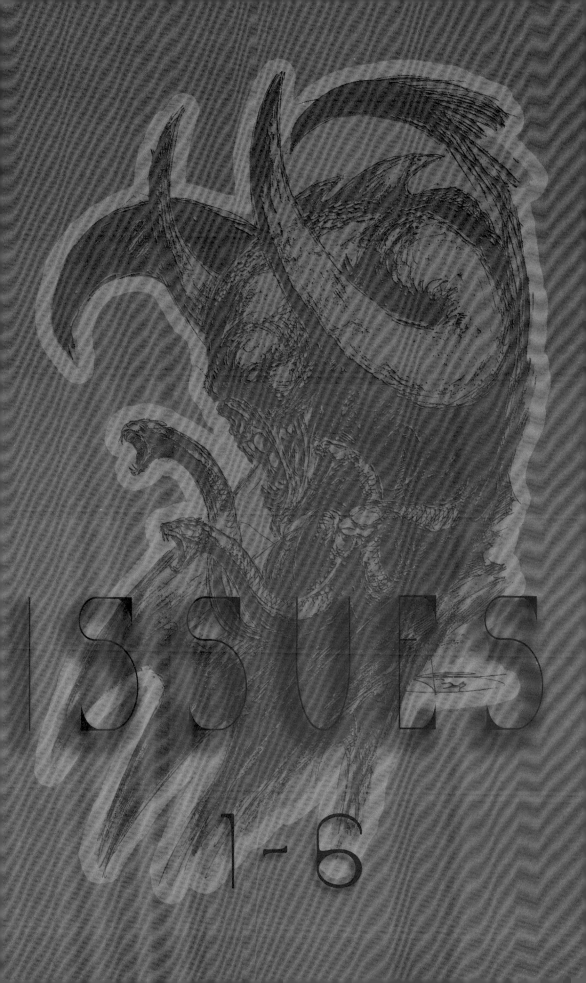

ISSUES

1-6

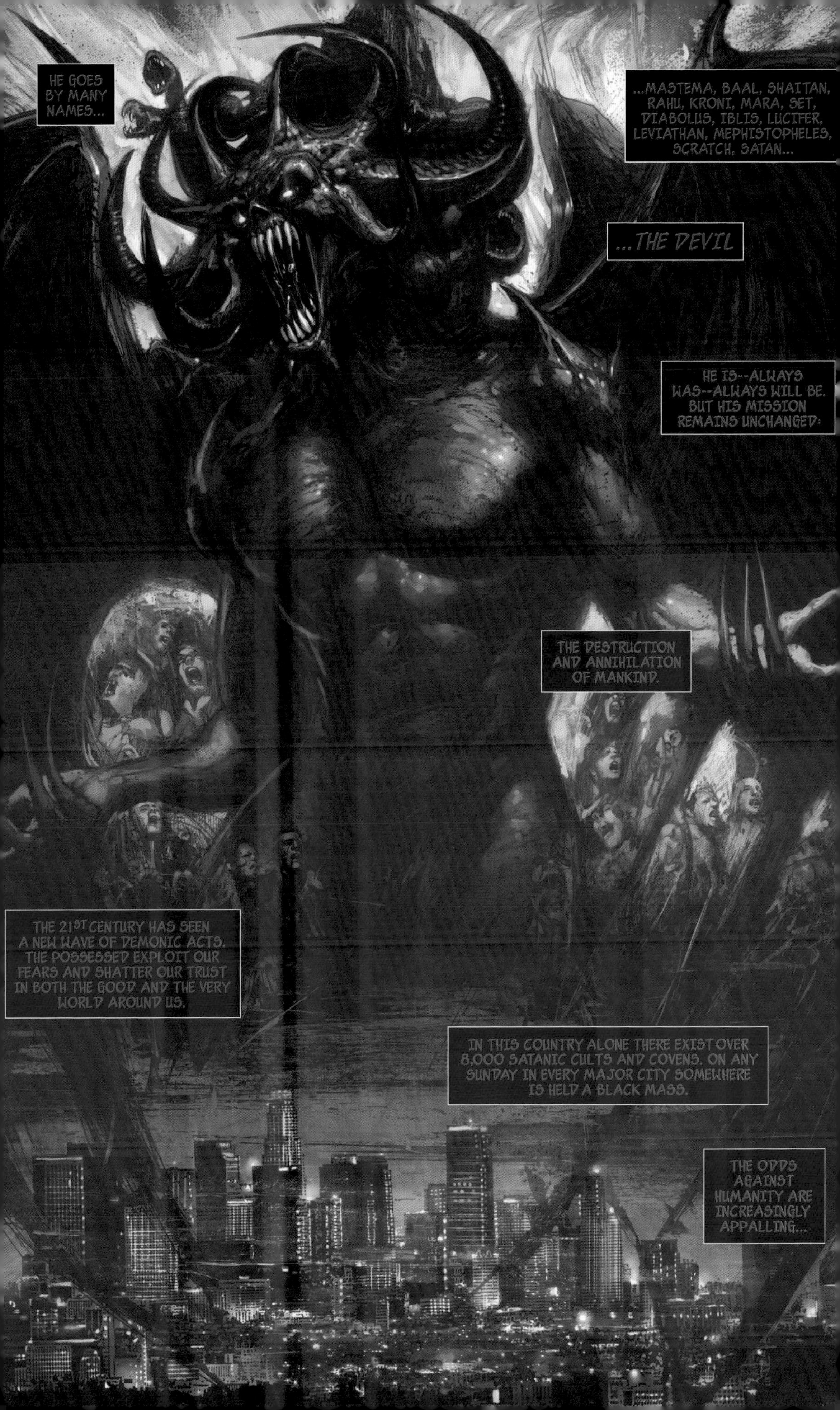
HE GOES BY MANY NAMES...
...MASTEMA, BAAL, SHAITAN, RAHU, KRONI, MARA, SET, DIABOLUS, IBLIS, LUCIFER, LEVIATHAN, MEPHISTOPHELES, SCRATCH, SATAN...
...THE DEVIL
HE IS--ALWAYS WAS--ALWAYS WILL BE. BUT HIS MISSION REMAINS UNCHANGED:
THE DESTRUCTION AND ANNIHILATION OF MANKIND.
THE 21ST CENTURY HAS SEEN A NEW WAVE OF DEMONIC ACTS. THE POSSESSED EXPLOIT OUR FEARS AND SHATTER OUR TRUST IN BOTH THE GOOD AND THE VERY WORLD AROUND US.
IN THIS COUNTRY ALONE THERE EXIST OVER 8,000 SATANIC CULTS AND COVENS. ON ANY SUNDAY IN EVERY MAJOR CITY SOMEWHERE IS HELD A BLACK MASS.
THE ODDS AGAINST HUMANITY ARE INCREASINGLY APPALLING...

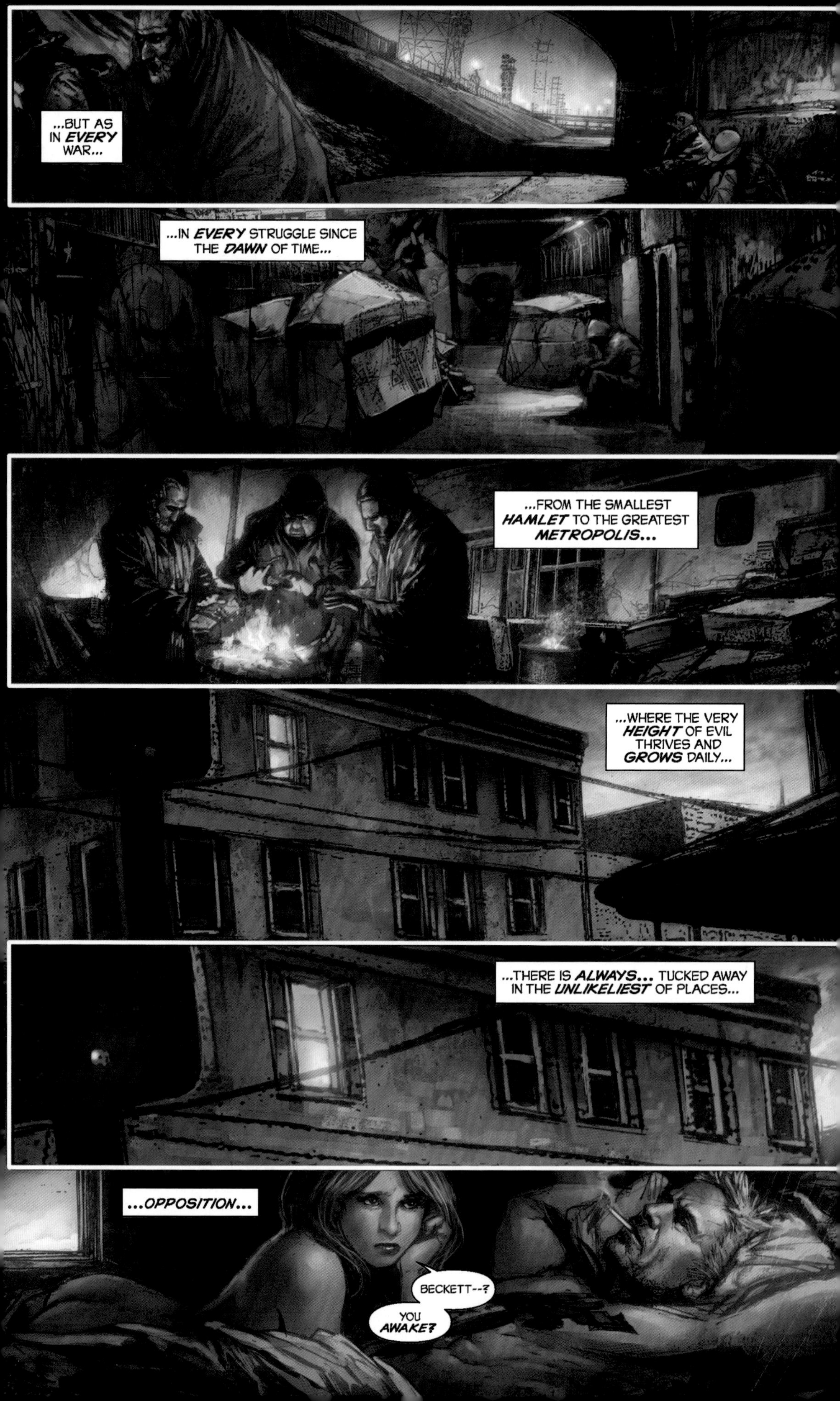
...BUT AS IN EVERY WAR...
...IN EVERY STRUGGLE SINCE THE DAWN OF TIME...
...FROM THE SMALLEST HAMLET TO THE GREATEST METROPOLIS...
...WHERE THE VERY HEIGHT OF EVIL THRIVES AND GROWS DAILY...
...THERE IS ALWAYS... TUCKED AWAY IN THE UNLIKELIEST OF PLACES...
...OPPOSITION...
BECKETT--?
YOU AWAKE?

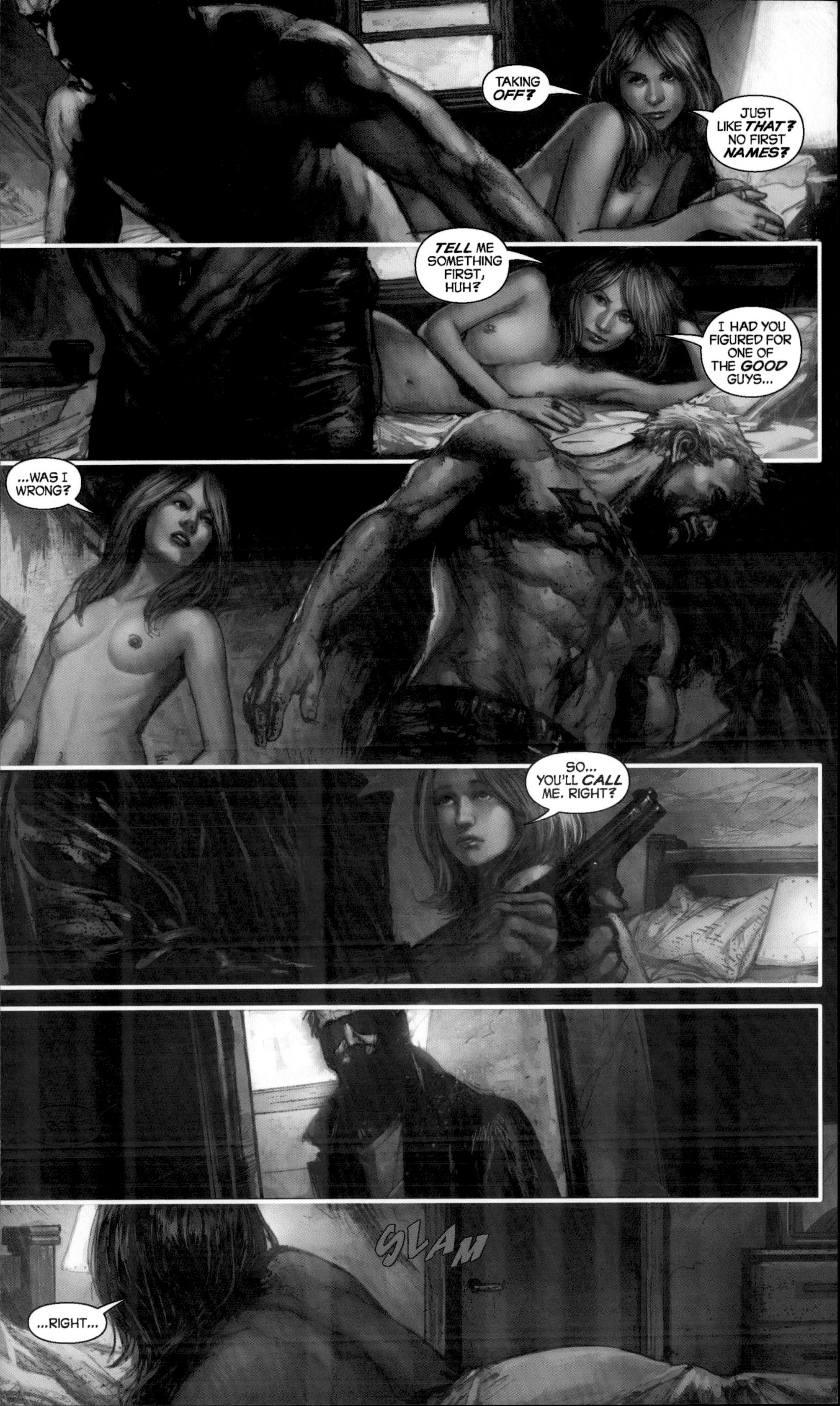
TAKING OFF?
JUST LIKE THAT? NO FIRST NAMES?
TELL ME SOMETHING FIRST, HUH?
I HAD YOU FIGURED FOR ONE OF THE GOOD GUYS...
...WAS I WRONG?
SO... YOU'LL CALL ME. RIGHT?
SLAM
...RIGHT...

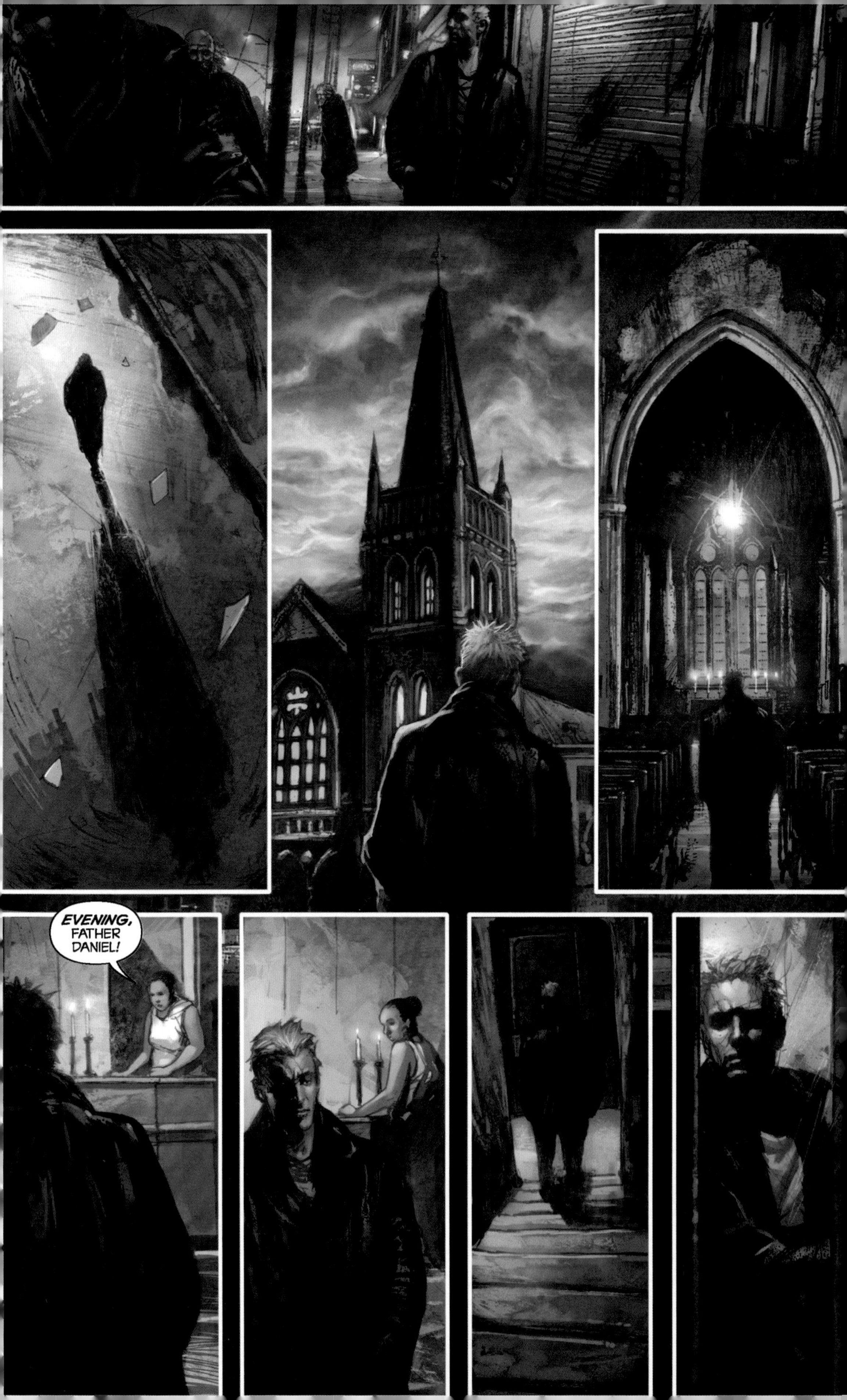
EVENING, FATHER DANIEL!

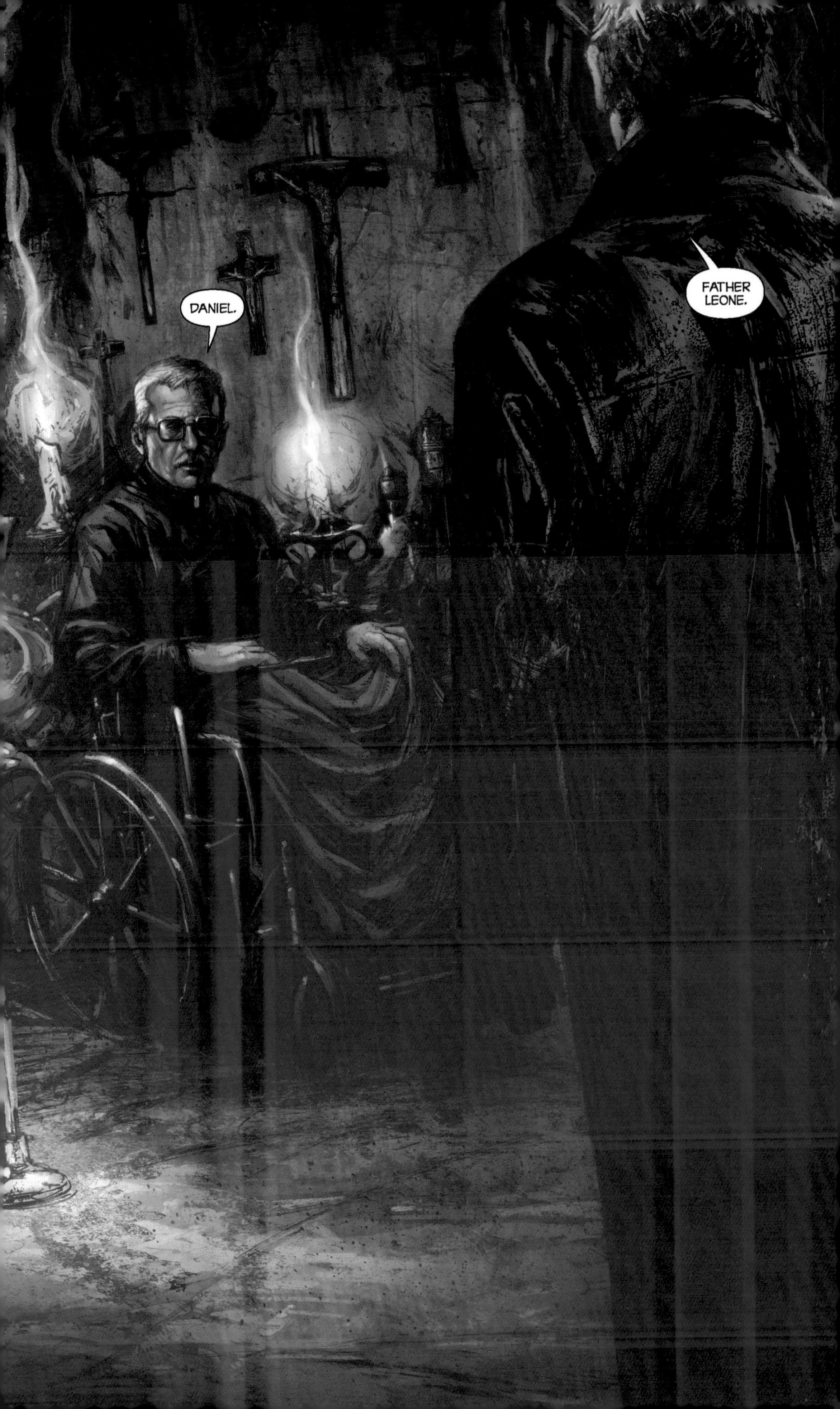
DANIEL.
FATHER LEONE.

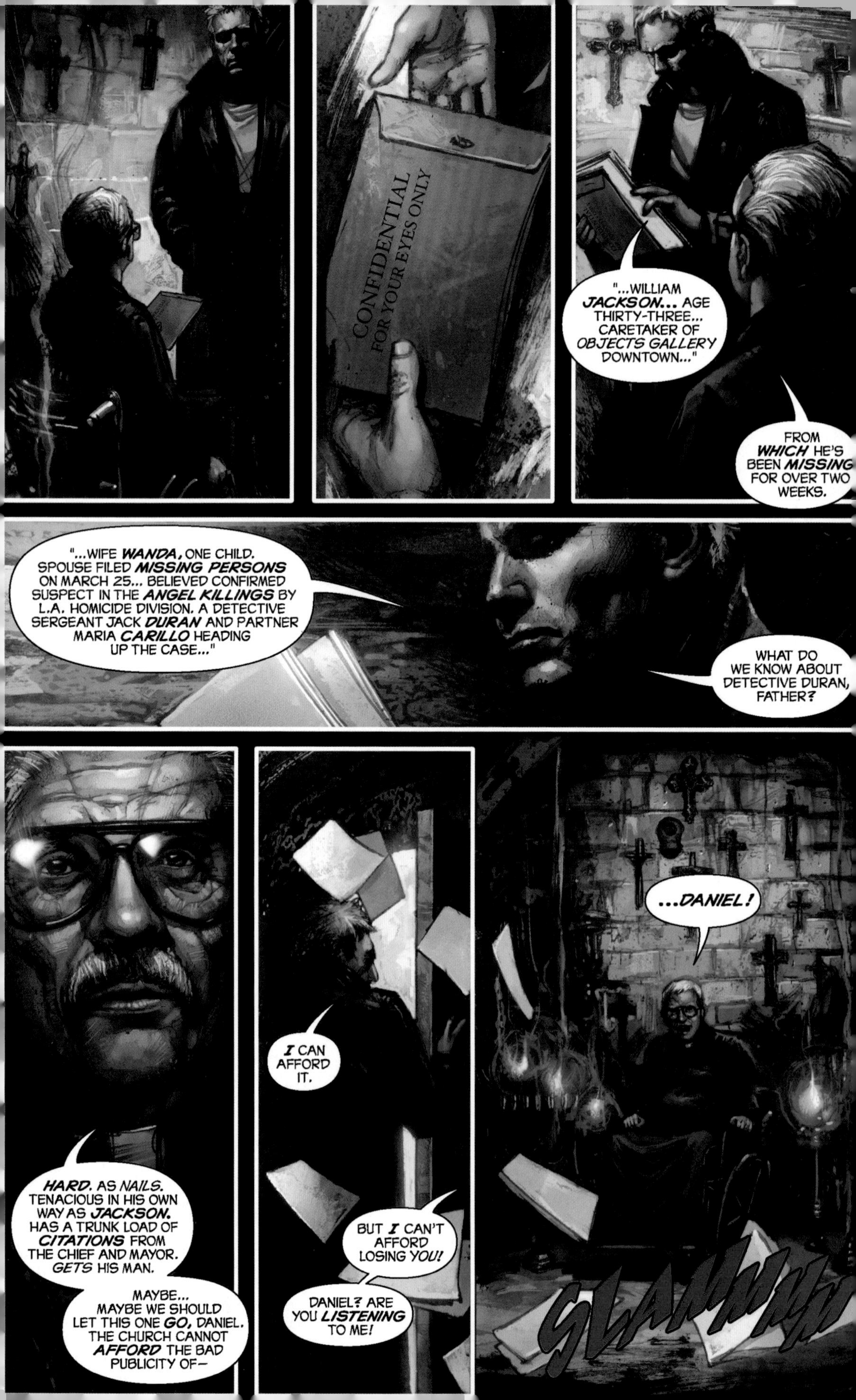
CONFIDENTIAL FOR YOUR EYES ONLY
"...WILLIAM JACKSON... AGE THIRTY-THREE... CARETAKER OF OBJECTS GALLERY DOWNTOWN..."
FROM WHICH HE'S BEEN MISSING FOR OVER TWO WEEKS.
"...WIFE WANDA, ONE CHILD. SPOUSE FILED MISSING PERSONS ON MARCH 25... BELIEVED CONFIRMED SUSPECT IN THE ANGEL KILLINGS BY L.A. HOMICIDE DIVISION. A DETECTIVE SERGEANT JACK DURAN AND PARTNER MARIA CARILLO HEADING UP THE CASE..."
WHAT DO WE KNOW ABOUT DETECTIVE DURAN, FATHER?
HARD. AS NAILS. TENACIOUS IN HIS OWN WAY AS JACKSON. HAS A TRUNK LOAD OF CITATIONS FROM THE CHIEF AND MAYOR. GETS HIS MAN.
MAYBE... MAYBE WE SHOULD LET THIS ONE GO, DANIEL. THE CHURCH CANNOT AFFORD THE BAD PUBLICITY OF—
I CAN AFFORD IT.
BUT I CAN'T AFFORD LOSING YOU!
DANIEL? ARE YOU LISTENING TO ME!
...DANIEL!
SLAMMM

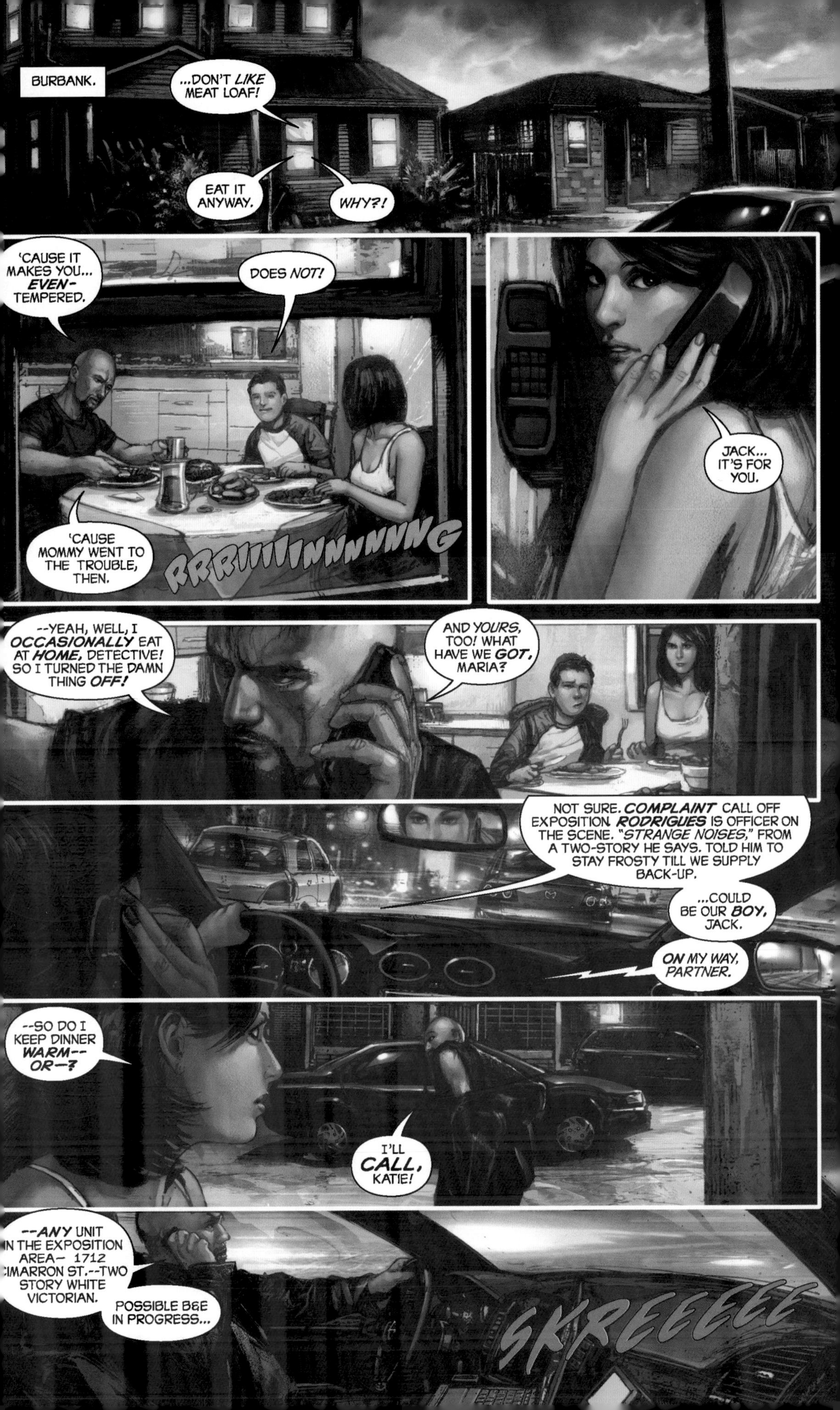
BURBANK.
...DON'T LIKE MEAT LOAF!
EAT IT ANYWAY.
WHY?!
'CAUSE IT MAKES YOU... EVEN-TEMPERED.
DOES NOT!
'CAUSE MOMMY WENT TO THE TROUBLE, THEN.
RRRIIIIINNNNNNG
JACK... IT'S FOR YOU.
--YEAH, WELL, I OCCASIONALLY EAT AT HOME, DETECTIVE! SO I TURNED THE DAMN THING OFF!
AND YOURS, TOO! WHAT HAVE WE GOT, MARIA?
NOT SURE. COMPLAINT CALL OFF EXPOSITION. RODRIGUES IS OFFICER ON THE SCENE. "STRANGE NOISES," FROM A TWO-STORY HE SAYS. TOLD HIM TO STAY FROSTY TILL WE SUPPLY BACK-UP.
...COULD BE OUR BOY, JACK.
ON MY WAY, PARTNER.
--SO DO I KEEP DINNER WARM--OR--?
I'LL CALL, KATIE!
--ANY UNIT IN THE EXPOSITION AREA-- 1712 CIMARRON ST.--TWO STORY WHITE VICTORIAN.
POSSIBLE B&E IN PROGRESS...
SKREEEEEE

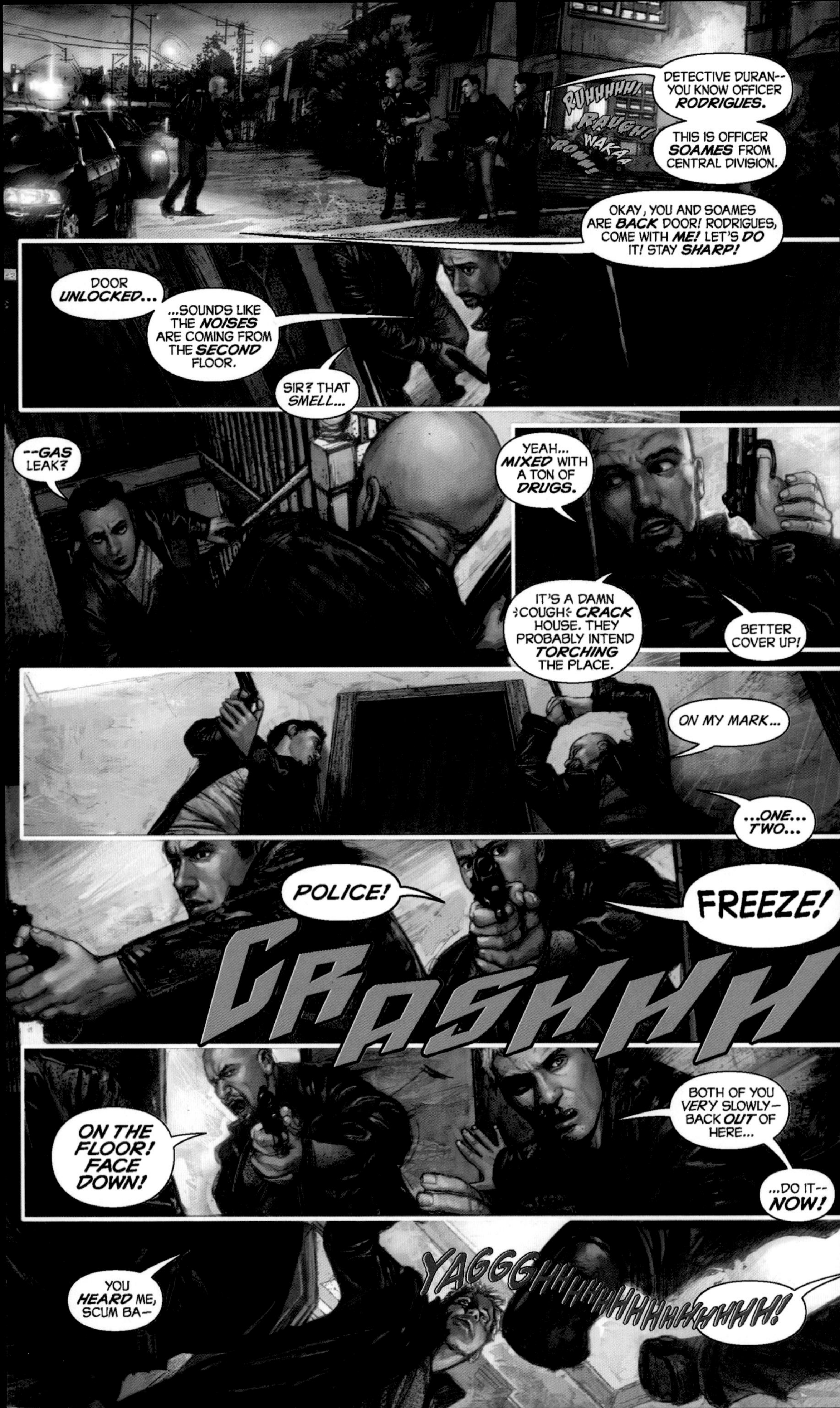
RUHHHH!
RAUGH!
WAKAA
ROMM!
DETECTIVE DURAN-- YOU KNOW OFFICER RODRIGUES.
THIS IS OFFICER SOAMES FROM CENTRAL DIVISION.
OKAY, YOU AND SOAMES ARE BACK DOOR! RODRIGUES, COME WITH ME! LET'S DO IT! STAY SHARP!
DOOR UNLOCKED...
...SOUNDS LIKE THE NOISES ARE COMING FROM THE SECOND FLOOR.
SIR? THAT SMELL...
--GAS LEAK?
YEAH... MIXED WITH A TON OF DRUGS.
IT'S A DAMN *COUGH* CRACK HOUSE. THEY PROBABLY INTEND TORCHING THE PLACE.
BETTER COVER UP!
ON MY MARK...
...ONE... TWO...
POLICE!
FREEZE!
CRASHHH
ON THE FLOOR! FACE DOWN!
BOTH OF YOU VERY SLOWLY— BACK OUT OF HERE...
...DO IT-- NOW!
YOU HEARD ME, SCUM BA—
YAGGGHHHHHHHHHHHHHHH!

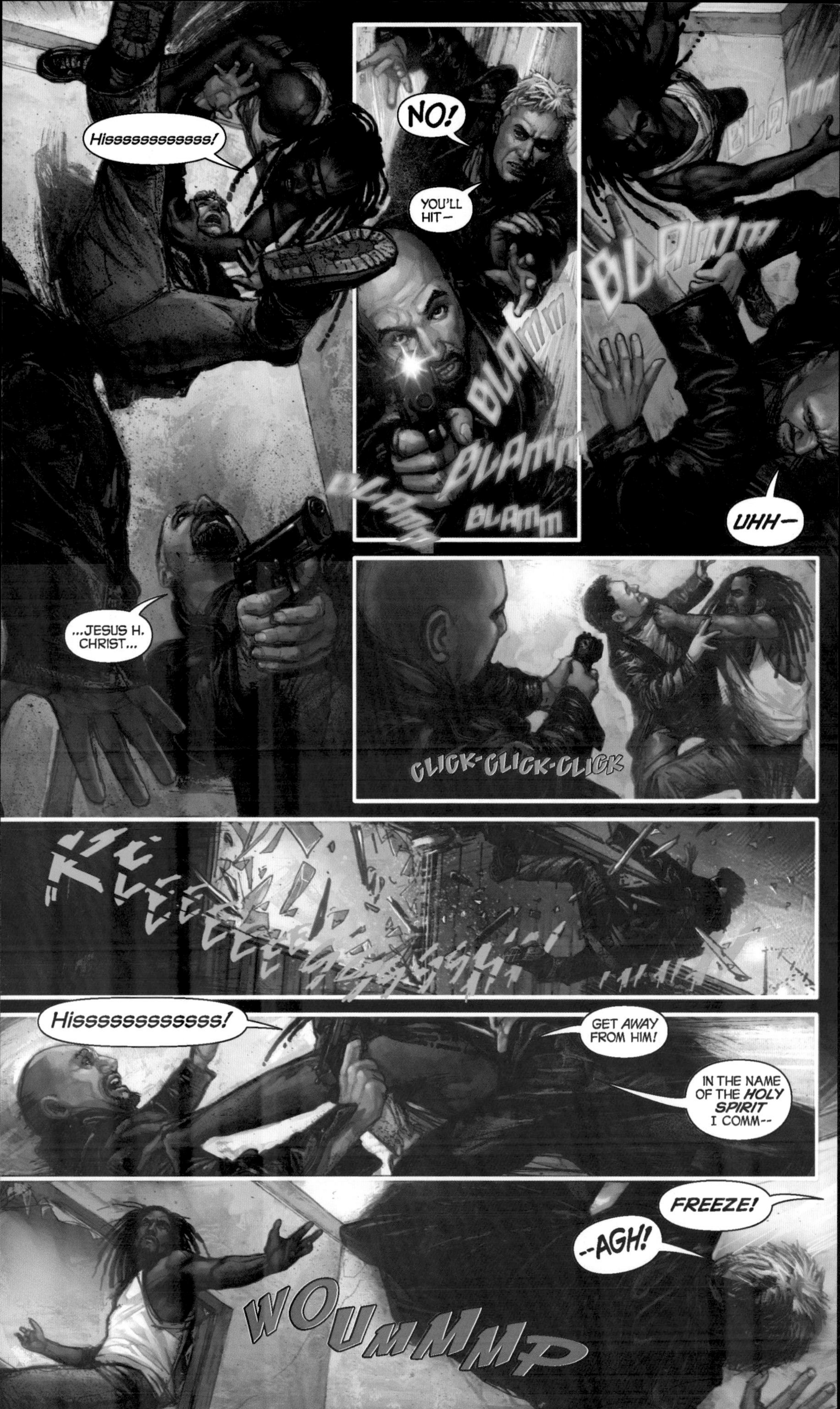
Hisssssssssssss!
NO!
YOU'LL HIT—
BLAMM
BLAMM
BLAMM
BLAMM
BLAMM
BLAMM
BLAMM
UHH—
...JESUS H. CHRIST...
CLICK-CLICK-CLICK
Hisssssssssssss!
GET AWAY FROM HIM!
IN THE NAME OF THE HOLY SPIRIT I COMM--
FREEZE!
--AGH!
WOUMMMP

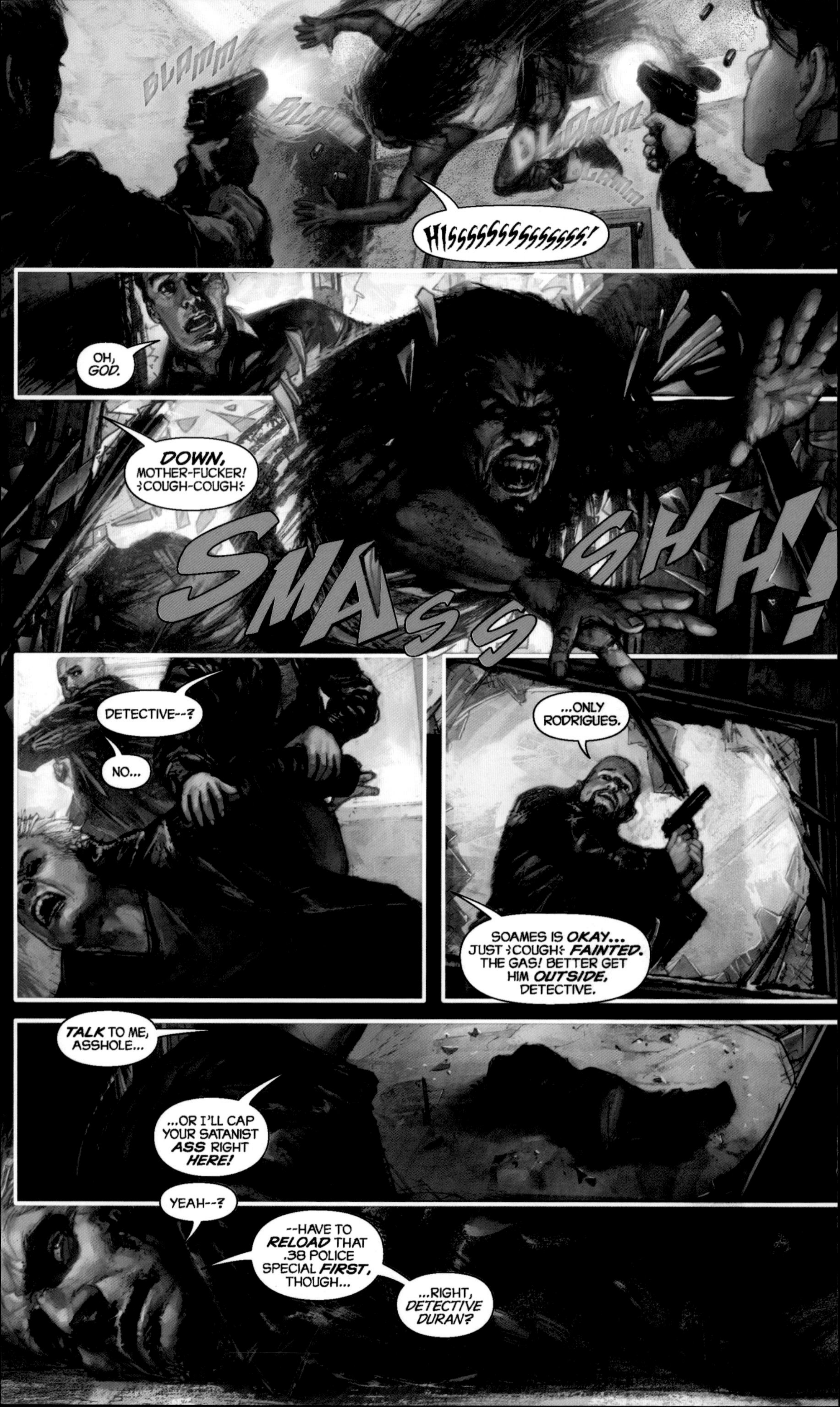
BLAMM
BLAM
BLAMM
BLAMM
HISSSSSSSSSSSSSS!
OH, GOD.
DOWN, MOTHER-FUCKER! COUGH-COUGH
SMASSSHH!
DETECTIVE--?
NO...
...ONLY RODRIGUES.
SOAMES IS OKAY... JUST COUGH FAINTED. THE GAS! BETTER GET HIM OUTSIDE, DETECTIVE.
TALK TO ME, ASSHOLE...
...OR I'LL CAP YOUR SATANIST ASS RIGHT HERE!
YEAH--?
--HAVE TO RELOAD THAT .38 POLICE SPECIAL FIRST, THOUGH...
...RIGHT, DETECTIVE DURAN?

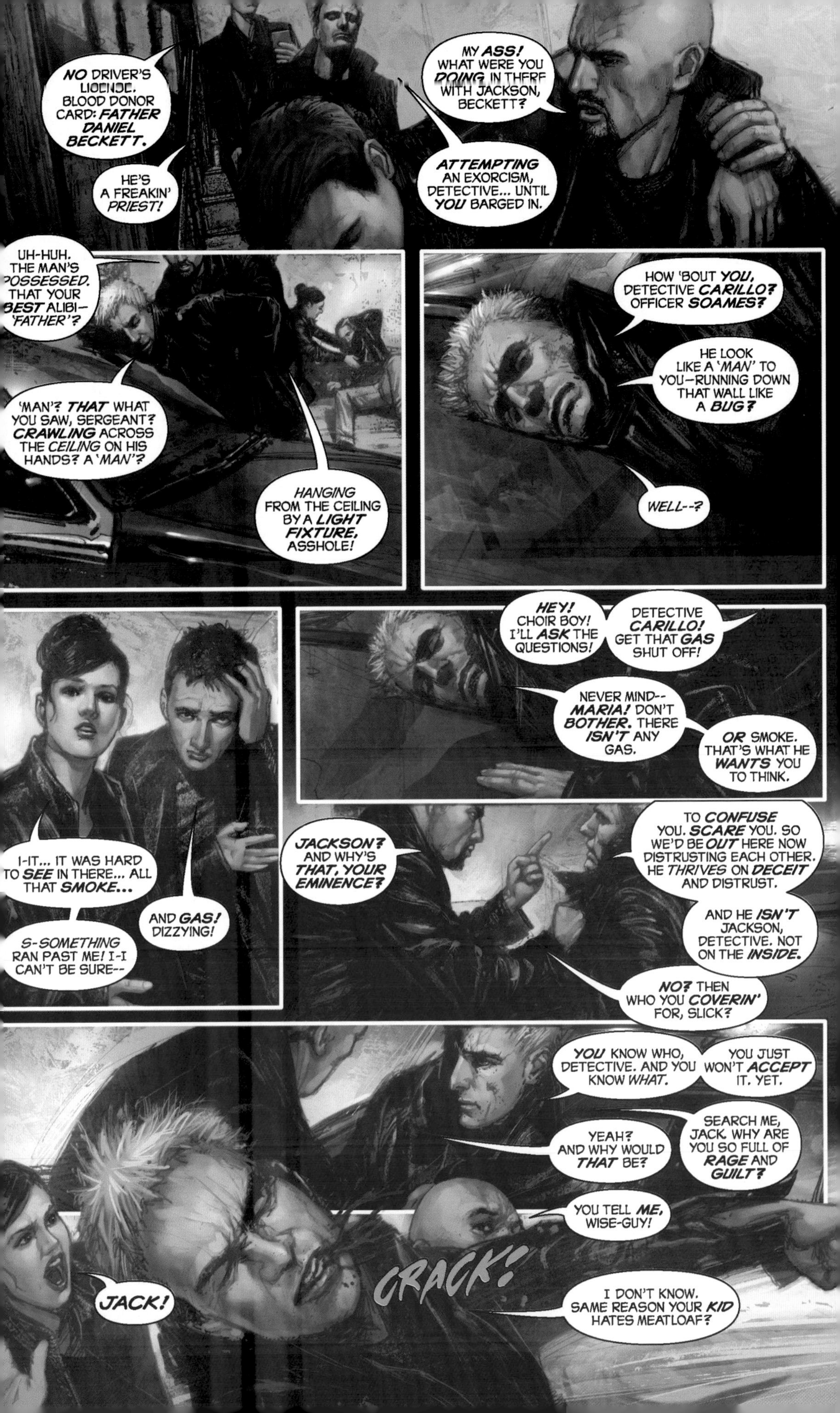
NO DRIVER'S LICENSE. BLOOD DONOR CARD: FATHER DANIEL BECKETT.
HE'S A FREAKIN' PRIEST!
MY ASS! WHAT WERE YOU DOING IN THERE WITH JACKSON, BECKETT?
ATTEMPTING AN EXORCISM, DETECTIVE... UNTIL YOU BARGED IN.
UH-HUH. THE MAN'S POSSESSED. THAT YOUR BEST ALIBI-'FATHER'?
'MAN'? THAT WHAT YOU SAW, SERGEANT? CRAWLING ACROSS THE CEILING ON HIS HANDS? A 'MAN'?
HANGING FROM THE CEILING BY A LIGHT FIXTURE, ASSHOLE!
HOW 'BOUT YOU, DETECTIVE CARILLO? OFFICER SOAMES?
HE LOOK LIKE A 'MAN' TO YOU—RUNNING DOWN THAT WALL LIKE A BUG?
WELL--?
I-IT... IT WAS HARD TO SEE IN THERE... ALL THAT SMOKE...
AND GAS! DIZZYING!
S-SOMETHING RAN PAST ME! I-I CAN'T BE SURE--
HEY! CHOIR BOY! I'LL ASK THE QUESTIONS!
DETECTIVE CARILLO! GET THAT GAS SHUT OFF!
NEVER MIND-- MARIA! DON'T BOTHER. THERE ISN'T ANY GAS.
OR SMOKE. THAT'S WHAT HE WANTS YOU TO THINK.
JACKSON? AND WHY'S THAT, YOUR EMINENCE?
TO CONFUSE YOU. SCARE YOU. SO WE'D BE OUT HERE NOW DISTRUSTING EACH OTHER. HE THRIVES ON DECEIT AND DISTRUST.
AND HE ISN'T JACKSON, DETECTIVE. NOT ON THE INSIDE.
NO? THEN WHO YOU COVERIN' FOR, SLICK?
YOU KNOW WHO, DETECTIVE. AND YOU KNOW WHAT.
YOU JUST WON'T ACCEPT IT. YET.
YEAH? AND WHY WOULD THAT BE?
SEARCH ME, JACK. WHY ARE YOU SO FULL OF RAGE AND GUILT?
YOU TELL ME, WISE-GUY!
CRACK!
JACK!
I DON'T KNOW. SAME REASON YOUR KID HATES MEATLOAF?

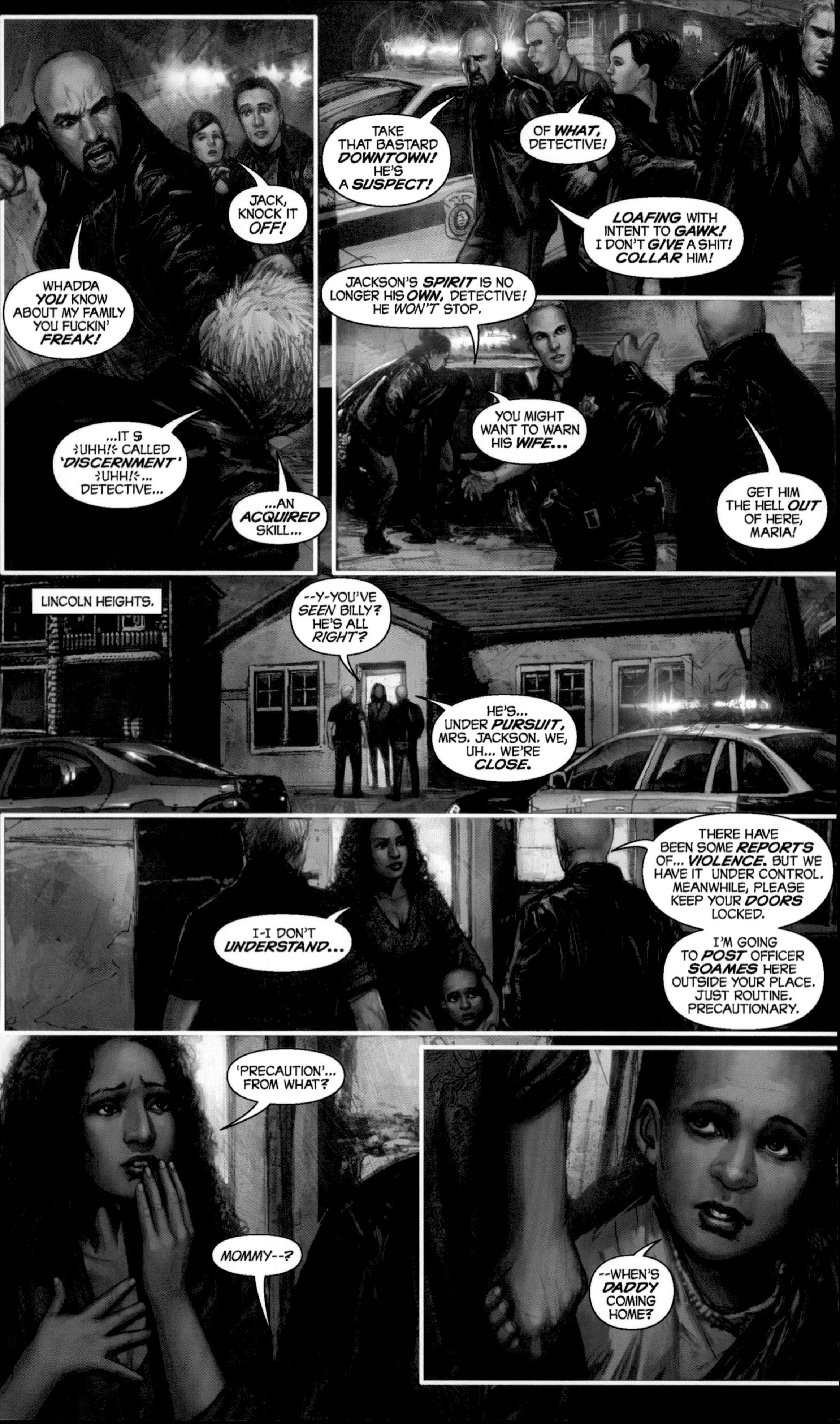
JACK, KNOCK IT OFF!
WHADDA YOU KNOW ABOUT MY FAMILY YOU FUCKIN' FREAK!
...IT S UHH! CALLED 'DISCERNMENT' UHH! ... DETECTIVE...
...AN ACQUIRED SKILL...
TAKE THAT BASTARD DOWNTOWN! HE'S A SUSPECT!
OF WHAT, DETECTIVE!
LOAFING WITH INTENT TO GAWK! I DON'T GIVE A SHIT! COLLAR HIM!
JACKSON'S SPIRIT IS NO LONGER HIS OWN, DETECTIVE! HE WON'T STOP.
YOU MIGHT WANT TO WARN HIS WIFE...
GET HIM THE HELL OUT OF HERE, MARIA!
LINCOLN HEIGHTS.
--Y-YOU'VE SEEN BILLY? HE'S ALL RIGHT?
HE'S... UNDER PURSUIT, MRS. JACKSON. WE, UH... WE'RE CLOSE.
I-I DON'T UNDERSTAND...
THERE HAVE BEEN SOME REPORTS OF... VIOLENCE. BUT WE HAVE IT UNDER CONTROL. MEANWHILE, PLEASE KEEP YOUR DOORS LOCKED.
I'M GOING TO POST OFFICER SOAMES HERE OUTSIDE YOUR PLACE. JUST ROUTINE. PRECAUTIONARY.
'PRECAUTION'... FROM WHAT?
MOMMY--?
--WHEN'S DADDY COMING HOME?

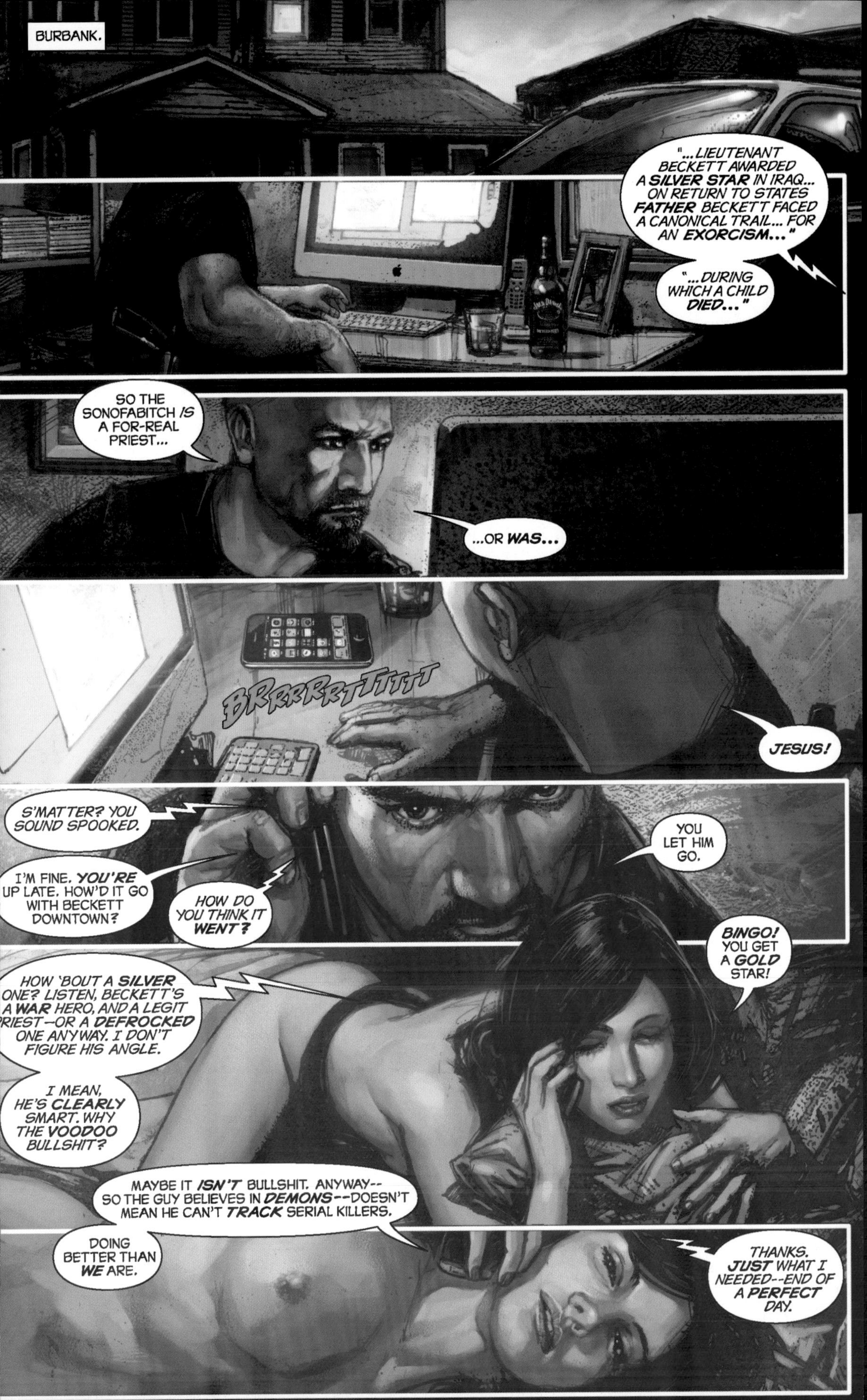

BURBANK.
"...LIEUTENANT BECKETT AWARDED A SILVER STAR IN IRAQ... ON RETURN TO STATES FATHER BECKETT FACED A CANONICAL TRAIL... FOR AN EXORCISM..."
"...DURING WHICH A CHILD DIED..."
SO THE SONOFABITCH IS A FOR-REAL PRIEST...
...OR WAS...
BRRRRRTTTTTT
JESUS!
S'MATTER? YOU SOUND SPOOKED.
I'M FINE. YOU'RE UP LATE. HOW'D IT GO WITH BECKETT DOWNTOWN?
HOW DO YOU THINK IT WENT?
YOU LET HIM GO.
BINGO! YOU GET A GOLD STAR!
HOW 'BOUT A SILVER ONE? LISTEN, BECKETT'S A WAR HERO, AND A LEGIT PRIEST--OR A DEFROCKED ONE ANYWAY. I DON'T FIGURE HIS ANGLE.
I MEAN, HE'S CLEARLY SMART. WHY THE VOODOO BULLSHIT?
MAYBE IT ISN'T BULLSHIT. ANYWAY-- SO THE GUY BELIEVES IN DEMONS--DOESN'T MEAN HE CAN'T TRACK SERIAL KILLERS.
DOING BETTER THAN WE ARE.
THANKS. JUST WHAT I NEEDED--END OF A PERFECT DAY.

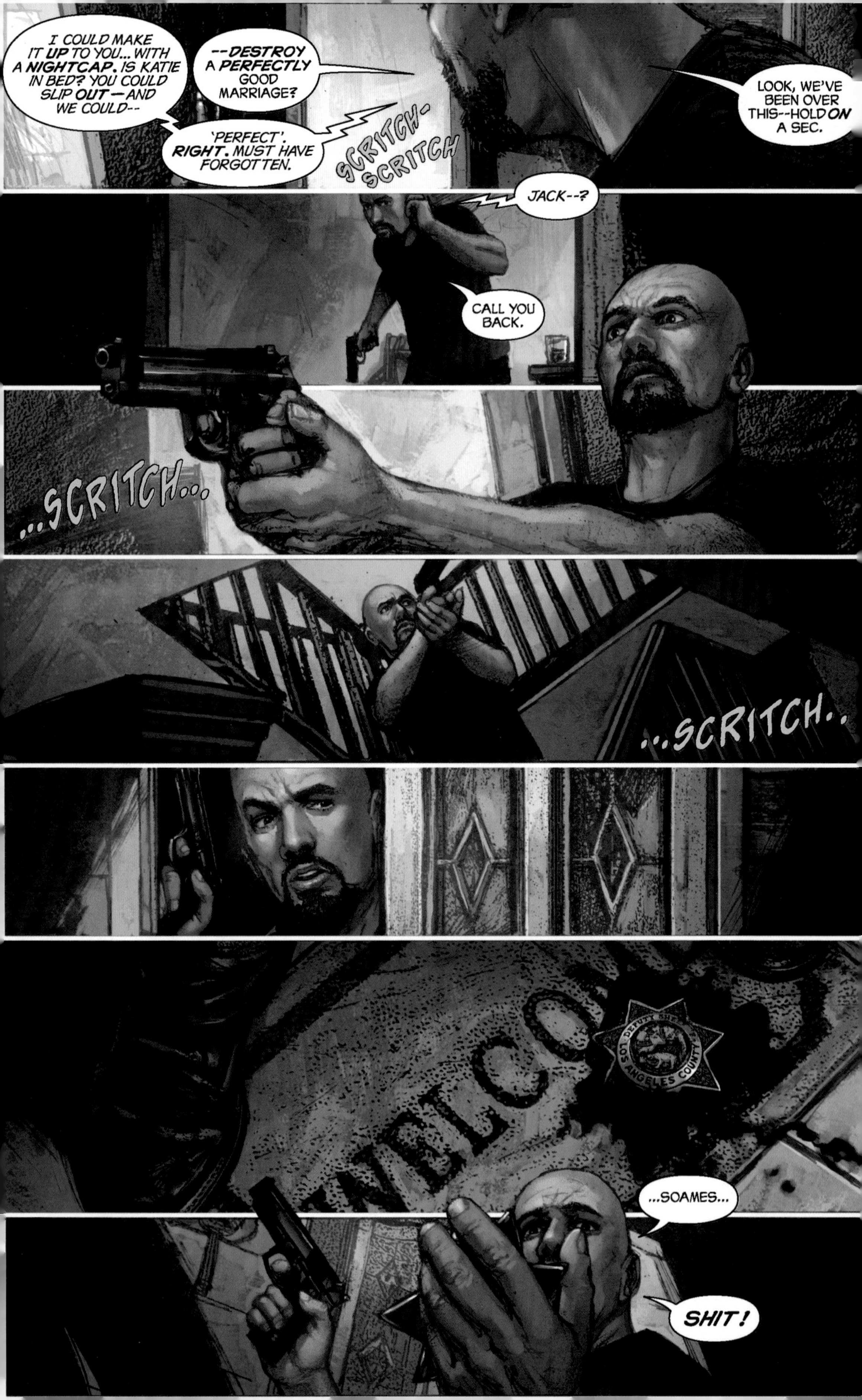
I COULD MAKE IT UP TO YOU... WITH A NIGHTCAP. IS KATIE IN BED? YOU COULD SLIP OUT—AND WE COULD--
--DESTROY A PERFECTLY GOOD MARRIAGE?
'PERFECT'. RIGHT. MUST HAVE FORGOTTEN.
SCRITCH-SCRITCH
LOOK, WE'VE BEEN OVER THIS--HOLD ON A SEC.
JACK--?
CALL YOU BACK.
...SCRITCH...
...SCRITCH..
DEPUTY SHERIFF
LOS ANGELES COUNTY
...SOAMES...
SHIT!

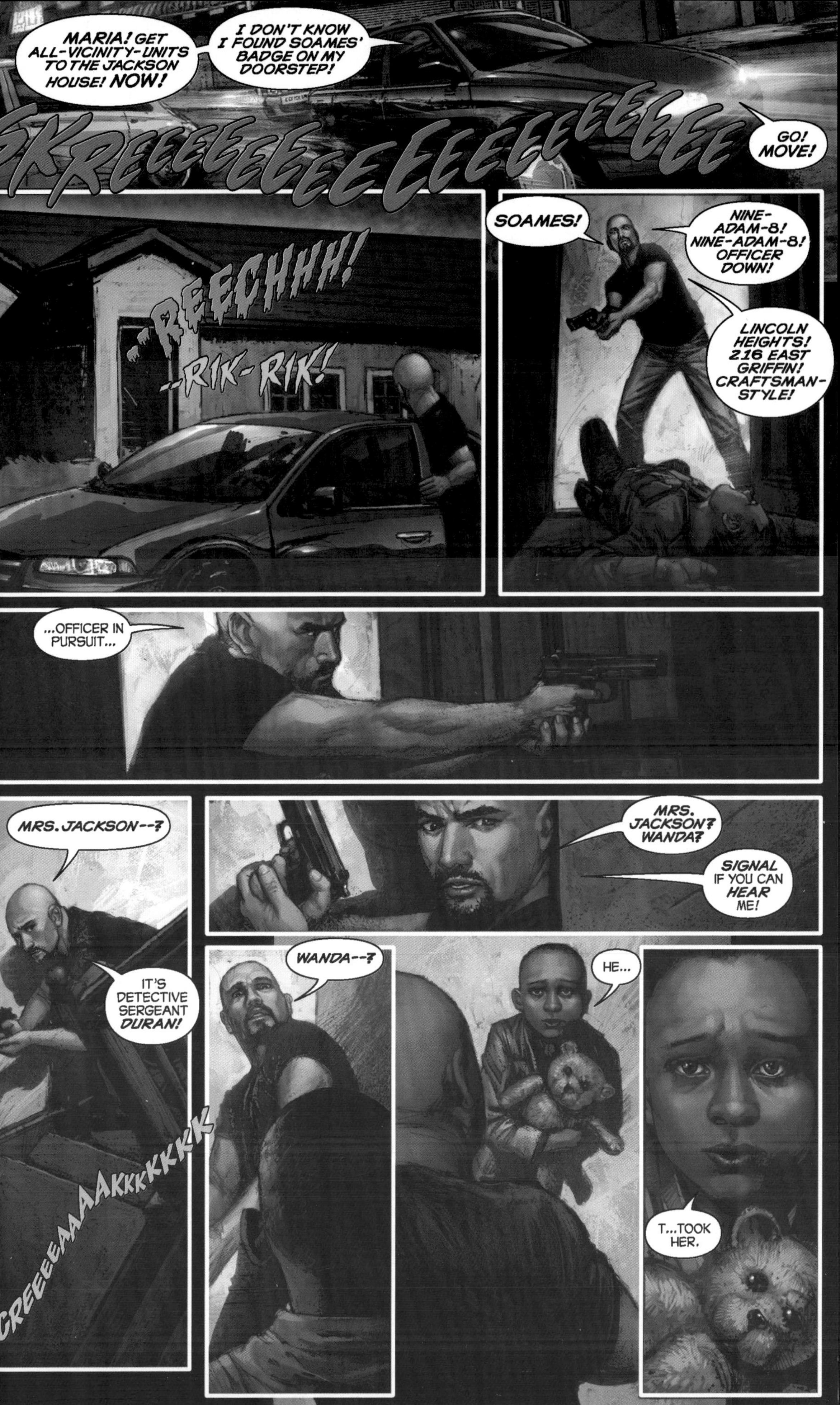
MARIA! GET ALL-VICINITY-UNITS TO THE JACKSON HOUSE! NOW!
I DON'T KNOW I FOUND SOAMES' BADGE ON MY DOORSTEP!
SKREEEEEEEEEEEEEEEEEEE
GO! MOVE!
..REECHHH!
..RIK-RIK!
SOAMES!
NINE-ADAM-8! NINE-ADAM-8! OFFICER DOWN!
LINCOLN HEIGHTS! 216 EAST GRIFFIN! CRAFTSMAN-STYLE!
...OFFICER IN PURSUIT...
MRS. JACKSON--?
IT'S DETECTIVE SERGEANT DURAN!
CREEEEAAAAKKKKKKK
MRS. JACKSON? WANDA?
SIGNAL IF YOU CAN HEAR ME!
WANDA--?
HE...
T...TOOK HER.

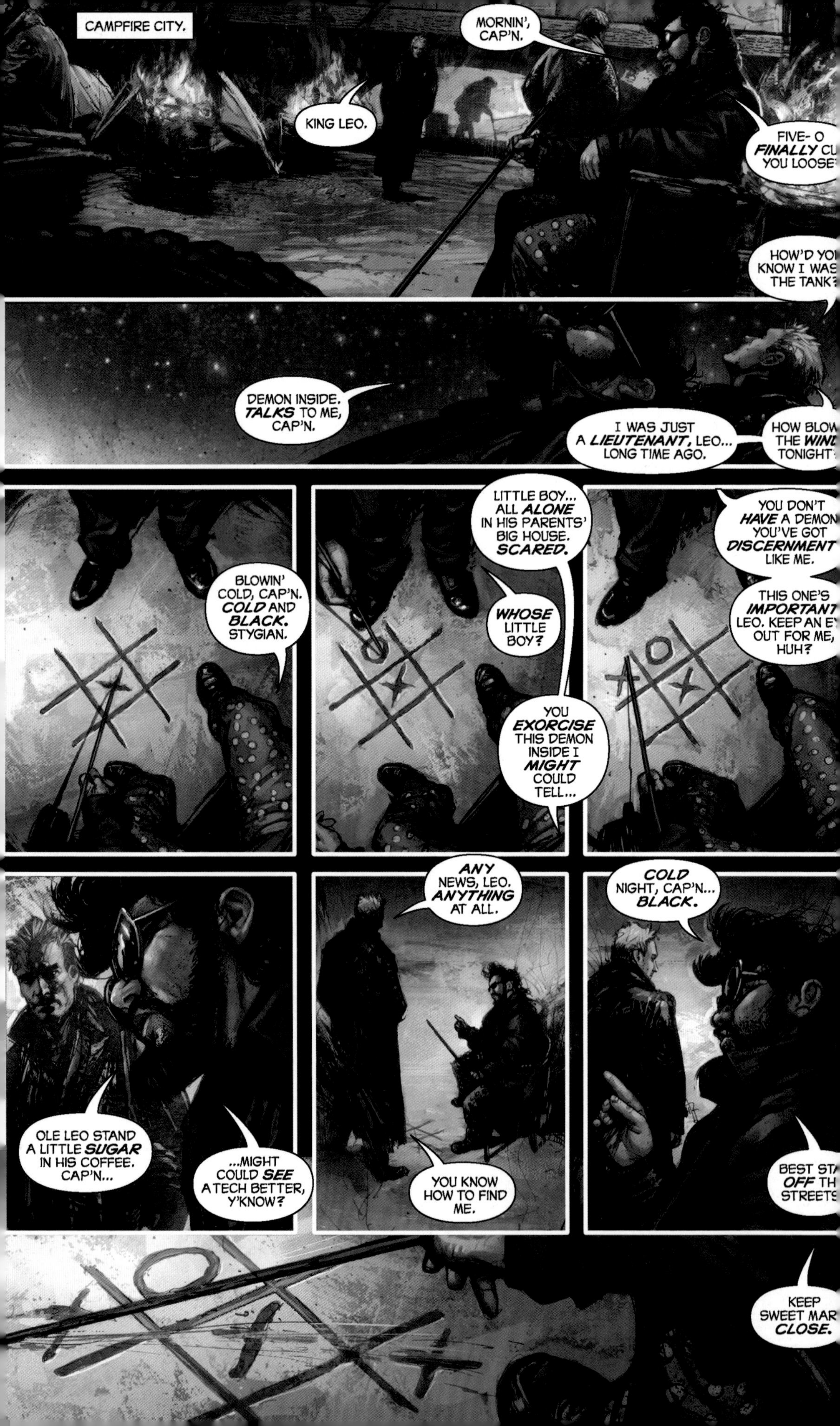

CAMPFIRE CITY.
MORNIN', CAP'N.
KING LEO.
FIVE- O FINALLY CU YOU LOOSE?
HOW'D YO KNOW I WAS THE TANK?
DEMON INSIDE. TALKS TO ME, CAP'N.
I WAS JUST A LIEUTENANT, LEO... LONG TIME AGO.
HOW BLOW THE WIND TONIGHT?
BLOWIN' COLD, CAP'N. COLD AND BLACK. STYGIAN.
LITTLE BOY... ALL ALONE IN HIS PARENTS' BIG HOUSE. SCARED.
WHOSE LITTLE BOY?
YOU EXORCISE THIS DEMON INSIDE I MIGHT COULD TELL...
YOU DON'T HAVE A DEMON YOU'VE GOT DISCERNMENT LIKE ME.
THIS ONE'S IMPORTANT LEO. KEEP AN E OUT FOR ME, HUH?
OLE LEO STAND A LITTLE SUGAR IN HIS COFFEE. CAP'N...
...MIGHT COULD SEE A TECH BETTER, Y'KNOW?
ANY NEWS, LEO. ANYTHING AT ALL.
YOU KNOW HOW TO FIND ME.
COLD NIGHT, CAP'N... BLACK.
BEST STA OFF TH STREETS
KEEP SWEET MAR CLOSE.

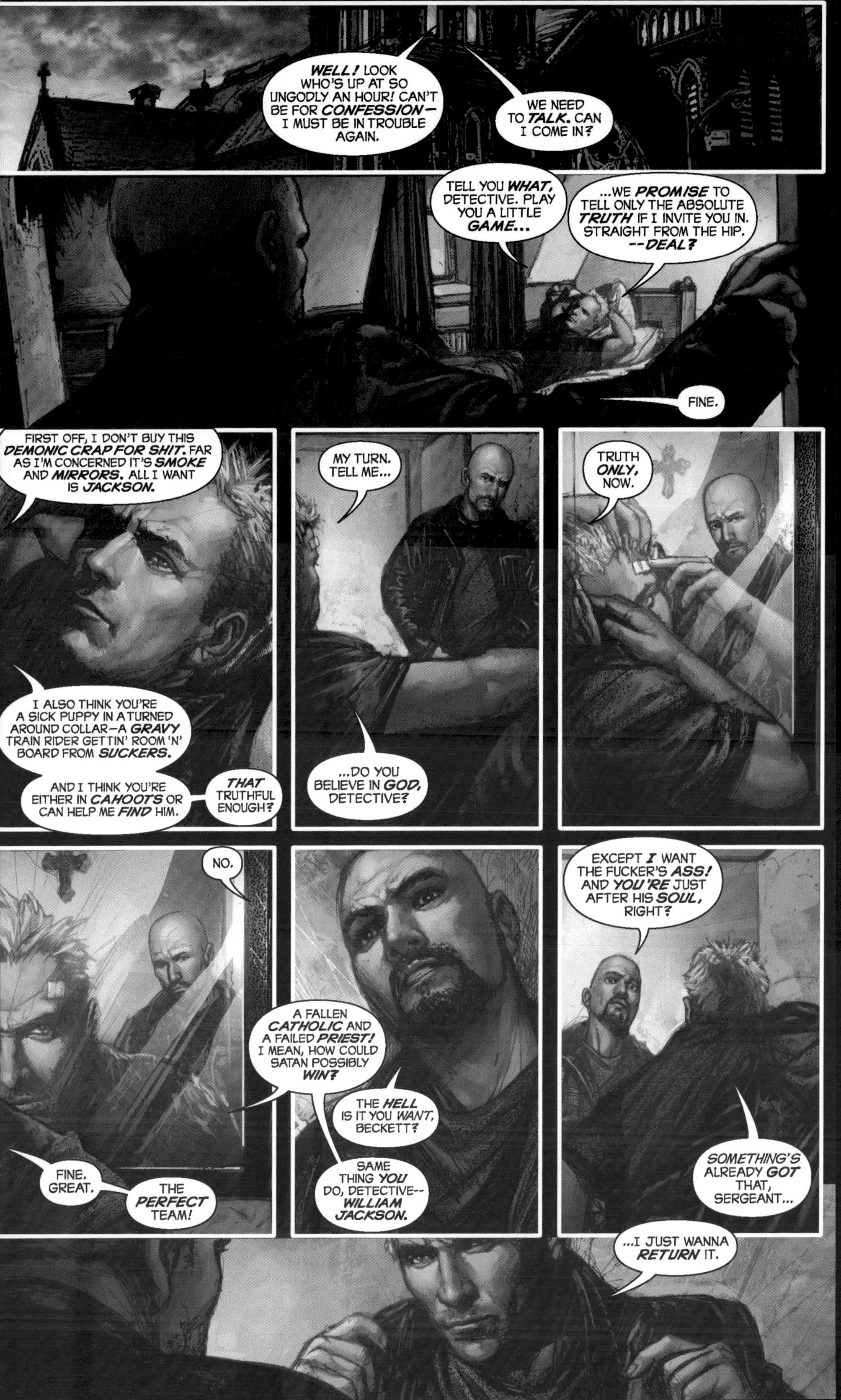

WELL! LOOK WHO'S UP AT SO UNGODLY AN HOUR! CAN'T BE FOR CONFESSION— I MUST BE IN TROUBLE AGAIN.
WE NEED TO TALK. CAN I COME IN?
TELL YOU WHAT, DETECTIVE. PLAY YOU A LITTLE GAME...
...WE PROMISE TO TELL ONLY THE ABSOLUTE TRUTH IF I INVITE YOU IN. STRAIGHT FROM THE HIP. --DEAL?
FINE.
FIRST OFF, I DON'T BUY THIS DEMONIC CRAP FOR SHIT. FAR AS I'M CONCERNED IT'S SMOKE AND MIRRORS. ALL I WANT IS JACKSON.
I ALSO THINK YOU'RE A SICK PUPPY IN A TURNED AROUND COLLAR—A GRAVY TRAIN RIDER GETTIN' ROOM 'N' BOARD FROM SUCKERS.
AND I THINK YOU'RE EITHER IN CAHOOTS OR CAN HELP ME FIND HIM.
THAT TRUTHFUL ENOUGH?
MY TURN. TELL ME...
...DO YOU BELIEVE IN GOD, DETECTIVE?
TRUTH ONLY, NOW.
NO.
A FALLEN CATHOLIC AND A FAILED PRIEST! I MEAN, HOW COULD SATAN POSSIBLY WIN?
FINE. GREAT.
THE PERFECT TEAM!
THE HELL IS IT YOU WANT, BECKETT?
SAME THING YOU DO, DETECTIVE-- WILLIAM JACKSON.
EXCEPT I WANT THE FUCKER'S ASS! AND YOU'RE JUST AFTER HIS SOUL, RIGHT?
SOMETHING'S ALREADY GOT THAT, SERGEANT...
...I JUST WANNA RETURN IT.

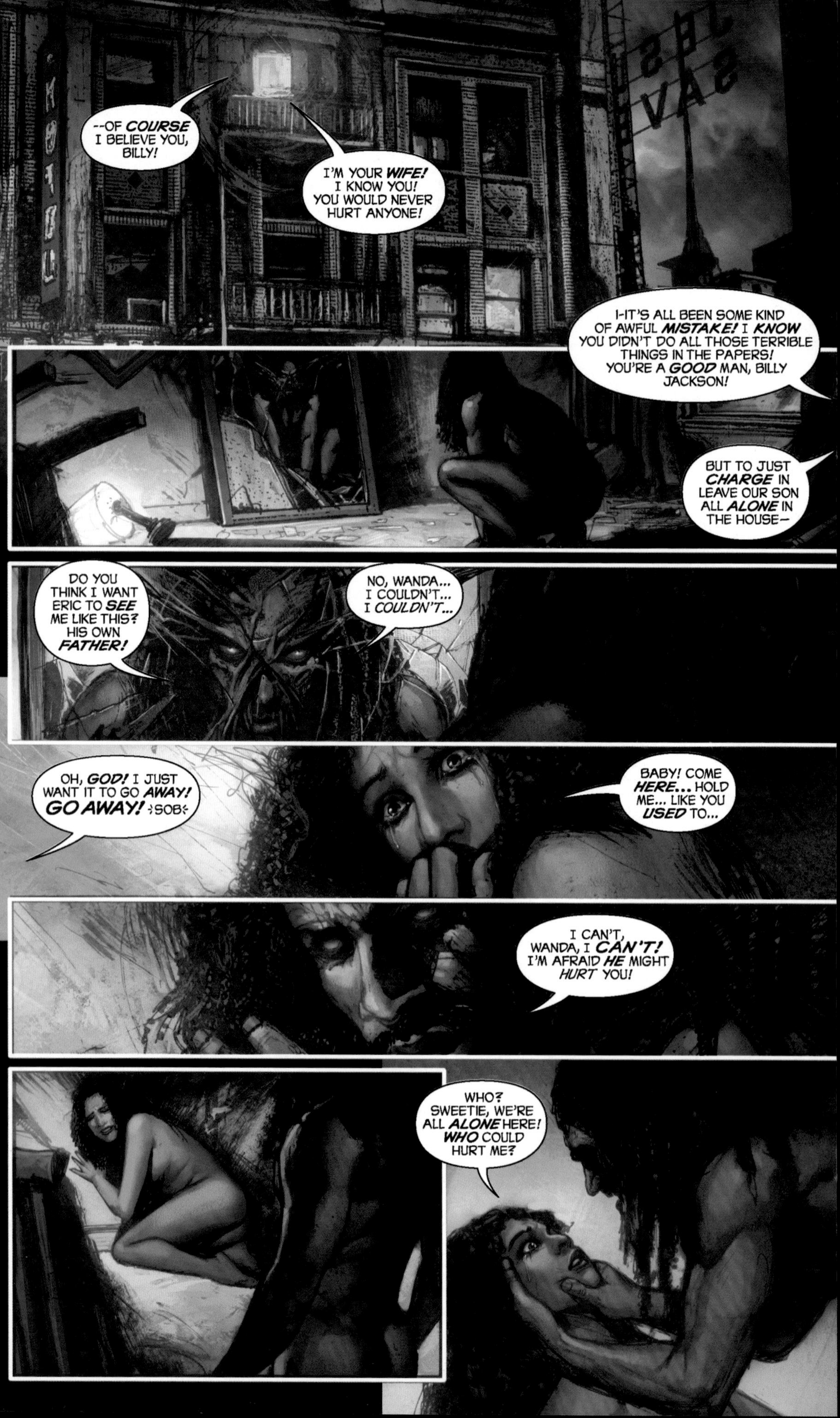
--OF COURSE I BELIEVE YOU, BILLY!
I'M YOUR WIFE! I KNOW YOU! YOU WOULD NEVER HURT ANYONE!
I-IT'S ALL BEEN SOME KIND OF AWFUL MISTAKE! I KNOW YOU DIDN'T DO ALL THOSE TERRIBLE THINGS IN THE PAPERS! YOU'RE A GOOD MAN, BILLY JACKSON!
BUT TO JUST CHARGE IN LEAVE OUR SON ALL ALONE IN THE HOUSE--
DO YOU THINK I WANT ERIC TO SEE ME LIKE THIS? HIS OWN FATHER!
NO, WANDA... I COULDN'T... I COULDN'T...
OH, GOD! I JUST WANT IT TO GO AWAY! GO AWAY! SOB
BABY! COME HERE... HOLD ME... LIKE YOU USED TO...
I CAN'T, WANDA, I CAN'T! I'M AFRAID HE MIGHT HURT YOU!
WHO? SWEETIE, WE'RE ALL ALONE HERE! WHO COULD HURT ME?

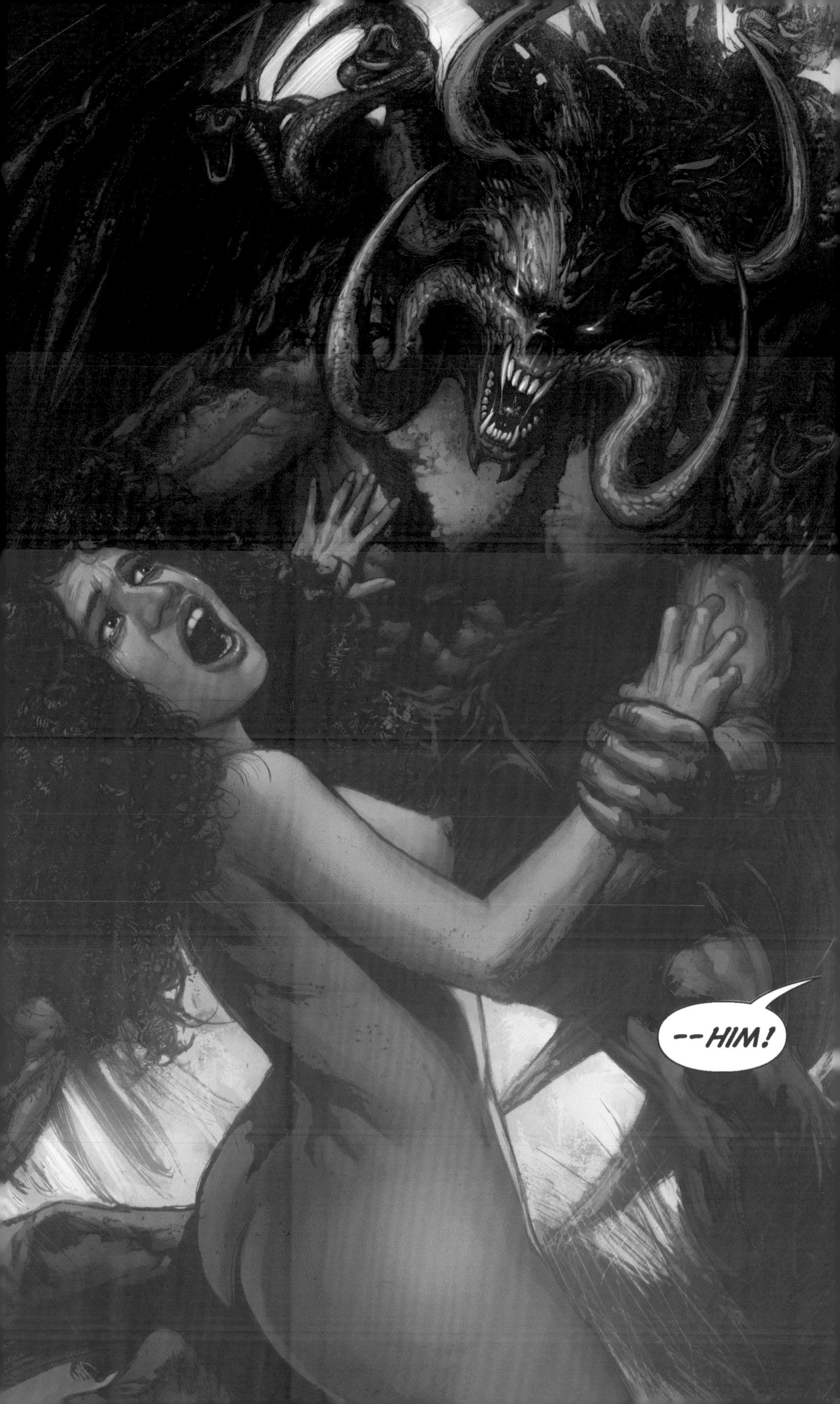
--HIM!

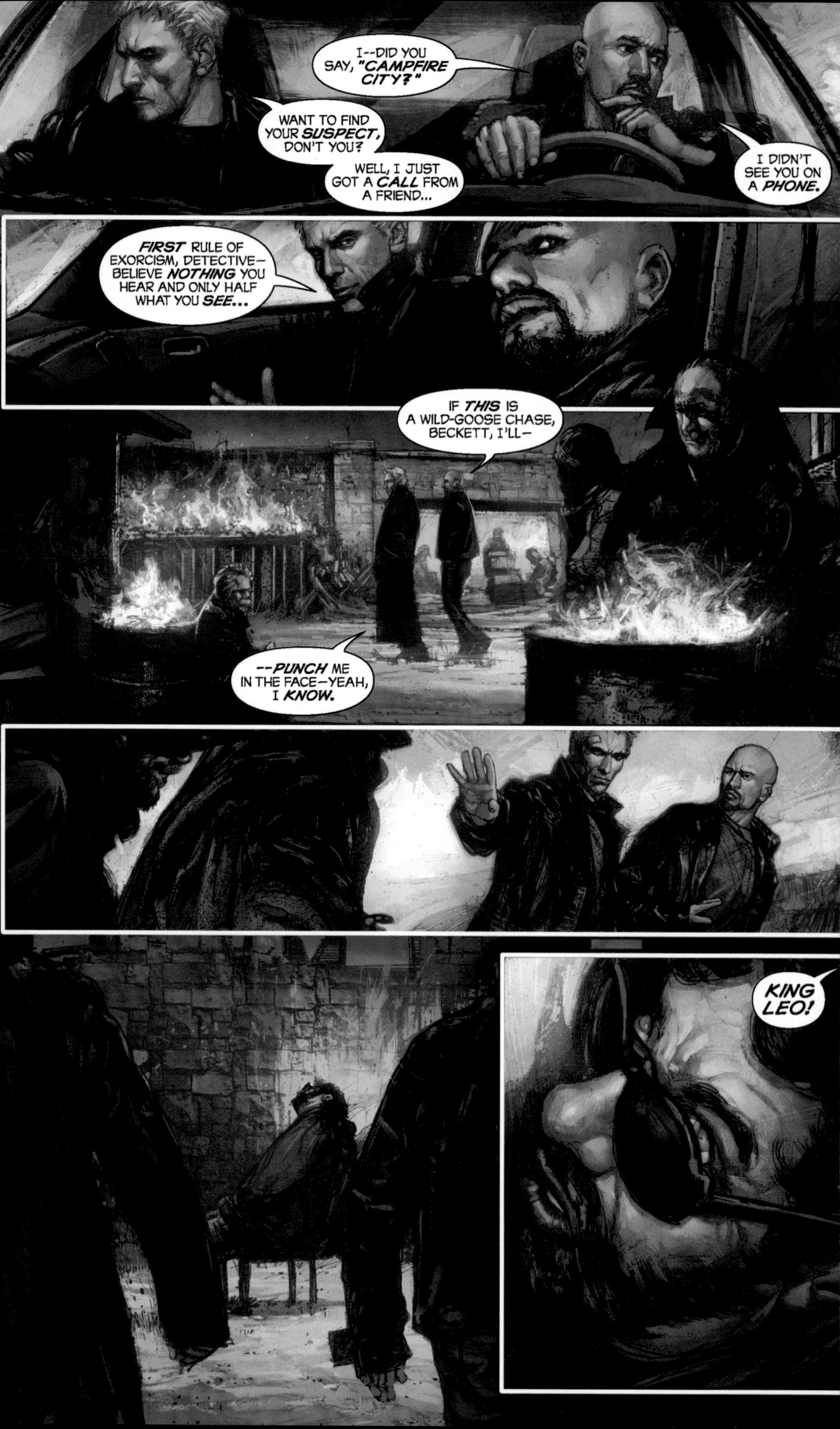
I--DID YOU SAY, "CAMPFIRE CITY?"
WANT TO FIND YOUR SUSPECT, DON'T YOU?
WELL, I JUST GOT A CALL FROM A FRIEND...
I DIDN'T SEE YOU ON A PHONE.
FIRST RULE OF EXORCISM, DETECTIVE-BELIEVE NOTHING YOU HEAR AND ONLY HALF WHAT YOU SEE...
IF THIS IS A WILD-GOOSE CHASE, BECKETT, I'LL-
--PUNCH ME IN THE FACE-YEAH, I KNOW.
KING LEO!

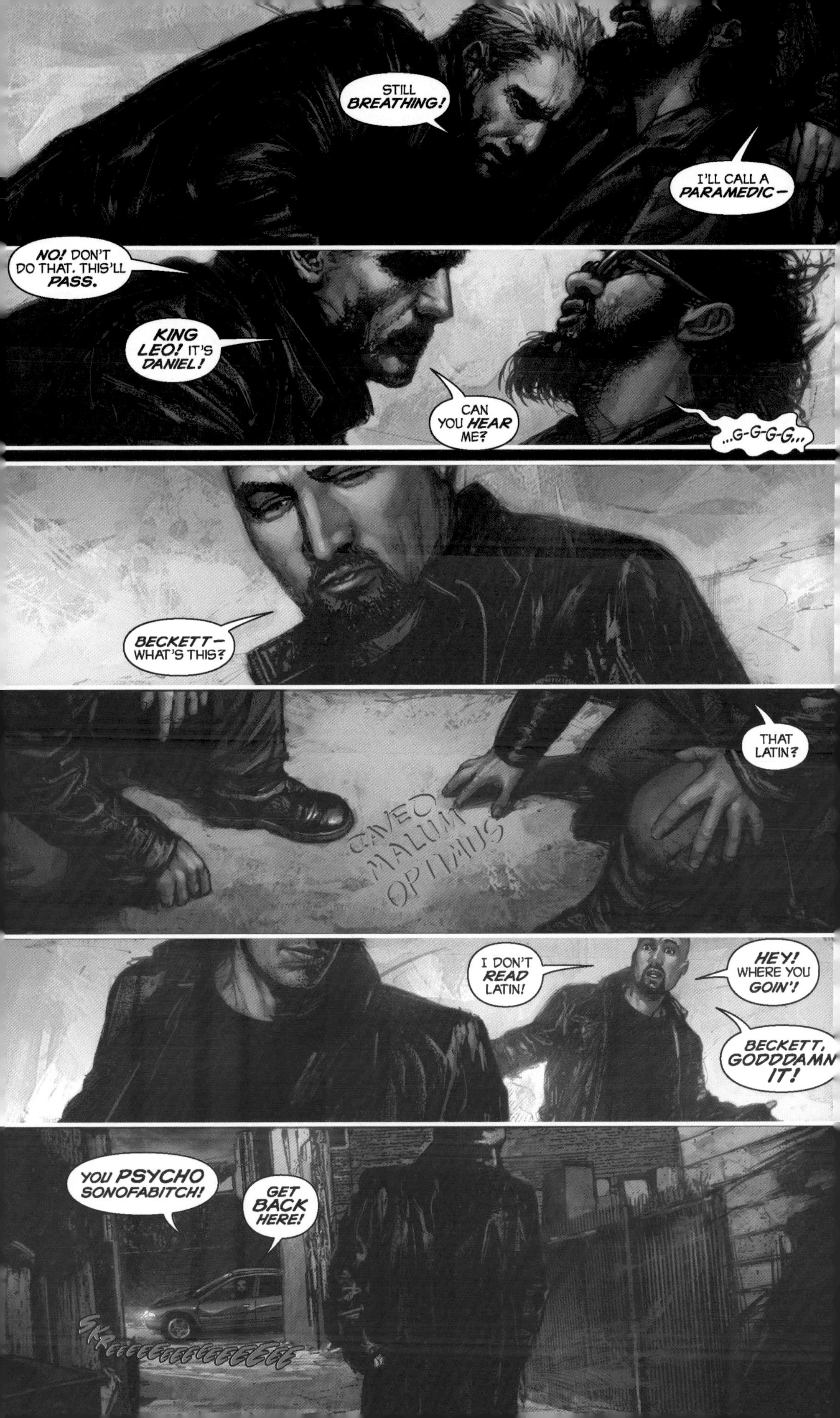
STILL BREATHING!
I'LL CALL A PARAMEDIC—
NO! DON'T DO THAT. THIS'LL PASS.
KING LEO! IT'S DANIEL!
CAN YOU HEAR ME?
...G-G-G-G...
BECKETT— WHAT'S THIS?
THAT LATIN?
CAVEO MALUM OPTIMUS
I DON'T READ LATIN!
HEY! WHERE YOU GOIN'!
BECKETT, GODDDAMN IT!
YOU PSYCHO SONOFABITCH!
GET BACK HERE!
SKREEEEEEEEEEEEEEE

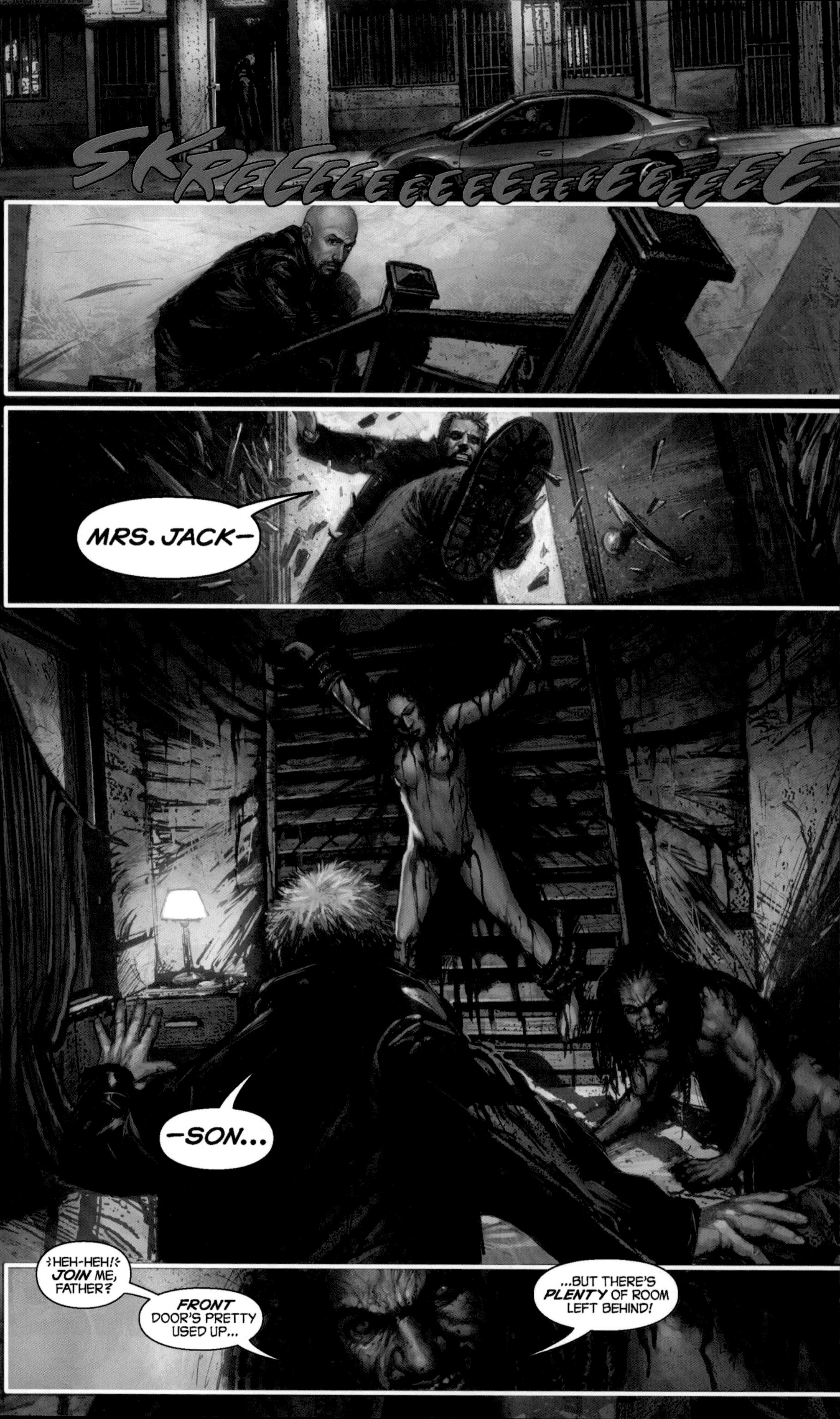
SKREEEEEEEEEEEEEEEEEEE
MRS. JACK—
—SON...
HEH-HEH! JOIN ME, FATHER?
FRONT DOOR'S PRETTY USED UP...
...BUT THERE'S PLENTY OF ROOM LEFT BEHIND!

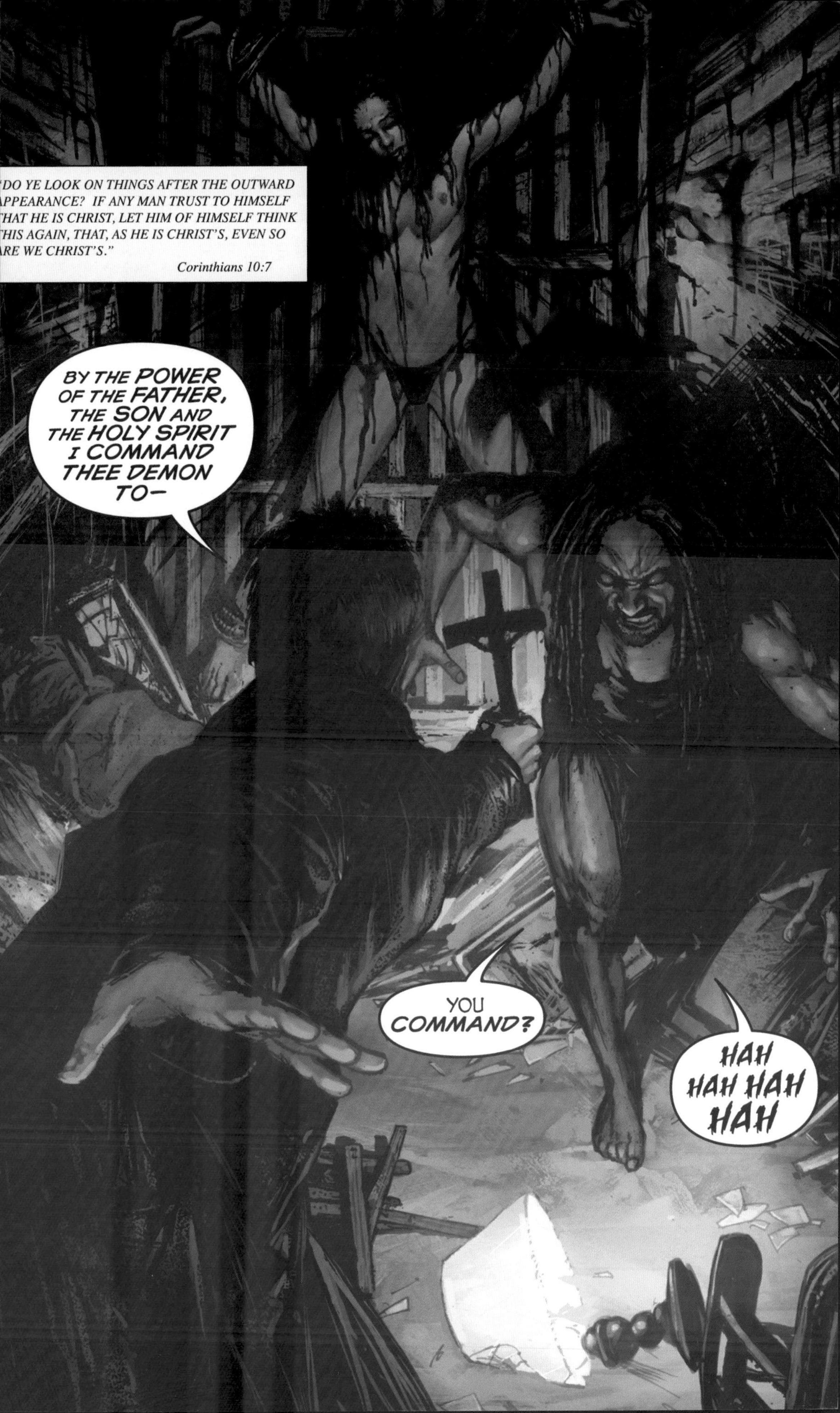
"DO YE LOOK ON THINGS AFTER THE OUTWARD APPEARANCE? IF ANY MAN TRUST TO HIMSELF THAT HE IS CHRIST, LET HIM OF HIMSELF THINK THIS AGAIN, THAT, AS HE IS CHRIST'S, EVEN SO ARE WE CHRIST'S."
Corinthians 10:7
BY THE POWER OF THE FATHER, THE SON AND THE HOLY SPIRIT I COMMAND THEE DEMON TO–
YOU COMMAND?
HAH HAH HAH HAH

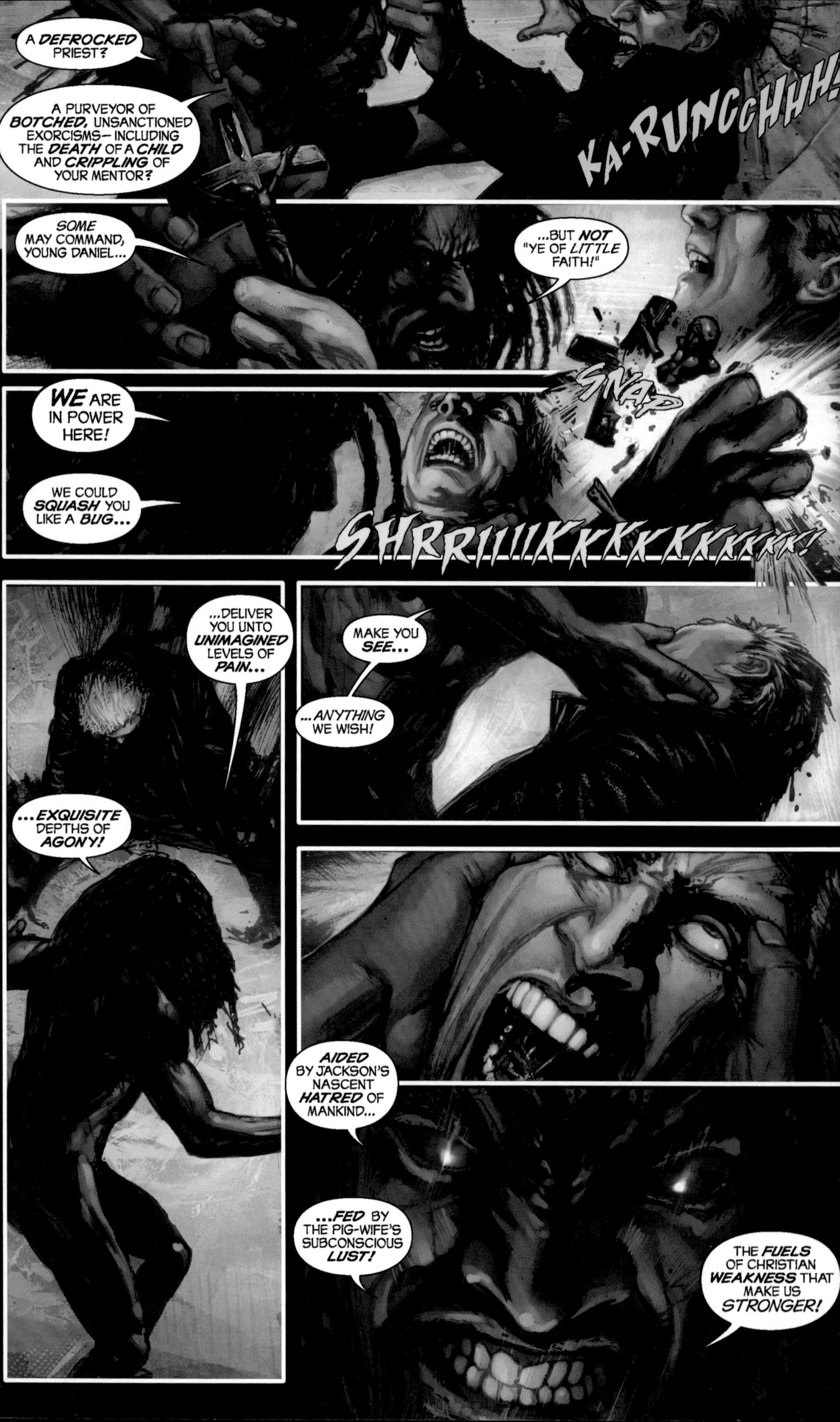
A DEFROCKED PRIEST?
A PURVEYOR OF BOTCHED, UNSANCTIONED EXORCISMS— INCLUDING THE DEATH OF A CHILD AND CRIPPLING OF YOUR MENTOR?
KA-RUNCCHHH!
SOME MAY COMMAND, YOUNG DANIEL...
...BUT NOT "YE OF LITTLE FAITH!"
SNAP
WE ARE IN POWER HERE!
WE COULD SQUASH YOU LIKE A BUG...
SHRRIIIIIKKKKKKKKKK!
...DELIVER YOU UNTO UNIMAGINED LEVELS OF PAIN...
...EXQUISITE DEPTHS OF AGONY!
MAKE YOU SEE...
...ANYTHING WE WISH!
AIDED BY JACKSON'S NASCENT HATRED OF MANKIND...
...FED BY THE PIG-WIFE'S SUBCONSCIOUS LUST!
THE FUELS OF CHRISTIAN WEAKNESS THAT MAKE US STRONGER!

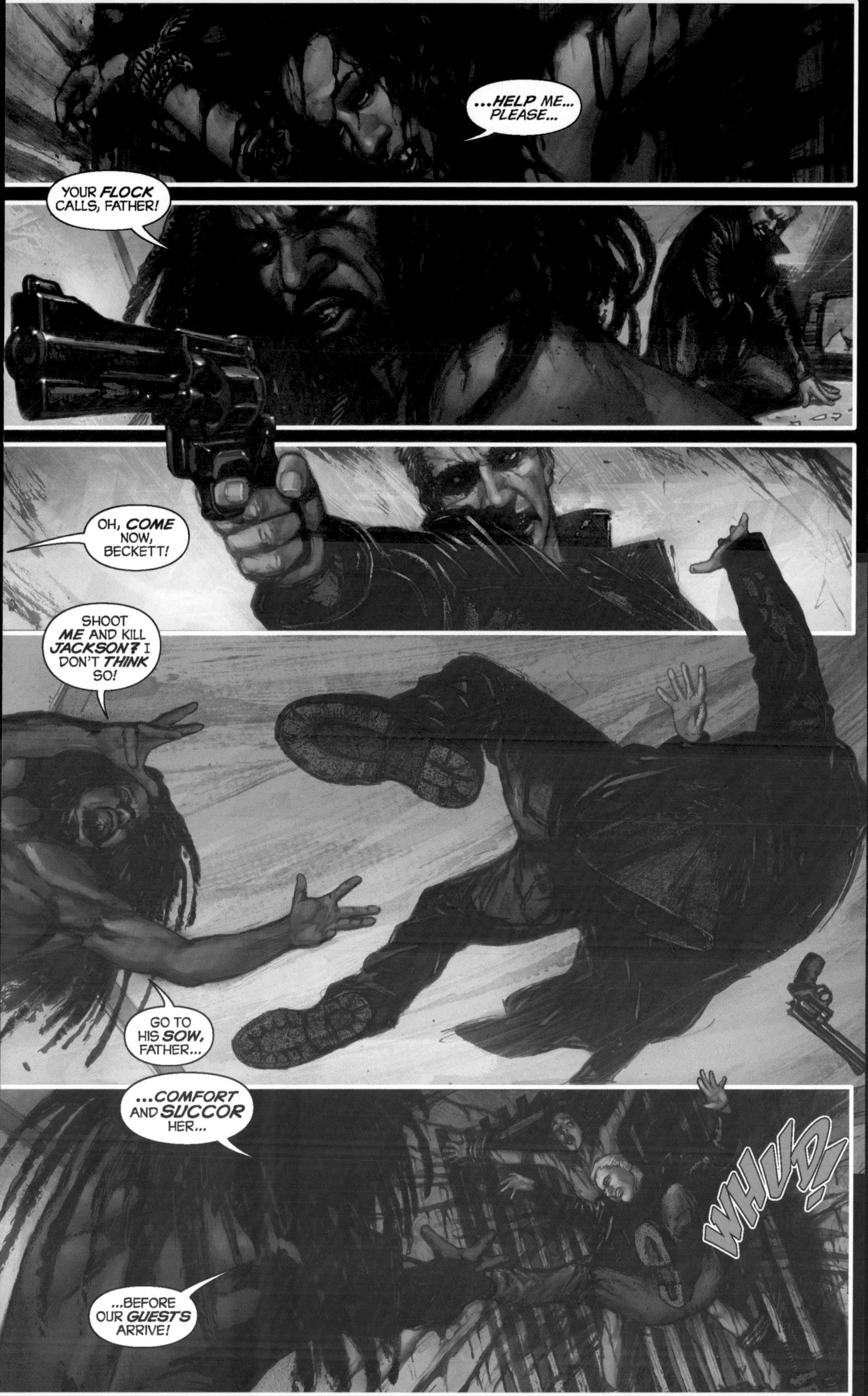
...HELP ME... PLEASE...
YOUR FLOCK CALLS, FATHER!
OH, COME NOW, BECKETT!
SHOOT ME AND KILL JACKSON? I DON'T THINK SO!
GO TO HIS SOW, FATHER...
...COMFORT AND SUCCOR HER...
...BEFORE OUR GUESTS ARRIVE!
WHUD!

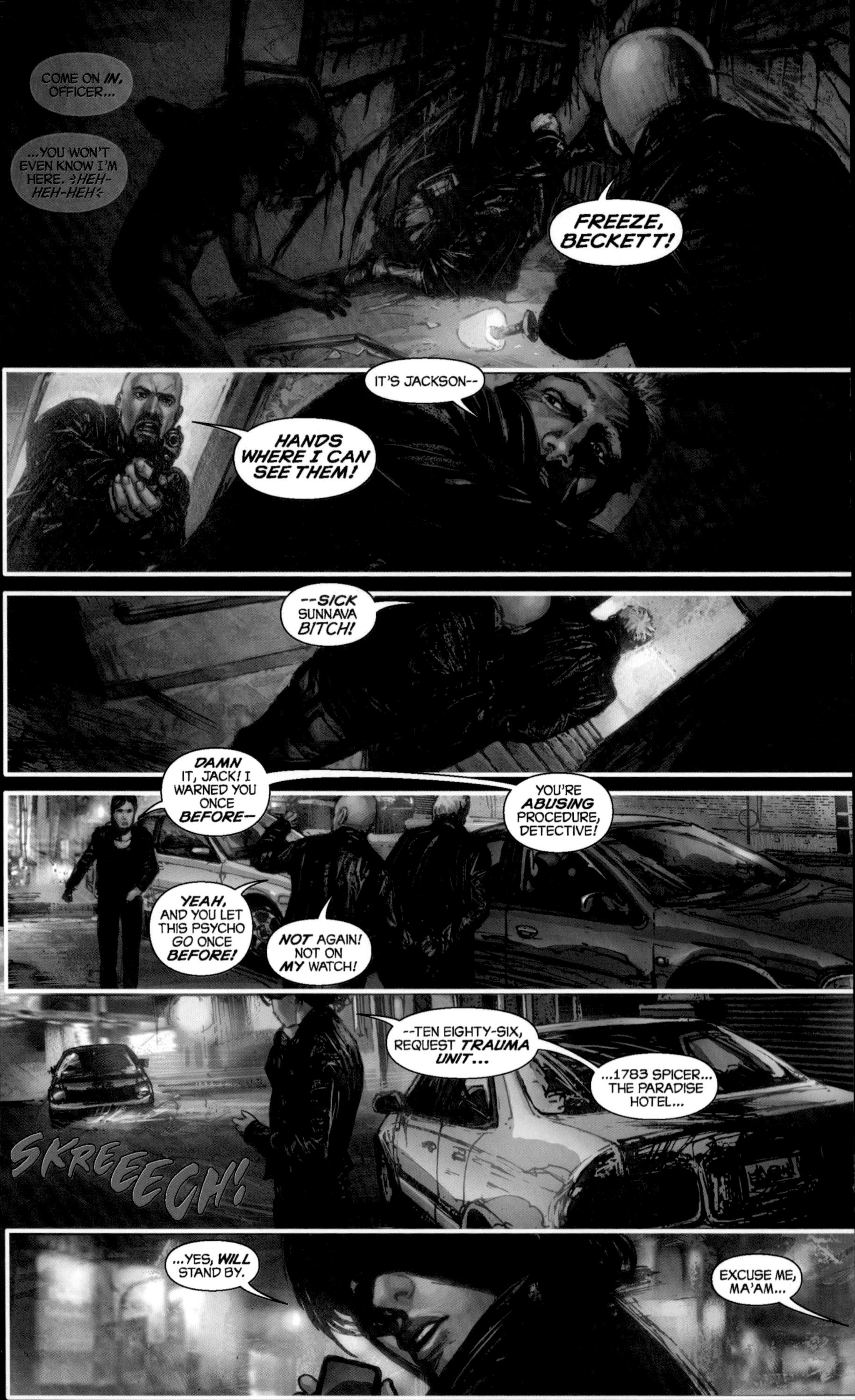
COME ON *IN*, OFFICER...
...YOU WON'T EVEN KNOW I'M HERE. ›HEH-HEH-HEH‹
FREEZE, BECKETT!
IT'S JACKSON--
HANDS WHERE I CAN SEE THEM!
--SICK SUNNAVA BITCH!
DAMN IT, JACK! I WARNED YOU ONCE BEFORE--
YOU'RE ABUSING PROCEDURE, DETECTIVE!
YEAH, AND YOU LET THIS PSYCHO GO ONCE BEFORE!
NOT AGAIN! NOT ON MY WATCH!
--TEN EIGHTY-SIX, REQUEST TRAUMA UNIT...
...1783 SPICER... THE PARADISE HOTEL...
SKREEECH!
...YES, WILL STAND BY.
EXCUSE ME, MA'AM...

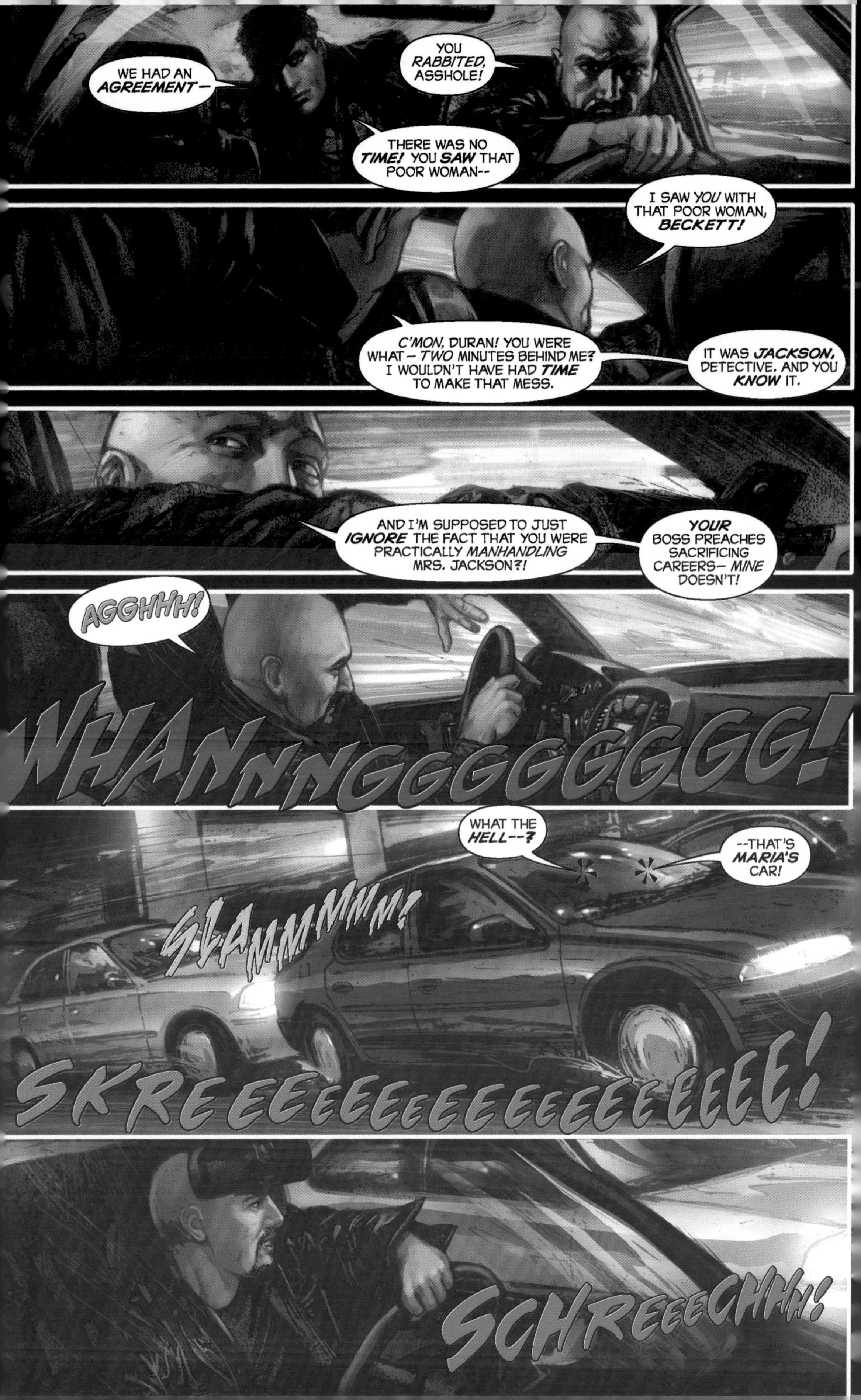

WE HAD AN AGREEMENT--
YOU RABBITED, ASSHOLE!
THERE WAS NO TIME! YOU SAW THAT POOR WOMAN--
I SAW YOU WITH THAT POOR WOMAN, BECKETT!
C'MON, DURAN! YOU WERE WHAT--TWO MINUTES BEHIND ME? I WOULDN'T HAVE HAD TIME TO MAKE THAT MESS.
IT WAS JACKSON, DETECTIVE. AND YOU KNOW IT.
AND I'M SUPPOSED TO JUST IGNORE THE FACT THAT YOU WERE PRACTICALLY MANHANDLING MRS. JACKSON?!
YOUR BOSS PREACHES SACRIFICING CAREERS--MINE DOESN'T!
AGGHHH!
WHANNNGGGGGGGG!
WHAT THE HELL--?
--THAT'S MARIA'S CAR!
SLAMMMMM!
SKREEEEEEEEEEEEEEEEE!
SCHREEECHHH!

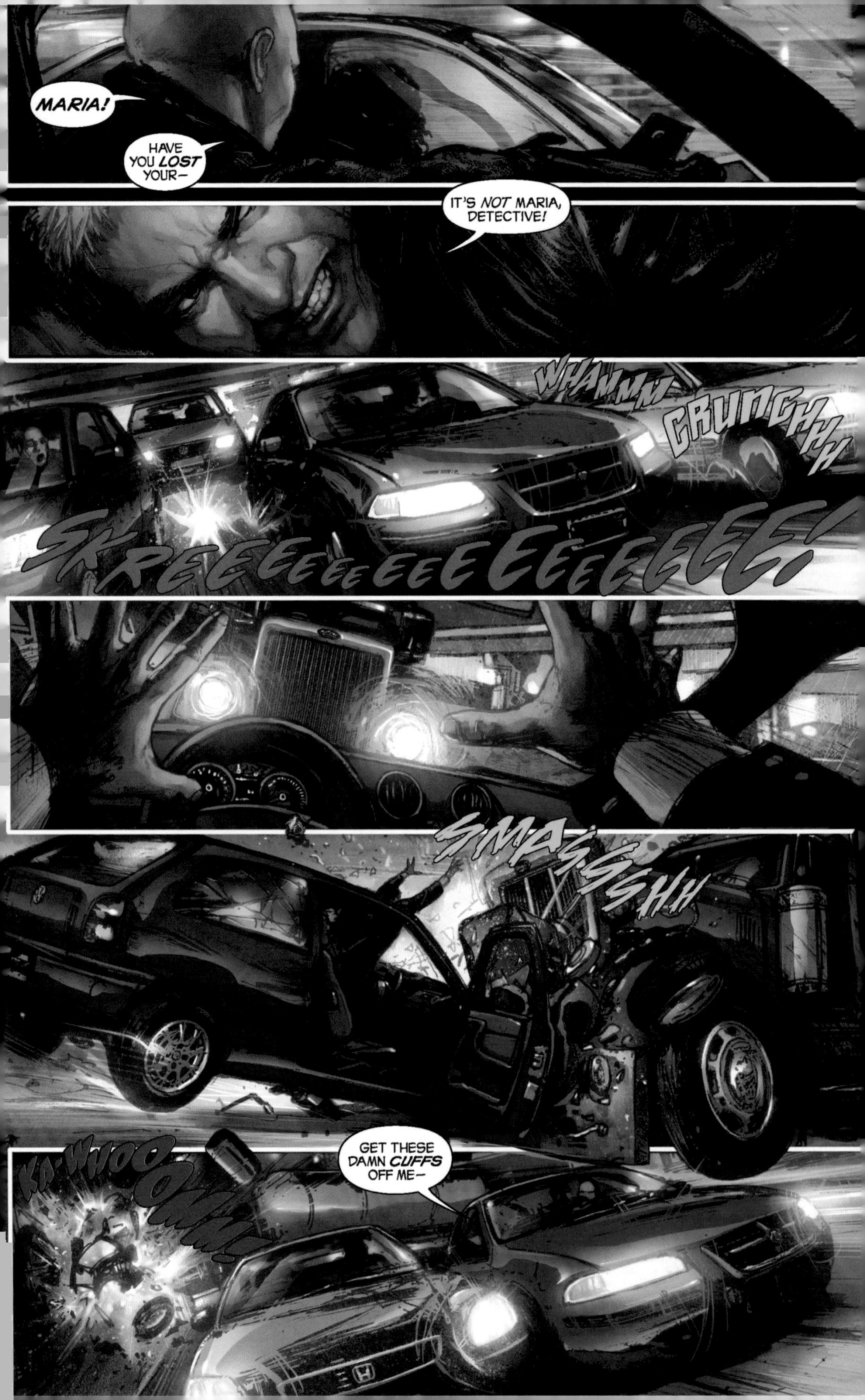
MARIA!
HAVE YOU LOST YOUR—
IT'S NOT MARIA, DETECTIVE!
WHAMMM
CRUNCHHH
SKREEEEEEEEEEEEEEEE!
SMASSSHH
KA-WHOOOOMM!
GET THESE DAMN CUFFS OFF ME—

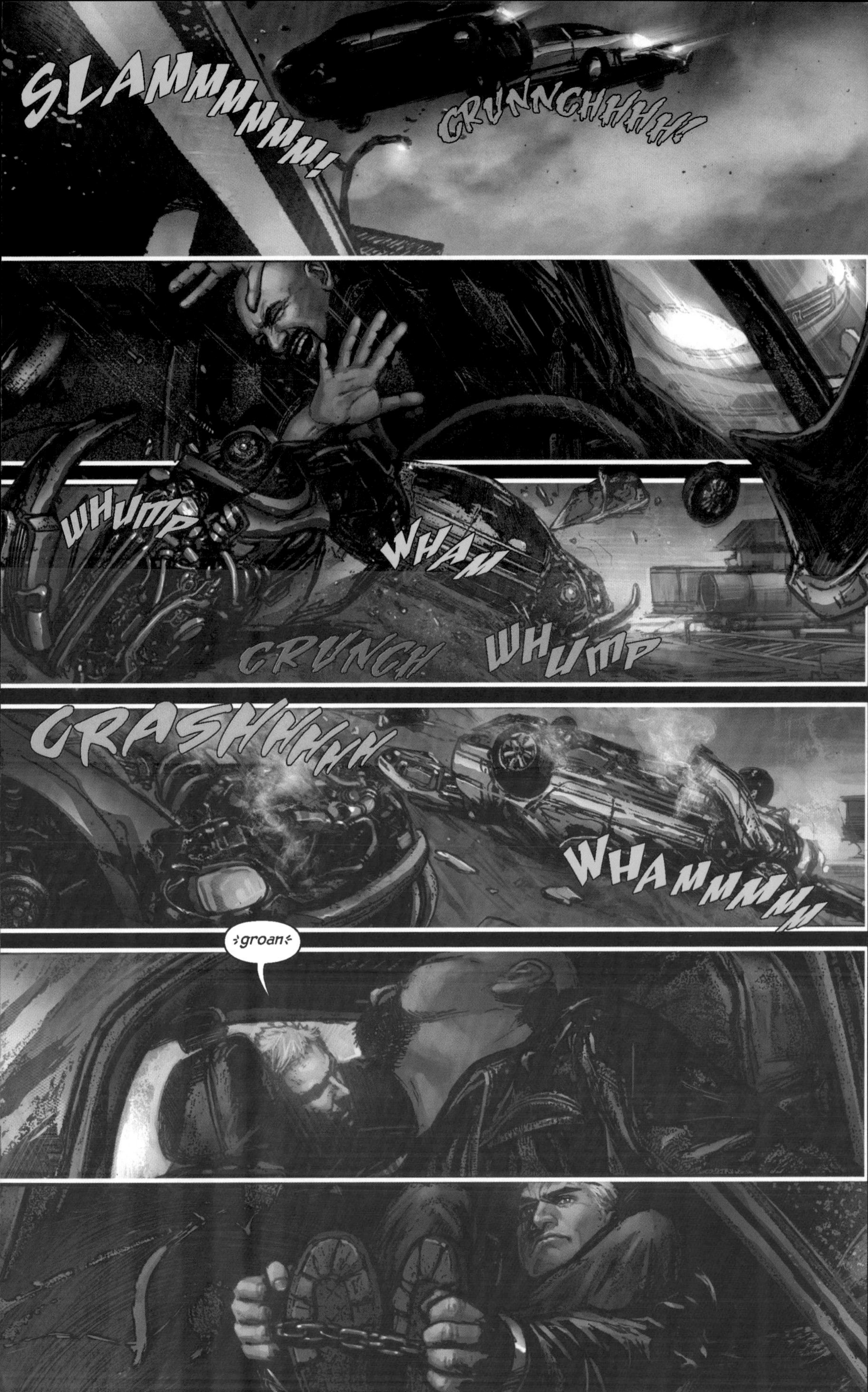
SLAMMMMMM!
CRUNNCHHHH!
WHUMP
WHAM
CRUNCH
WHUMP
CRASHHHHH
WHAMMMMM
groan

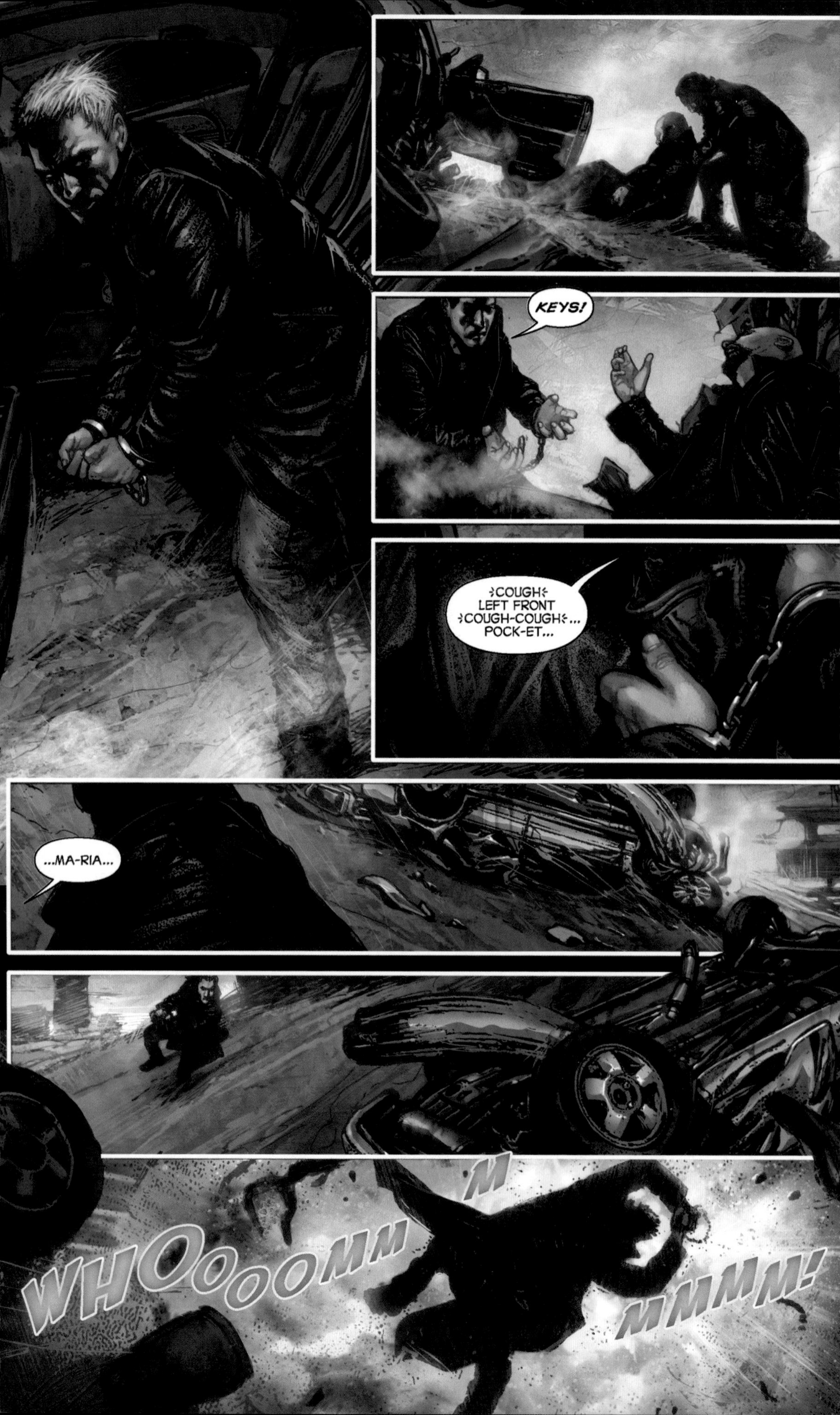
KEYS!
COUGH LEFT FRONT *COUGH-COUGH*... POCK-ET...
...MA-RIA...
WHOOOOOMMMMMMM!

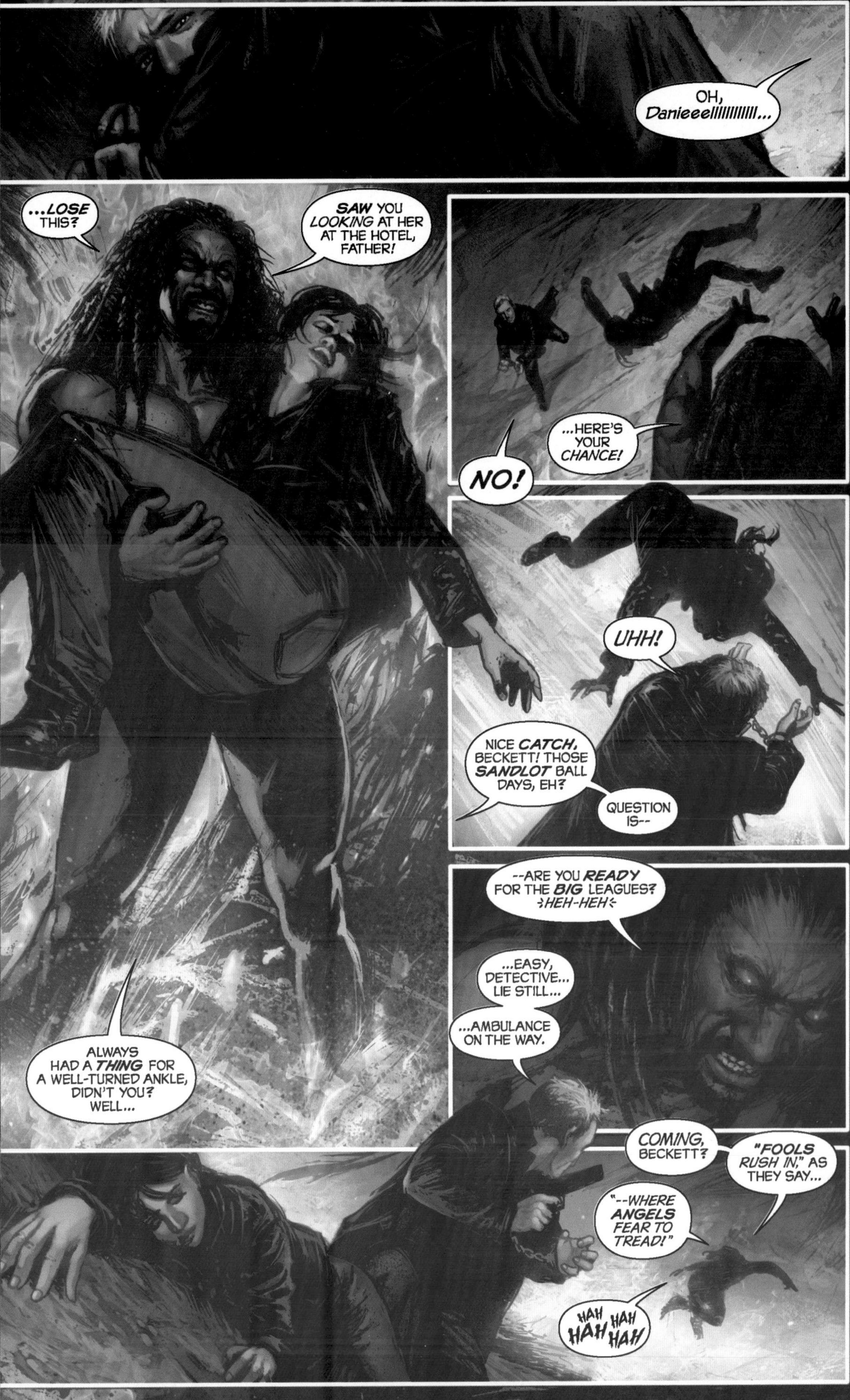
OH, Danieeelllllllllllll...
...LOSE THIS?
SAW YOU LOOKING AT HER AT THE HOTEL, FATHER!
ALWAYS HAD A THING FOR A WELL-TURNED ANKLE, DIDN'T YOU? WELL...
...HERE'S YOUR CHANCE!
NO!
UHH!
NICE CATCH, BECKETT! THOSE SANDLOT BALL DAYS, EH?
QUESTION IS--
--ARE YOU READY FOR THE BIG LEAGUES? HEH-HEH
...EASY, DETECTIVE... LIE STILL...
...AMBULANCE ON THE WAY.
COMING, BECKETT?
"FOOLS RUSH IN," AS THEY SAY...
"--WHERE ANGELS FEAR TO TREAD!"
HAH HAH HAH HAH

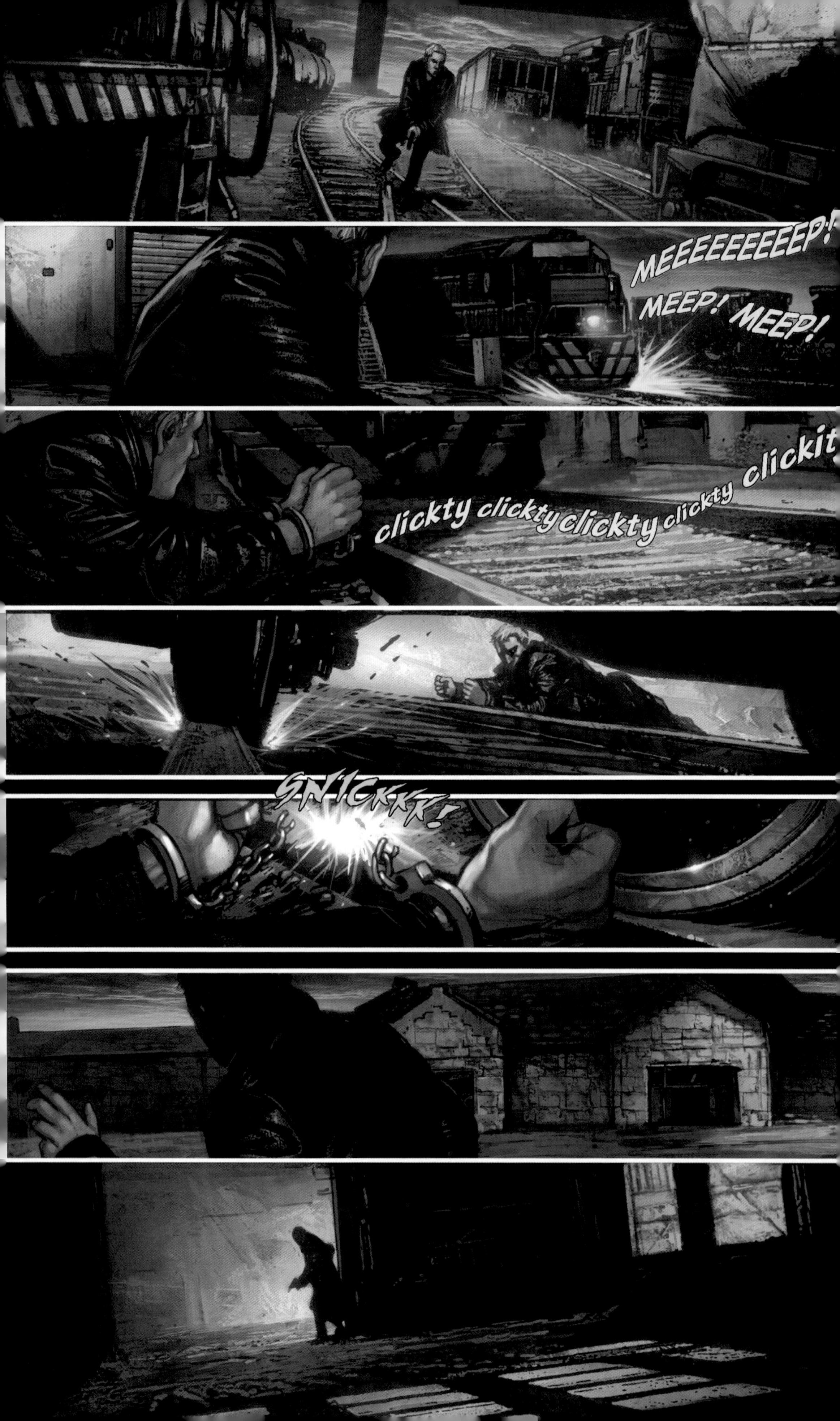
MEEEEEEEEEP!
MEEP! MEEP!
clickty clickty clickty clickty clickit
SNICKKK!

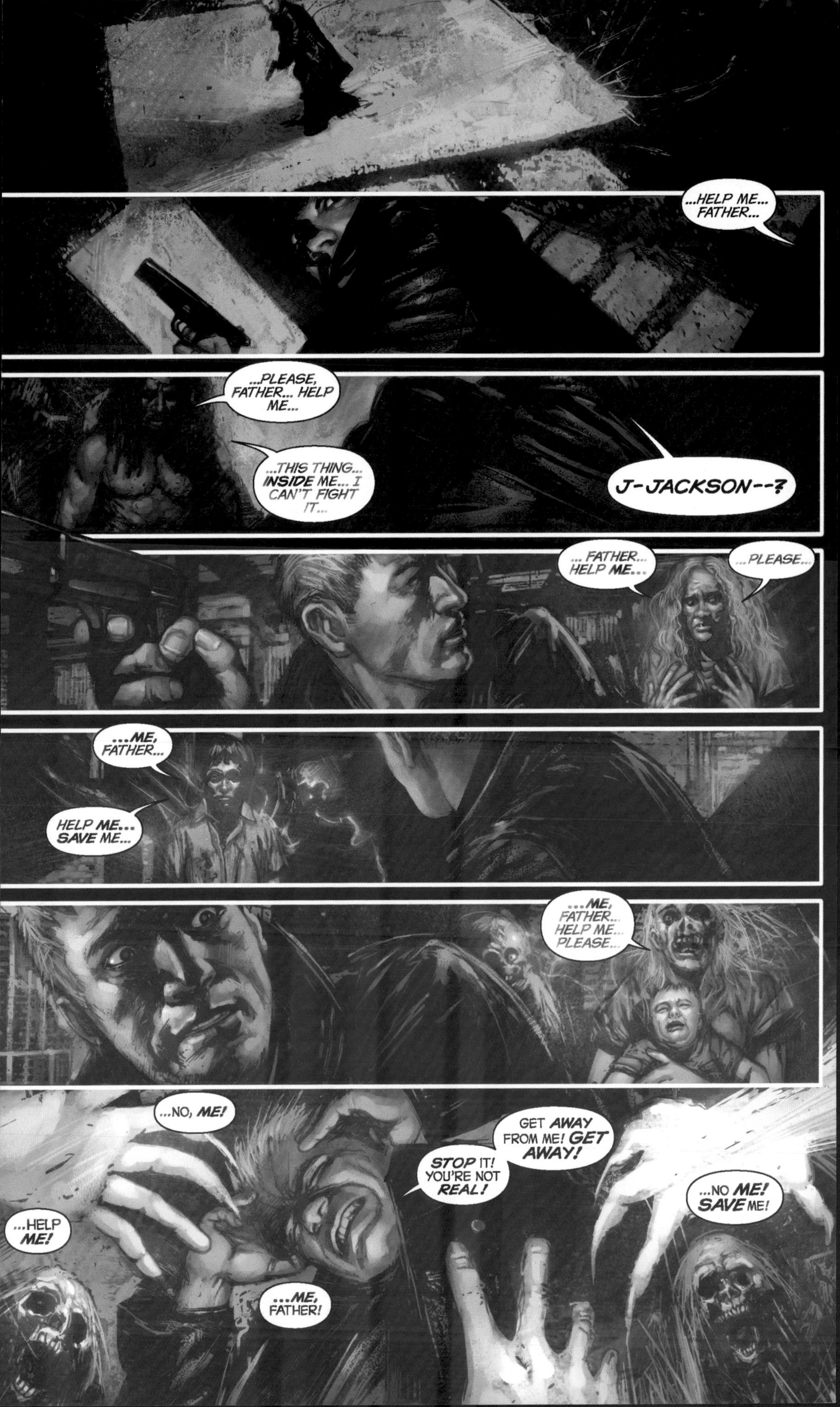
...HELP ME... FATHER...
...PLEASE, FATHER... HELP ME...
...THIS THING... INSIDE ME... I CAN'T FIGHT IT...
J-JACKSON--?
... FATHER... HELP ME...
...PLEASE...
...ME, FATHER...
HELP ME... SAVE ME...
...ME, FATHER... HELP ME... PLEASE...
...NO, ME!
GET AWAY FROM ME! GET AWAY!
STOP IT! YOU'RE NOT REAL!
...NO ME! SAVE ME!
...HELP ME!
...ME, FATHER!

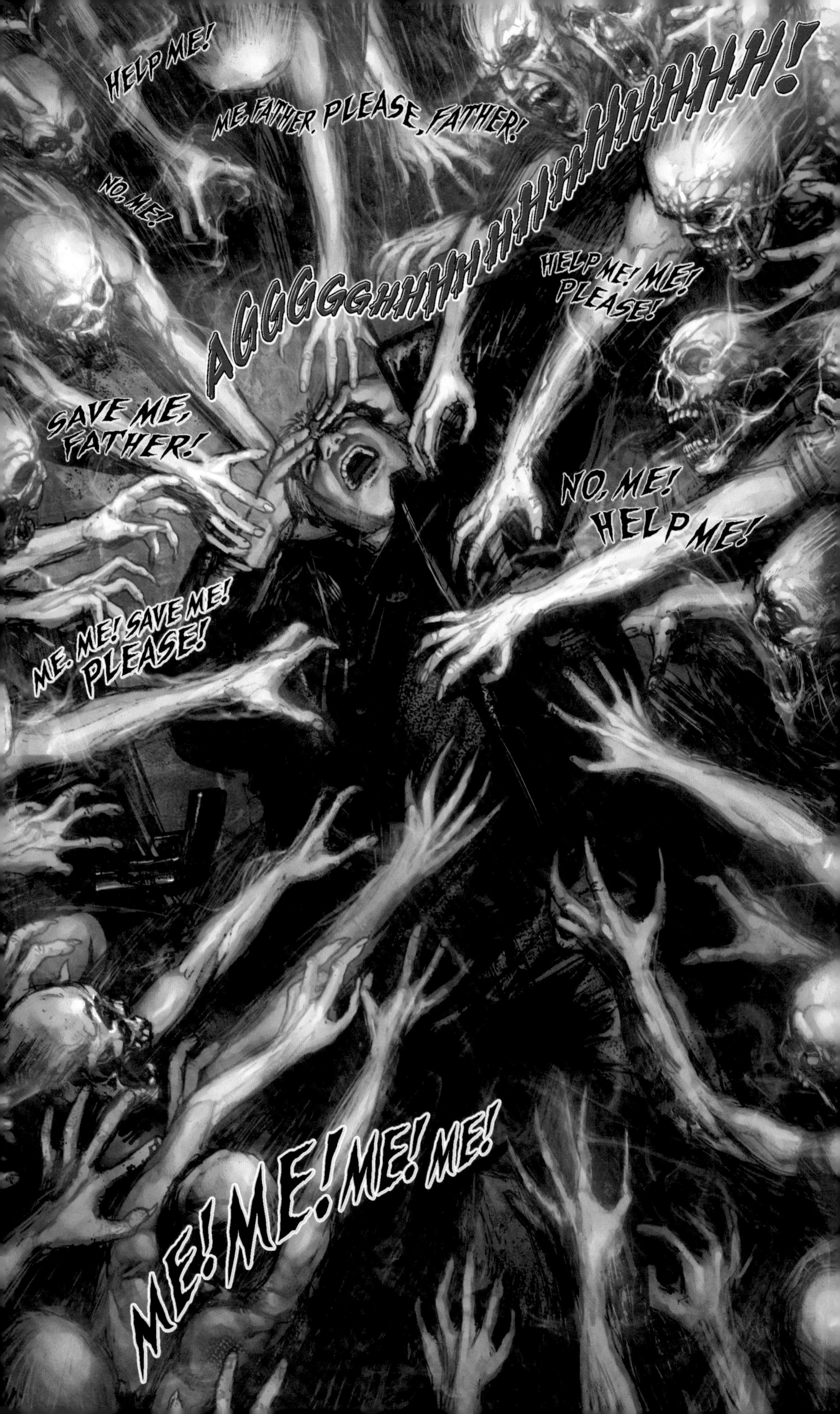

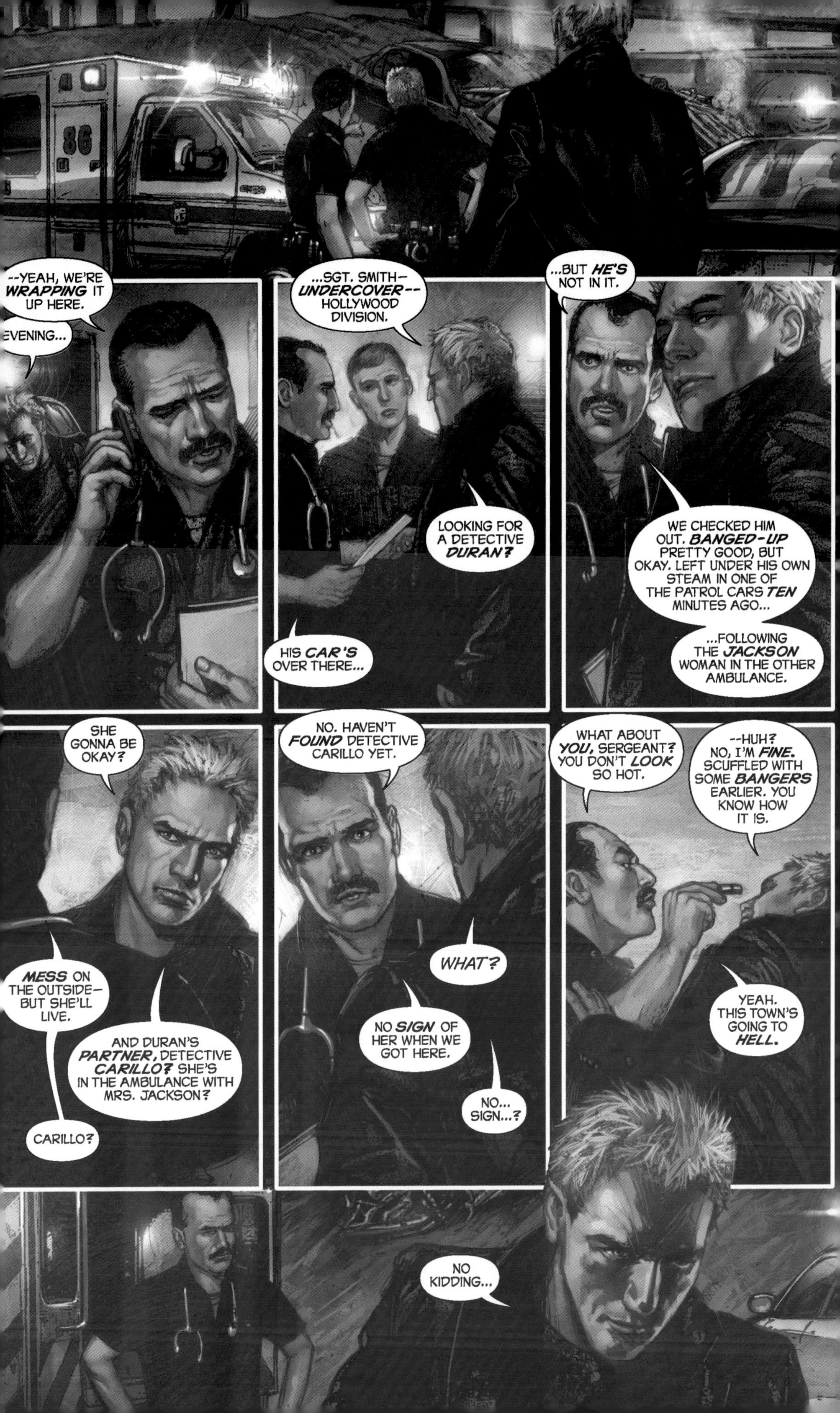
--YEAH, WE'RE WRAPPING IT UP HERE.
EVENING...
...SGT. SMITH—UNDERCOVER--HOLLYWOOD DIVISION.
LOOKING FOR A DETECTIVE DURAN?
HIS CAR'S OVER THERE...
...BUT HE'S NOT IN IT.
WE CHECKED HIM OUT. BANGED-UP PRETTY GOOD, BUT OKAY. LEFT UNDER HIS OWN STEAM IN ONE OF THE PATROL CARS TEN MINUTES AGO...
...FOLLOWING THE JACKSON WOMAN IN THE OTHER AMBULANCE.
SHE GONNA BE OKAY?
MESS ON THE OUTSIDE—BUT SHE'LL LIVE.
AND DURAN'S PARTNER, DETECTIVE CARILLO? SHE'S IN THE AMBULANCE WITH MRS. JACKSON?
CARILLO?
NO. HAVEN'T FOUND DETECTIVE CARILLO YET.
WHAT?
NO SIGN OF HER WHEN WE GOT HERE.
NO... SIGN...?
WHAT ABOUT YOU, SERGEANT? YOU DON'T LOOK SO HOT.
--HUH? NO, I'M FINE. SCUFFLED WITH SOME BANGERS EARLIER. YOU KNOW HOW IT IS.
YEAH. THIS TOWN'S GOING TO HELL.
NO KIDDING...

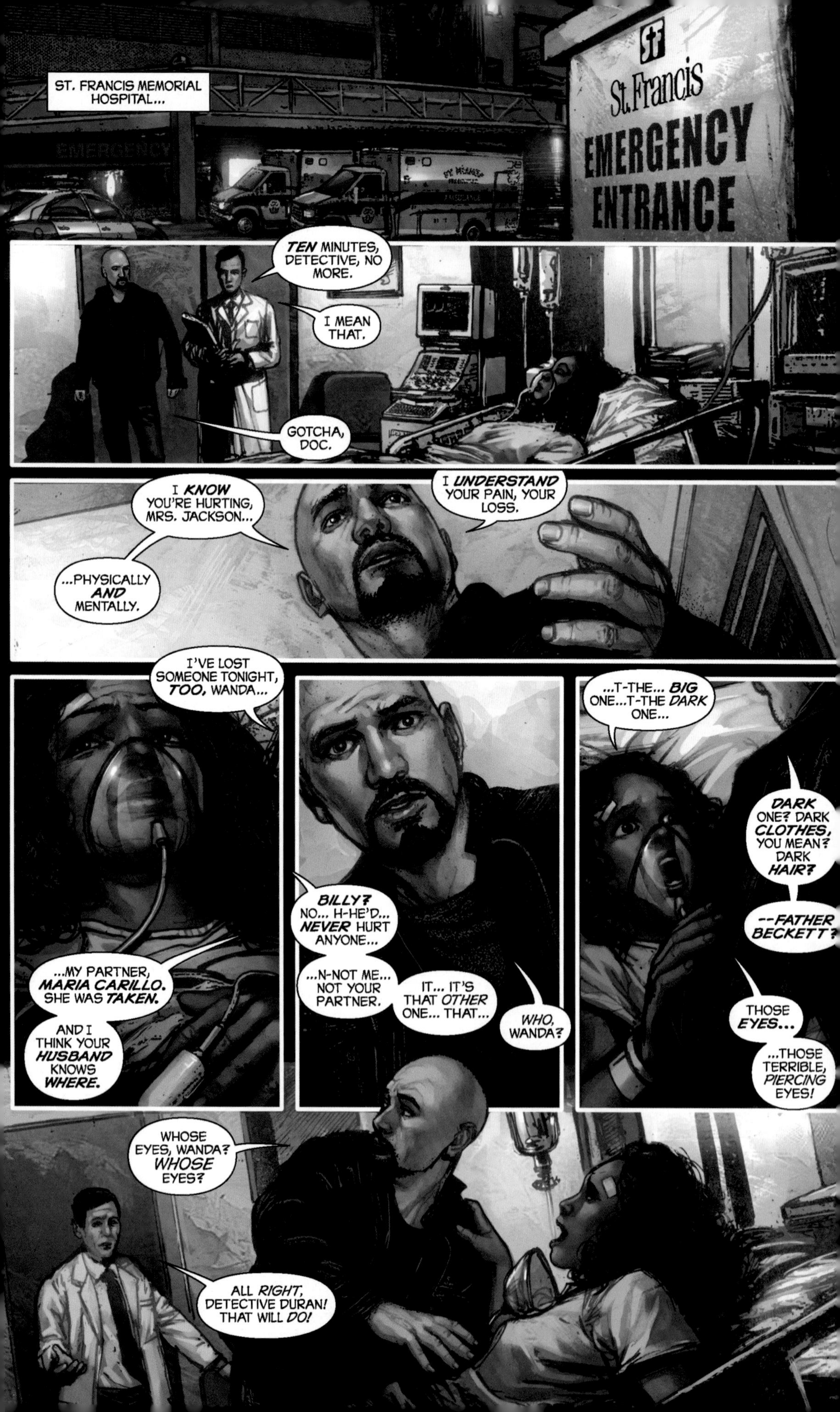

ST. FRANCIS MEMORIAL HOSPITAL...
St. Francis
EMERGENCY ENTRANCE
TEN MINUTES, DETECTIVE, NO MORE.
I MEAN THAT.
GOTCHA, DOC.
I KNOW YOU'RE HURTING, MRS. JACKSON...
...PHYSICALLY AND MENTALLY.
I UNDERSTAND YOUR PAIN, YOUR LOSS.
I'VE LOST SOMEONE TONIGHT, TOO, WANDA...
...MY PARTNER, MARIA CARILLO. SHE WAS TAKEN.
AND I THINK YOUR HUSBAND KNOWS WHERE.
BILLY? NO... H-HE'D... NEVER HURT ANYONE...
...N-NOT ME... NOT YOUR PARTNER.
IT... IT'S THAT OTHER ONE... THAT...
WHO, WANDA?
...T-THE... BIG ONE...T-THE DARK ONE...
DARK ONE? DARK CLOTHES, YOU MEAN? DARK HAIR?
--FATHER BECKETT?
THOSE EYES...
...THOSE TERRIBLE, PIERCING EYES!
WHOSE EYES, WANDA? WHOSE EYES?
ALL RIGHT, DETECTIVE DURAN! THAT WILL DO!

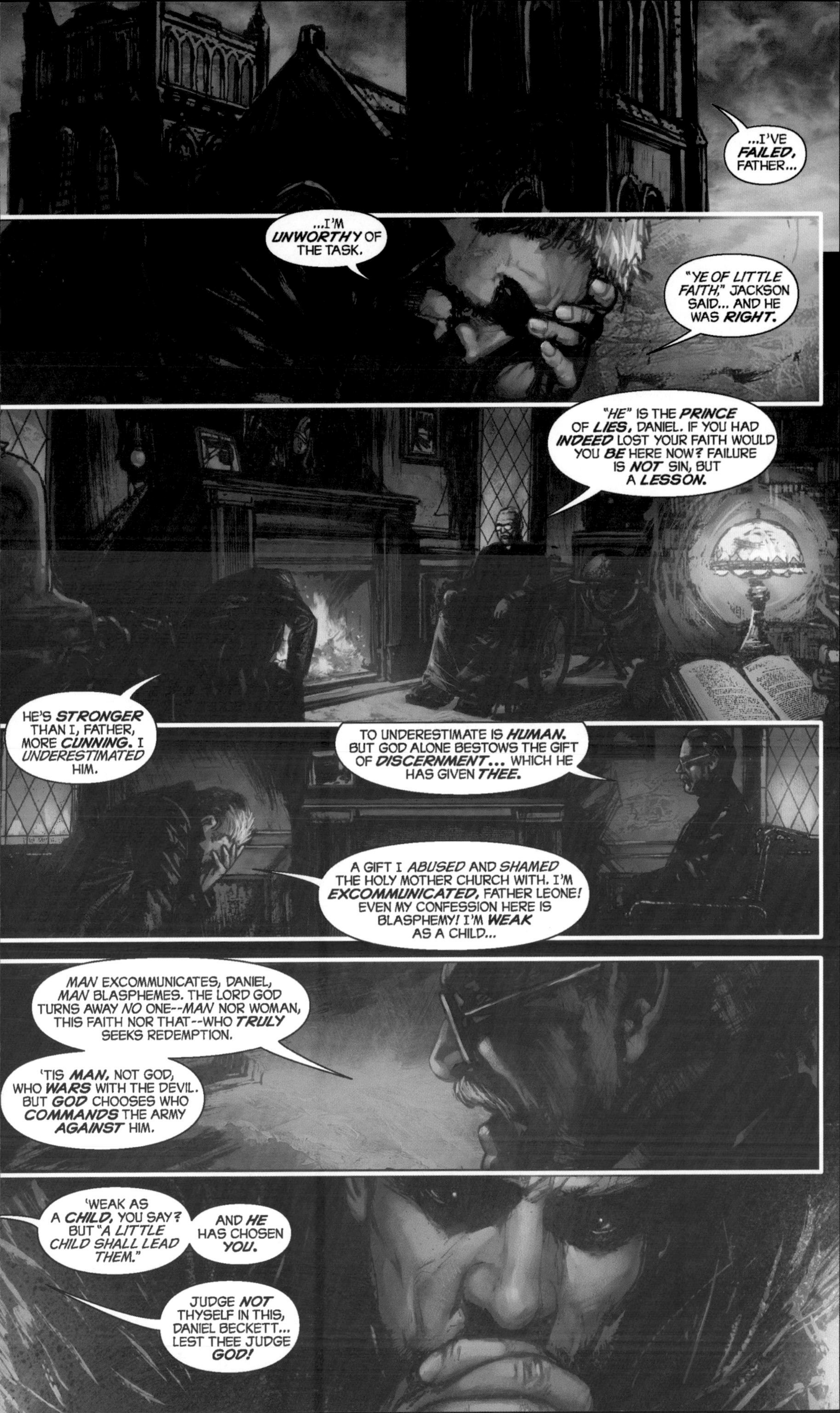
...I'VE FAILED, FATHER...
...I'M UNWORTHY OF THE TASK.
"YE OF LITTLE FAITH," JACKSON SAID... AND HE WAS RIGHT.
"HE" IS THE PRINCE OF LIES, DANIEL. IF YOU HAD INDEED LOST YOUR FAITH WOULD YOU BE HERE NOW? FAILURE IS NOT SIN, BUT A LESSON.
HE'S STRONGER THAN I, FATHER, MORE CUNNING. I UNDERESTIMATED HIM.
TO UNDERESTIMATE IS HUMAN. BUT GOD ALONE BESTOWS THE GIFT OF DISCERNMENT... WHICH HE HAS GIVEN THEE.
A GIFT I ABUSED AND SHAMED THE HOLY MOTHER CHURCH WITH. I'M EXCOMMUNICATED, FATHER LEONE! EVEN MY CONFESSION HERE IS BLASPHEMY! I'M WEAK AS A CHILD...
MAN EXCOMMUNICATES, DANIEL, MAN BLASPHEMES. THE LORD GOD TURNS AWAY NO ONE--MAN NOR WOMAN, THIS FAITH NOR THAT--WHO TRULY SEEKS REDEMPTION.
'TIS MAN, NOT GOD, WHO WARS WITH THE DEVIL. BUT GOD CHOOSES WHO COMMANDS THE ARMY AGAINST HIM.
'WEAK AS A CHILD,' YOU SAY? BUT "A LITTLE CHILD SHALL LEAD THEM."
AND HE HAS CHOSEN YOU.
JUDGE NOT THYSELF IN THIS, DANIEL BECKETT... LEST THEE JUDGE GOD!

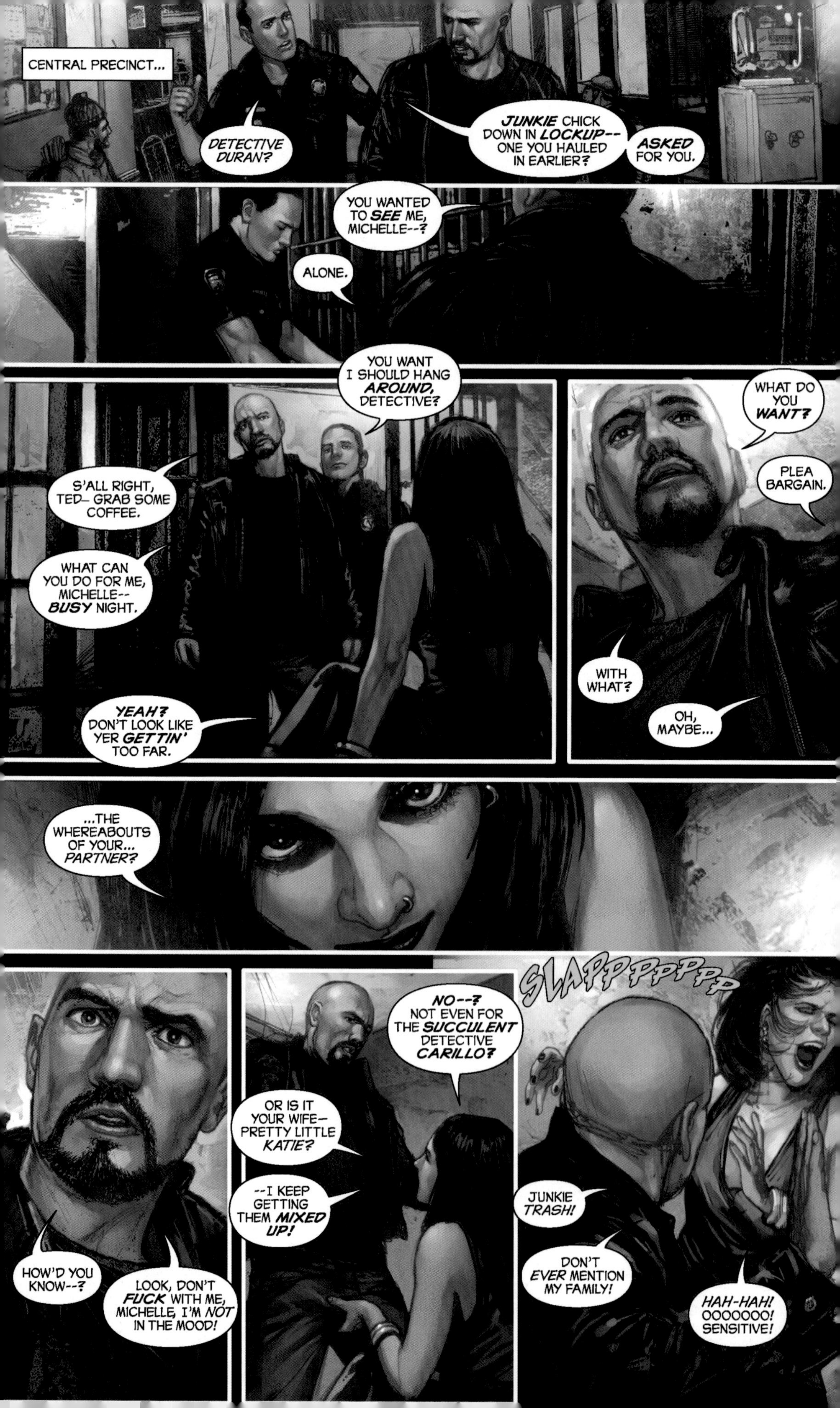
CENTRAL PRECINCT...
DETECTIVE DURAN?
JUNKIE CHICK DOWN IN LOCKUP-- ONE YOU HAULED IN EARLIER?
ASKED FOR YOU.
YOU WANTED TO SEE ME, MICHELLE--?
ALONE.
YOU WANT I SHOULD HANG AROUND, DETECTIVE?
S'ALL RIGHT, TED– GRAB SOME COFFEE.
WHAT CAN YOU DO FOR ME, MICHELLE-- BUSY NIGHT.
YEAH? DON'T LOOK LIKE YER GETTIN' TOO FAR.
WHAT DO YOU WANT?
PLEA BARGAIN.
WITH WHAT?
OH, MAYBE...
...THE WHEREABOUTS OF YOUR... PARTNER?
HOW'D YOU KNOW--?
LOOK, DON'T FUCK WITH ME, MICHELLE, I'M NOT IN THE MOOD!
NO--? NOT EVEN FOR THE SUCCULENT DETECTIVE CARILLO?
OR IS IT YOUR WIFE– PRETTY LITTLE KATIE?
--I KEEP GETTING THEM MIXED UP!
SLAPPPPPPP
JUNKIE TRASH!
DON'T EVER MENTION MY FAMILY!
HAH-HAH! OOOOOOO! SENSITIVE!

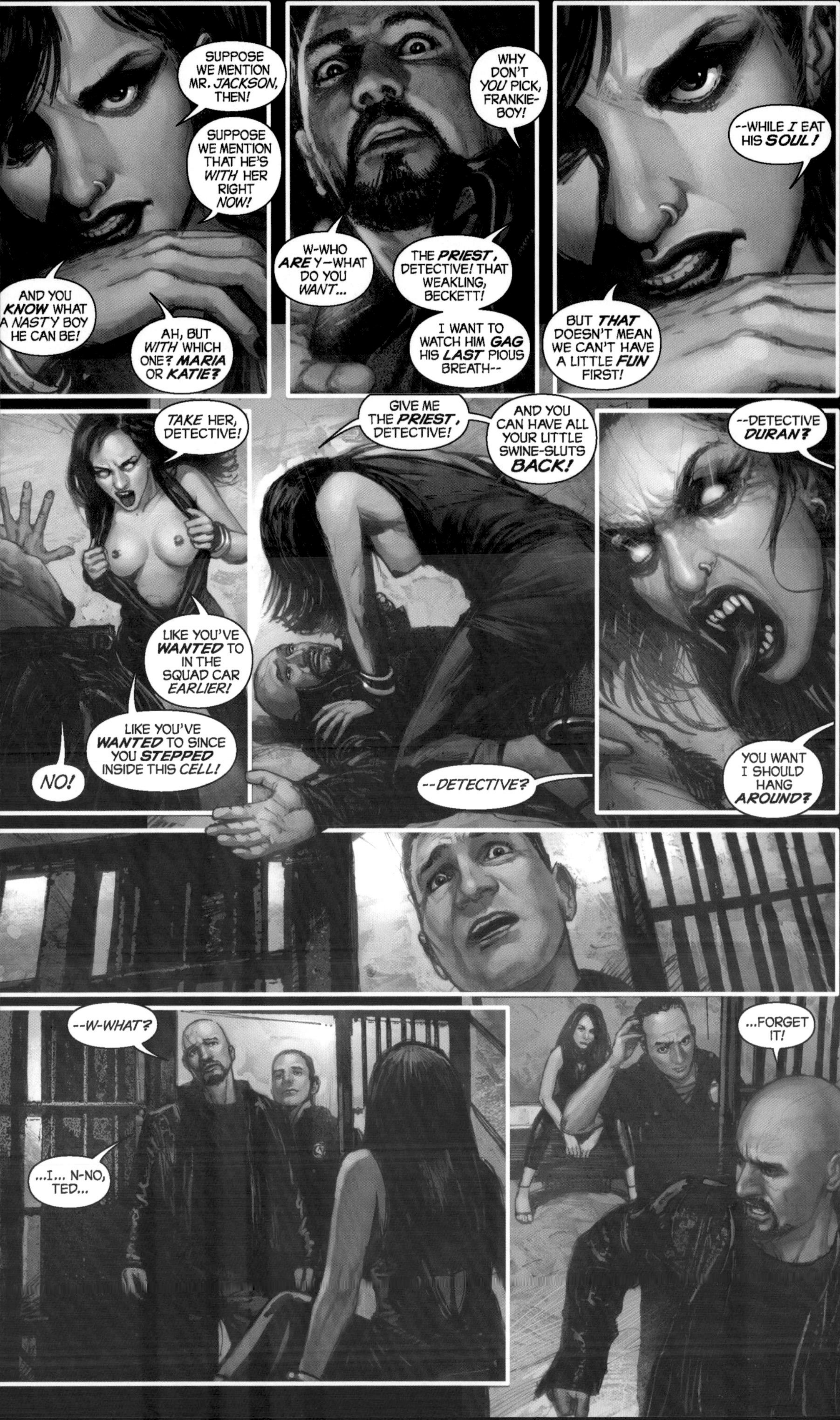
SUPPOSE WE MENTION MR. JACKSON, THEN!
SUPPOSE WE MENTION THAT HE'S WITH HER RIGHT NOW!
AND YOU KNOW WHAT A NASTY BOY HE CAN BE!
AH, BUT WITH WHICH ONE? MARIA OR KATIE?
WHY DON'T YOU PICK, FRANKIE-BOY!
W-WHO ARE Y—WHAT DO YOU WANT...
THE PRIEST, DETECTIVE! THAT WEAKLING, BECKETT!
I WANT TO WATCH HIM GAG HIS LAST PIOUS BREATH--
--WHILE I EAT HIS SOUL!
BUT THAT DOESN'T MEAN WE CAN'T HAVE A LITTLE FUN FIRST!
TAKE HER, DETECTIVE!
LIKE YOU'VE WANTED TO IN THE SQUAD CAR EARLIER!
LIKE YOU'VE WANTED TO SINCE YOU STEPPED INSIDE THIS CELL!
NO!
GIVE ME THE PRIEST, DETECTIVE!
AND YOU CAN HAVE ALL YOUR LITTLE SWINE-SLUTS BACK!
--DETECTIVE?
--DETECTIVE DURAN?
YOU WANT I SHOULD HANG AROUND?
--W-WHAT?
...I... N-NO, TED...
...FORGET IT!

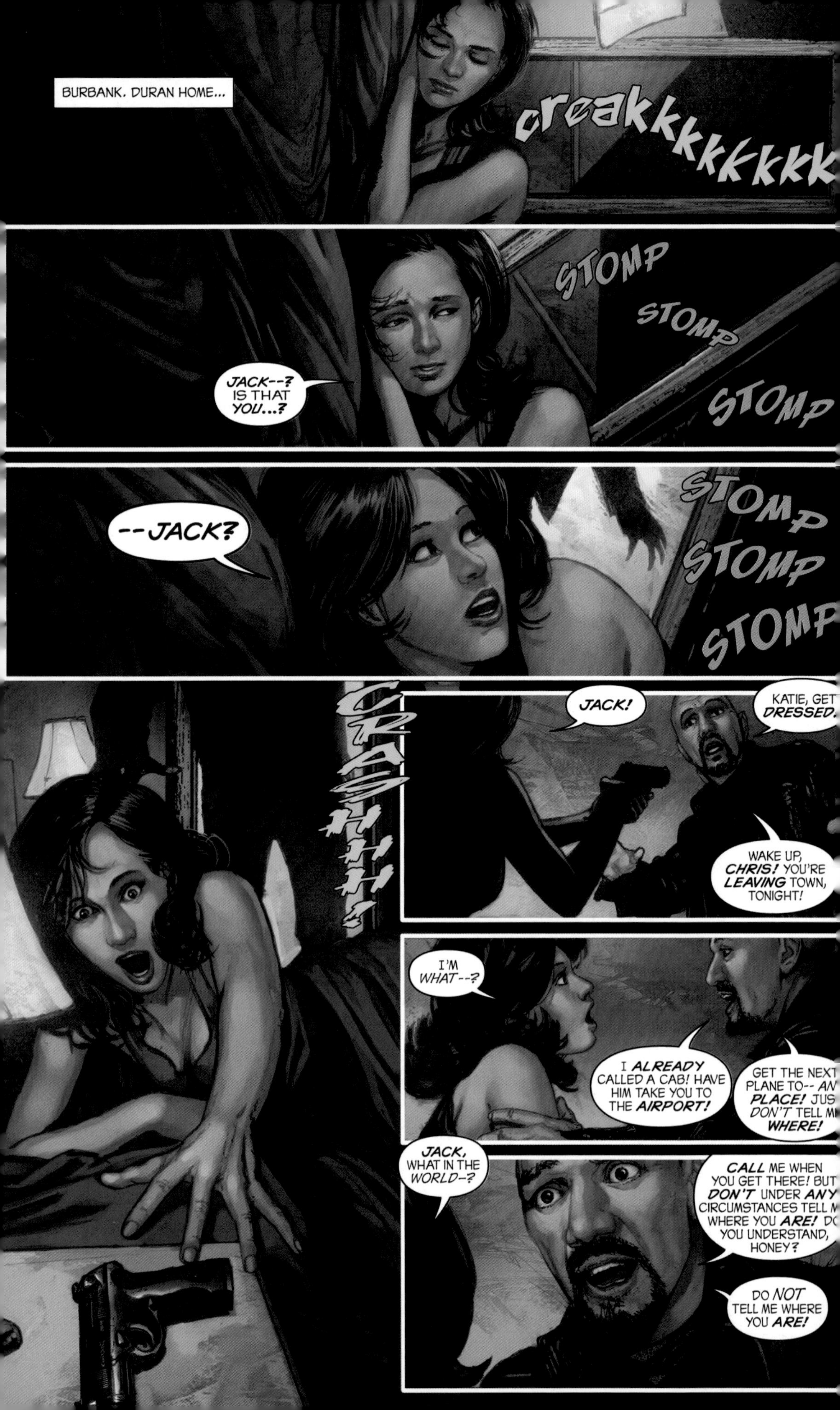
BURBANK. DURAN HOME...
creakkkkkkkk
STOMP
STOMP
STOMP
JACK--? IS THAT YOU...?
STOMP
STOMP
STOMP
--JACK?
CRASHHHH!
JACK!
KATIE, GET DRESSED.
WAKE UP, CHRIS! YOU'RE LEAVING TOWN, TONIGHT!
I'M WHAT--?
I ALREADY CALLED A CAB! HAVE HIM TAKE YOU TO THE AIRPORT!
JACK, WHAT IN THE WORLD--?
CALL ME WHEN YOU GET THERE! BUT DON'T UNDER ANY CIRCUMSTANCES TELL WHERE YOU ARE! DO YOU UNDERSTAND, HONEY?
DO NOT TELL ME WHERE YOU ARE!

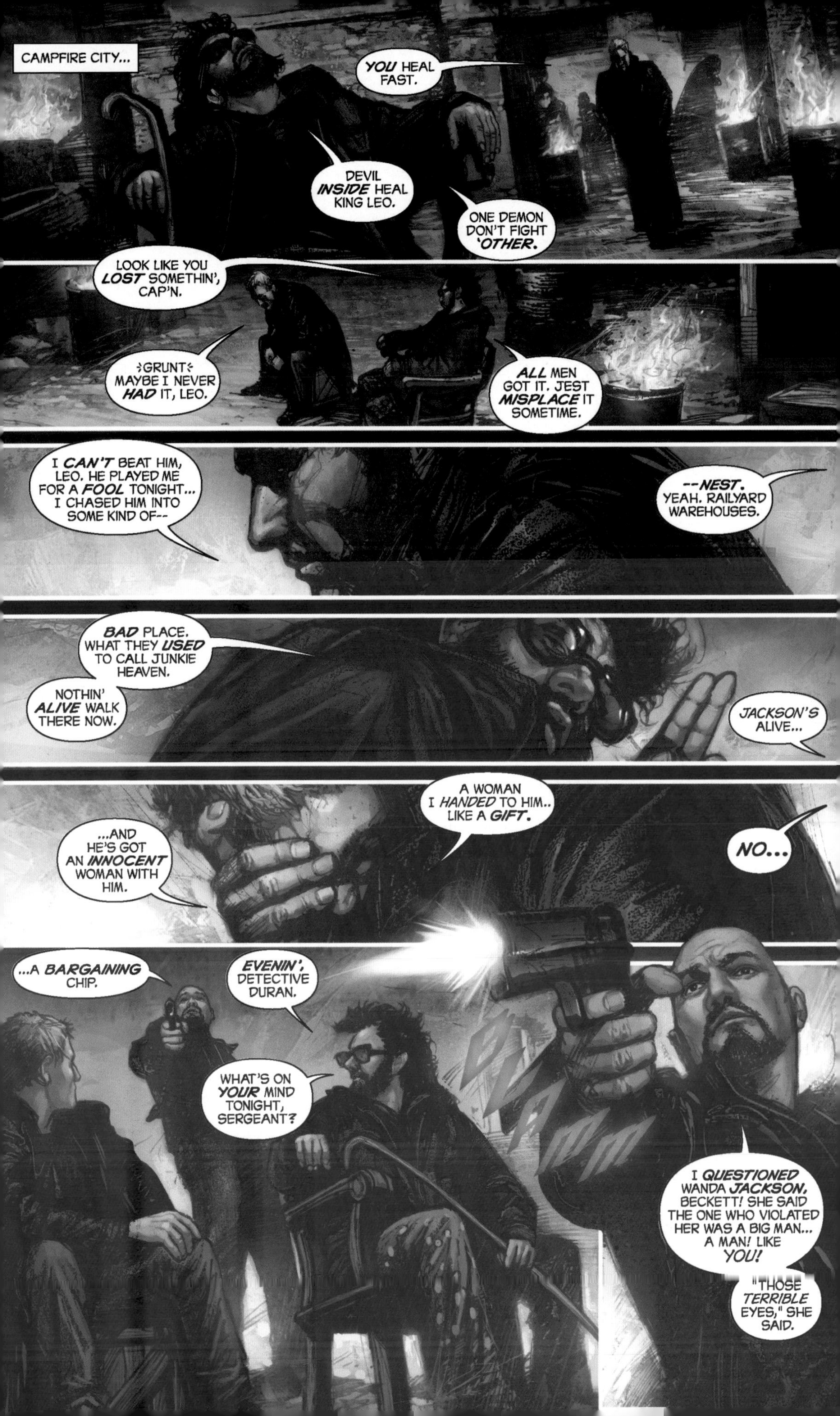
CAMPFIRE CITY...
YOU HEAL FAST.
DEVIL INSIDE HEAL KING LEO.
ONE DEMON DON'T FIGHT 'OTHER.
LOOK LIKE YOU LOST SOMETHIN', CAP'N.
GRUNT MAYBE I NEVER HAD IT, LEO.
ALL MEN GOT IT. JEST MISPLACE IT SOMETIME.
I CAN'T BEAT HIM, LEO. HE PLAYED ME FOR A FOOL TONIGHT... I CHASED HIM INTO SOME KIND OF--
--NEST. YEAH. RAILYARD WAREHOUSES.
BAD PLACE. WHAT THEY USED TO CALL JUNKIE HEAVEN.
NOTHIN' ALIVE WALK THERE NOW.
JACKSON'S ALIVE...
...AND HE'S GOT AN INNOCENT WOMAN WITH HIM.
A WOMAN I HANDED TO HIM.. LIKE A GIFT.
NO...
...A BARGAINING CHIP.
EVENIN', DETECTIVE DURAN.
WHAT'S ON YOUR MIND TONIGHT, SERGEANT?
I QUESTIONED WANDA JACKSON, BECKETT! SHE SAID THE ONE WHO VIOLATED HER WAS A BIG MAN... A MAN! LIKE YOU!
"THOSE TERRIBLE EYES," SHE SAID.

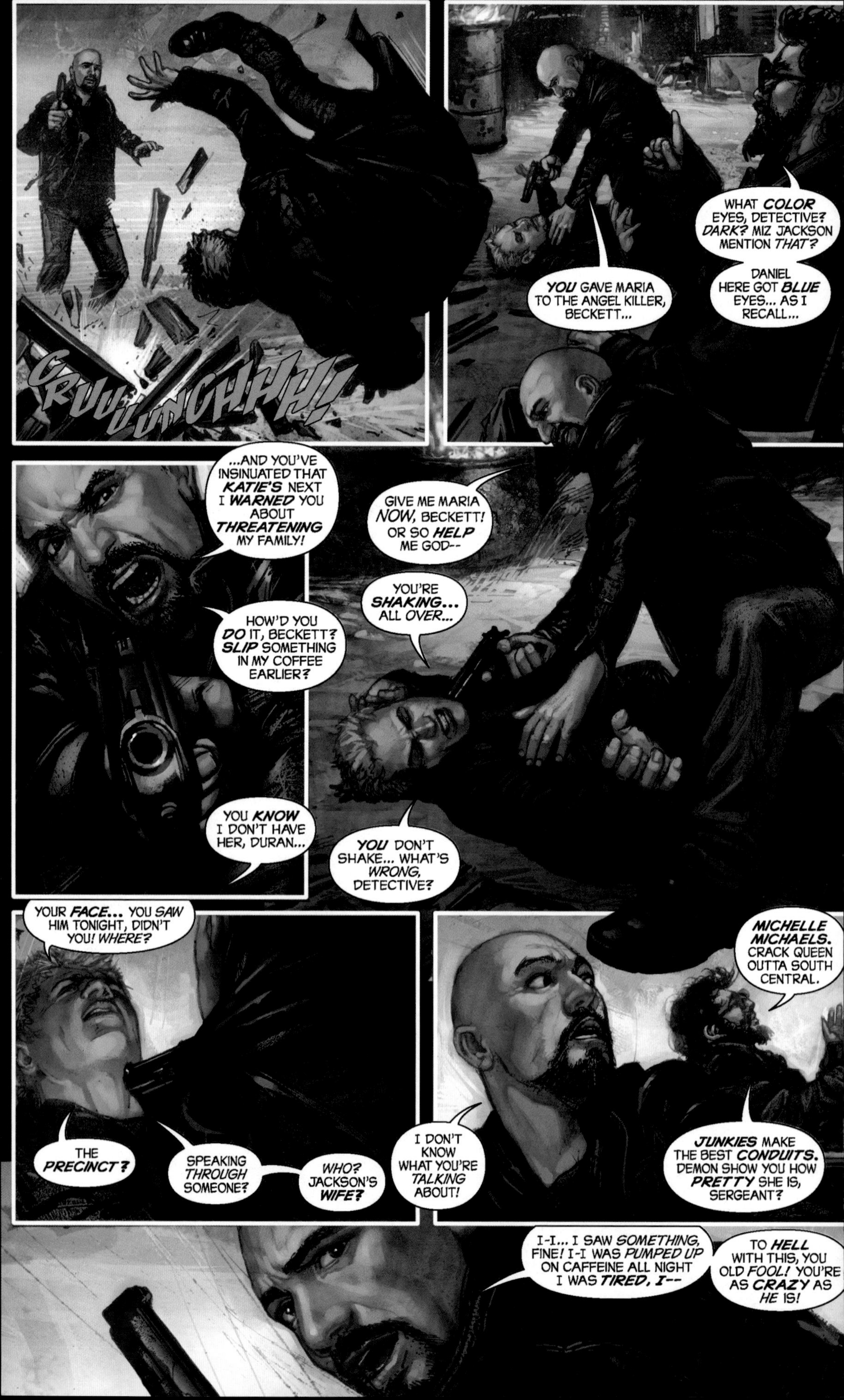
CRUUUUNCHHH!!
YOU GAVE MARIA TO THE ANGEL KILLER, BECKETT...
WHAT COLOR EYES, DETECTIVE? DARK? MIZ JACKSON MENTION THAT?
DANIEL HERE GOT BLUE EYES... AS I RECALL...
GIVE ME MARIA NOW, BECKETT! OR SO HELP ME GOD--
YOU'RE SHAKING... ALL OVER...
YOU DON'T SHAKE... WHAT'S WRONG, DETECTIVE?
...AND YOU'VE INSINUATED THAT KATIE'S NEXT I WARNED YOU ABOUT THREATENING MY FAMILY!
HOW'D YOU DO IT, BECKETT? SLIP SOMETHING IN MY COFFEE EARLIER?
YOU KNOW I DON'T HAVE HER, DURAN...
YOUR FACE... YOU SAW HIM TONIGHT, DIDN'T YOU! WHERE?
THE PRECINCT?
SPEAKING THROUGH SOMEONE?
WHO? JACKSON'S WIFE?
I DON'T KNOW WHAT YOU'RE TALKING ABOUT!
MICHELLE MICHAELS. CRACK QUEEN OUTTA SOUTH CENTRAL.
JUNKIES MAKE THE BEST CONDUITS. DEMON SHOW YOU HOW PRETTY SHE IS, SERGEANT?
I-I... I SAW SOMETHING, FINE! I-I WAS PUMPED UP ON CAFFEINE ALL NIGHT I WAS TIRED, I--
TO HELL WITH THIS, YOU OLD FOOL! YOU'RE AS CRAZY AS HE IS!

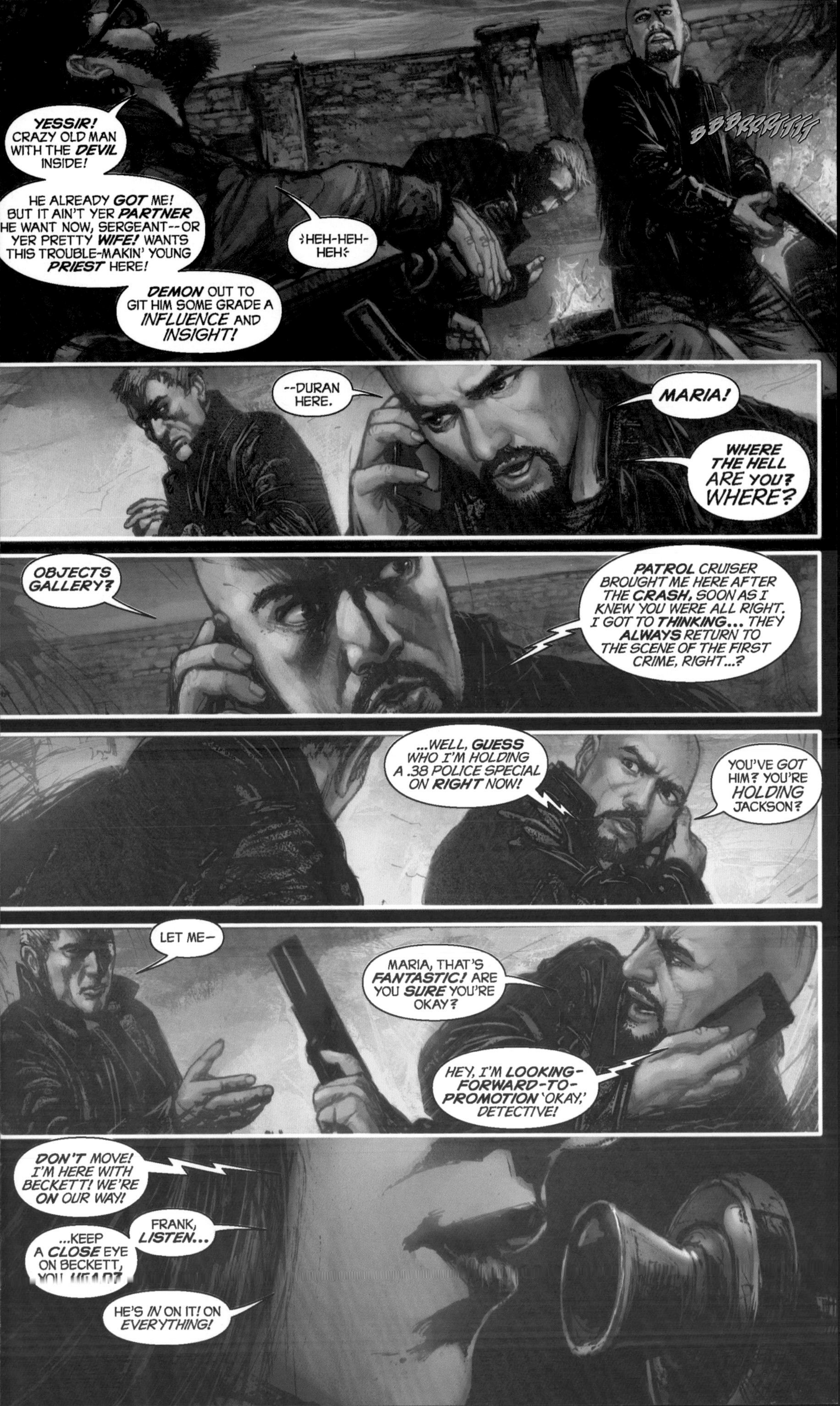
YESSIR! CRAZY OLD MAN WITH THE DEVIL INSIDE!
HE ALREADY GOT ME! BUT IT AIN'T YER PARTNER HE WANT NOW, SERGEANT--OR YER PRETTY WIFE! WANTS THIS TROUBLE-MAKIN' YOUNG PRIEST HERE!
DEMON OUT TO GIT HIM SOME GRADE A INFLUENCE AND INSIGHT!
HEH-HEH-HEH
--DURAN HERE.
MARIA!
WHERE THE HELL ARE YOU? WHERE?
OBJECTS GALLERY?
PATROL CRUISER BROUGHT ME HERE AFTER THE CRASH, SOON AS I KNEW YOU WERE ALL RIGHT. I GOT TO THINKING... THEY ALWAYS RETURN TO THE SCENE OF THE FIRST CRIME, RIGHT...?
...WELL, GUESS WHO I'M HOLDING A .38 POLICE SPECIAL ON RIGHT NOW!
YOU'VE GOT HIM? YOU'RE HOLDING JACKSON?
LET ME--
MARIA, THAT'S FANTASTIC! ARE YOU SURE YOU'RE OKAY?
HEY, I'M LOOKING-FORWARD-TO-PROMOTION 'OKAY,' DETECTIVE!
DON'T MOVE! I'M HERE WITH BECKETT! WE'RE ON OUR WAY!
FRANK, LISTEN...
...KEEP A CLOSE EYE ON BECKETT,
HE'S IN ON IT! ON EVERYTHING!

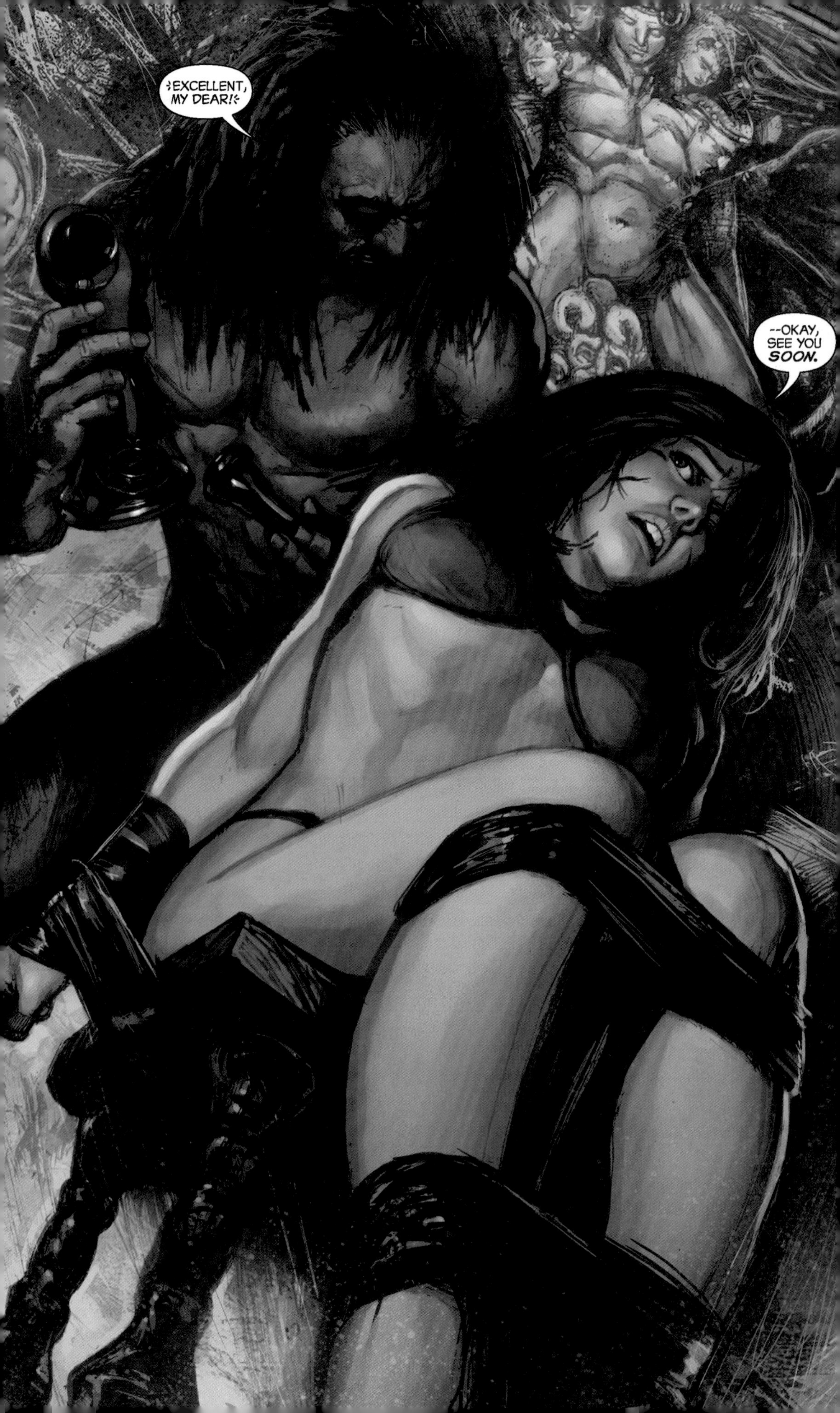
EXCELLENT, MY DEAR!
--OKAY, SEE YOU **SOON.**

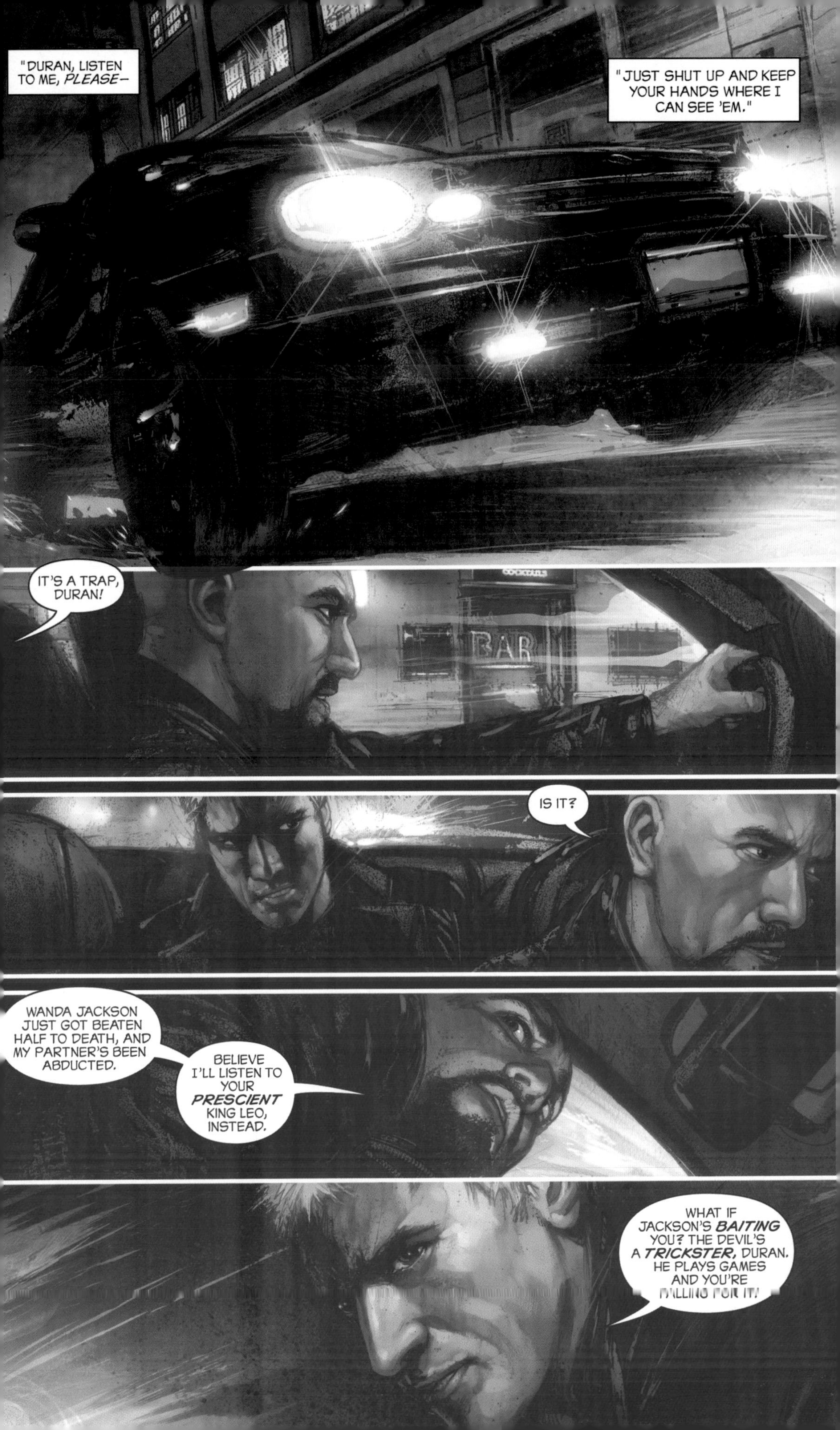
"DURAN, LISTEN TO ME, *PLEASE*–
"JUST SHUT UP AND KEEP YOUR HANDS WHERE I CAN SEE 'EM."
COCKTAILS
BAR
IT'S A TRAP, DURAN!
IS IT?
WANDA JACKSON JUST GOT BEATEN HALF TO DEATH, AND MY PARTNER'S BEEN ABDUCTED.
BELIEVE I'LL LISTEN TO YOUR ***PRESCIENT*** KING LEO, INSTEAD.
WHAT IF JACKSON'S ***BAITING*** YOU? THE DEVIL'S A ***TRICKSTER,*** DURAN. HE PLAYS GAMES AND YOU'RE

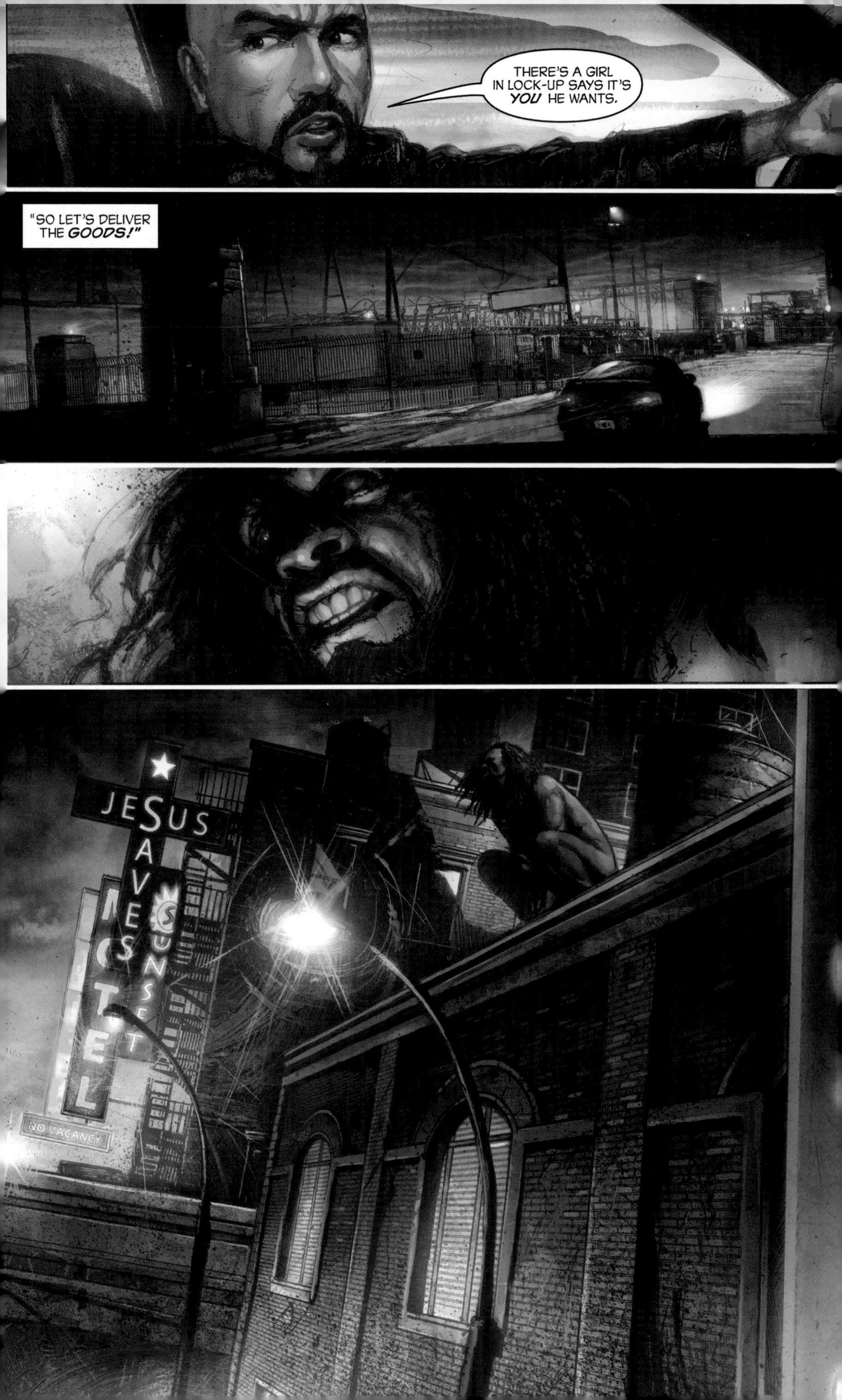

THERE'S A GIRL IN LOCK-UP SAYS IT'S *YOU* HE WANTS.
"SO LET'S DELIVER THE *GOODS!*"
JESUS SAVES
MOTEL
SUNSET
NO VACANCY

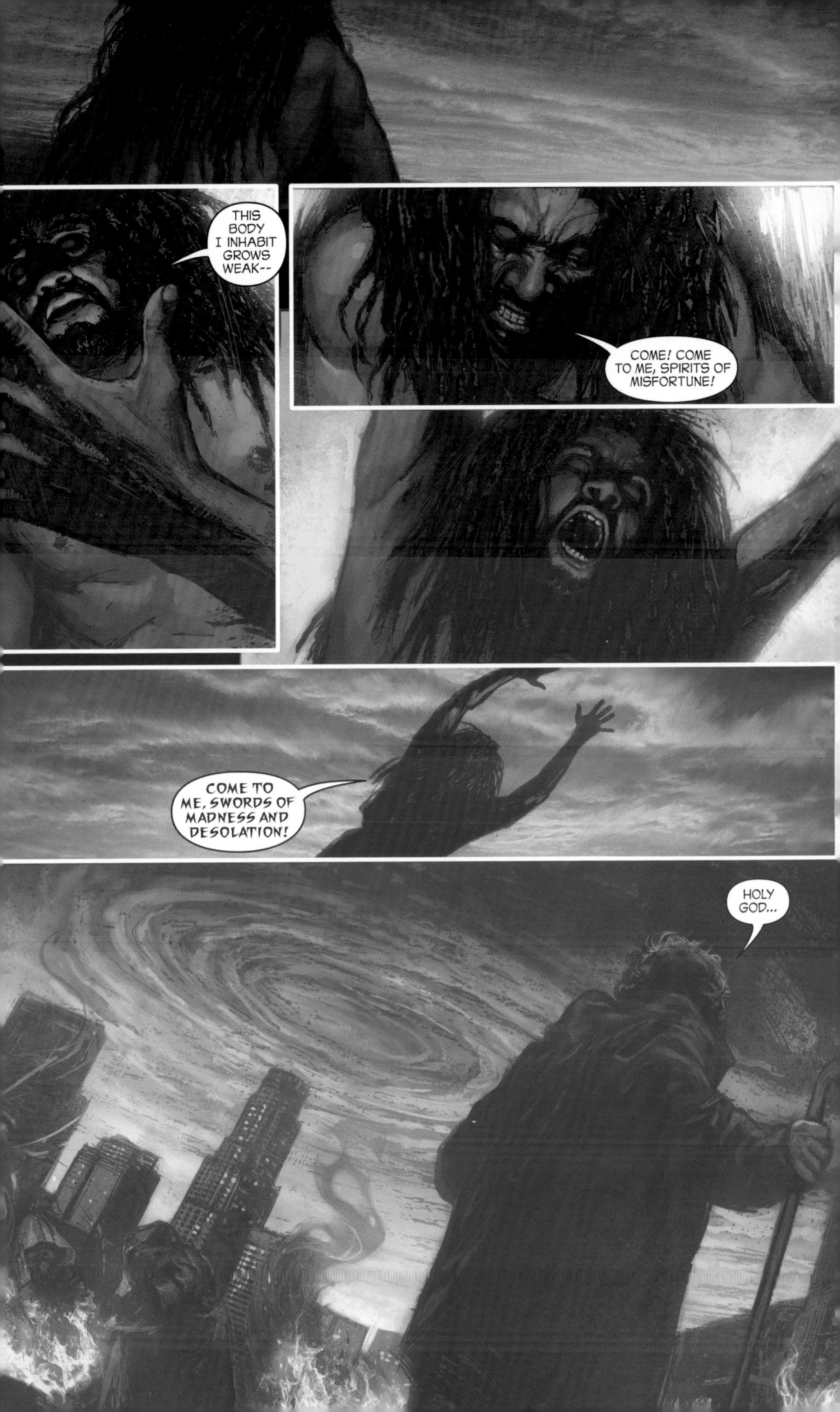
THIS BODY I INHABIT GROWS WEAK--
COME! COME TO ME, SPIRITS OF MISFORTUNE!
COME TO ME, SWORDS OF MADNESS AND DESOLATION!
HOLY GOD...

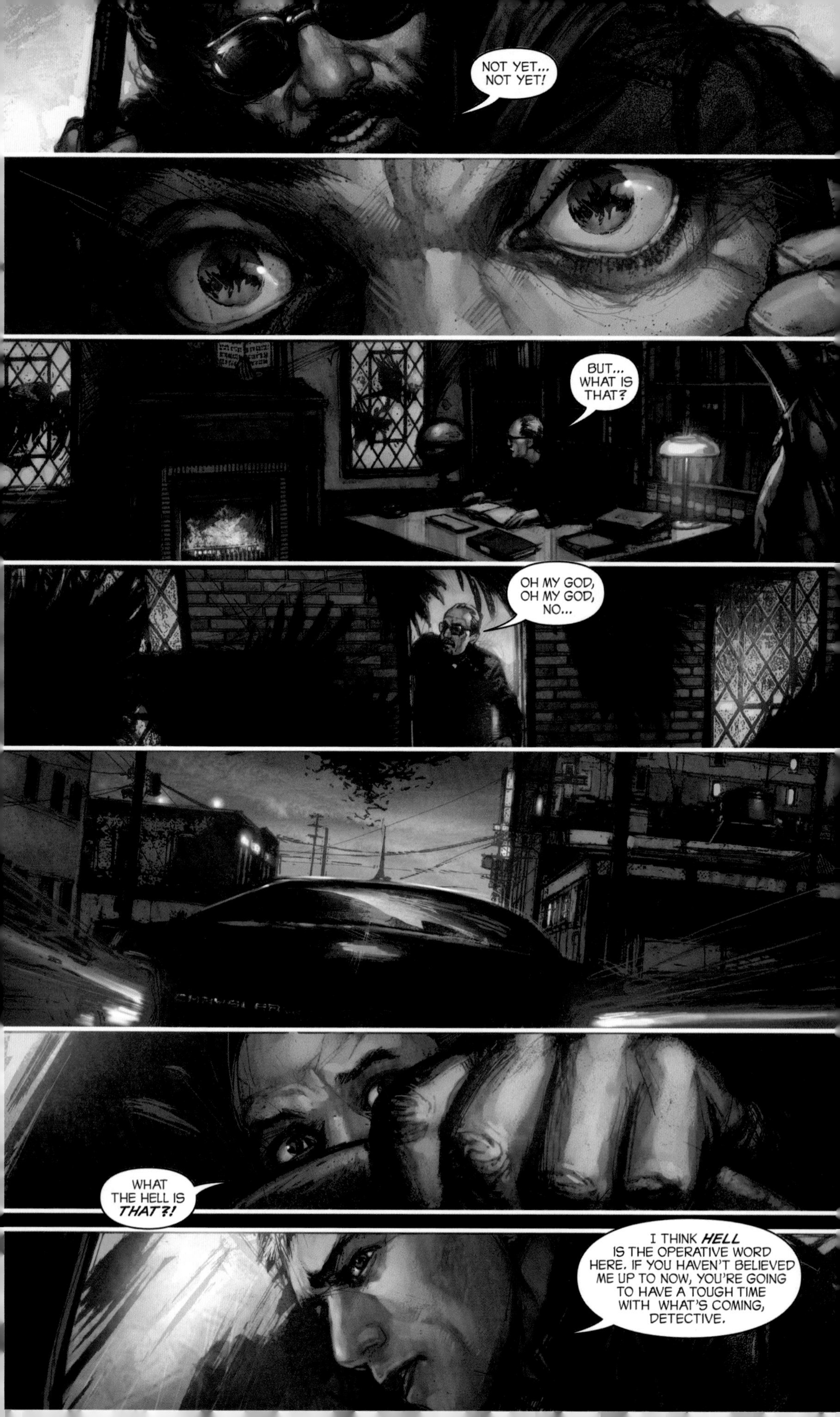
NOT YET... NOT YET!
BUT... WHAT IS THAT?
OH MY GOD, OH MY GOD, NO...
WHAT THE HELL IS *THAT?!*
I THINK **HELL** IS THE OPERATIVE WORD HERE. IF YOU HAVEN'T BELIEVED ME UP TO NOW, YOU'RE GOING TO HAVE A TOUGH TIME WITH WHAT'S COMING, DETECTIVE.

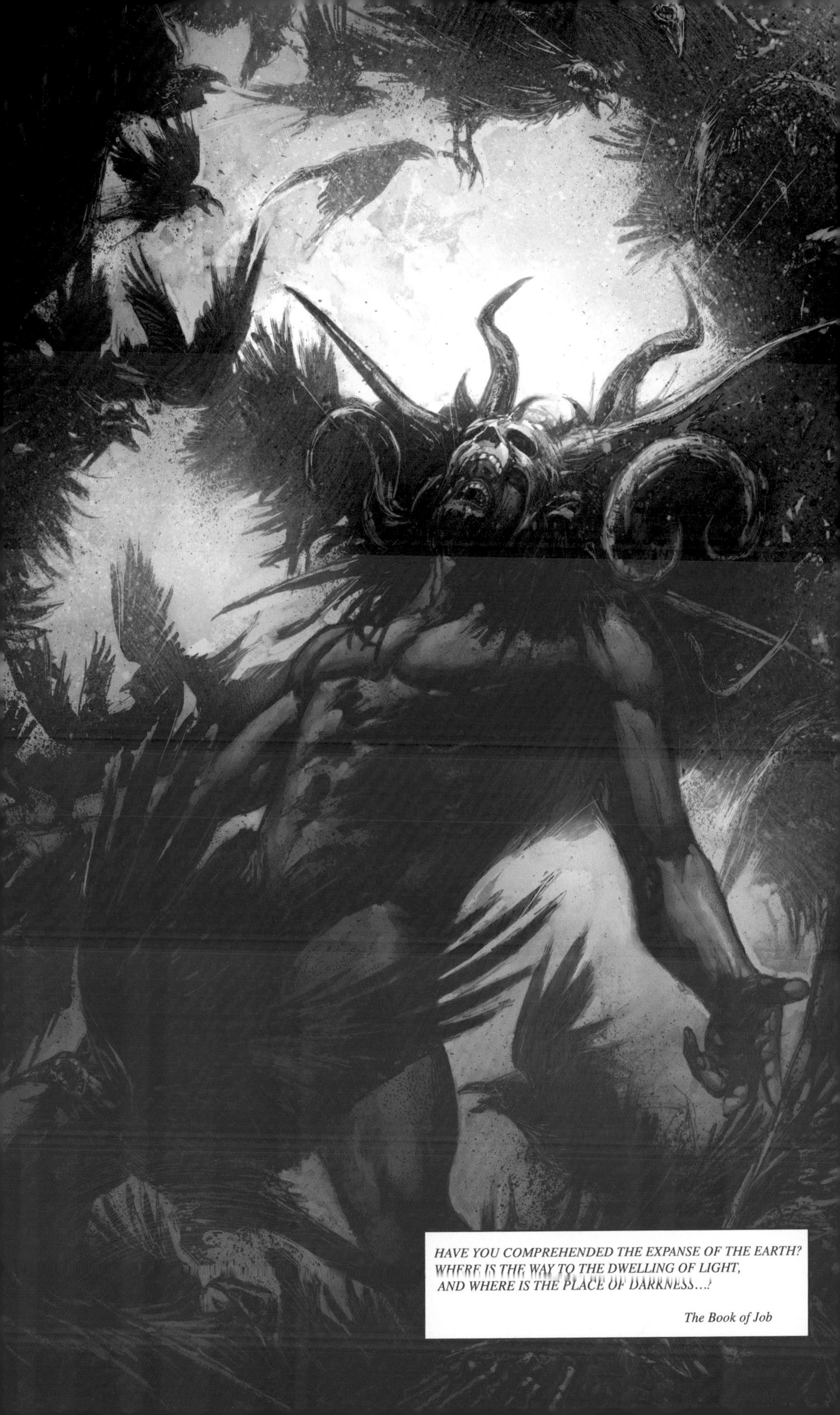
HAVE YOU COMPREHENDED THE EXPANSE OF THE EARTH?
WHERE IS THE WAY TO THE DWELLING OF LIGHT,
AND WHERE IS THE PLACE OF DARKNESS…?
The Book of Job

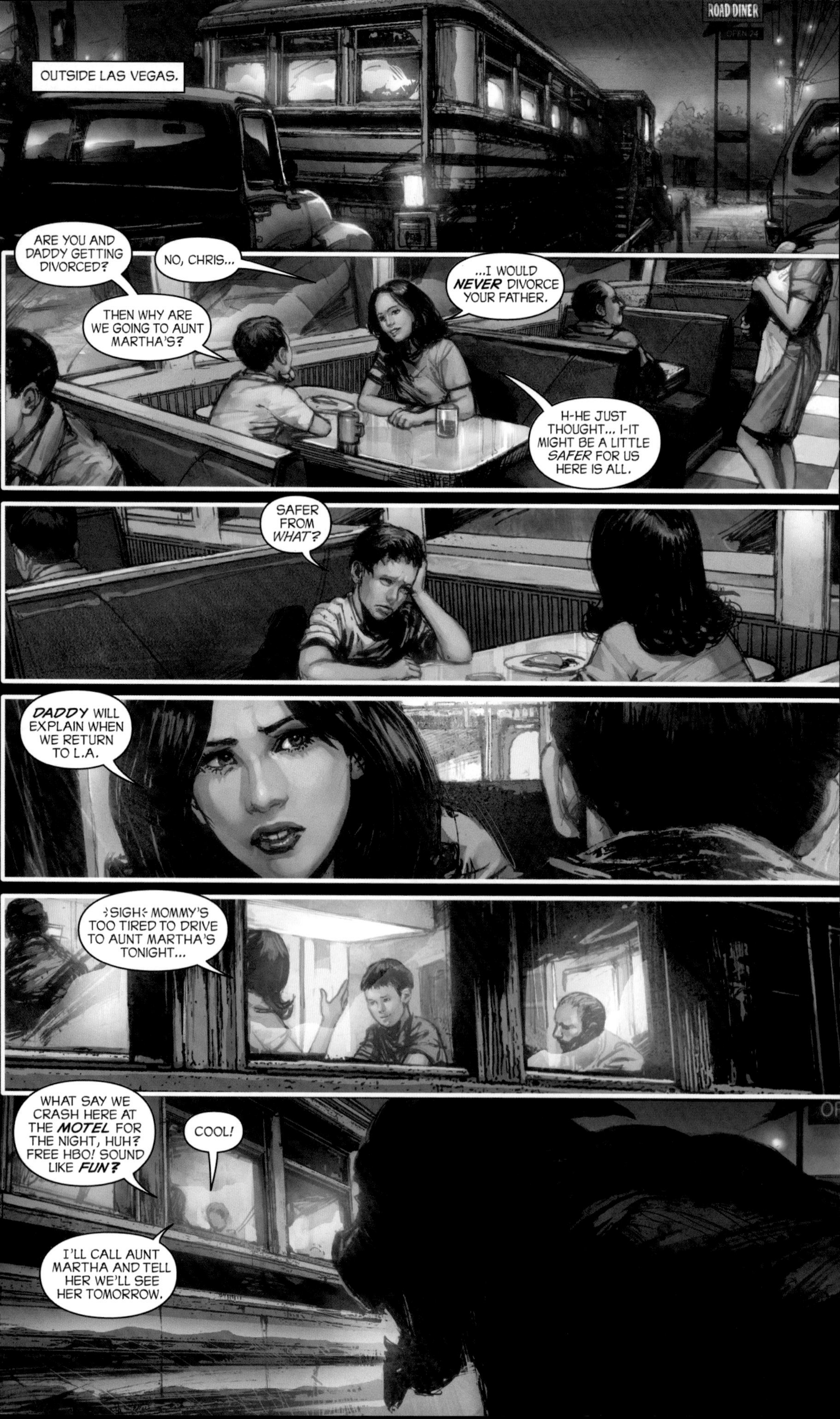
OUTSIDE LAS VEGAS.
ROAD DINER
OPEN 24
ARE YOU AND DADDY GETTING DIVORCED?
NO, CHRIS...
...I WOULD NEVER DIVORCE YOUR FATHER.
THEN WHY ARE WE GOING TO AUNT MARTHA'S?
H-HE JUST THOUGHT... I-IT MIGHT BE A LITTLE SAFER FOR US HERE IS ALL.
SAFER FROM WHAT?
DADDY WILL EXPLAIN WHEN WE RETURN TO L.A.
SIGH MOMMY'S TOO TIRED TO DRIVE TO AUNT MARTHA'S TONIGHT...
WHAT SAY WE CRASH HERE AT THE MOTEL FOR THE NIGHT, HUH? FREE HBO! SOUND LIKE FUN?
COOL!
I'LL CALL AUNT MARTHA AND TELL HER WE'LL SEE HER TOMORROW.

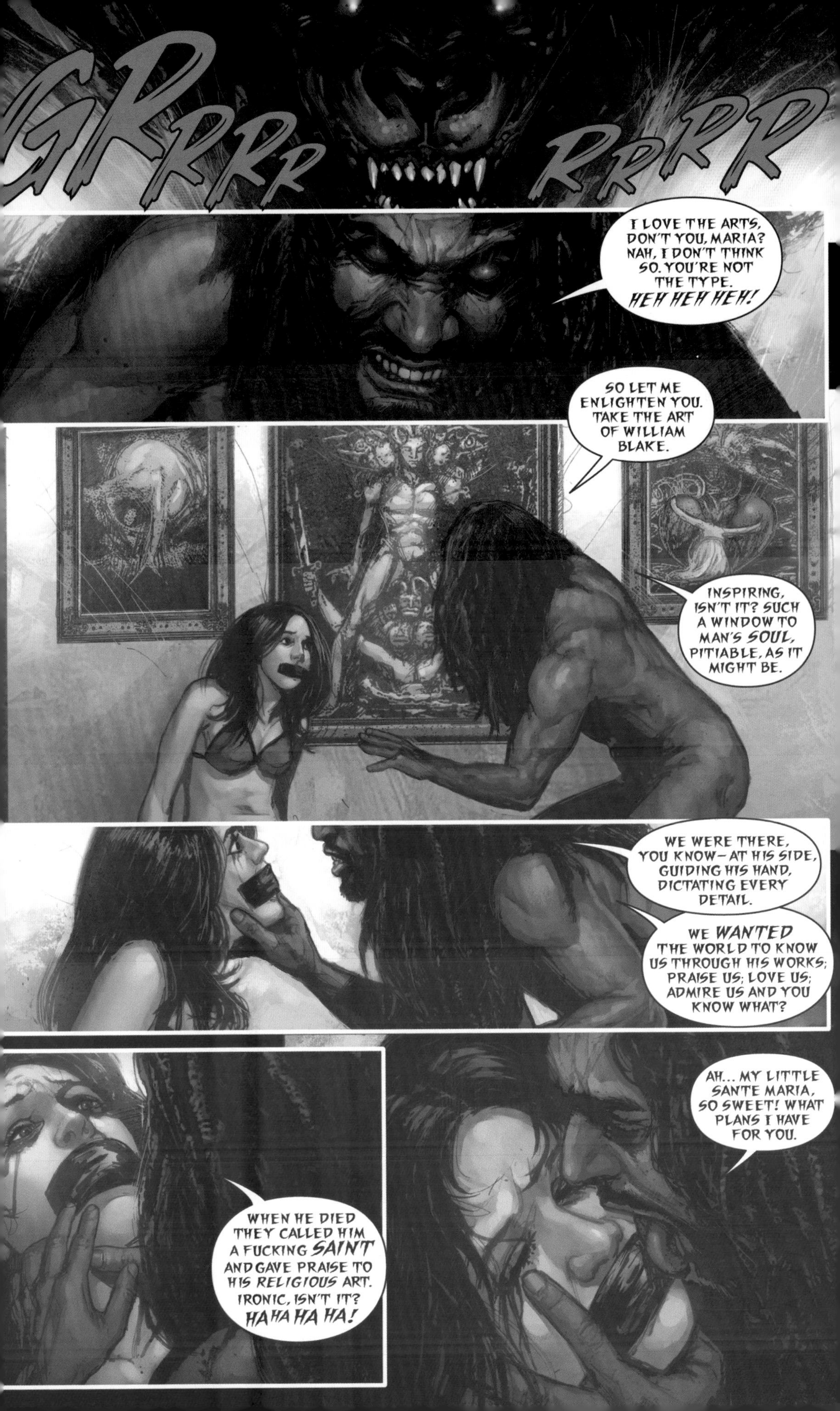
GRRRR RRRRR
I LOVE THE ARTS, DON'T YOU, MARIA? NAH, I DON'T THINK SO. YOU'RE NOT THE TYPE. HEH HEH HEH!
SO LET ME ENLIGHTEN YOU. TAKE THE ART OF WILLIAM BLAKE.
INSPIRING, ISN'T IT? SUCH A WINDOW TO MAN'S SOUL, PITIABLE, AS IT MIGHT BE.
WE WERE THERE, YOU KNOW—AT HIS SIDE, GUIDING HIS HAND, DICTATING EVERY DETAIL.
WE WANTED THE WORLD TO KNOW US THROUGH HIS WORKS; PRAISE US; LOVE US; ADMIRE US AND YOU KNOW WHAT?
WHEN HE DIED THEY CALLED HIM A FUCKING SAINT AND GAVE PRAISE TO HIS RELIGIOUS ART. IRONIC, ISN'T IT? HA HA HA HA!
AH... MY LITTLE SANTE MARIA, SO SWEET! WHAT PLANS I HAVE FOR YOU.

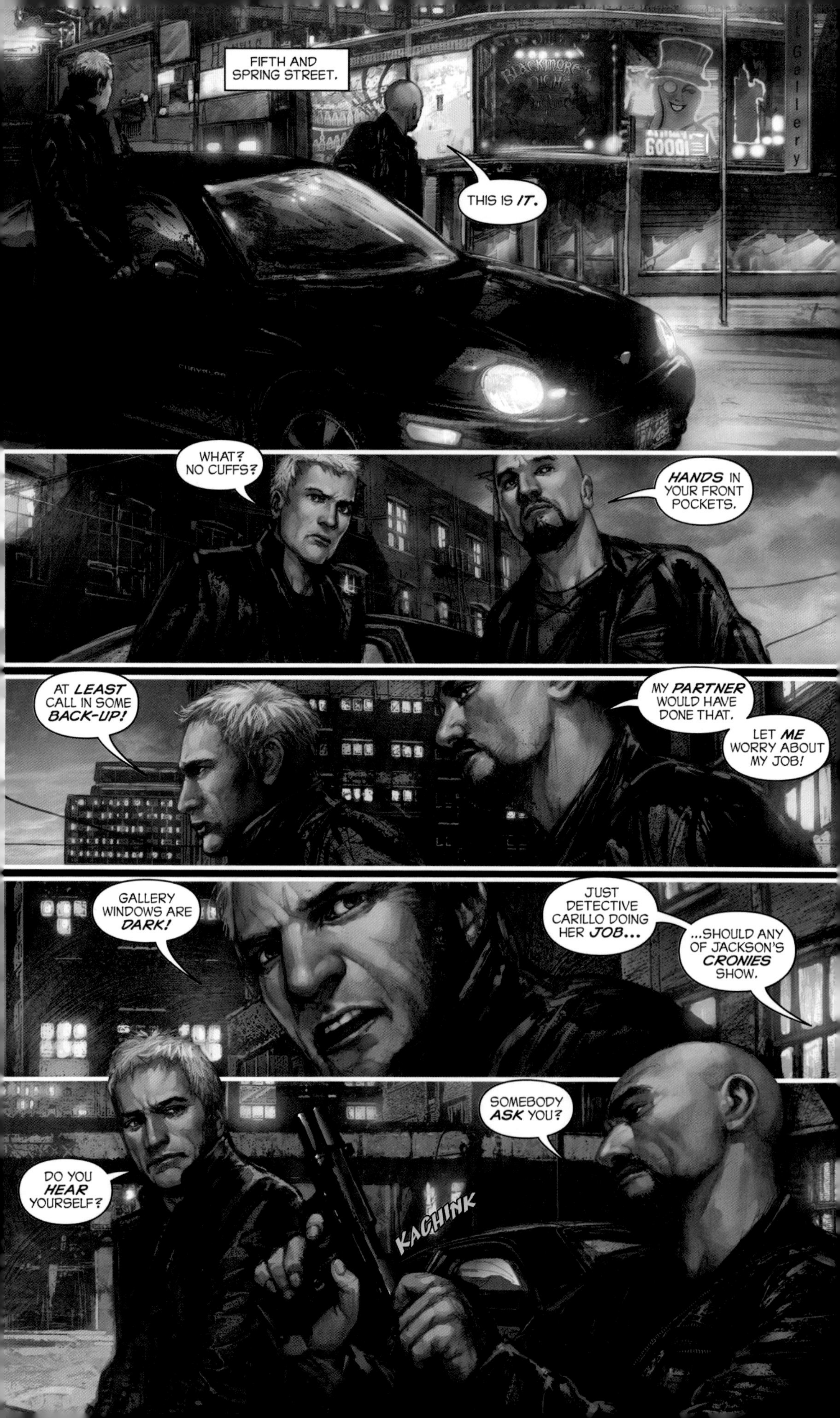
FIFTH AND SPRING STREET.
THIS IS IT.
WHAT? NO CUFFS?
HANDS IN YOUR FRONT POCKETS.
AT LEAST CALL IN SOME BACK-UP!
MY PARTNER WOULD HAVE DONE THAT.
LET ME WORRY ABOUT MY JOB!
GALLERY WINDOWS ARE DARK!
JUST DETECTIVE CARILLO DOING HER JOB...
...SHOULD ANY OF JACKSON'S CRONIES SHOW.
SOMEBODY ASK YOU?
DO YOU HEAR YOURSELF?
KACHINK

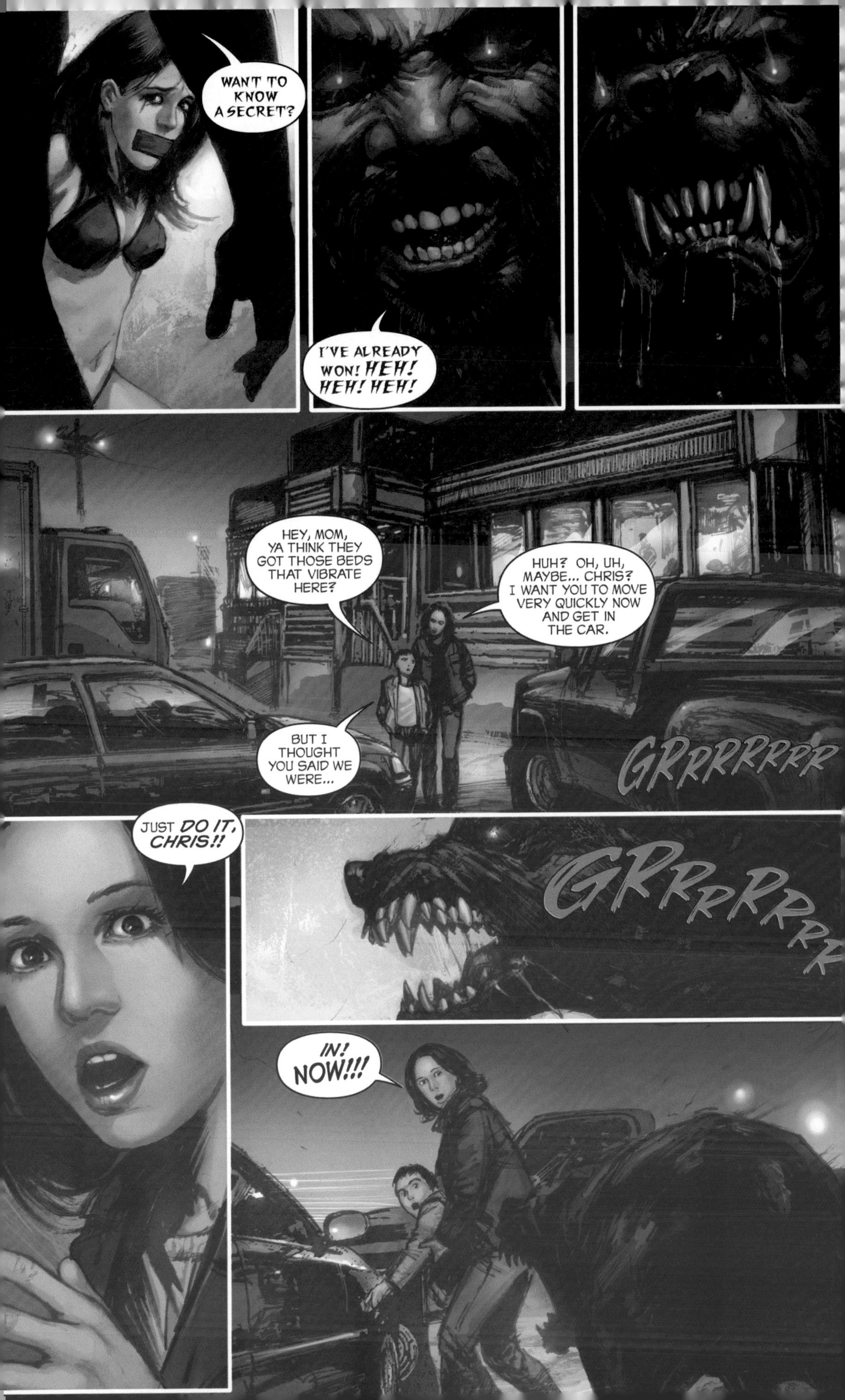
WANT TO KNOW A SECRET?
I'VE ALREADY WON! HEH! HEH! HEH!
HEY, MOM, YA THINK THEY GOT THOSE BEDS THAT VIBRATE HERE?
HUH? OH, UH, MAYBE... CHRIS? I WANT YOU TO MOVE VERY QUICKLY NOW AND GET IN THE CAR.
BUT I THOUGHT YOU SAID WE WERE...
GRRRRRRR
JUST DO IT, CHRIS!!
GRRRRRRRR
IN! NOW!!!

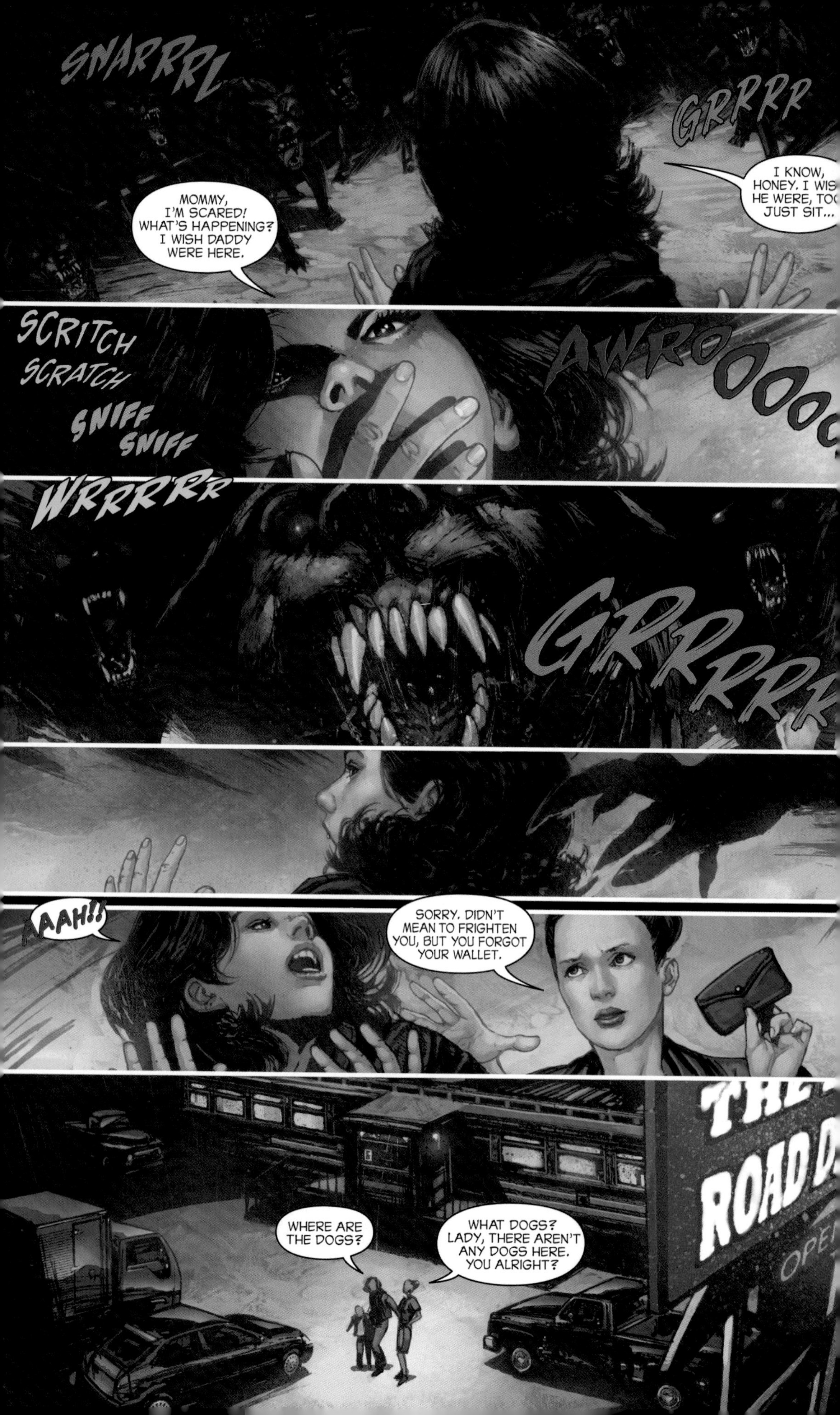
SNARRRL
GRRRR
MOMMY, I'M SCARED! WHAT'S HAPPENING? I WISH DADDY WERE HERE.
I KNOW, HONEY. I WIS HE WERE, TO JUST SIT...
SCRITCH SCRATCH
SNIFF SNIFF
AWROOOOO
WRRRRR
GRRRRR
AAAH!!
SORRY. DIDN'T MEAN TO FRIGHTEN YOU, BUT YOU FORGOT YOUR WALLET.
WHERE ARE THE DOGS?
WHAT DOGS? LADY, THERE AREN'T ANY DOGS HERE. YOU ALRIGHT?
ROAD

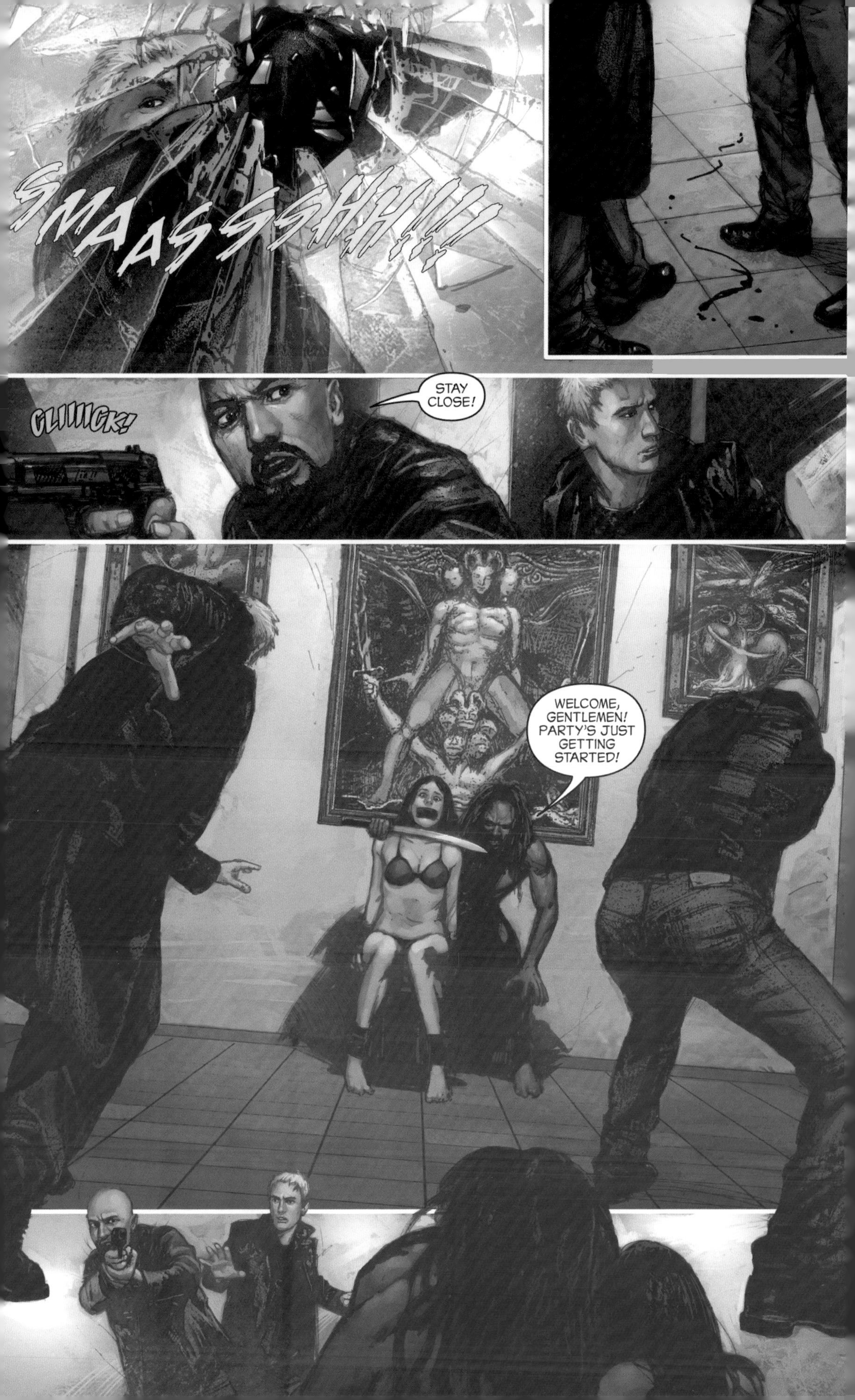
SMAASSSHH!!!!
GLIIIICK!
STAY CLOSE!
WELCOME, GENTLEMEN! PARTY'S JUST GETTING STARTED!

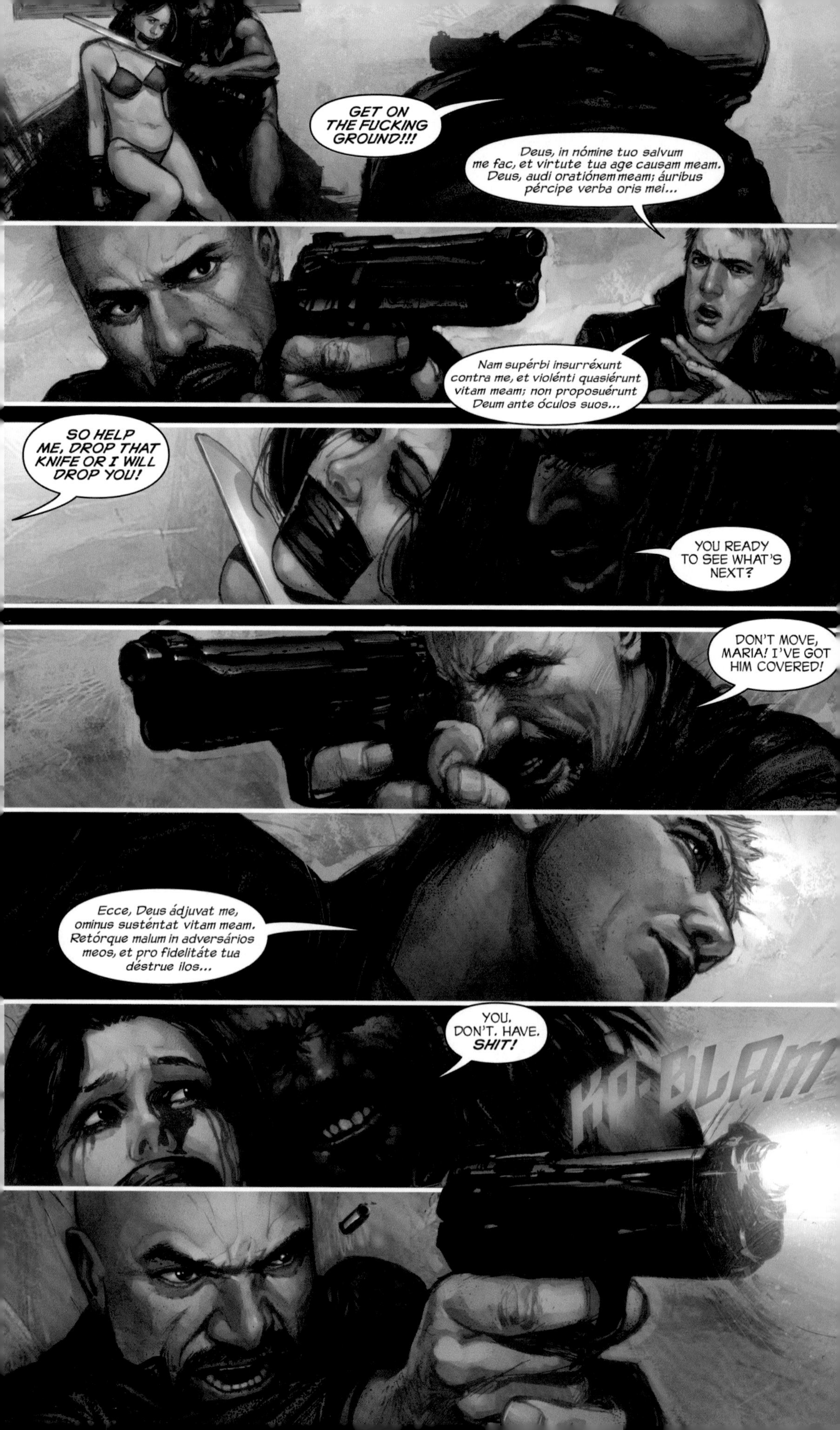
GET ON THE FUCKING GROUND!!!
Deus, in nómine tuo salvum me fac, et virtute tua age causam meam. Deus, audi oratiónem meam; áuribus pércipe verba oris mei...
Nam supérbi insurréxunt contra me, et violénti quasiérunt vitam meam; non proposuérunt Deum ante óculos suos...
SO HELP ME, DROP THAT KNIFE OR I WILL DROP YOU!
YOU READY TO SEE WHAT'S NEXT?
DON'T MOVE, MARIA! I'VE GOT HIM COVERED!
Ecce, Deus ádjuvat me, ominus susténtat vitam meam. Retórque malum in adversários meos, et pro fidelitáte tua déstrue ilos...
YOU. DON'T. HAVE. SHIT!
KO-BLAM

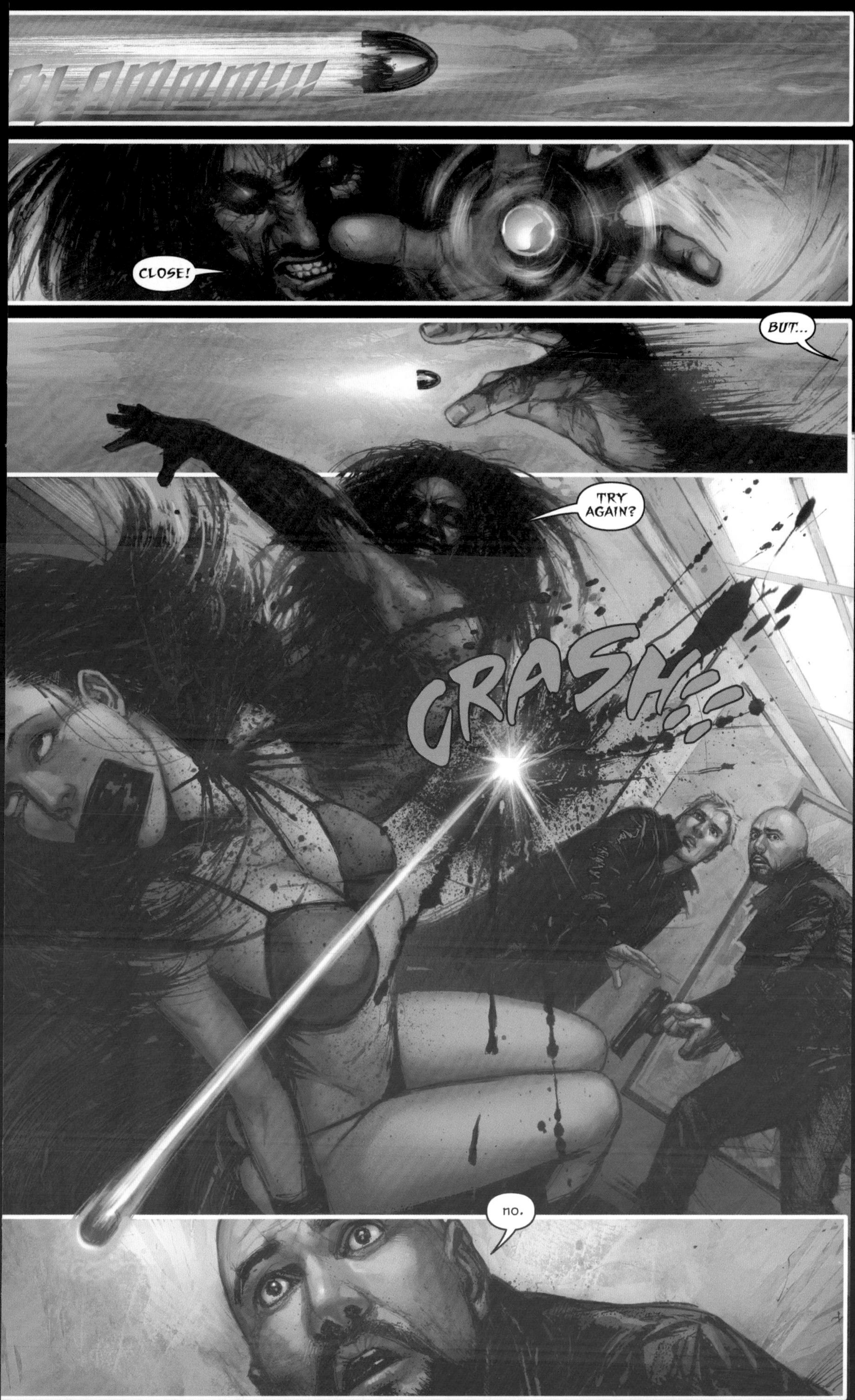
CLOSE!
BUT...
TRY AGAIN?
CRASH!!
no.

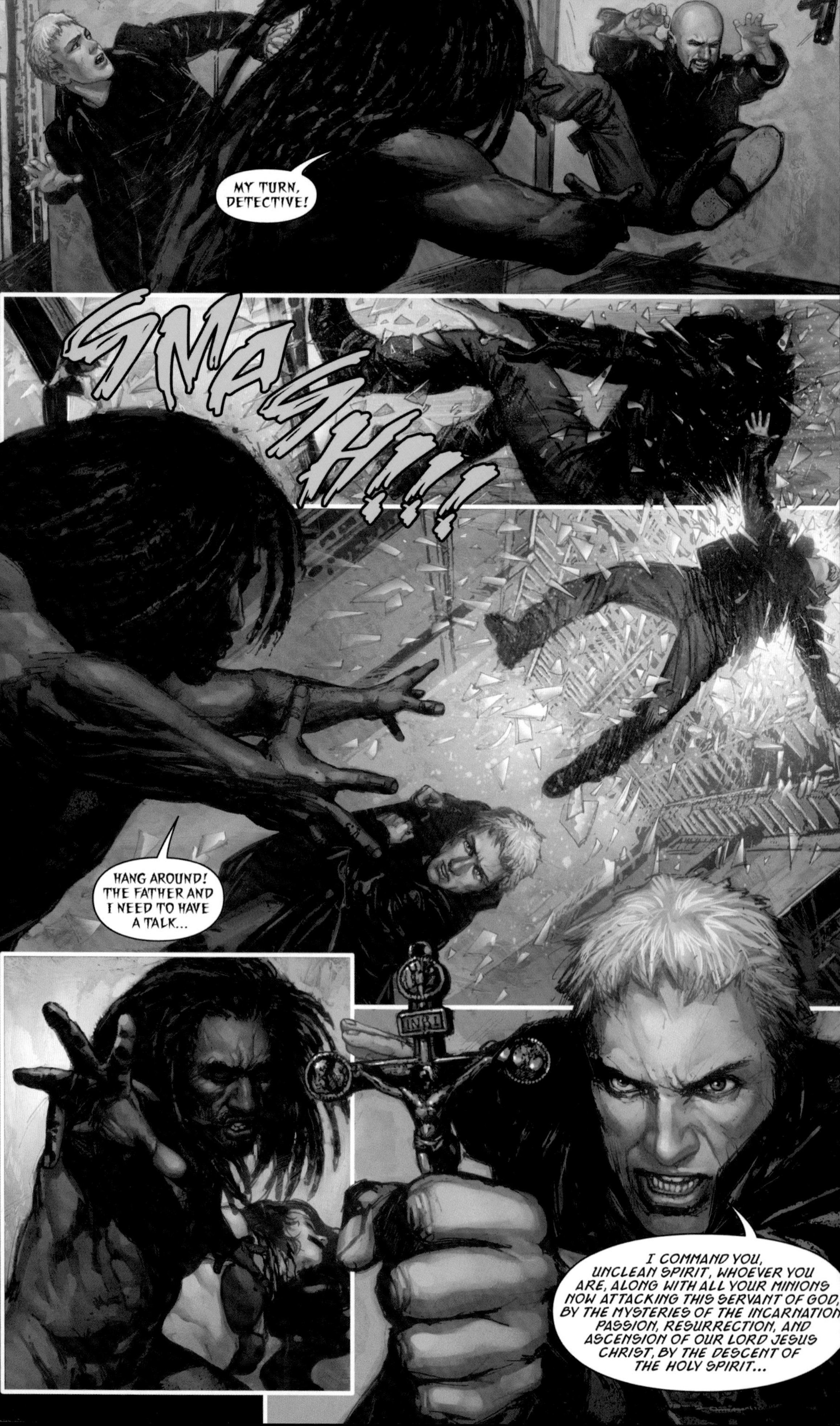
MY TURN, DETECTIVE!
SMASH!!!
HANG AROUND! THE FATHER AND I NEED TO HAVE A TALK...
I COMMAND YOU, UNCLEAN SPIRIT, WHOEVER YOU ARE, ALONG WITH ALL YOUR MINIONS NOW ATTACKING THIS SERVANT OF GOD, BY THE MYSTERIES OF THE INCARNATION, PASSION, RESURRECTION, AND ASCENSION OF OUR LORD JESUS CHRIST, BY THE DESCENT OF THE HOLY SPIRIT...

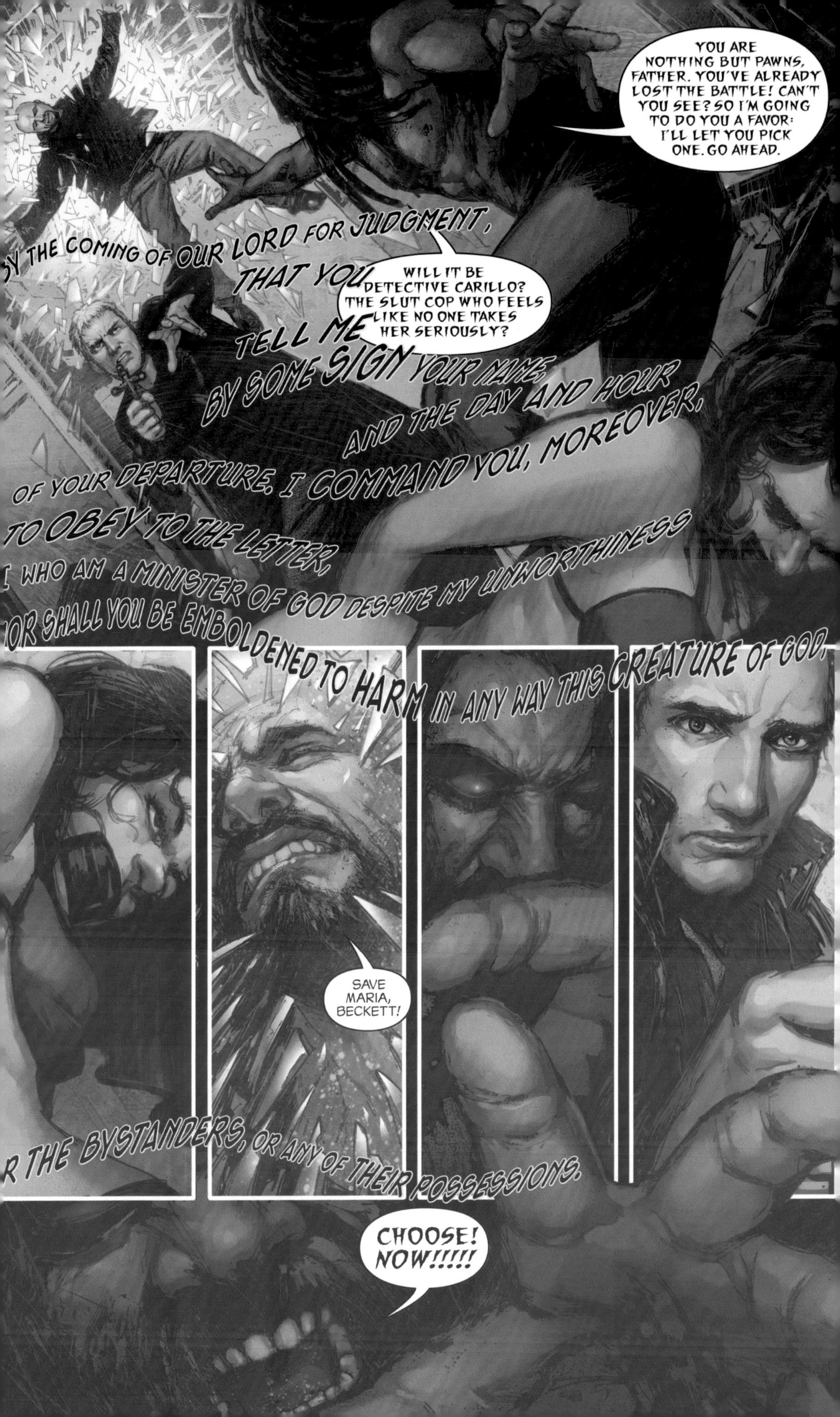
YOU ARE NOTHING BUT PAWNS, FATHER. YOU'VE ALREADY LOST THE BATTLE! CAN'T YOU SEE? SO I'M GOING TO DO YOU A FAVOR: I'LL LET YOU PICK ONE. GO AHEAD.
BY THE COMING OF OUR LORD FOR JUDGMENT,
THAT YOU
WILL IT BE DETECTIVE CARILLO? THE SLUT COP WHO FEELS LIKE NO ONE TAKES HER SERIOUSLY?
TELL ME
BY SOME SIGN YOUR NAME,
AND THE DAY AND HOUR
OF YOUR DEPARTURE. I COMMAND YOU, MOREOVER,
TO OBEY TO THE LETTER,
I WHO AM A MINISTER OF GOD DESPITE MY UNWORTHINESS
NOR SHALL YOU BE EMBOLDENED TO HARM IN ANY WAY THIS CREATURE OF GOD,
SAVE MARIA, BECKETT!
OR THE BYSTANDERS, OR ANY OF THEIR POSSESSIONS.
CHOOSE! NOW!!!!!

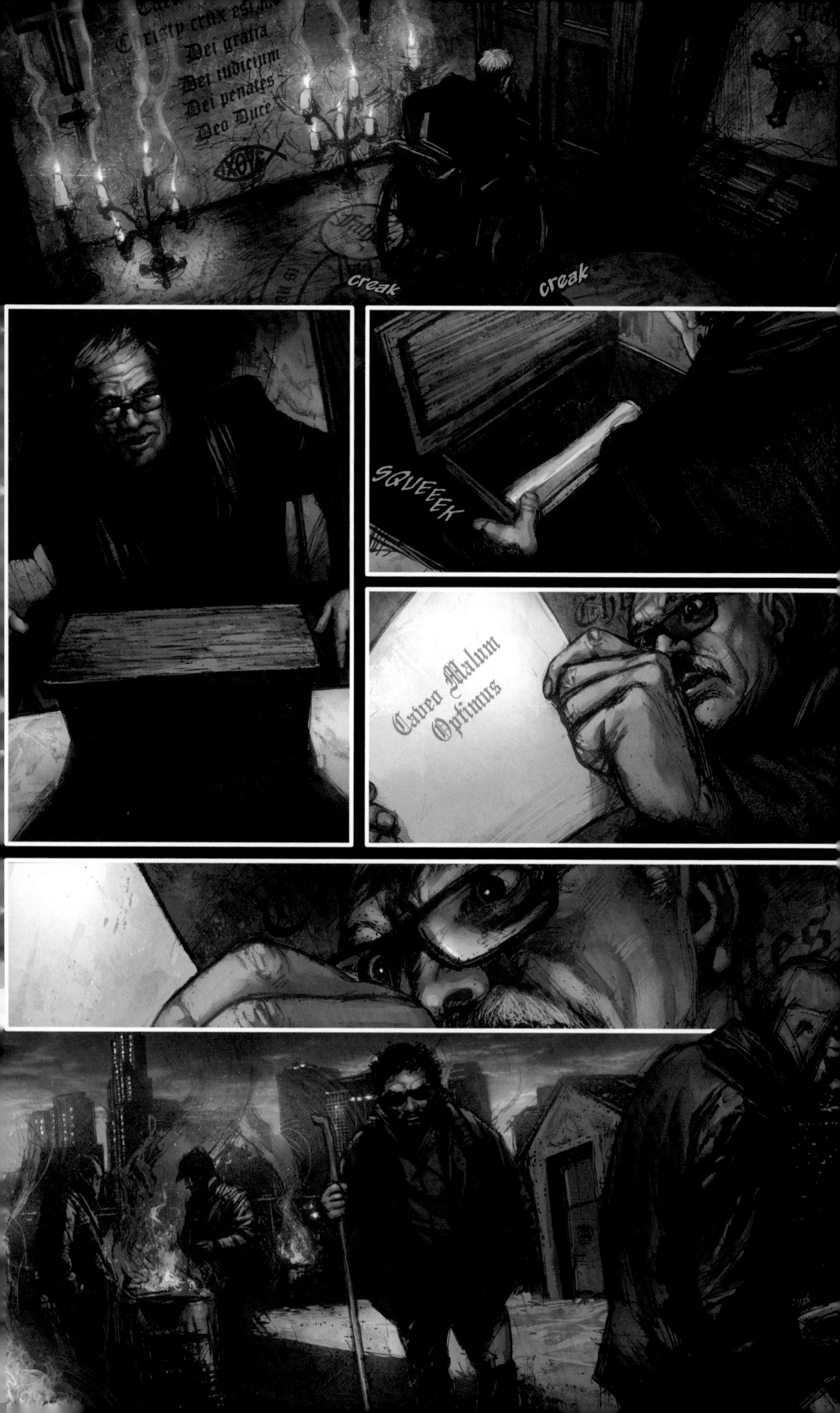
Dei gratia
Dei iudicium
Dei penates
Deo Duce
creak
creak
SQUEEEK
Caveo Malum
Optimus

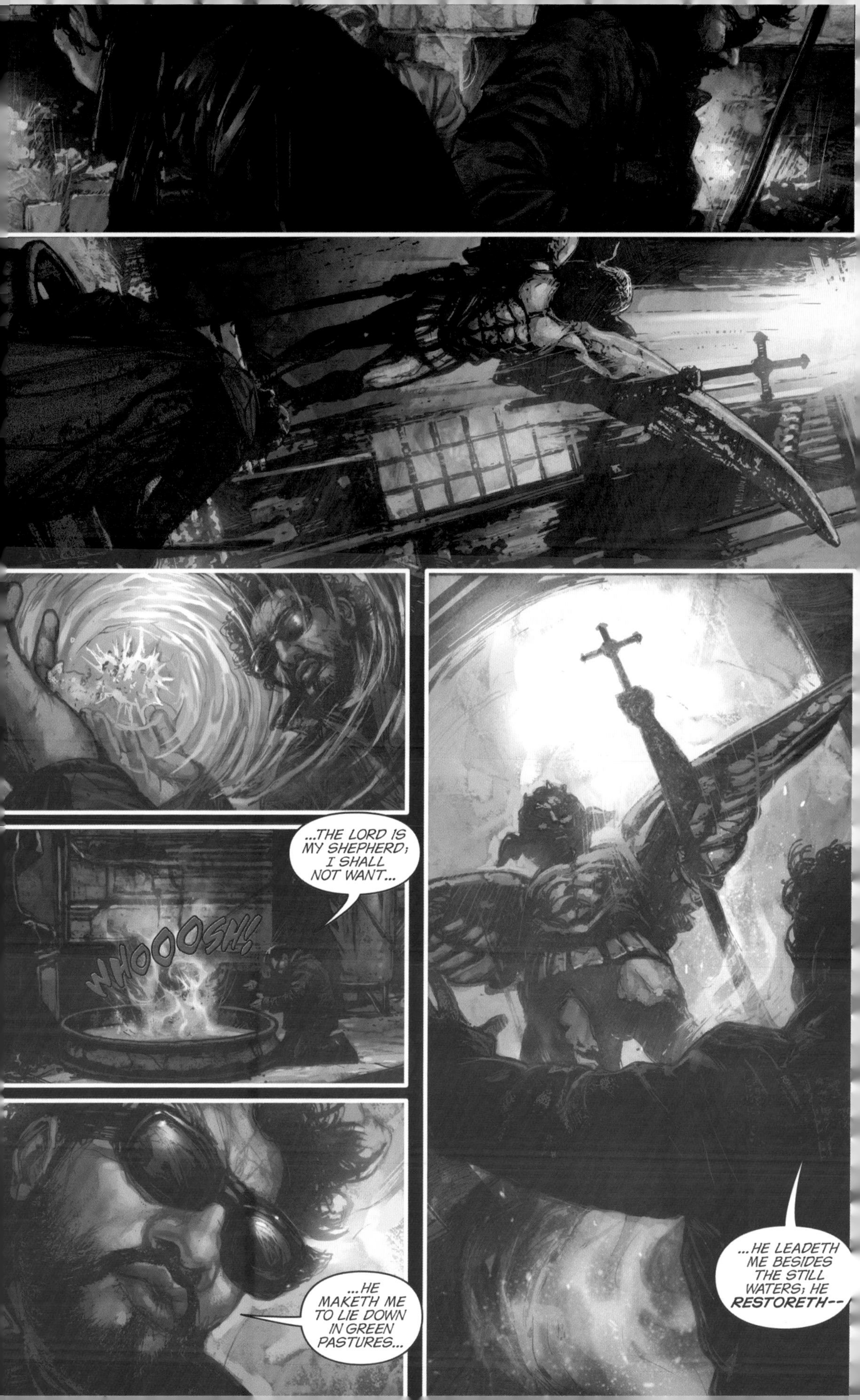

...THE LORD IS MY SHEPHERD; I SHALL NOT WANT...
WHOOOSH!
...HE MAKETH ME TO LIE DOWN IN GREEN PASTURES...
...HE LEADETH ME BESIDES THE STILL WATERS; HE **RESTORETH--**

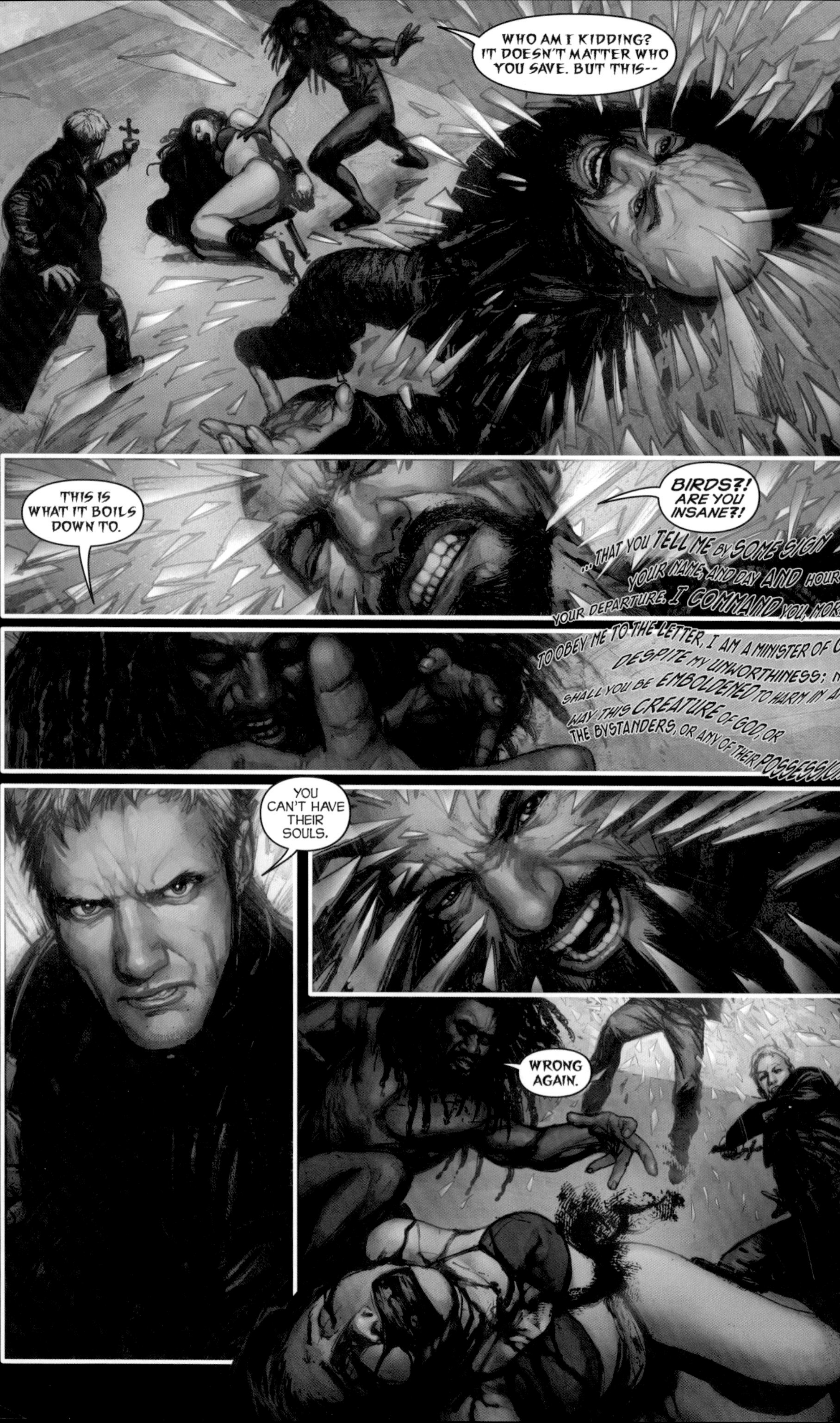
WHO AM I KIDDING? IT DOESN'T MATTER WHO YOU SAVE. BUT THIS--
THIS IS WHAT IT BOILS DOWN TO.
BIRDS?! ARE YOU INSANE?!
...THAT YOU TELL ME BY SOME SIGN YOUR NAME, AND DAY AND HOUR YOUR DEPARTURE. I COMMAND YOU, MOR
TO OBEY ME TO THE LETTER, I AM A MINISTER OF G
DESPITE MY UNWORTHINESS; N
SHALL YOU BE EMBOLDENED TO HARM IN A
WAY THIS CREATURE OF GOD, OR THE BYSTANDERS, OR ANY OF THEIR POSSESSI
YOU CAN'T HAVE THEIR SOULS.
WRONG AGAIN.

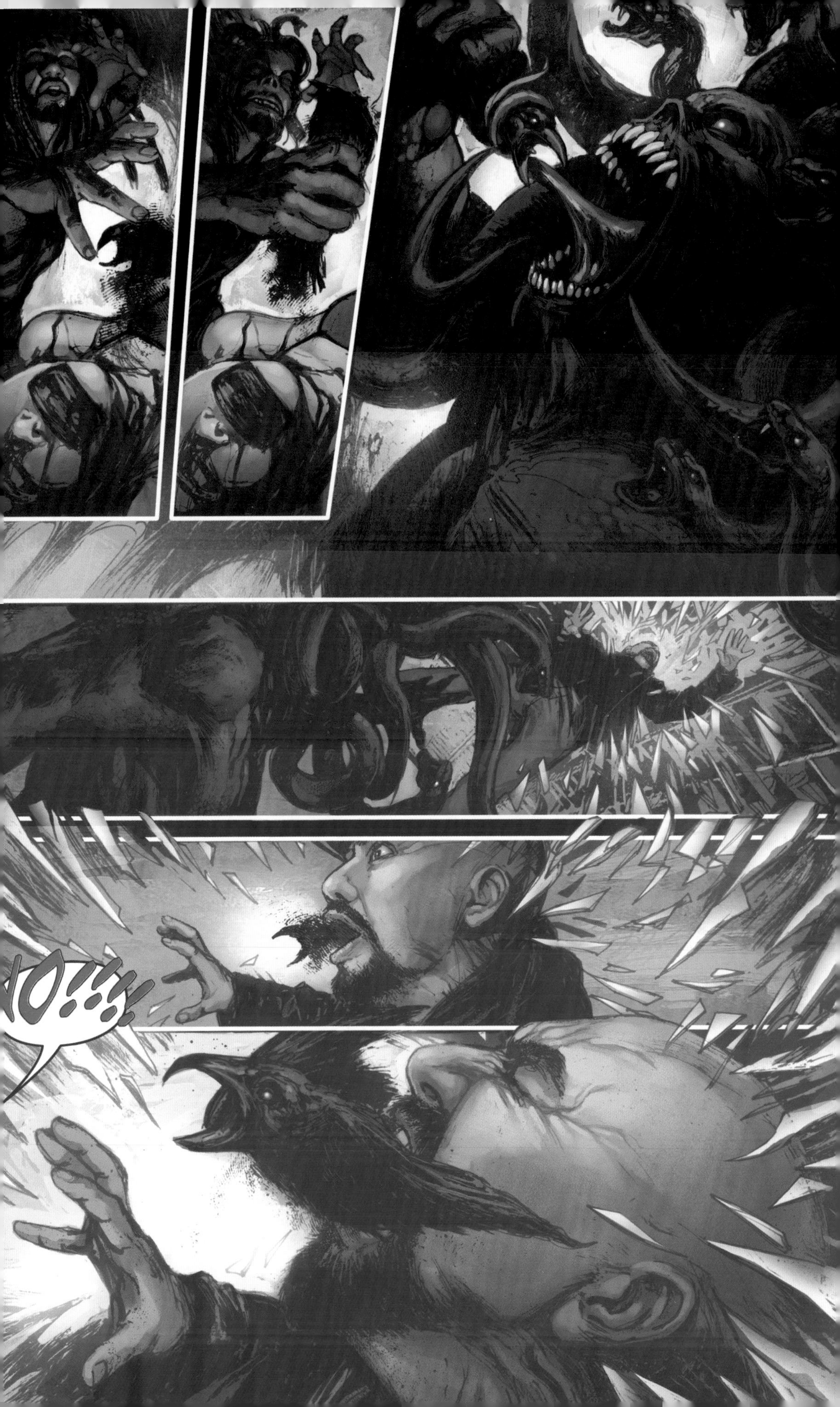
O!!!

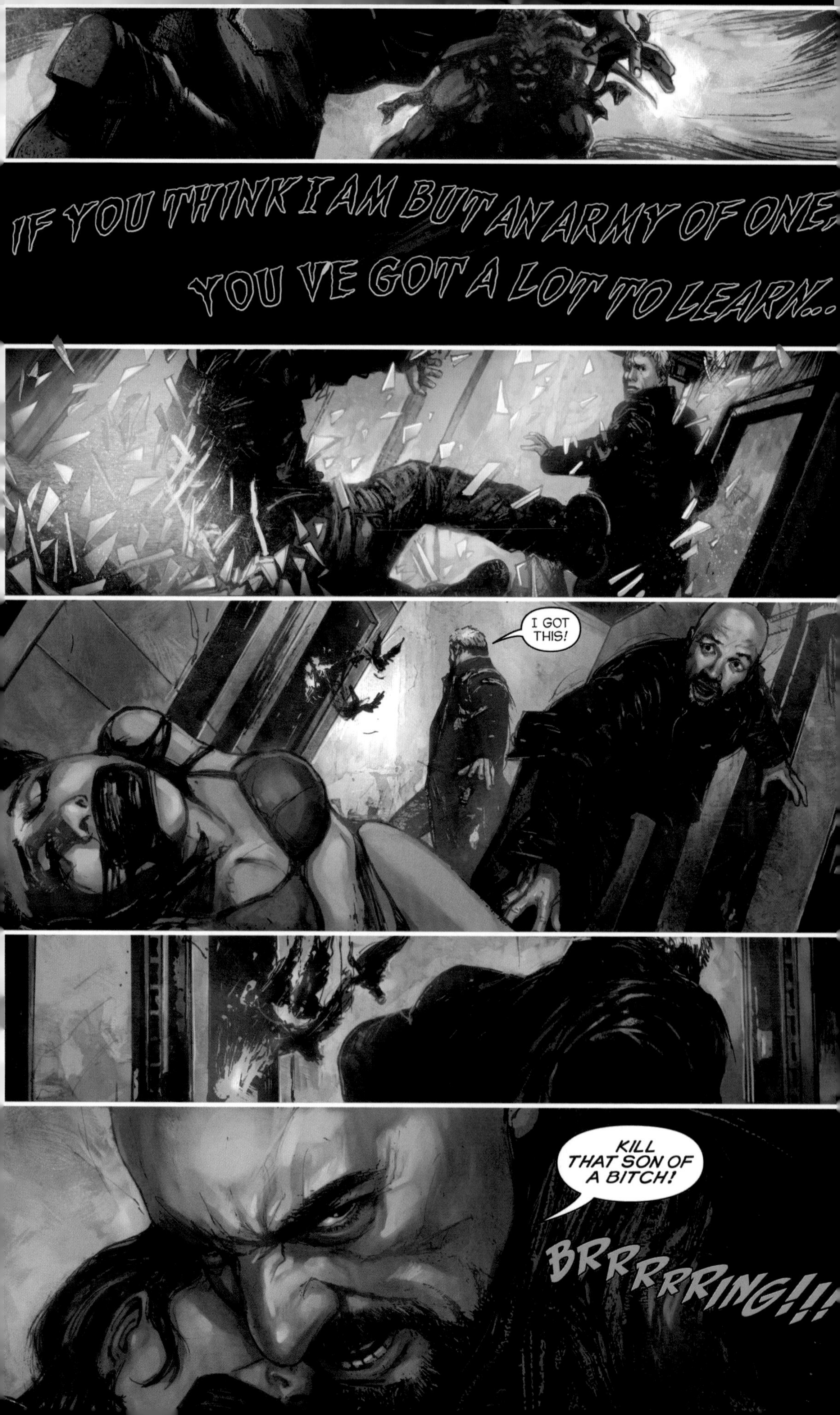
IF YOU THINK I AM BUT AN ARMY OF ONE,
YOU VE GOT A LOT TO LEARN...
I GOT THIS!
KILL THAT SON OF A BITCH!
BRRRRRING!!!

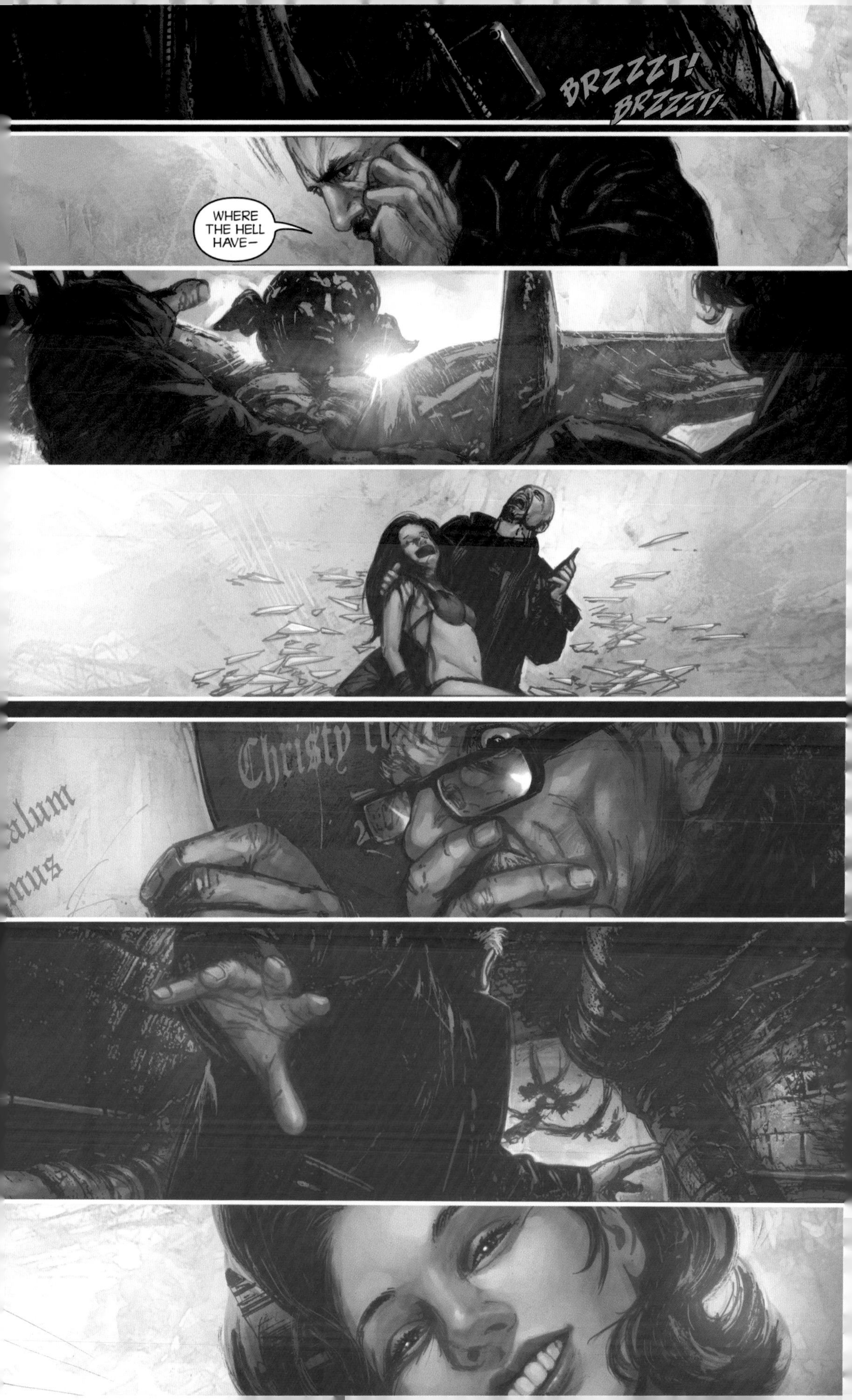
BRZZZT!
BRZZZT!
WHERE THE HELL HAVE–

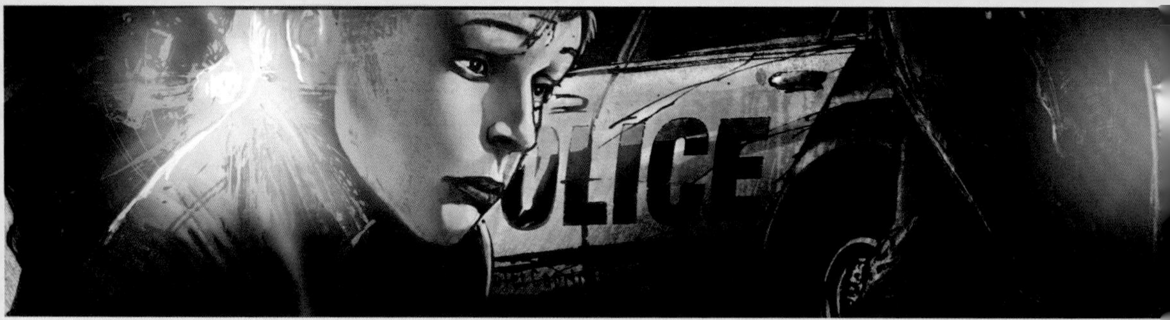

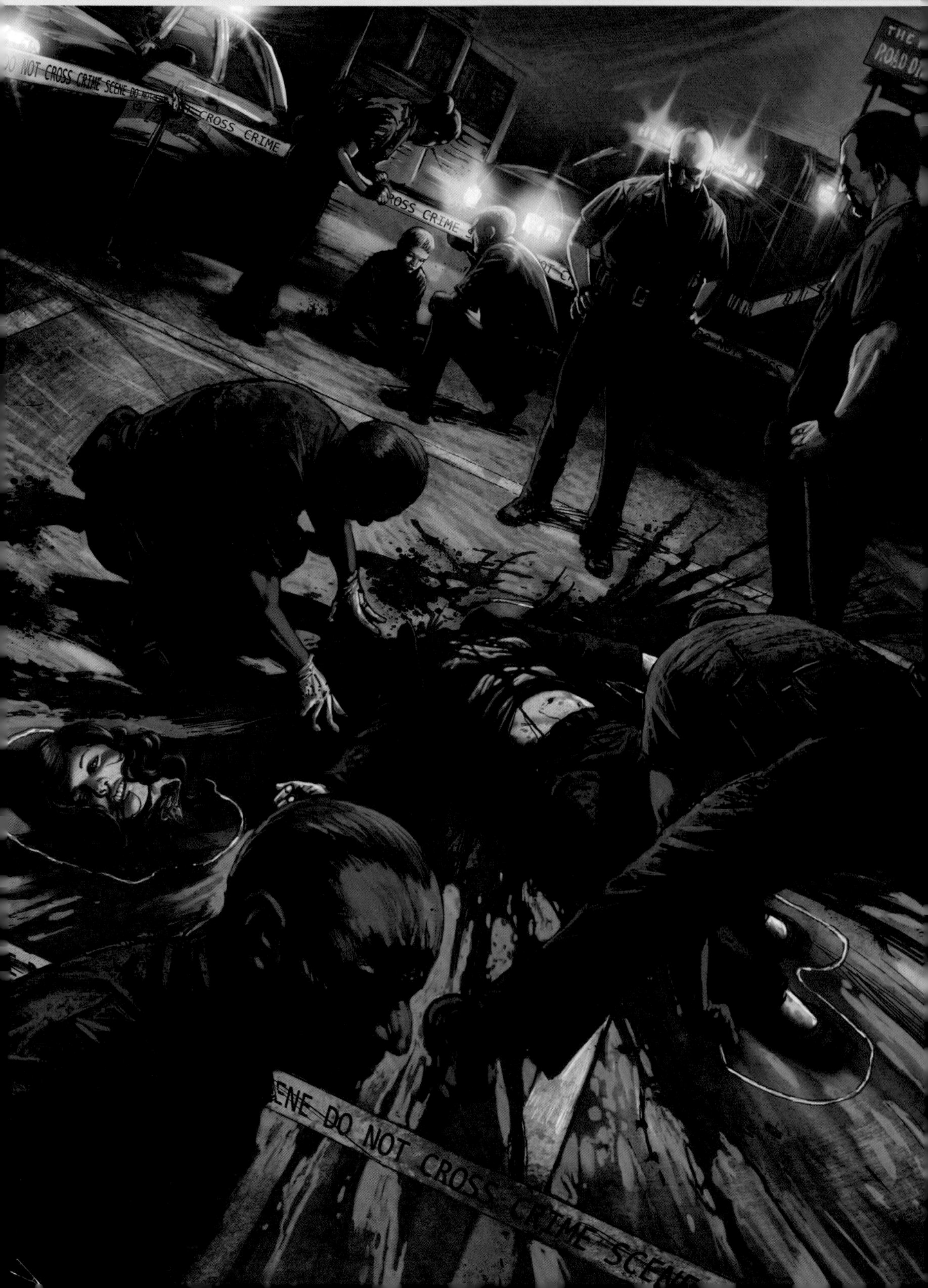
DO NOT CROSS CRIME SCENE
CROSS CRIME
CROSS CRIME
DO NOT CROSS CRIME SCENE

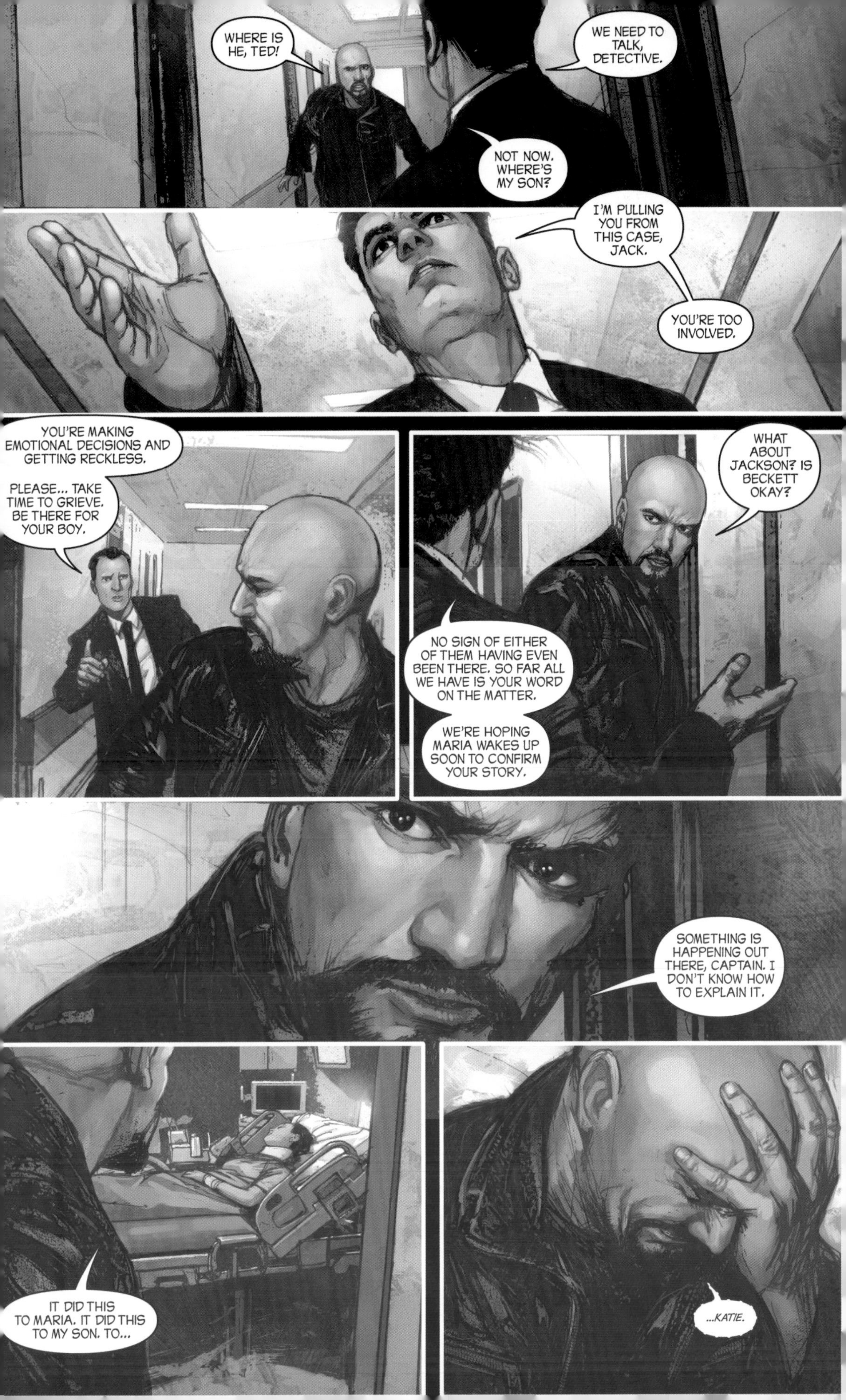
WHERE IS HE, TED!
WE NEED TO TALK, DETECTIVE.
NOT NOW. WHERE'S MY SON?
I'M PULLING YOU FROM THIS CASE, JACK.
YOU'RE TOO INVOLVED.
YOU'RE MAKING EMOTIONAL DECISIONS AND GETTING RECKLESS.
PLEASE... TAKE TIME TO GRIEVE. BE THERE FOR YOUR BOY.
WHAT ABOUT JACKSON? IS BECKETT OKAY?
NO SIGN OF EITHER OF THEM HAVING EVEN BEEN THERE. SO FAR ALL WE HAVE IS YOUR WORD ON THE MATTER.
WE'RE HOPING MARIA WAKES UP SOON TO CONFIRM YOUR STORY.
SOMETHING IS HAPPENING OUT THERE, CAPTAIN. I DON'T KNOW HOW TO EXPLAIN IT.
IT DID THIS TO MARIA. IT DID THIS TO MY SON. TO...
...KATIE.

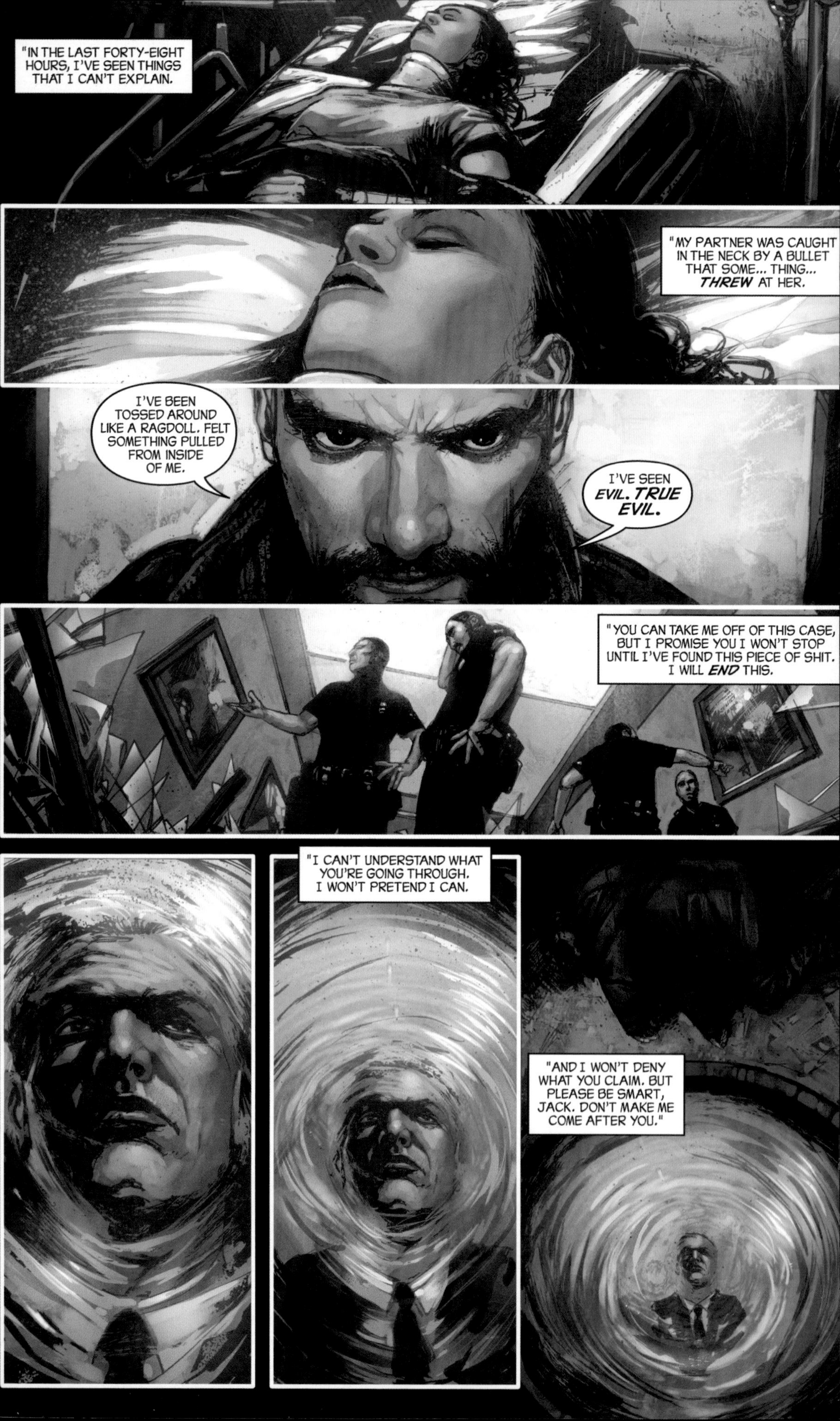
"IN THE LAST FORTY-EIGHT HOURS, I'VE SEEN THINGS THAT I CAN'T EXPLAIN.
"MY PARTNER WAS CAUGHT IN THE NECK BY A BULLET THAT SOME... THING... THREW AT HER.
I'VE BEEN TOSSED AROUND LIKE A RAGDOLL. FELT SOMETHING PULLED FROM INSIDE OF ME.
I'VE SEEN EVIL. TRUE EVIL.
"YOU CAN TAKE ME OFF OF THIS CASE, BUT I PROMISE YOU I WON'T STOP UNTIL I'VE FOUND THIS PIECE OF SHIT. I WILL END THIS.
"I CAN'T UNDERSTAND WHAT YOU'RE GOING THROUGH. I WON'T PRETEND I CAN.
"AND I WON'T DENY WHAT YOU CLAIM. BUT PLEASE BE SMART, JACK. DON'T MAKE ME COME AFTER YOU."

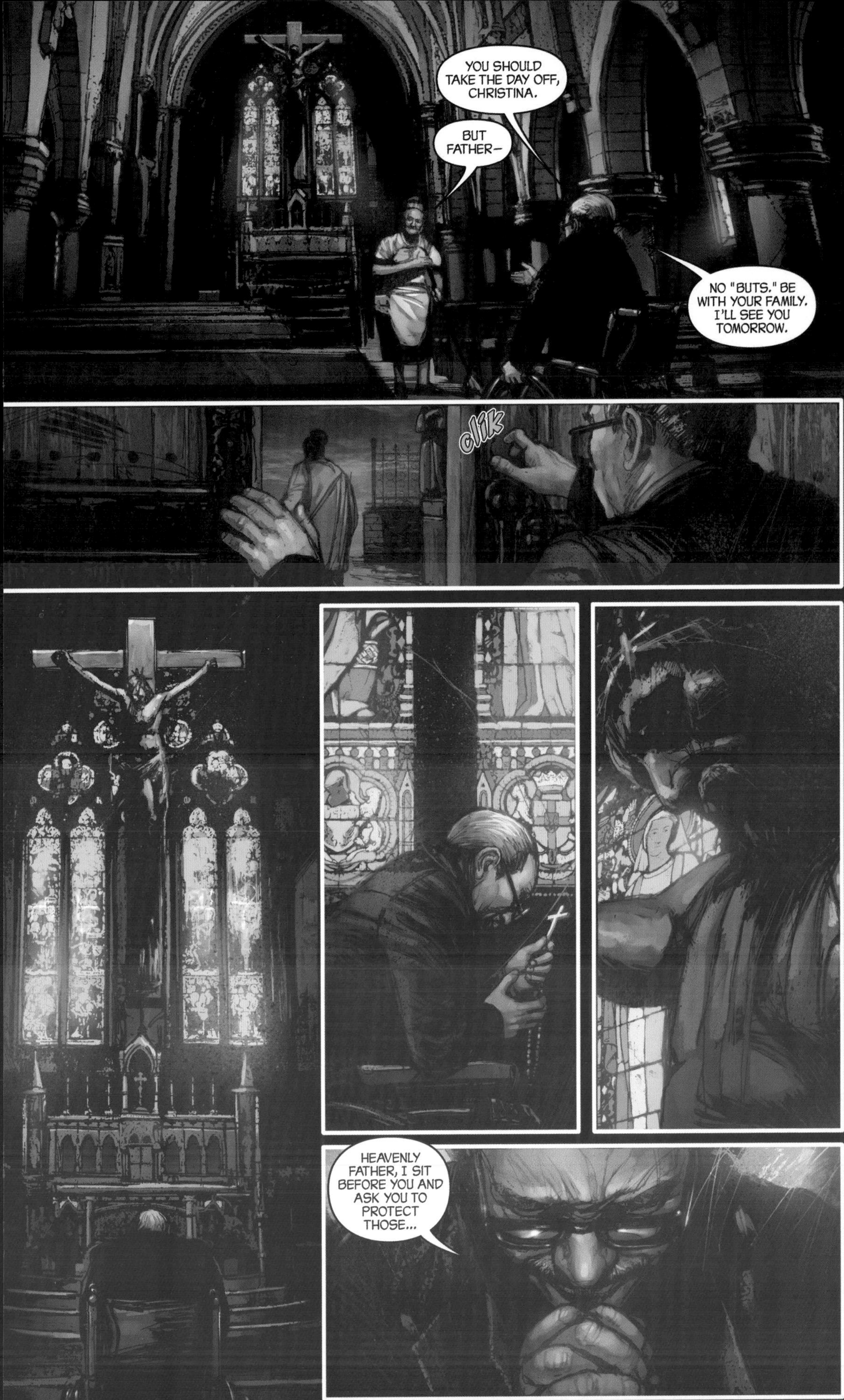
YOU SHOULD TAKE THE DAY OFF, CHRISTINA.
BUT FATHER–
NO "BUTS." BE WITH YOUR FAMILY. I'LL SEE YOU TOMORROW.
CLIK
HEAVENLY FATHER, I SIT BEFORE YOU AND ASK YOU TO PROTECT THOSE...

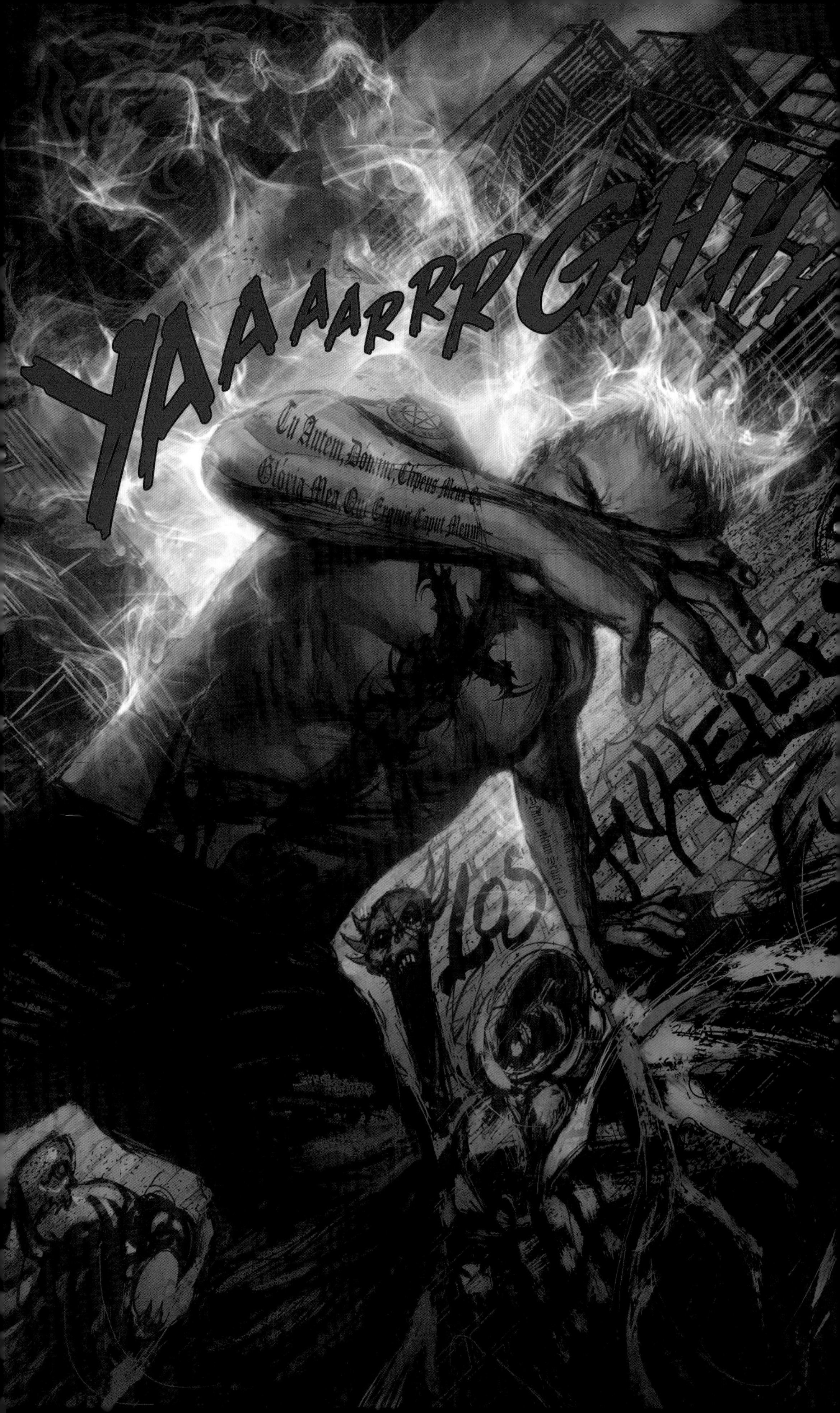
YAAAARRRGHHH
Tu Autem, Domine, Clipeus Meus Es
Glória Mea, Qui Erigis Caput Meum
LOS

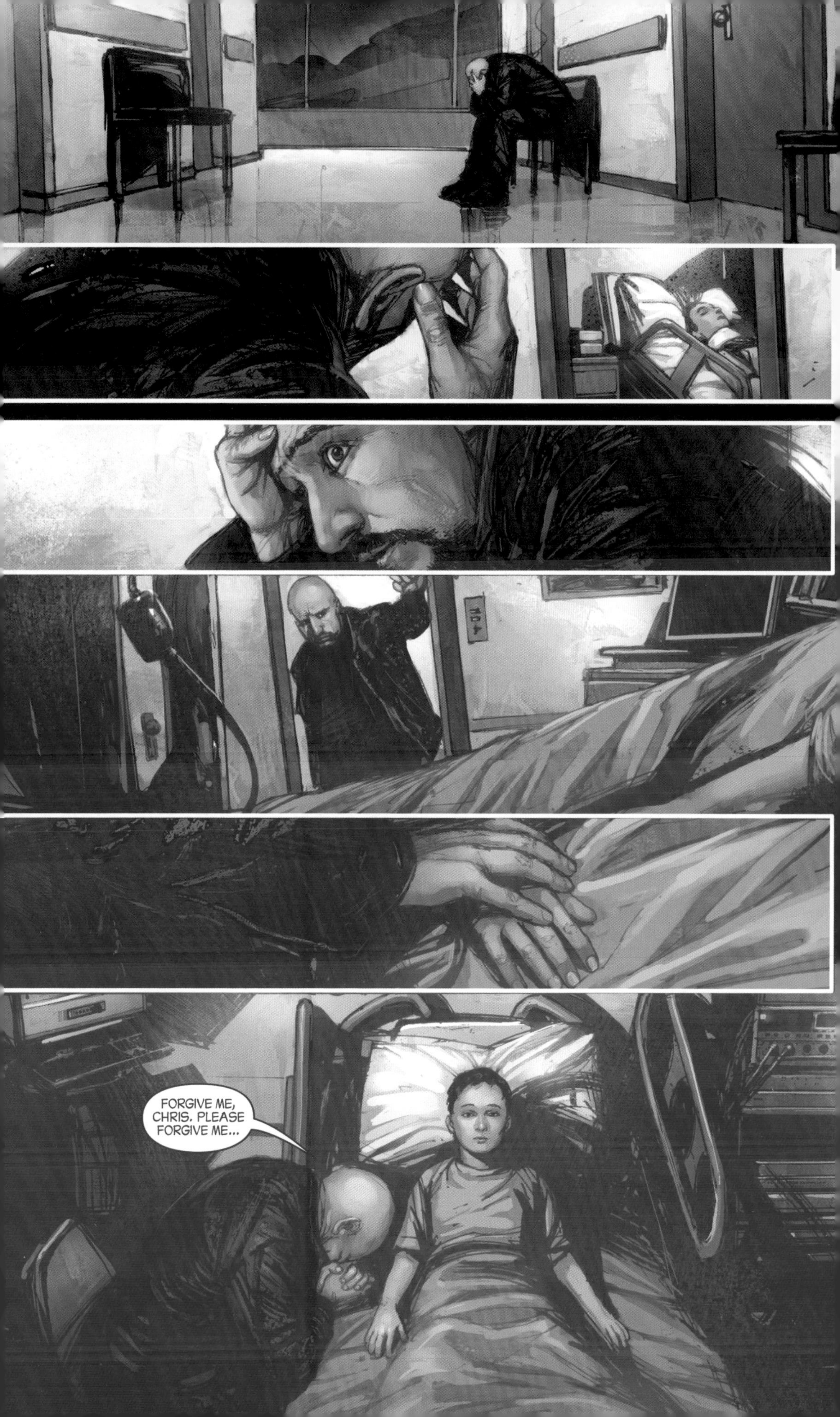
FORGIVE ME, CHRIS. PLEASE FORGIVE ME...

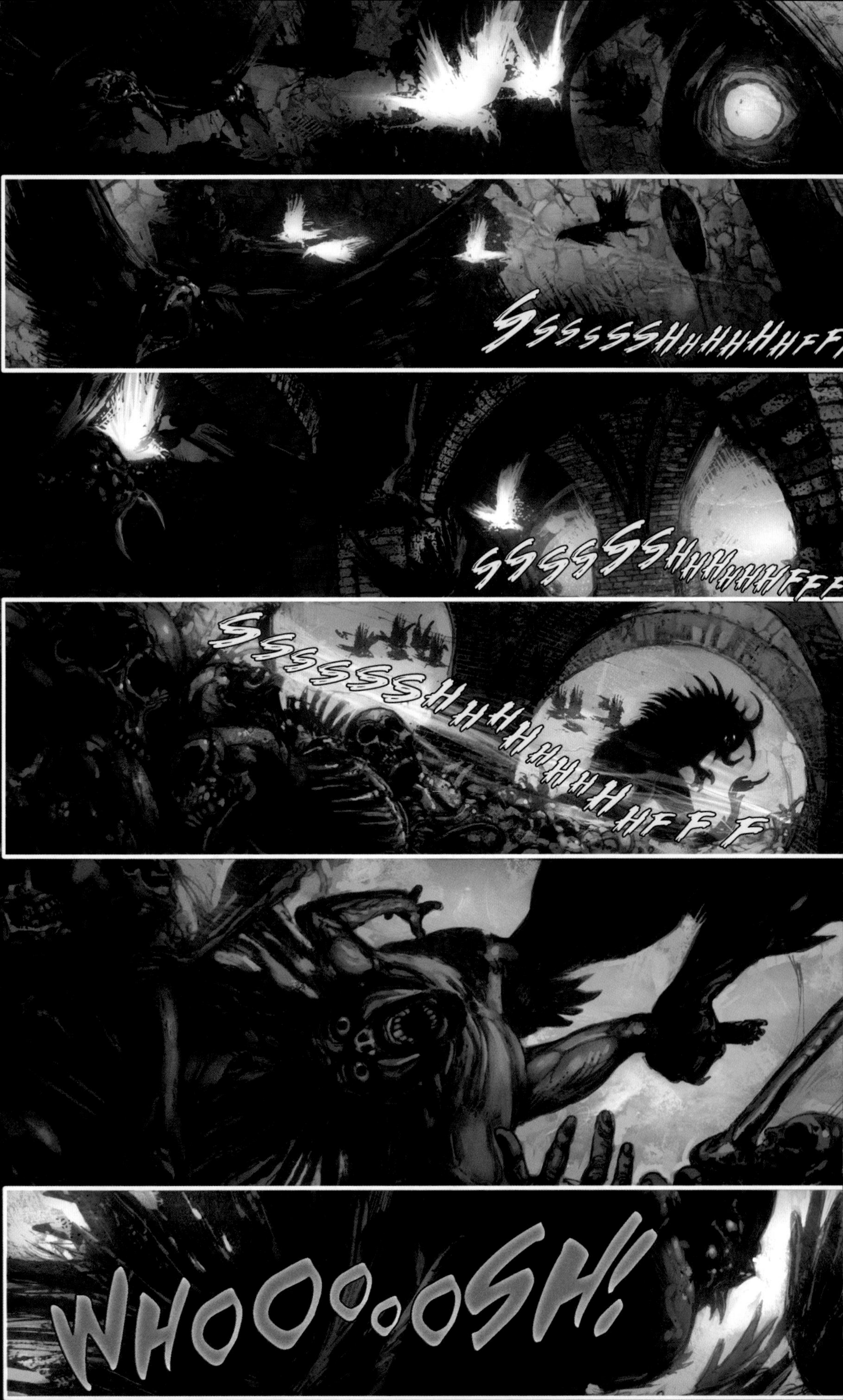
SSSSSSHHHHHFFF
SSSSSSHHHHHHFFF
SSSSSSSHHHHHHHHHHHHHFFF
WHOOOOSH!

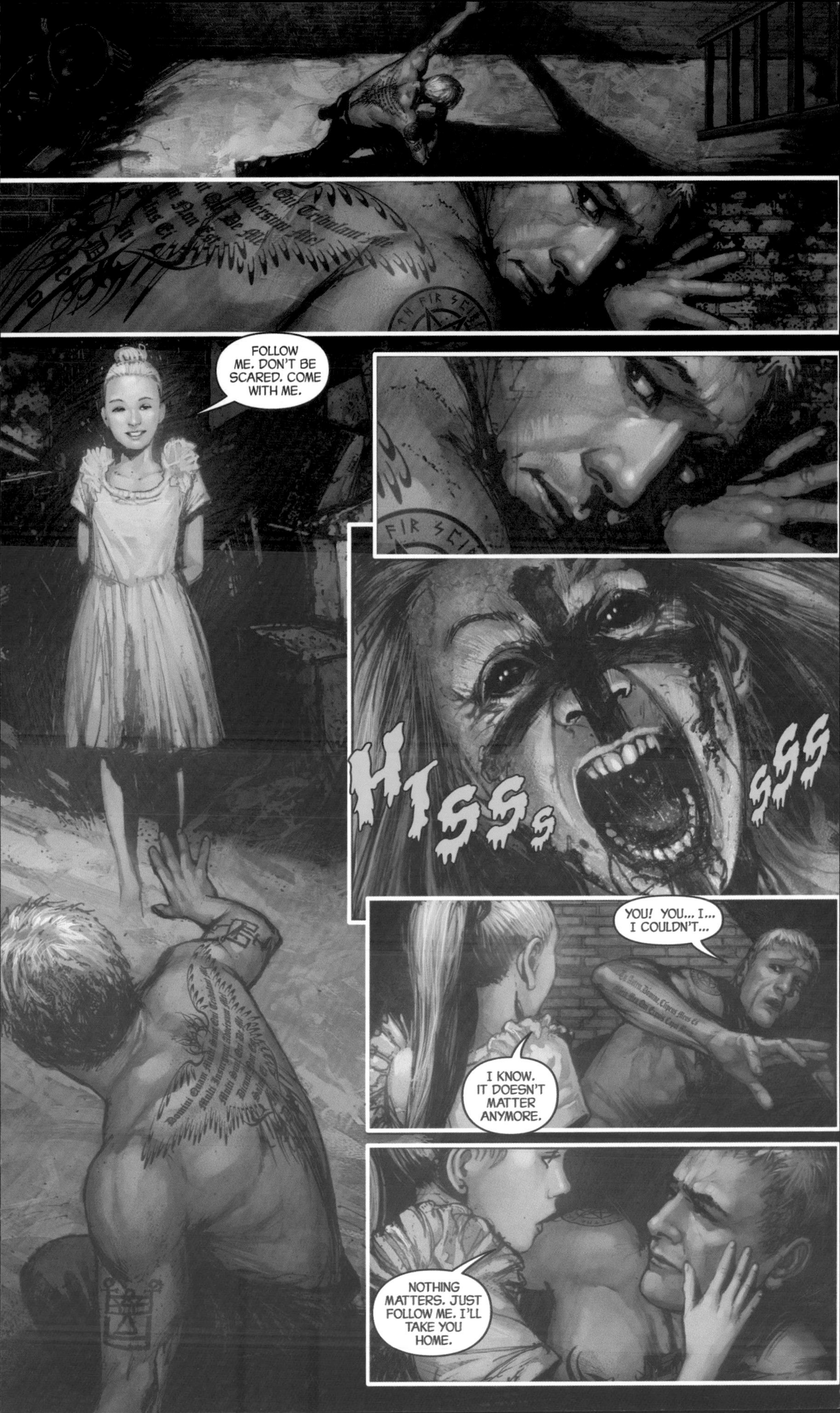
FOLLOW ME. DON'T BE SCARED. COME WITH ME.
HISSSSSS
YOU! YOU... I... I COULDN'T...
I KNOW. IT DOESN'T MATTER ANYMORE.
NOTHING MATTERS. JUST FOLLOW ME. I'LL TAKE YOU HOME.

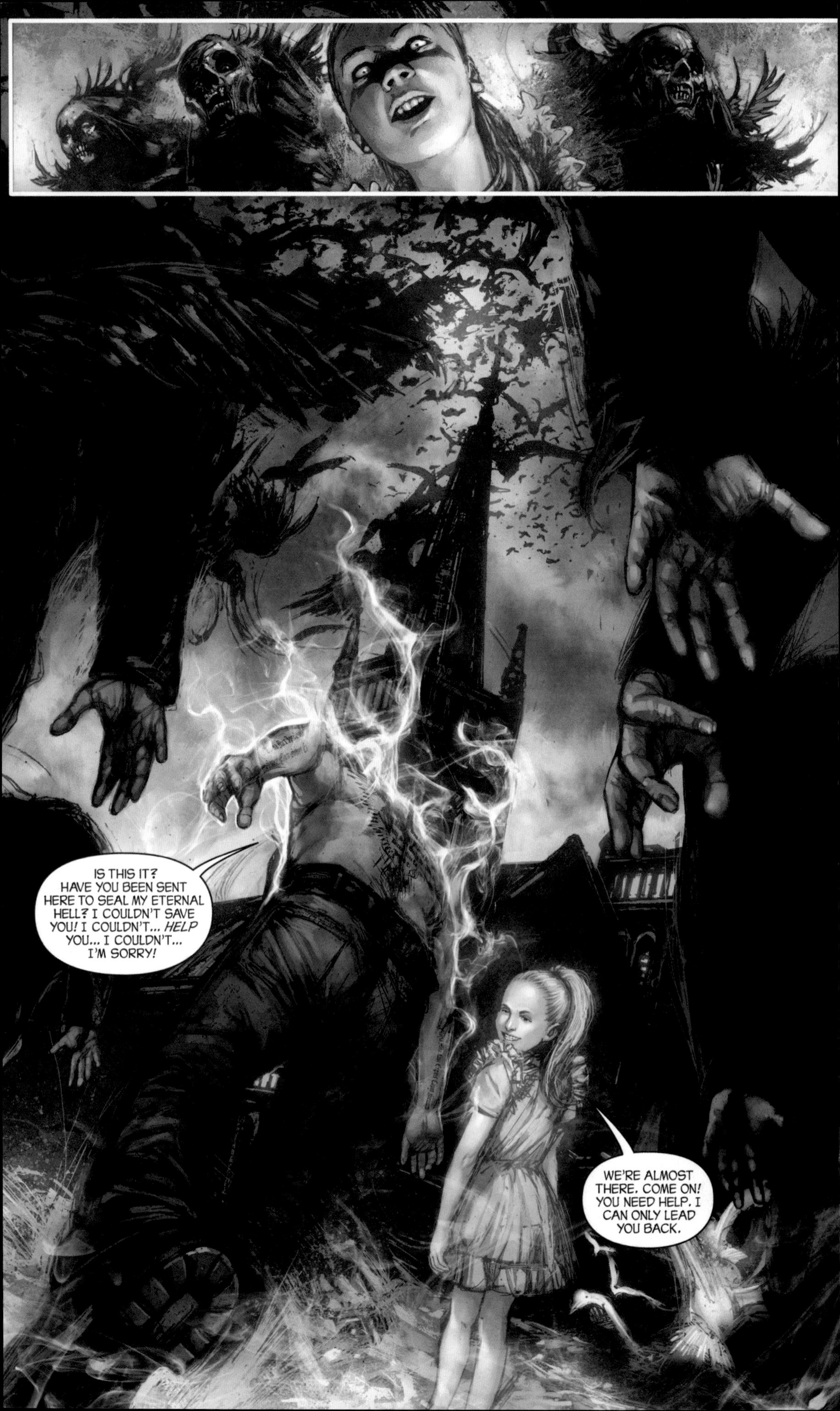
IS THIS IT? HAVE YOU BEEN SENT HERE TO SEAL MY ETERNAL HELL? I COULDN'T SAVE YOU! I COULDN'T... *HELP* YOU... I COULDN'T... I'M SORRY!
WE'RE ALMOST THERE. COME ON! YOU NEED HELP. I CAN ONLY LEAD YOU BACK.

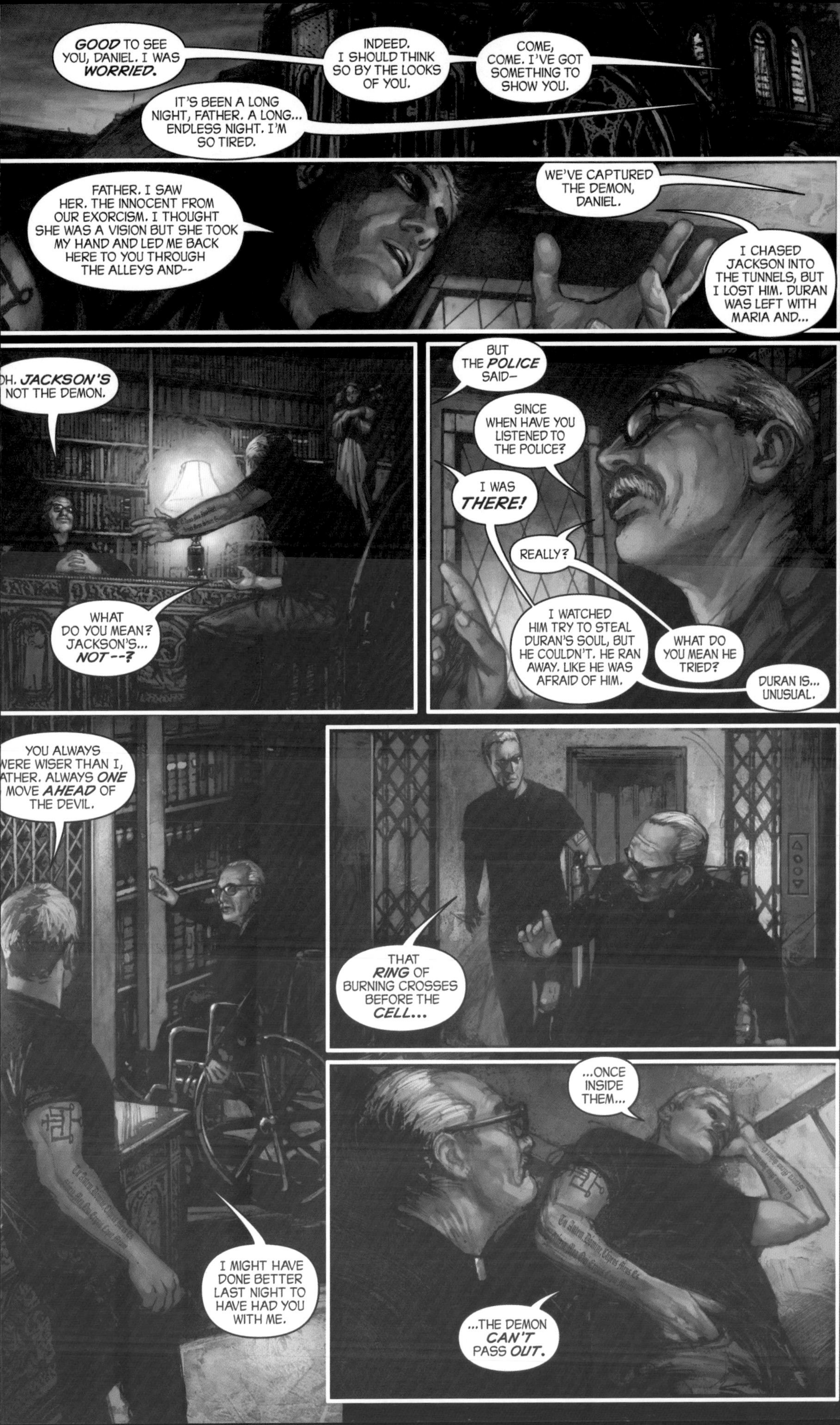
GOOD TO SEE YOU, DANIEL. I WAS WORRIED.
INDEED. I SHOULD THINK SO BY THE LOOKS OF YOU.
COME, COME. I'VE GOT SOMETHING TO SHOW YOU.
IT'S BEEN A LONG NIGHT, FATHER. A LONG... ENDLESS NIGHT. I'M SO TIRED.
FATHER. I SAW HER. THE INNOCENT FROM OUR EXORCISM. I THOUGHT SHE WAS A VISION BUT SHE TOOK MY HAND AND LED ME BACK HERE TO YOU THROUGH THE ALLEYS AND--
WE'VE CAPTURED THE DEMON, DANIEL.
I CHASED JACKSON INTO THE TUNNELS, BUT I LOST HIM. DURAN WAS LEFT WITH MARIA AND...
OH. JACKSON'S NOT THE DEMON.
WHAT DO YOU MEAN? JACKSON'S... NOT--?
BUT THE POLICE SAID–
SINCE WHEN HAVE YOU LISTENED TO THE POLICE?
I WAS THERE!
REALLY?
I WATCHED HIM TRY TO STEAL DURAN'S SOUL, BUT HE COULDN'T. HE RAN AWAY. LIKE HE WAS AFRAID OF HIM.
WHAT DO YOU MEAN HE TRIED?
DURAN IS... UNUSUAL.
YOU ALWAYS WERE WISER THAN I, FATHER. ALWAYS ONE MOVE AHEAD OF THE DEVIL.
I MIGHT HAVE DONE BETTER LAST NIGHT TO HAVE HAD YOU WITH ME.
THAT RING OF BURNING CROSSES BEFORE THE CELL...
...ONCE INSIDE THEM...
...THE DEMON CAN'T PASS OUT.

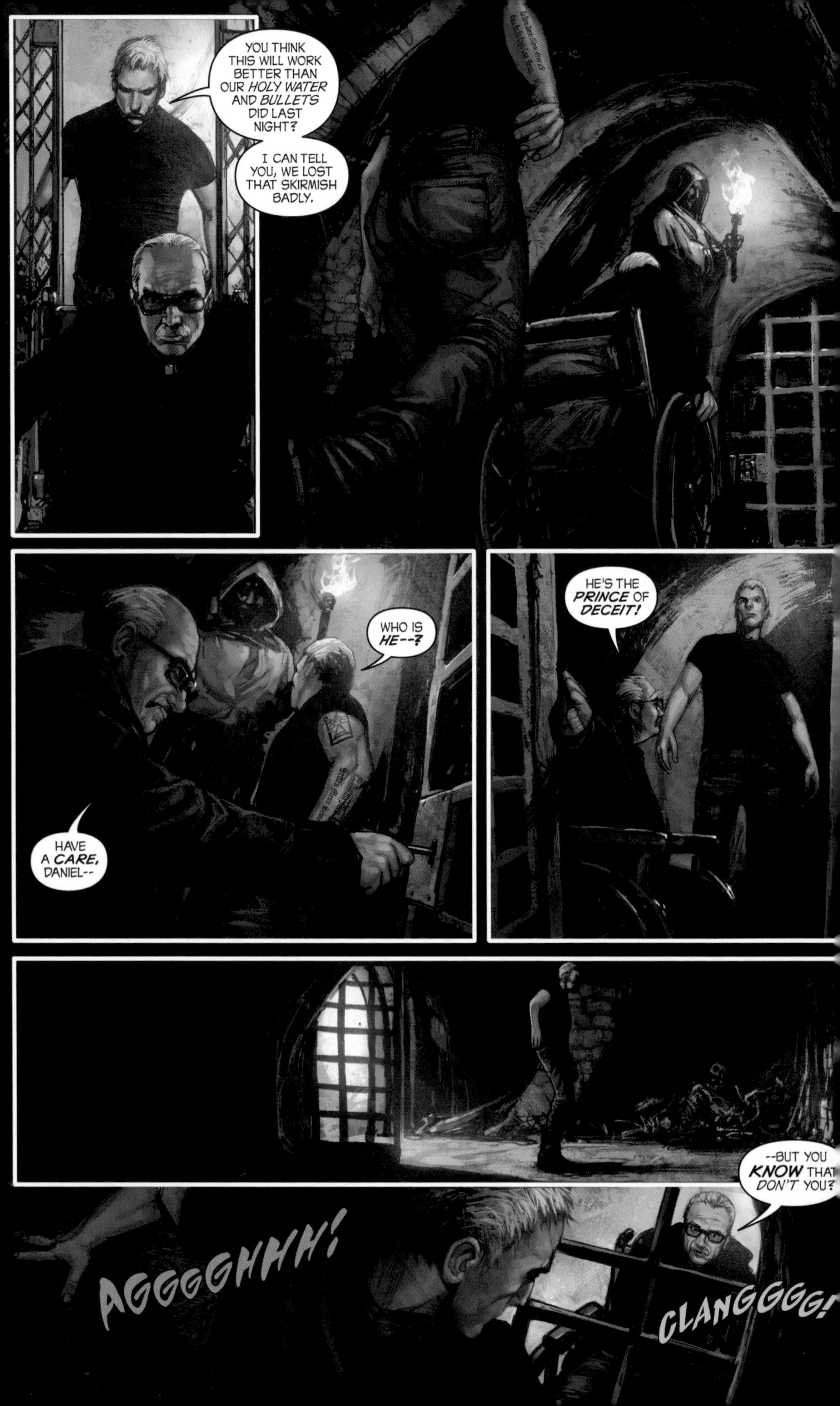

YOU THINK THIS WILL WORK BETTER THAN OUR HOLY WATER AND BULLETS DID LAST NIGHT?
I CAN TELL YOU, WE LOST THAT SKIRMISH BADLY.
WHO IS HE--?
HAVE A CARE, DANIEL--
HE'S THE PRINCE OF DECEIT!
--BUT YOU KNOW THAT DON'T YOU?
AGGGGHHH!
CLANGGGG!

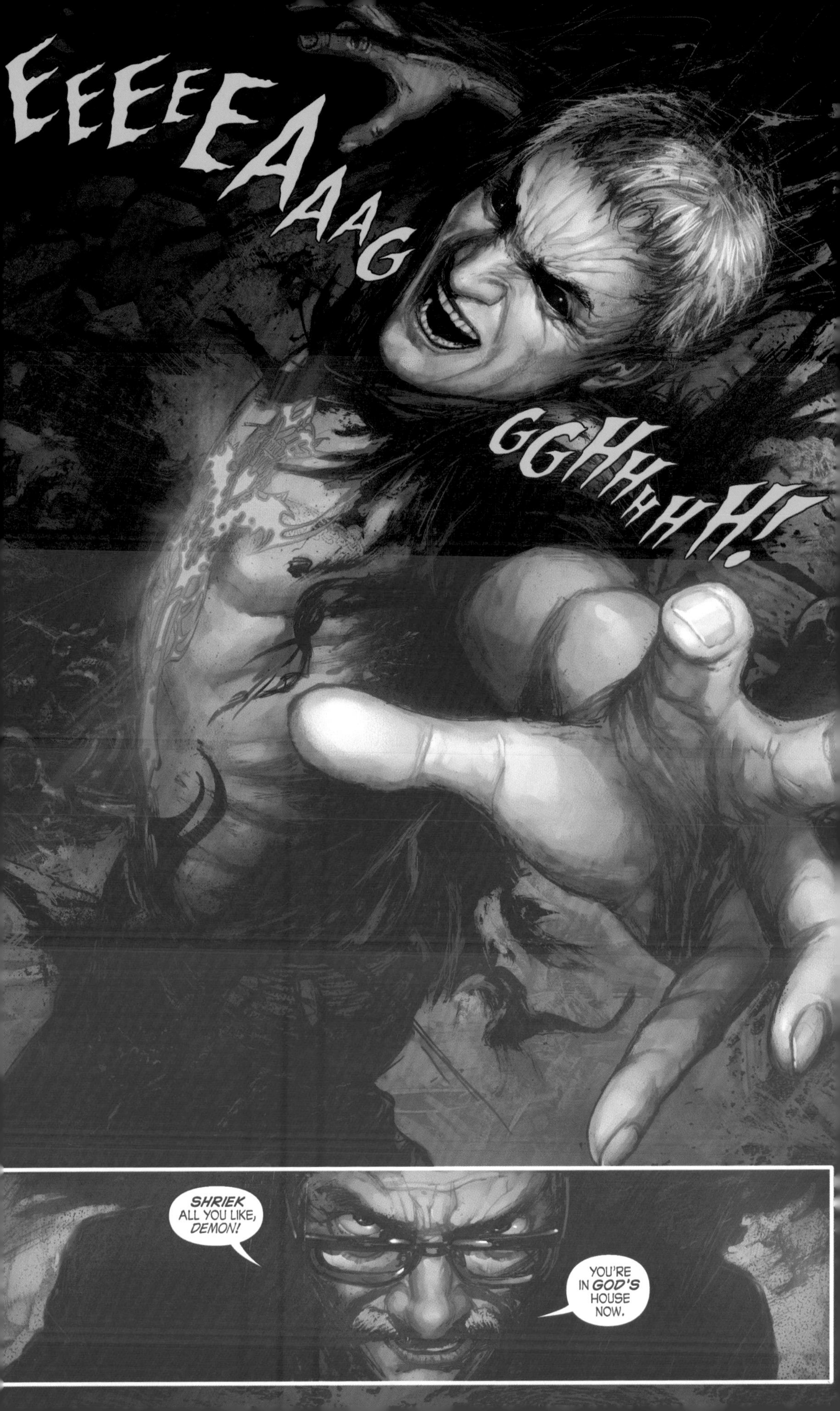
EEEEEAAAG
GGHHHHH!
SHRIEK ALL YOU LIKE, DEMON!
YOU'RE IN GOD'S HOUSE NOW.

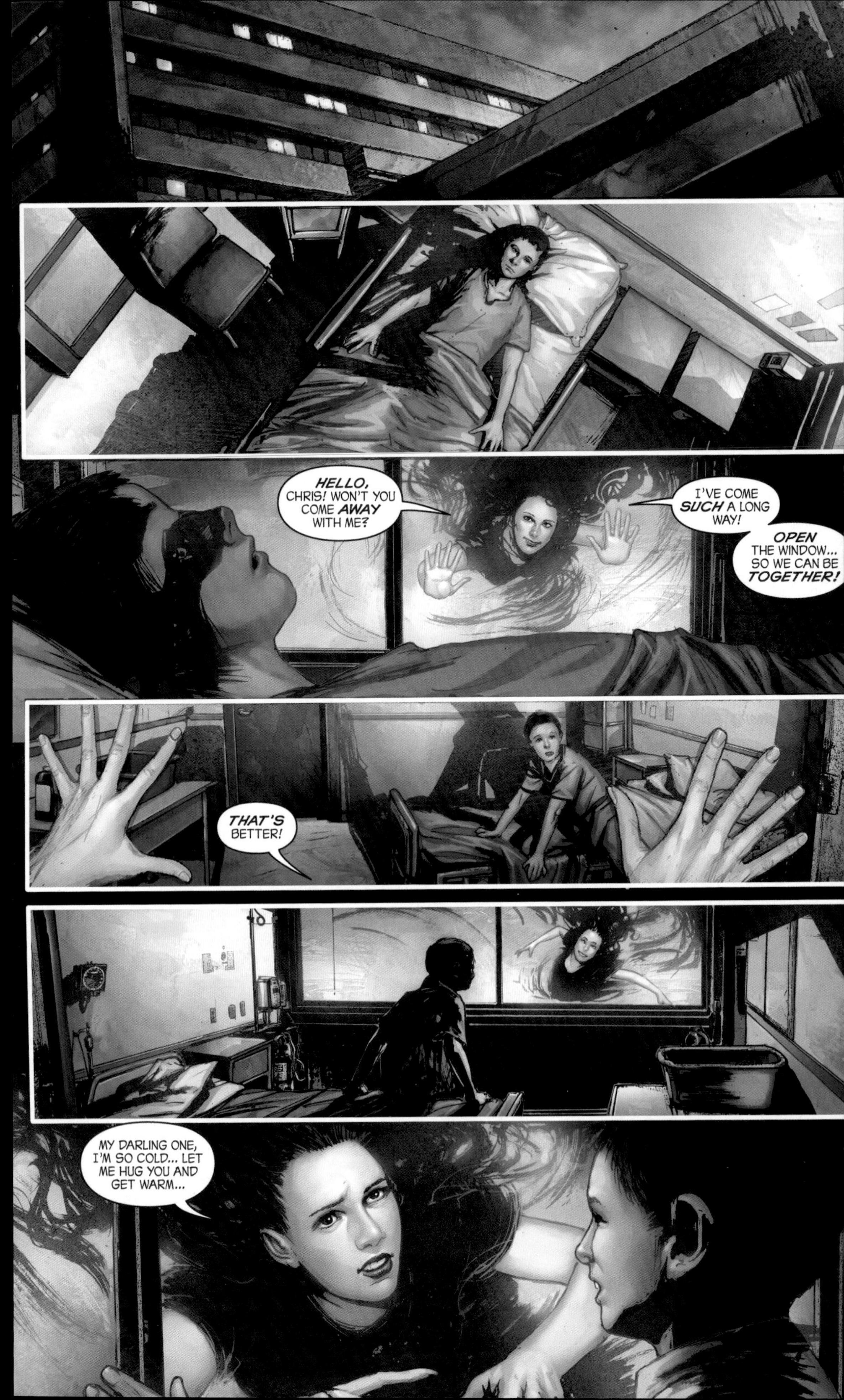
HELLO, CHRIS! WON'T YOU COME AWAY WITH ME?
I'VE COME SUCH A LONG WAY!
OPEN THE WINDOW... SO WE CAN BE TOGETHER!
THAT'S BETTER!
MY DARLING ONE, I'M SO COLD... LET ME HUG YOU AND GET WARM...

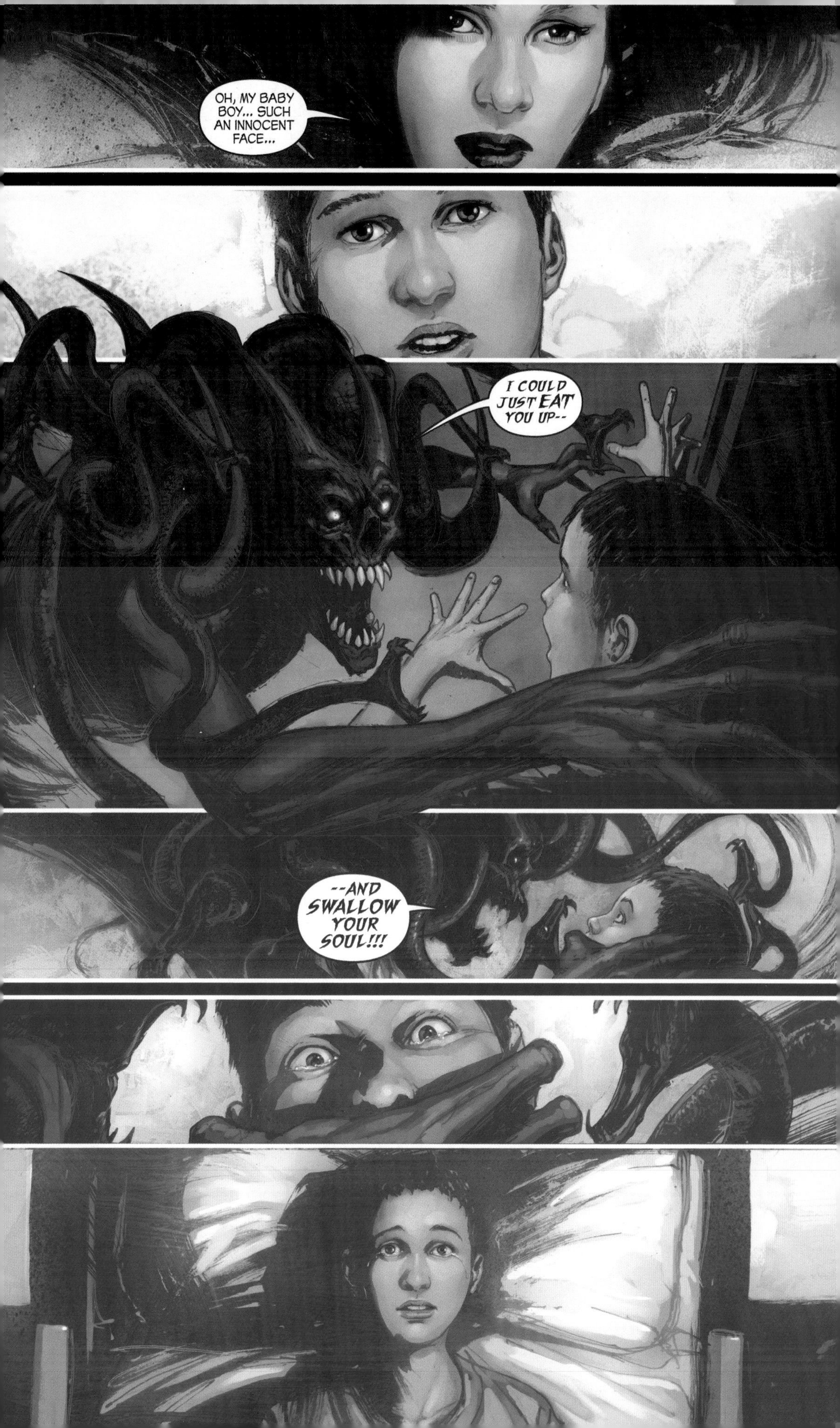
OH, MY BABY BOY... SUCH AN INNOCENT FACE...
I COULD JUST EAT YOU UP--
--AND SWALLOW YOUR SOUL!!!

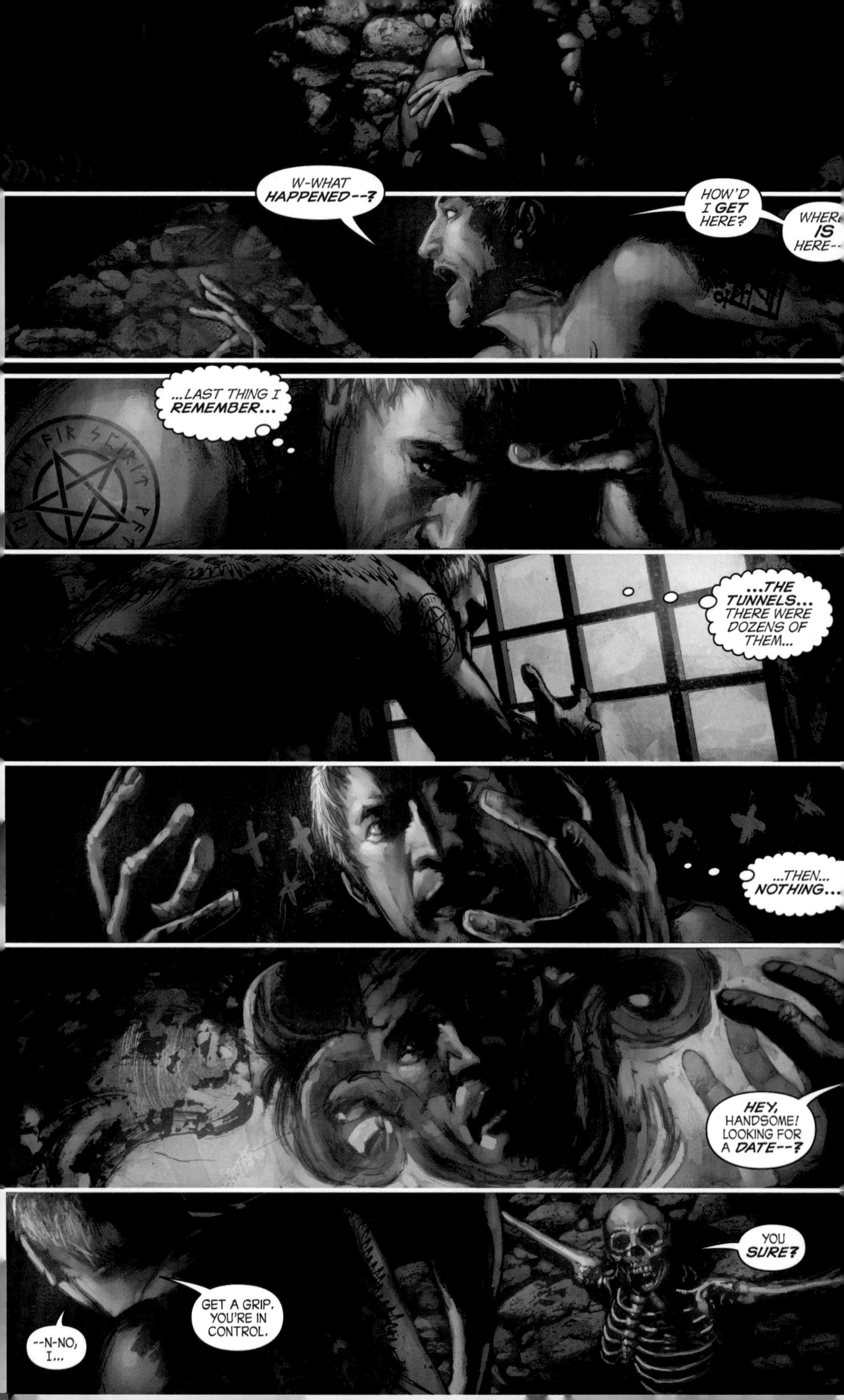
W-WHAT HAPPENED--?
HOW'D I GET HERE?
WHERE IS HERE--
...LAST THING I REMEMBER...
...THE TUNNELS... THERE WERE DOZENS OF THEM...
...THEN... NOTHING...
HEY, HANDSOME! LOOKING FOR A DATE--?
--N-NO, I...
GET A GRIP. YOU'RE IN CONTROL.
YOU SURE?

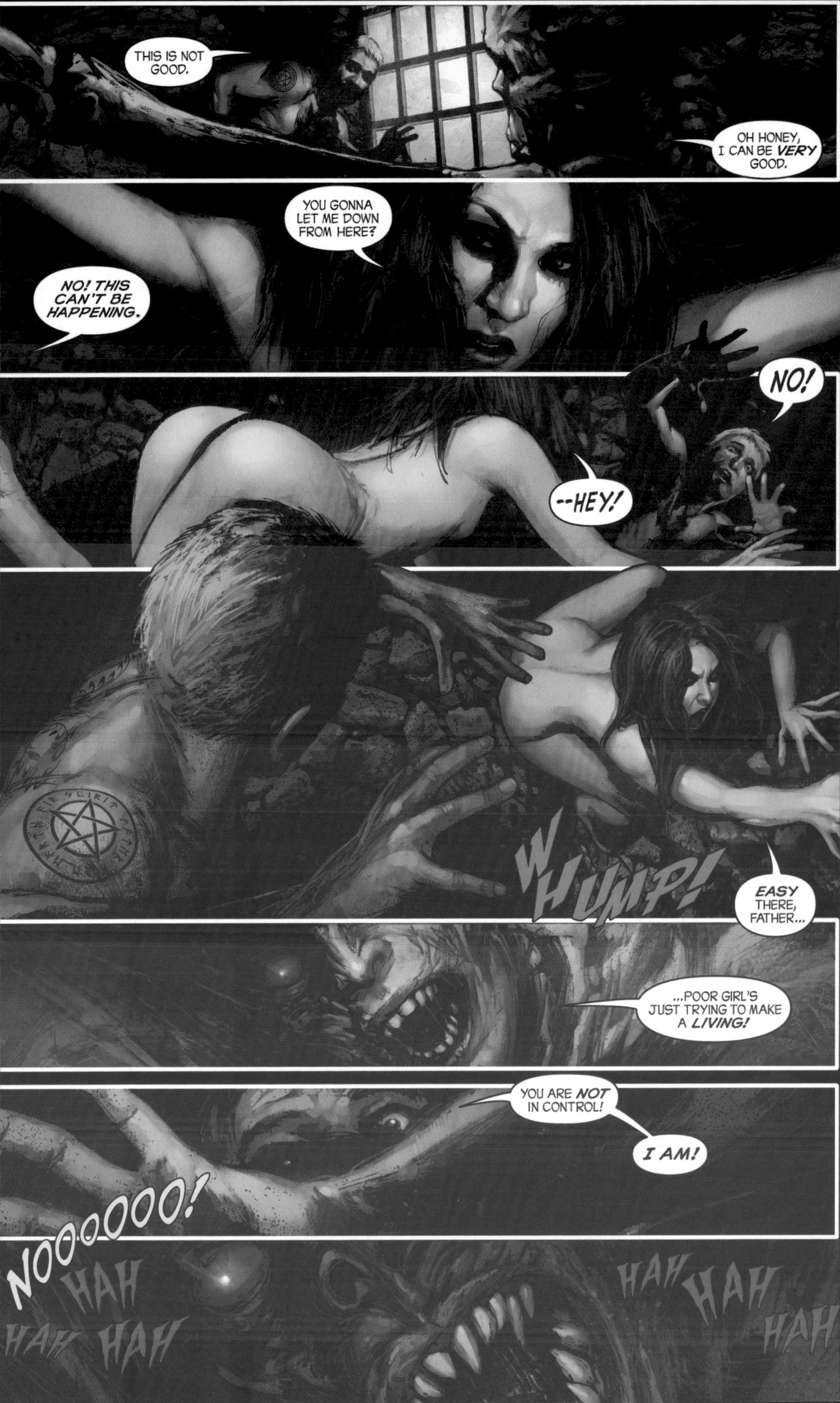
THIS IS NOT GOOD.
OH HONEY, I CAN BE VERY GOOD.
YOU GONNA LET ME DOWN FROM HERE?
NO! THIS CAN'T BE HAPPENING.
NO!
--HEY!
WHUMP!
EASY THERE, FATHER...
...POOR GIRL'S JUST TRYING TO MAKE A LIVING!
YOU ARE NOT IN CONTROL!
I AM!
NOOOOOO!
HAH HAH HAH HAH
HAH HAH HAH HAH

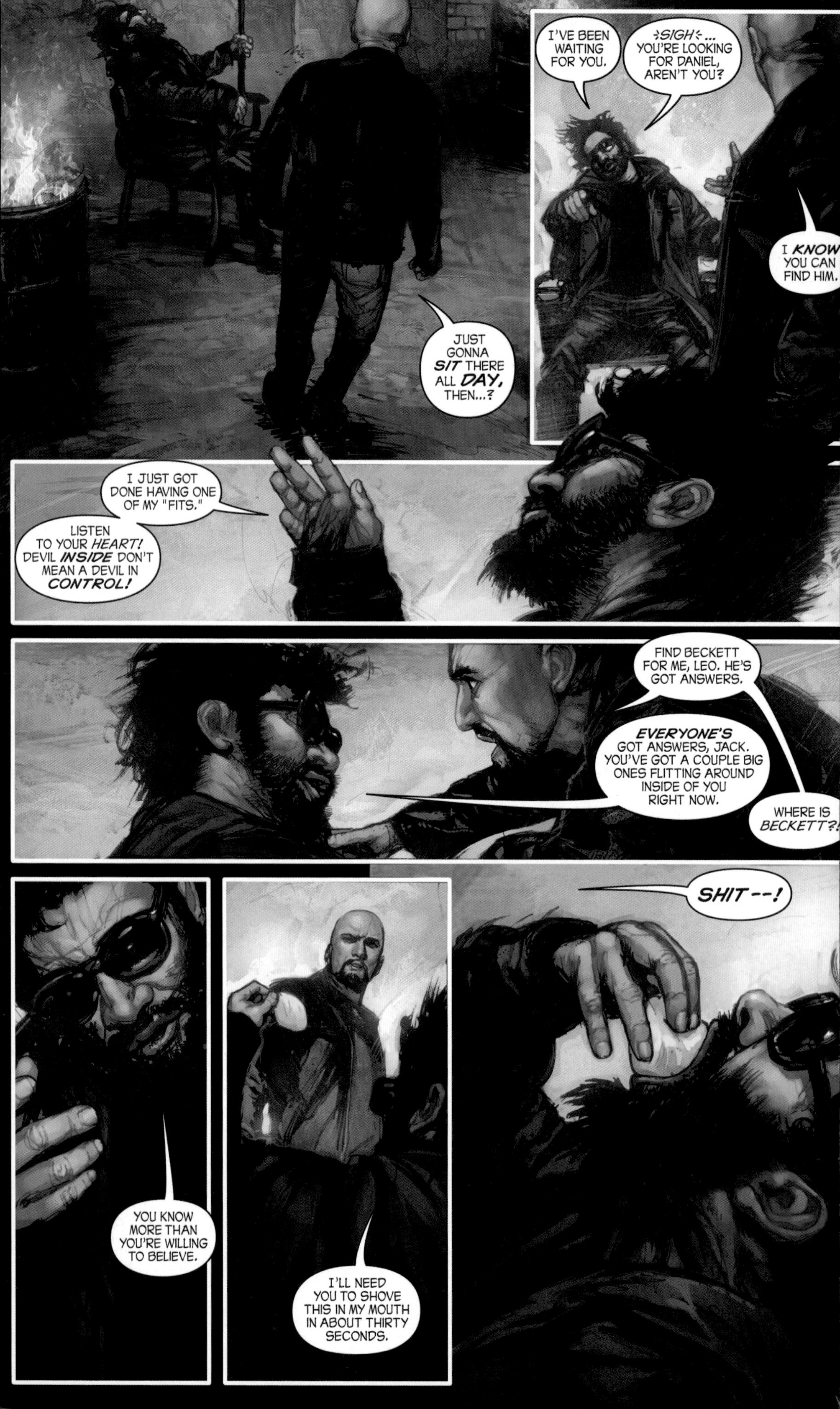
JUST GONNA SIT THERE ALL DAY, THEN...?
I'VE BEEN WAITING FOR YOU.
-SIGH-... YOU'RE LOOKING FOR DANIEL, AREN'T YOU?
I KNOW YOU CAN FIND HIM.
I JUST GOT DONE HAVING ONE OF MY "FITS."
LISTEN TO YOUR HEART! DEVIL INSIDE DON'T MEAN A DEVIL IN CONTROL!
FIND BECKETT FOR ME, LEO. HE'S GOT ANSWERS.
EVERYONE'S GOT ANSWERS, JACK. YOU'VE GOT A COUPLE BIG ONES FLITTING AROUND INSIDE OF YOU RIGHT NOW.
WHERE IS BECKETT?!
YOU KNOW MORE THAN YOU'RE WILLING TO BELIEVE.
I'LL NEED YOU TO SHOVE THIS IN MY MOUTH IN ABOUT THIRTY SECONDS.
SHIT--!

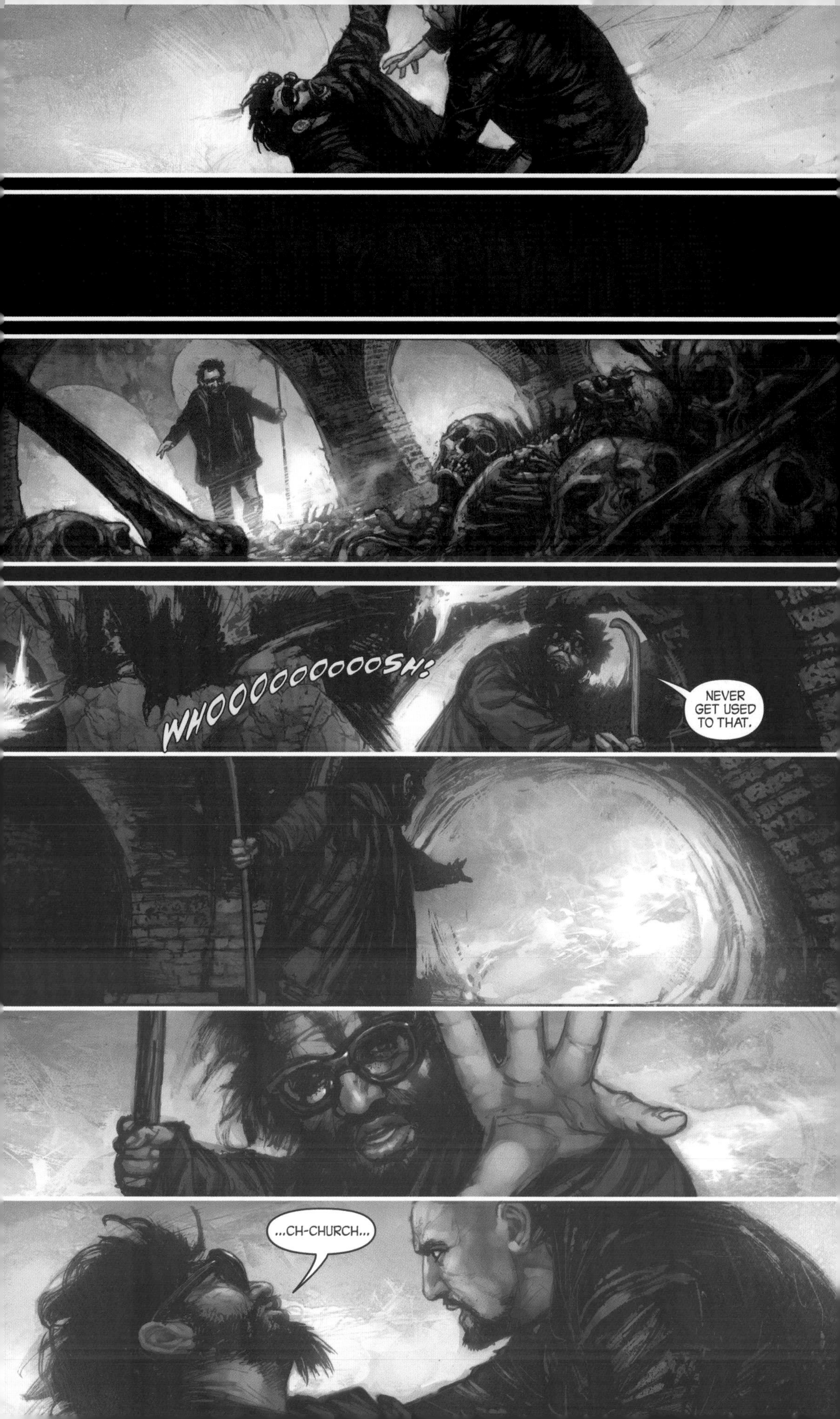
WHOOOOOOOOOOSH!
NEVER GET USED TO THAT.
...CH-CHURCH...

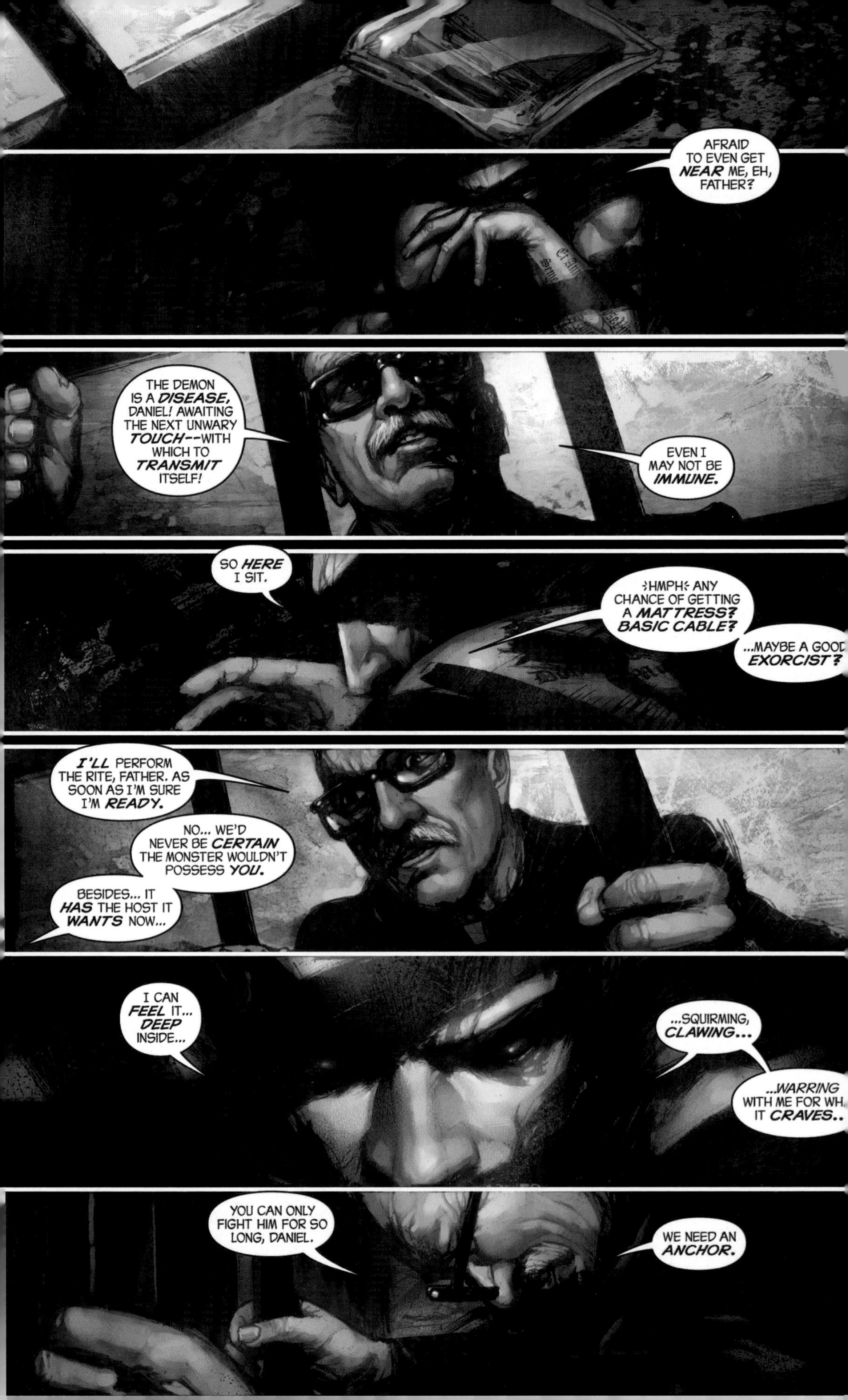
AFRAID TO EVEN GET NEAR ME, EH, FATHER?
THE DEMON IS A DISEASE, DANIEL! AWAITING THE NEXT UNWARY TOUCH--WITH WHICH TO TRANSMIT ITSELF!
EVEN I MAY NOT BE IMMUNE.
SO HERE I SIT.
HMPH ANY CHANCE OF GETTING A MATTRESS? BASIC CABLE?
...MAYBE A GOOD EXORCIST?
I'LL PERFORM THE RITE, FATHER. AS SOON AS I'M SURE I'M READY.
NO... WE'D NEVER BE CERTAIN THE MONSTER WOULDN'T POSSESS YOU.
BESIDES... IT HAS THE HOST IT WANTS NOW...
I CAN FEEL IT... DEEP INSIDE...
...SQUIRMING, CLAWING...
...WARRING WITH ME FOR WH IT CRAVES..
YOU CAN ONLY FIGHT HIM FOR SO LONG, DANIEL.
WE NEED AN ANCHOR.

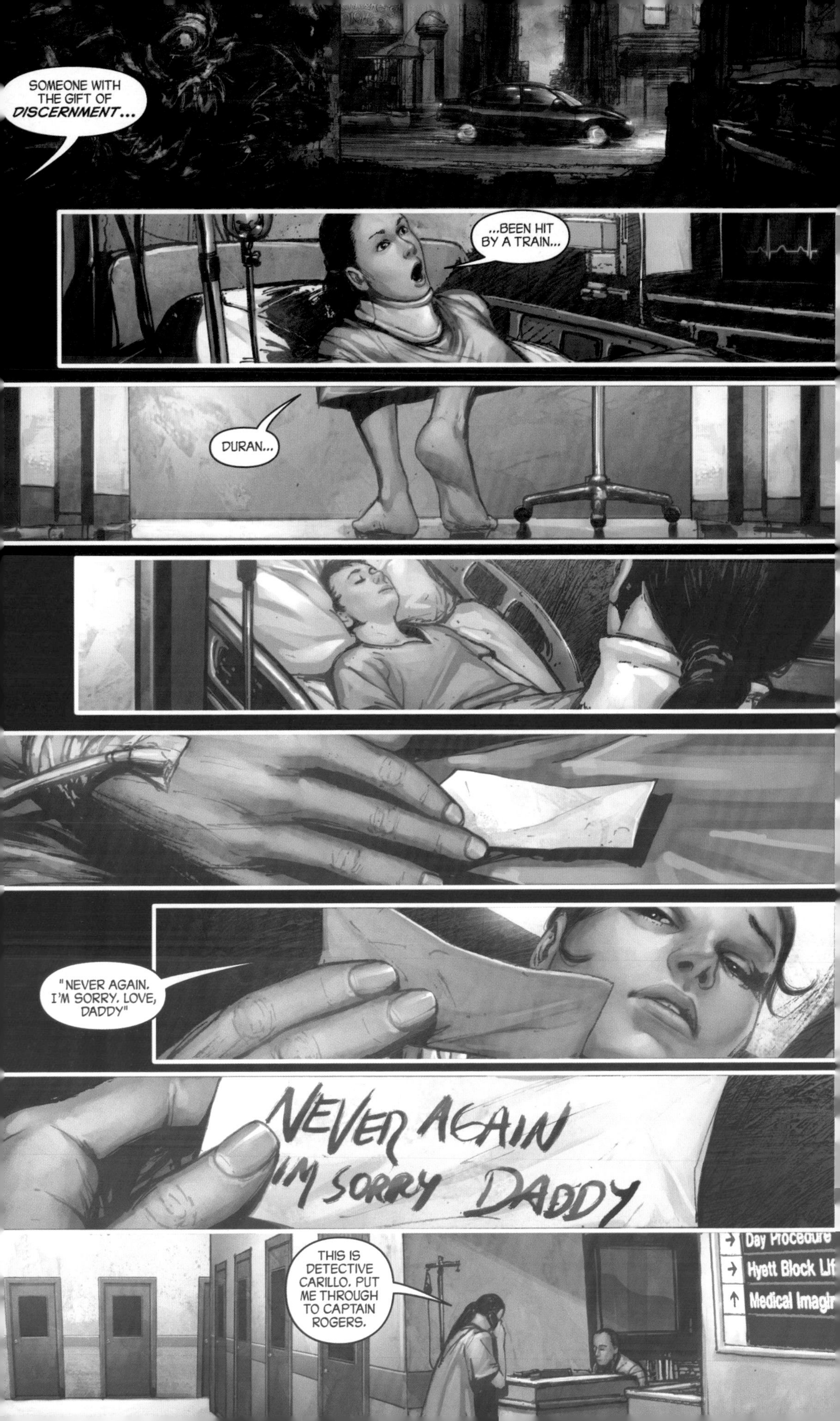
SOMEONE WITH THE GIFT OF *DISCERNMENT...*
...BEEN HIT BY A TRAIN...
DURAN...
"NEVER AGAIN. I'M SORRY. LOVE, DADDY"
NEVER AGAIN
I'M SORRY DADDY
THIS IS DETECTIVE CARILLO. PUT ME THROUGH TO CAPTAIN ROGERS.
Day Procedure
Hyett Block Lif
Medical Imagir

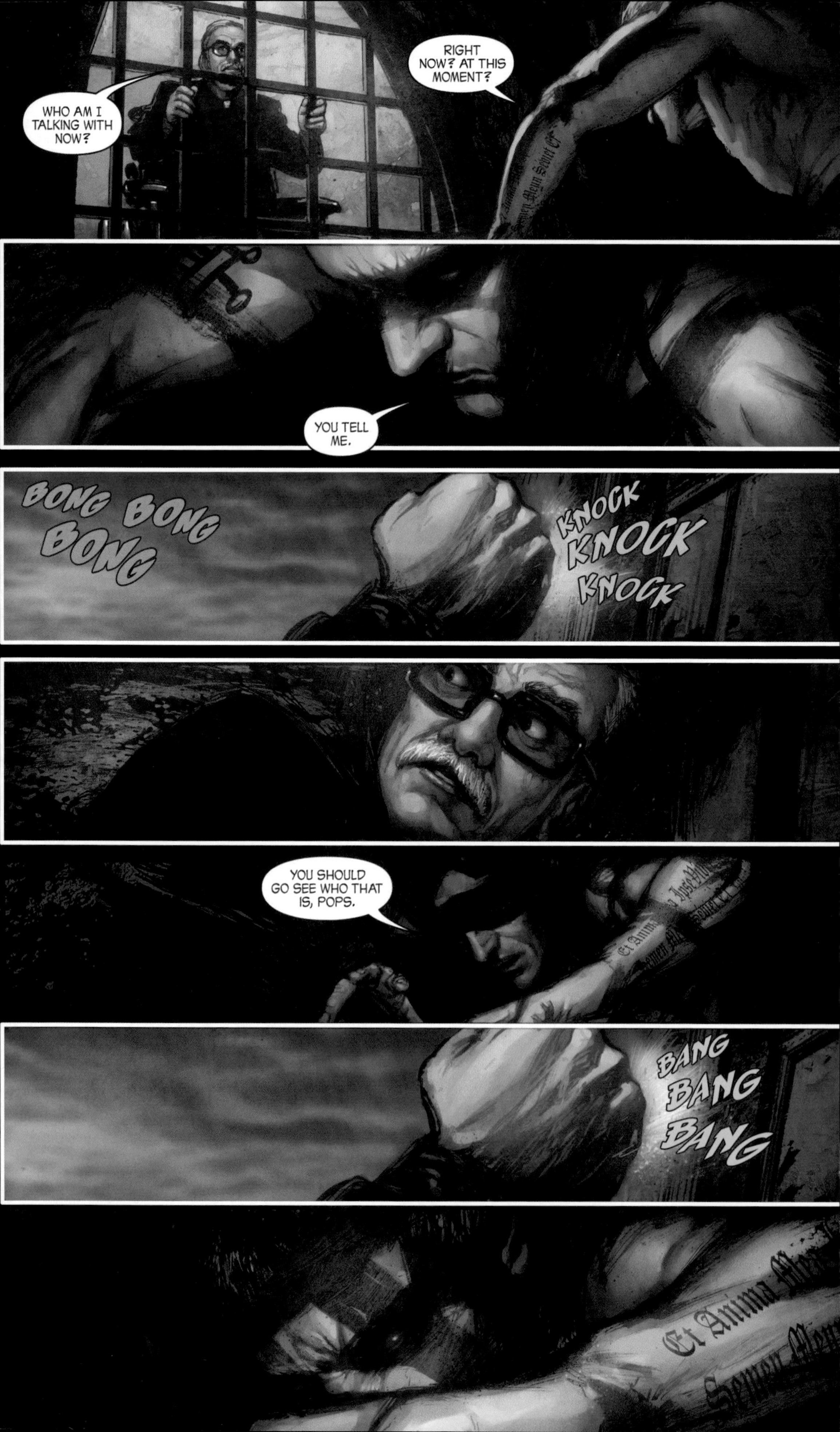
WHO AM I TALKING WITH NOW?
RIGHT NOW? AT THIS MOMENT?
YOU TELL ME.
BONG BONG BONG
KNOCK KNOCK KNOCK
YOU SHOULD GO SEE WHO THAT IS, POPS.
BANG BANG BANG

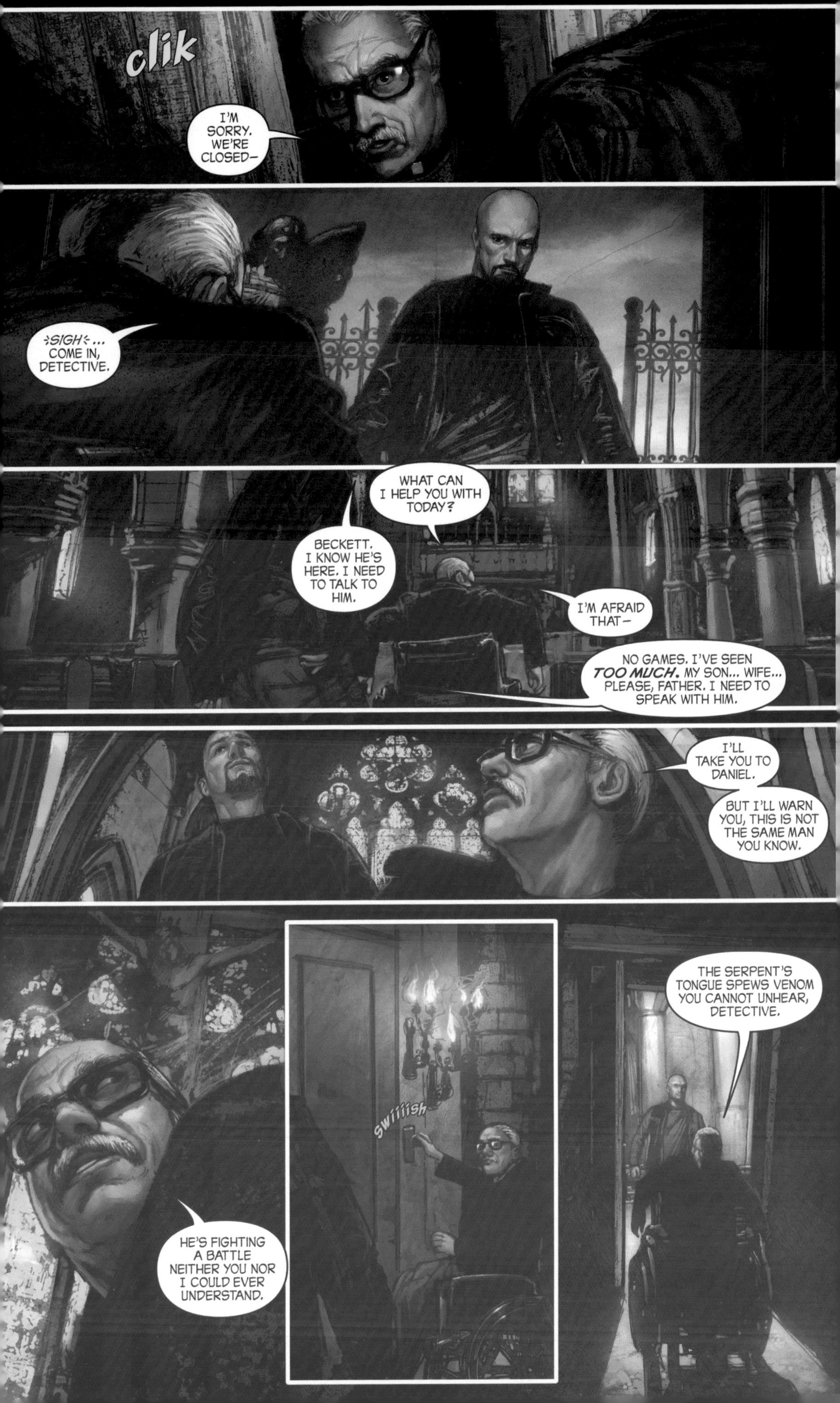
clik
I'M SORRY. WE'RE CLOSED—
⊰SIGH⊱... COME IN, DETECTIVE.
WHAT CAN I HELP YOU WITH TODAY?
BECKETT. I KNOW HE'S HERE. I NEED TO TALK TO HIM.
I'M AFRAID THAT—
NO GAMES. I'VE SEEN TOO MUCH. MY SON... WIFE... PLEASE, FATHER. I NEED TO SPEAK WITH HIM.
I'LL TAKE YOU TO DANIEL.
BUT I'LL WARN YOU, THIS IS NOT THE SAME MAN YOU KNOW.
HE'S FIGHTING A BATTLE NEITHER YOU NOR I COULD EVER UNDERSTAND.
SWIIIISH
THE SERPENT'S TONGUE SPEWS VENOM YOU CANNOT UNHEAR, DETECTIVE.

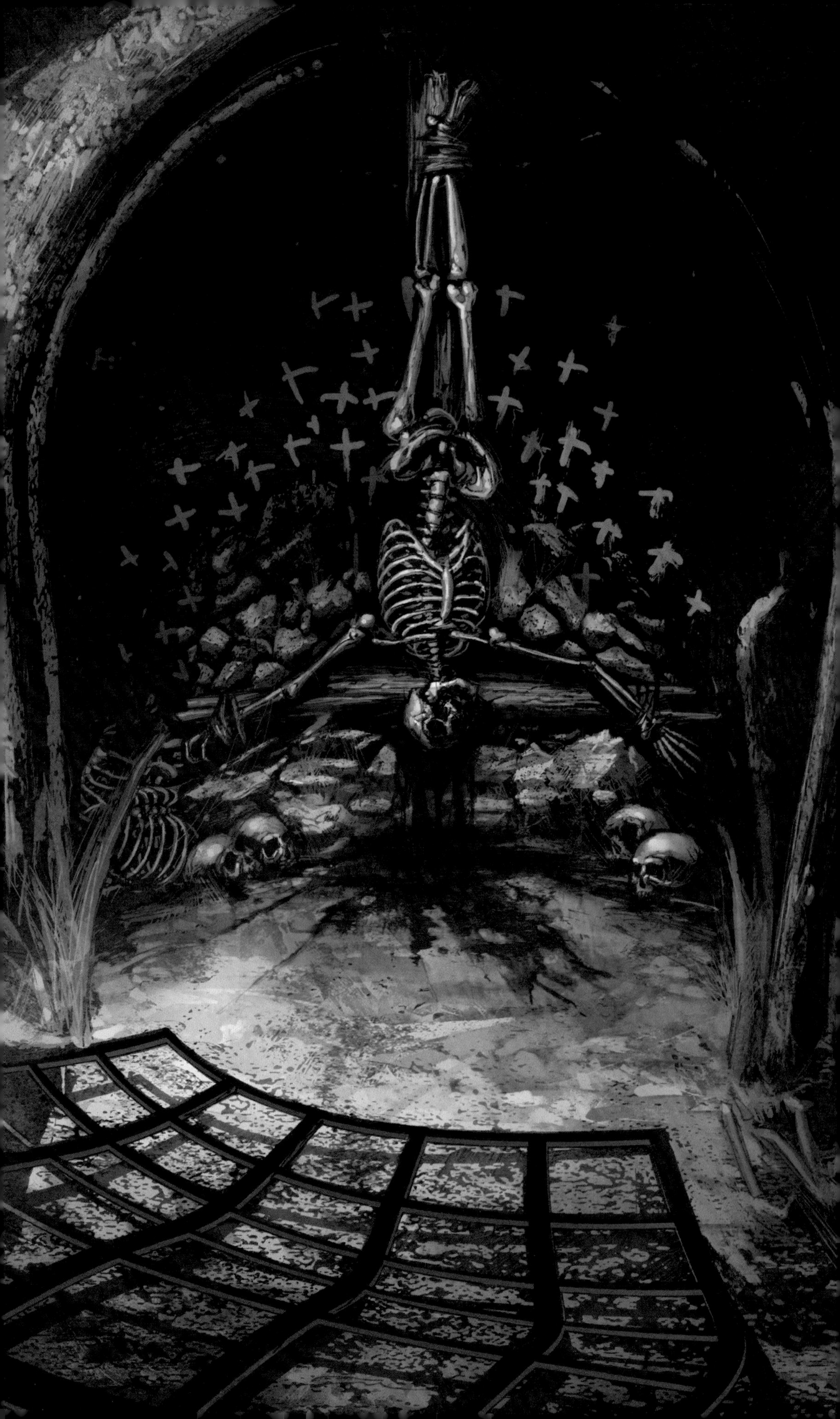

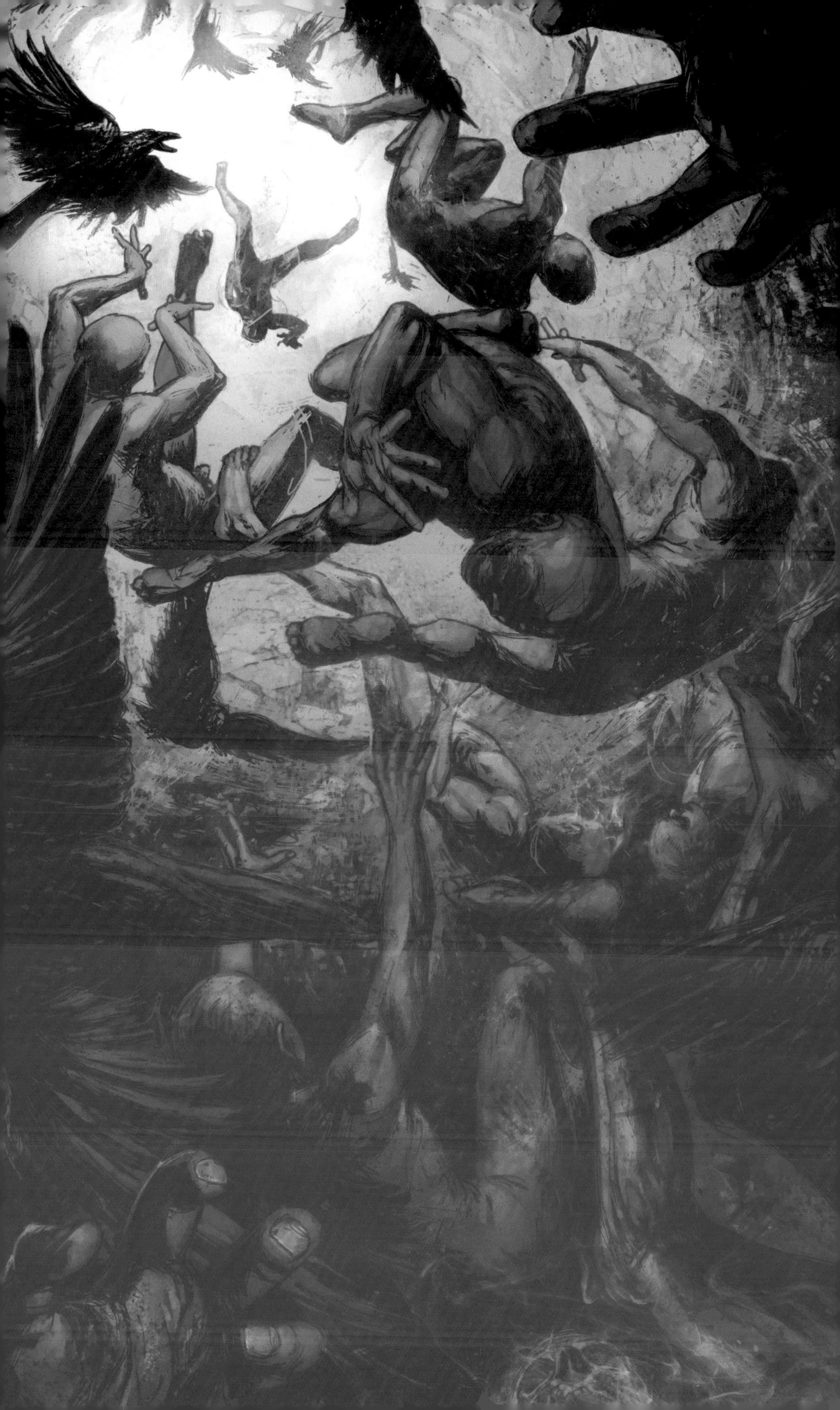

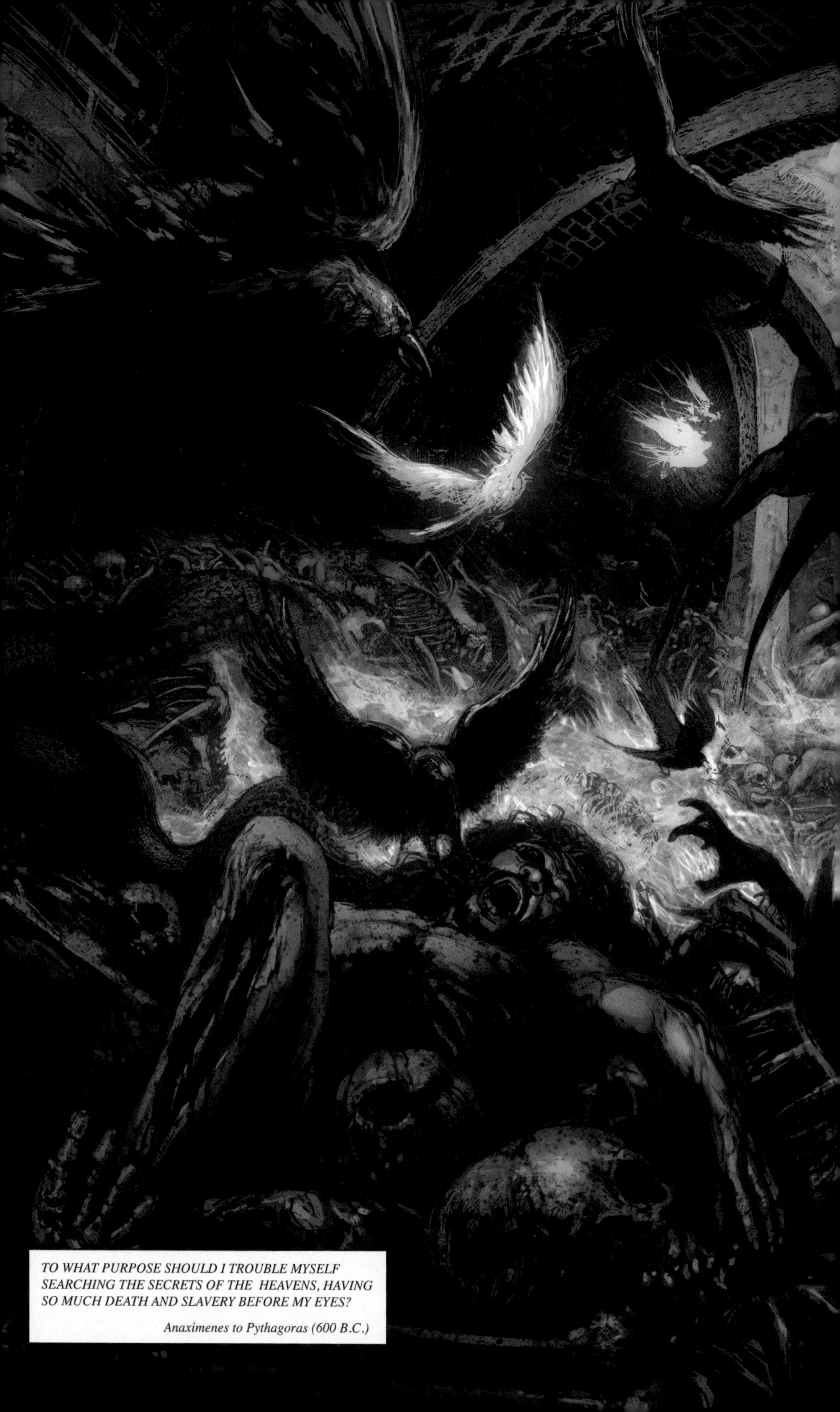

TO WHAT PURPOSE SHOULD I TROUBLE MYSELF SEARCHING THE SECRETS OF THE HEAVENS, HAVING SO MUCH DEATH AND SLAVERY BEFORE MY EYES?

Anaximenes to Pythagoras (600 B.C.)

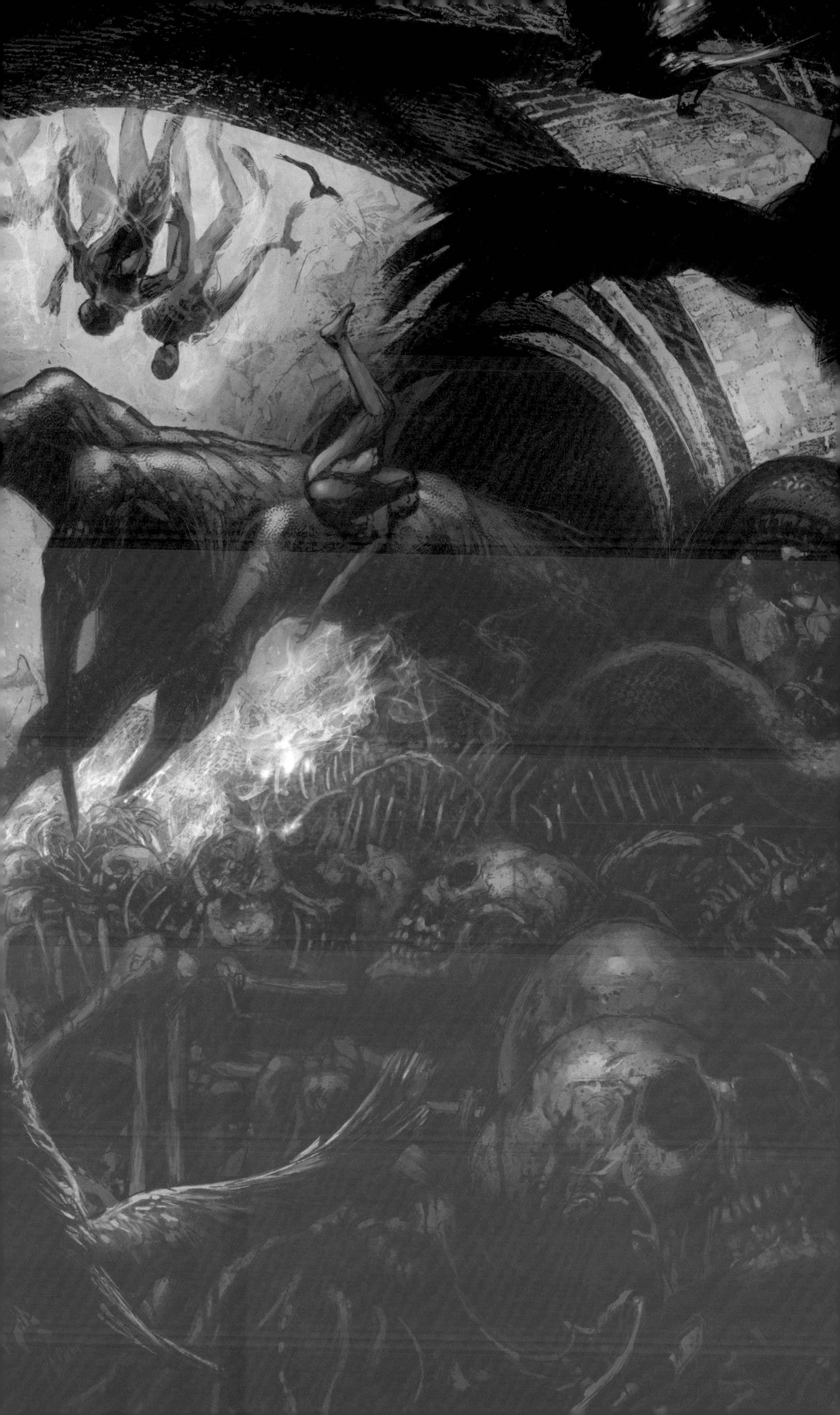

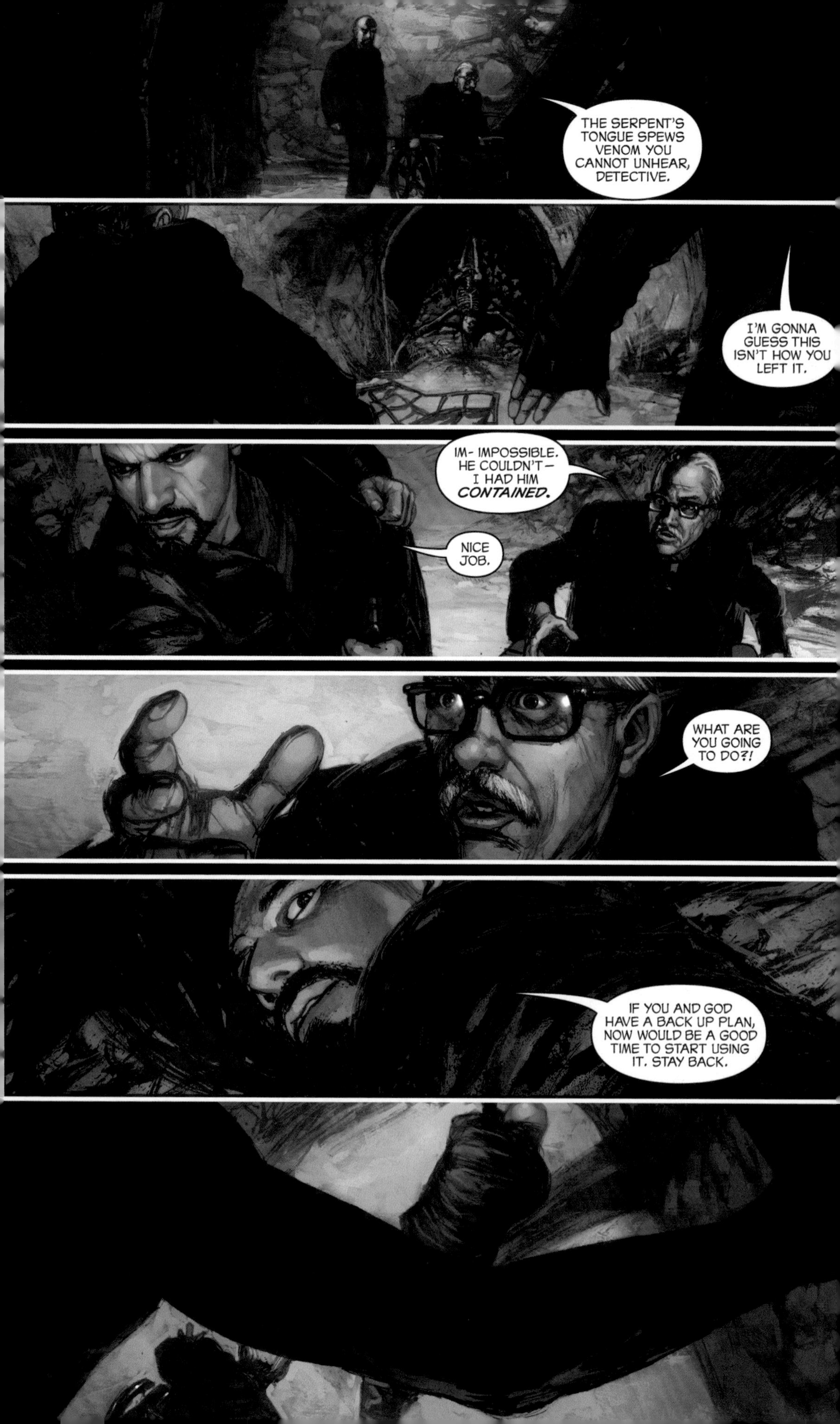
THE SERPENT'S TONGUE SPEWS VENOM YOU CANNOT UNHEAR, DETECTIVE.
I'M GONNA GUESS THIS ISN'T HOW YOU LEFT IT.
IM- IMPOSSIBLE. HE COULDN'T— I HAD HIM CONTAINED.
NICE JOB.
WHAT ARE YOU GOING TO DO?!
IF YOU AND GOD HAVE A BACK UP PLAN, NOW WOULD BE A GOOD TIME TO START USING IT. STAY BACK.

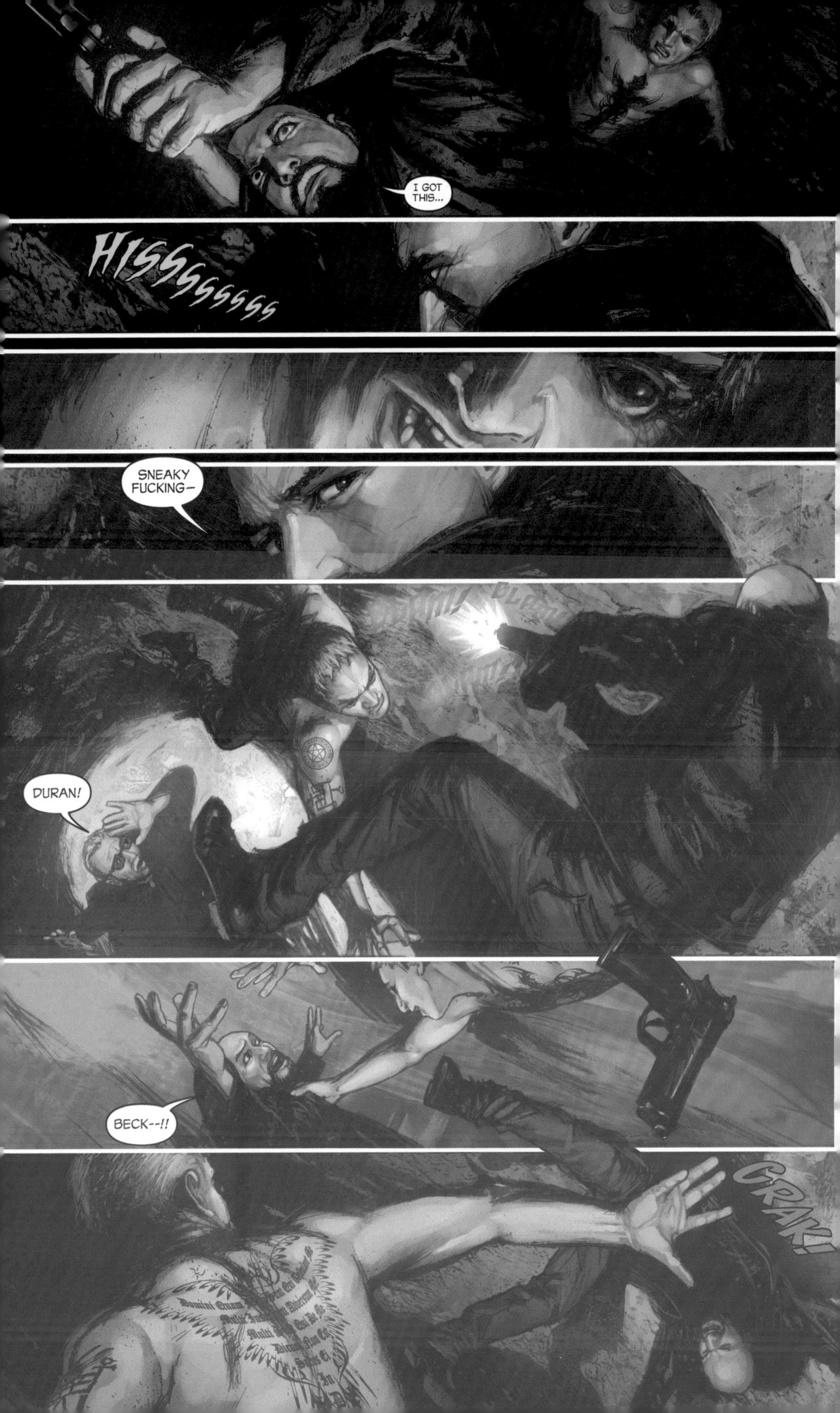
I GOT THIS...
HISSssssss
SNEAKY FUCKING—
DURAN!
BECK--!!
CRAK!!

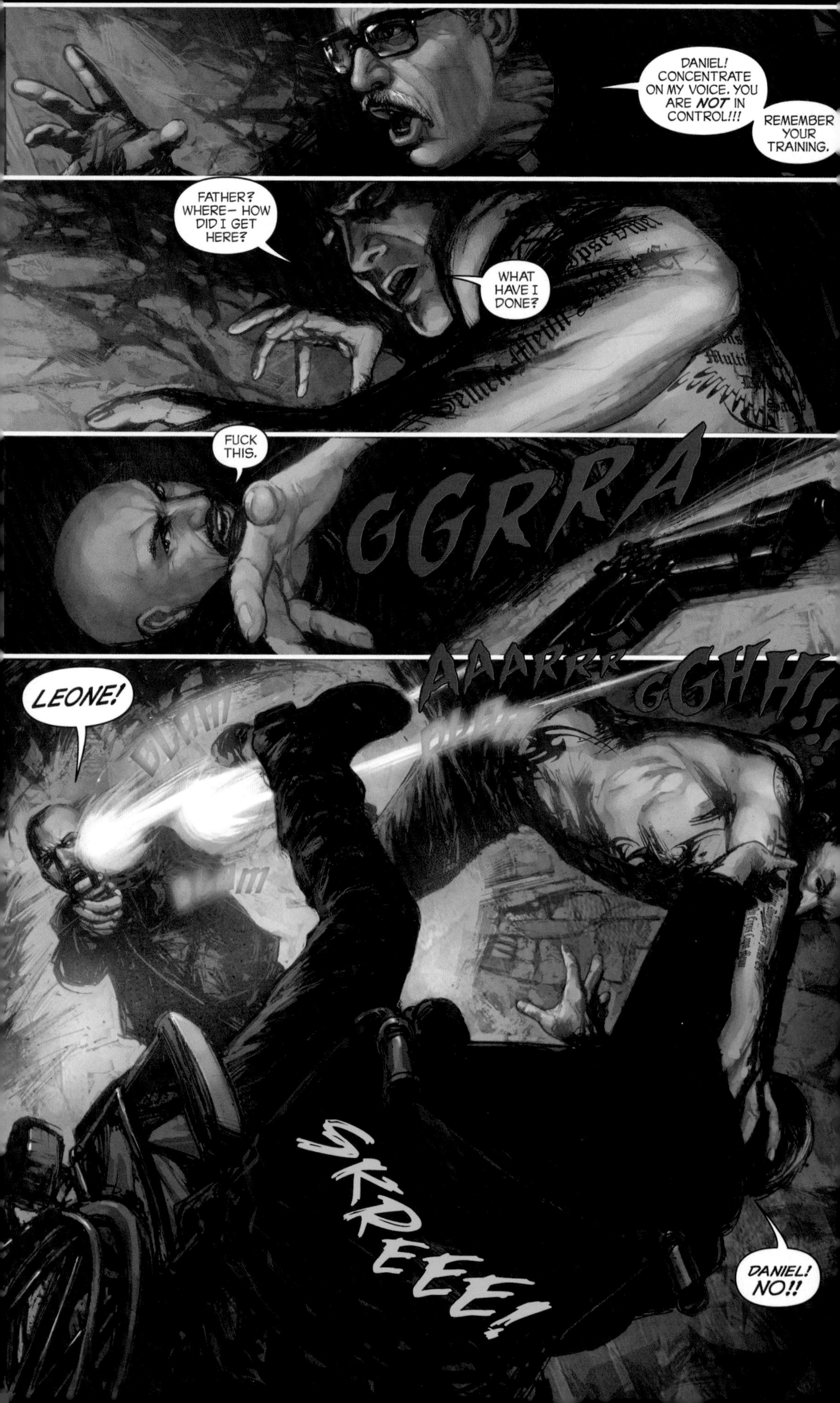
DANIEL! CONCENTRATE ON MY VOICE. YOU ARE *NOT* IN CONTROL!!!
REMEMBER YOUR TRAINING.
FATHER? WHERE— HOW DID I GET HERE?
WHAT HAVE I DONE?
FUCK THIS.
GGRRA
LEONE!
AAARRRGGHH!!!
SKREEE!
DANIEL! NO!!

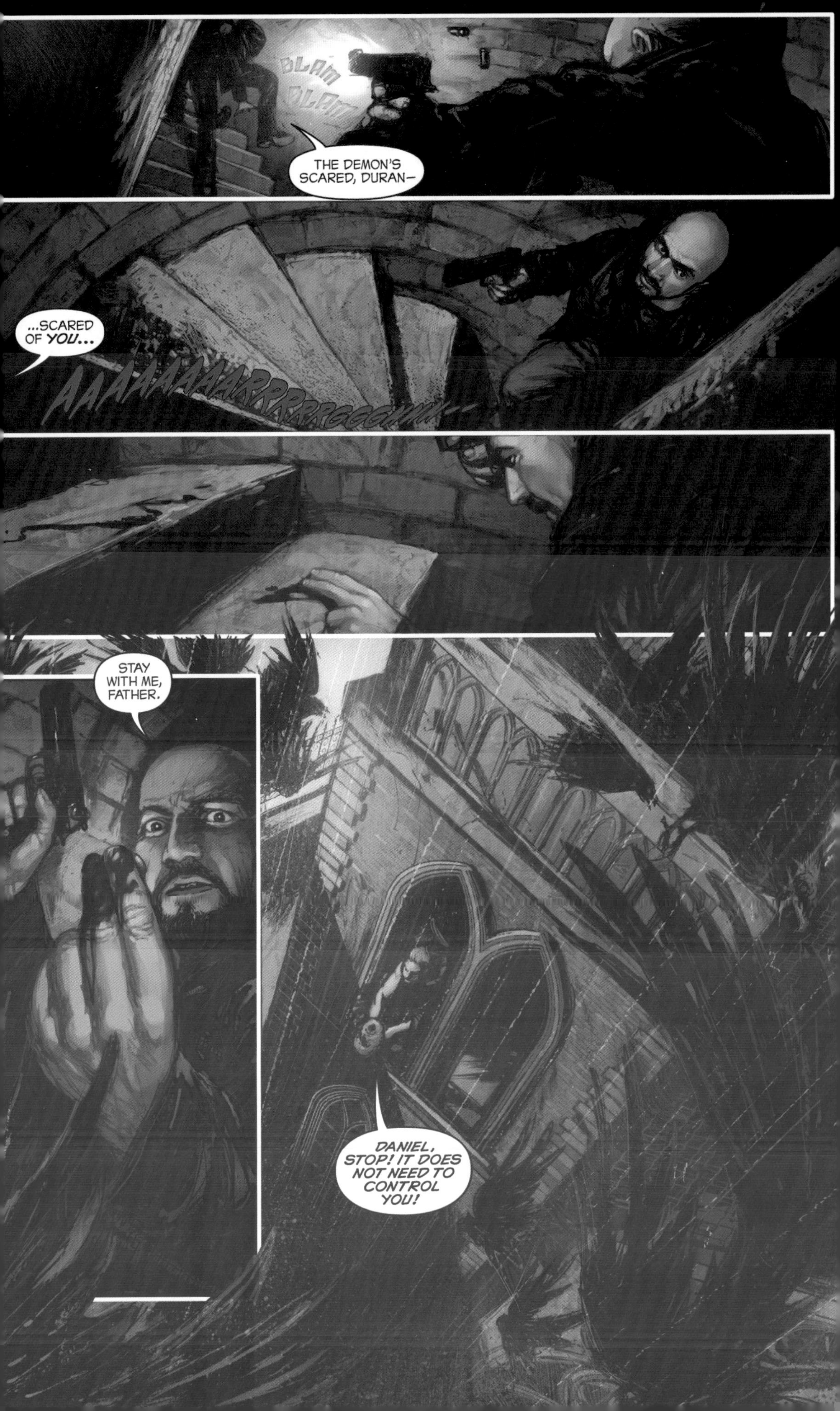
BLAM
BLAM
THE DEMON'S SCARED, DURAN—
...SCARED OF *YOU*...
AAAAAAAAARRRRRRGGGGHHH—
STAY WITH ME, FATHER.
DANIEL, STOP! IT DOES NOT NEED TO CONTROL YOU!

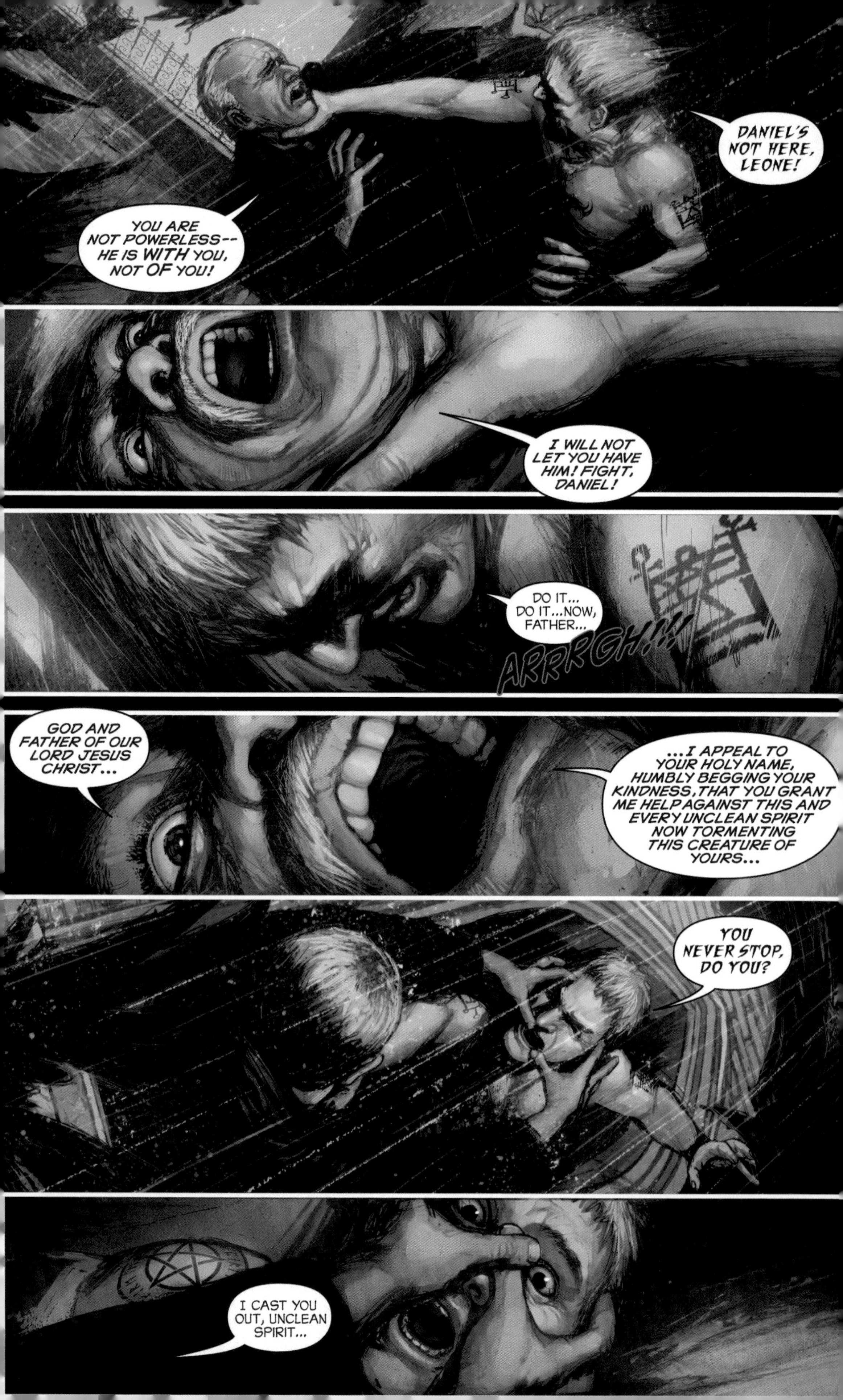
DANIEL'S NOT HERE, LEONE!
YOU ARE NOT POWERLESS-- HE IS WITH YOU, NOT OF YOU!
I WILL NOT LET YOU HAVE HIM! FIGHT, DANIEL!
DO IT... DO IT...NOW, FATHER...
ARRRGH!!!
GOD AND FATHER OF OUR LORD JESUS CHRIST...
...I APPEAL TO YOUR HOLY NAME, HUMBLY BEGGING YOUR KINDNESS, THAT YOU GRANT ME HELP AGAINST THIS AND EVERY UNCLEAN SPIRIT NOW TORMENTING THIS CREATURE OF YOURS...
YOU NEVER STOP, DO YOU?
I CAST YOU OUT, UNCLEAN SPIRIT...

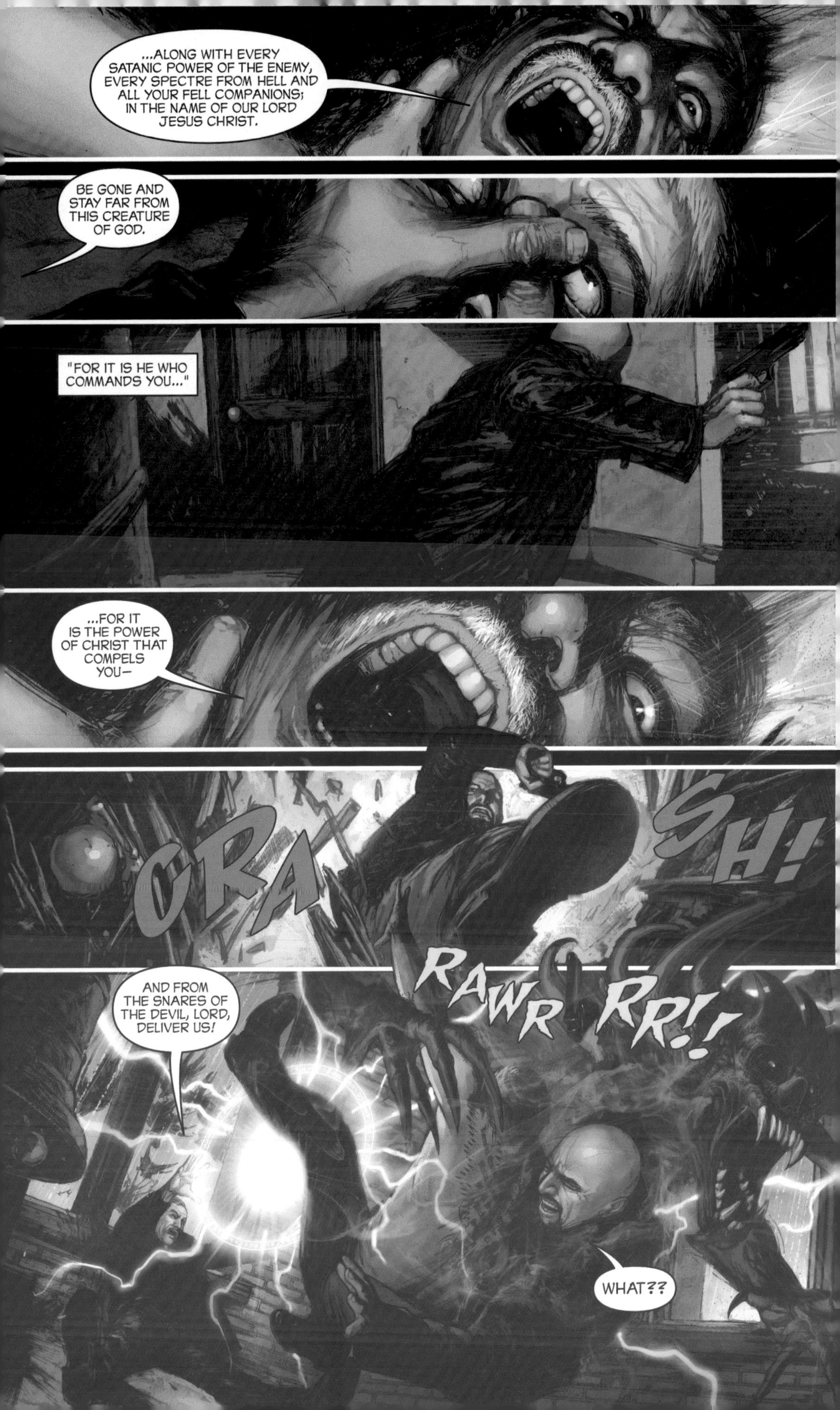
...ALONG WITH EVERY SATANIC POWER OF THE ENEMY, EVERY SPECTRE FROM HELL AND ALL YOUR FELL COMPANIONS; IN THE NAME OF OUR LORD JESUS CHRIST.
BE GONE AND STAY FAR FROM THIS CREATURE OF GOD.
"FOR IT IS HE WHO COMMANDS YOU..."
...FOR IT IS THE POWER OF CHRIST THAT COMPELS YOU—
CRASH!
RAWRRR!!
AND FROM THE SNARES OF THE DEVIL, LORD, DELIVER US!
WHAT??

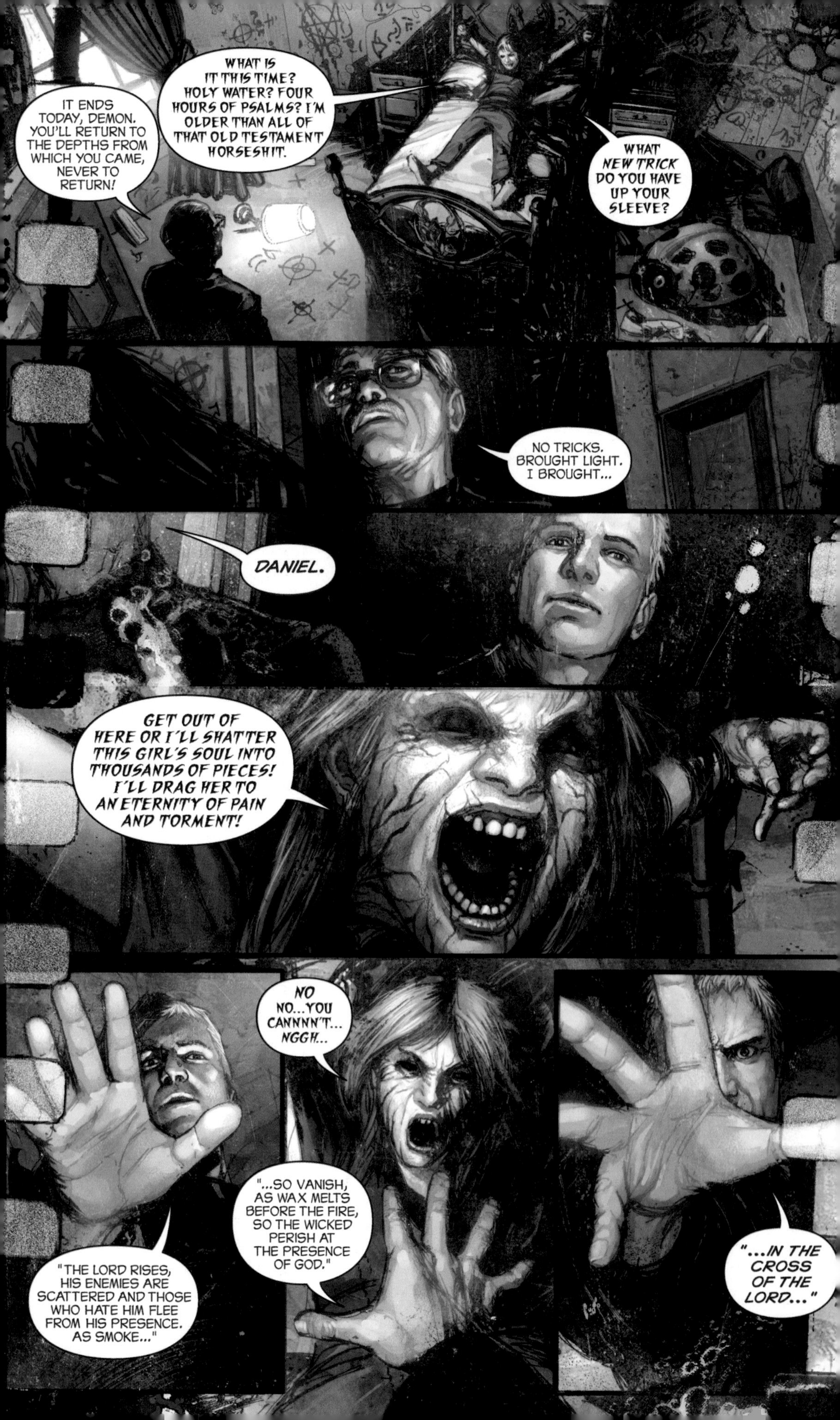
IT ENDS TODAY, DEMON. YOU'LL RETURN TO THE DEPTHS FROM WHICH YOU CAME, NEVER TO RETURN!
WHAT IS IT THIS TIME? HOLY WATER? FOUR HOURS OF PSALMS? I'M OLDER THAN ALL OF THAT OLD TESTAMENT HORSESHIT.
WHAT NEW TRICK DO YOU HAVE UP YOUR SLEEVE?
NO TRICKS. BROUGHT LIGHT. I BROUGHT...
DANIEL.
GET OUT OF HERE OR I'LL SHATTER THIS GIRL'S SOUL INTO THOUSANDS OF PIECES! I'LL DRAG HER TO AN ETERNITY OF PAIN AND TORMENT!
"THE LORD RISES, HIS ENEMIES ARE SCATTERED AND THOSE WHO HATE HIM FLEE FROM HIS PRESENCE. AS SMOKE..."
NO NO...YOU CANNNN'T... NGGH...
"...SO VANISH, AS WAX MELTS BEFORE THE FIRE, SO THE WICKED PERISH AT THE PRESENCE OF GOD."
"...IN THE CROSS OF THE LORD..."

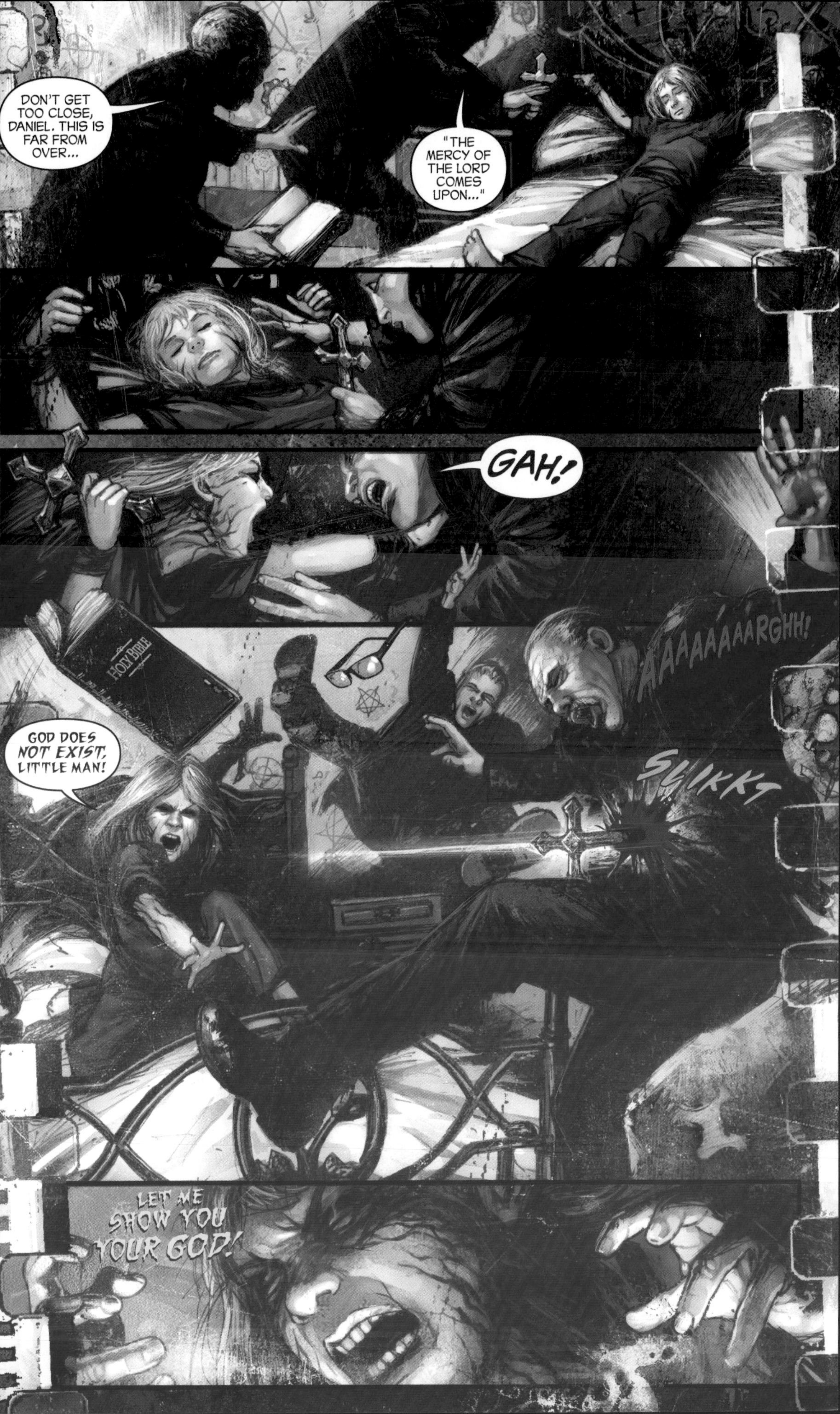
DON'T GET TOO CLOSE, DANIEL. THIS IS FAR FROM OVER...
"THE MERCY OF THE LORD COMES UPON..."
GAH!
HOLY BIBLE
AAAAAAAARGHH!
GOD DOES NOT EXIST, LITTLE MAN!
SLIKK!
LET ME SHOW YOU YOUR GOD!

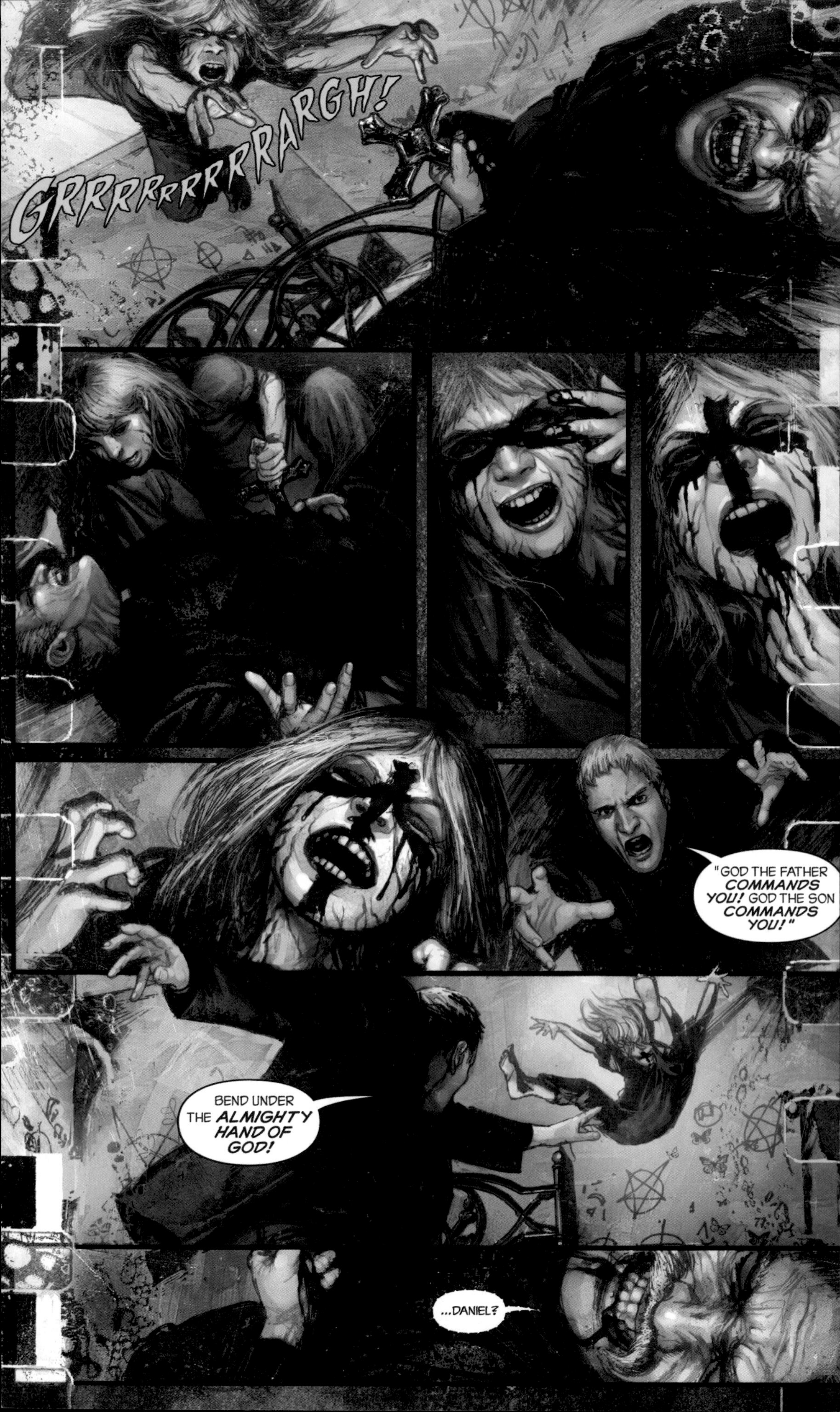
GRRRRRRRRRARGH!
"GOD THE FATHER COMMANDS YOU! GOD THE SON COMMANDS YOU!"
BEND UNDER THE ALMIGHTY HAND OF GOD!
...DANIEL?

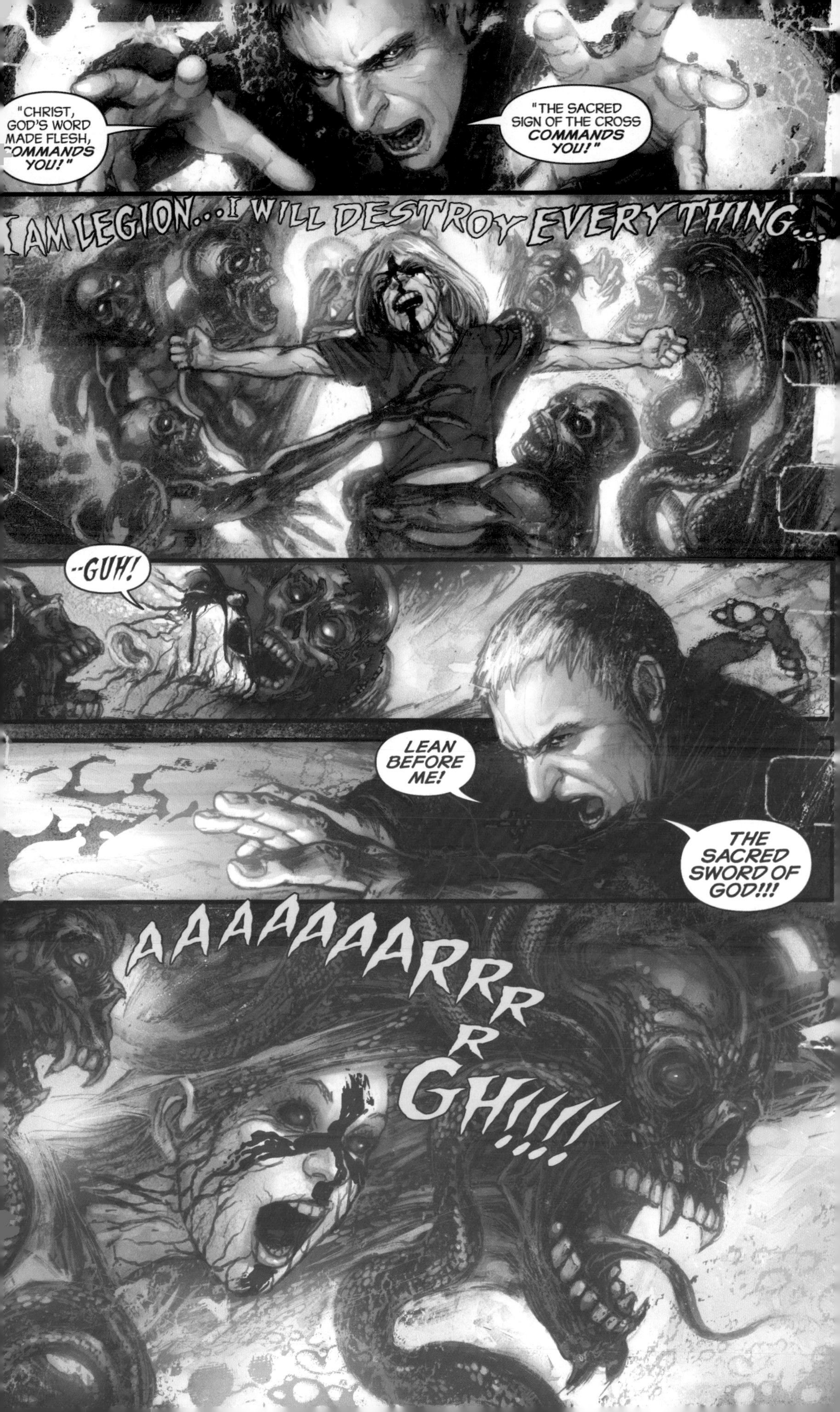
"CHRIST, GOD'S WORD MADE FLESH, COMMANDS YOU!"
"THE SACRED SIGN OF THE CROSS COMMANDS YOU!"
I AM LEGION...I WILL DESTROY EVERYTHING...
--GUH!
LEAN BEFORE ME!
THE SACRED SWORD OF GOD!!!
AAAAAAARRRRRGH!!!!

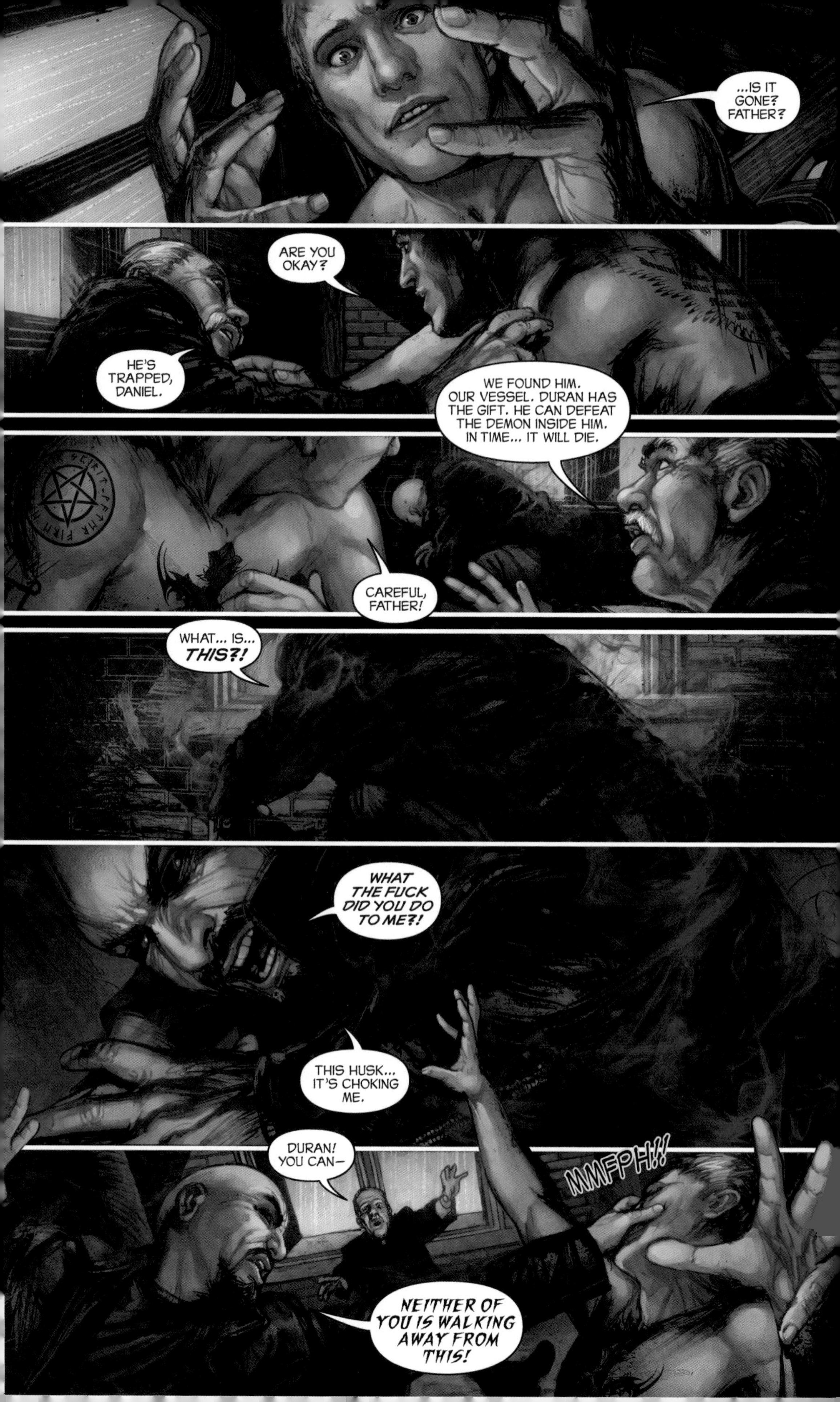

...IS IT GONE? FATHER?
ARE YOU OKAY?
HE'S TRAPPED, DANIEL.
WE FOUND HIM. OUR VESSEL. DURAN HAS THE GIFT. HE CAN DEFEAT THE DEMON INSIDE HIM. IN TIME... IT WILL DIE.
CAREFUL, FATHER!
WHAT... IS... THIS?!
WHAT THE FUCK DID YOU DO TO ME?!
THIS HUSK... IT'S CHOKING ME.
DURAN! YOU CAN—
MMFPH!!
NEITHER OF YOU IS WALKING AWAY FROM THIS!

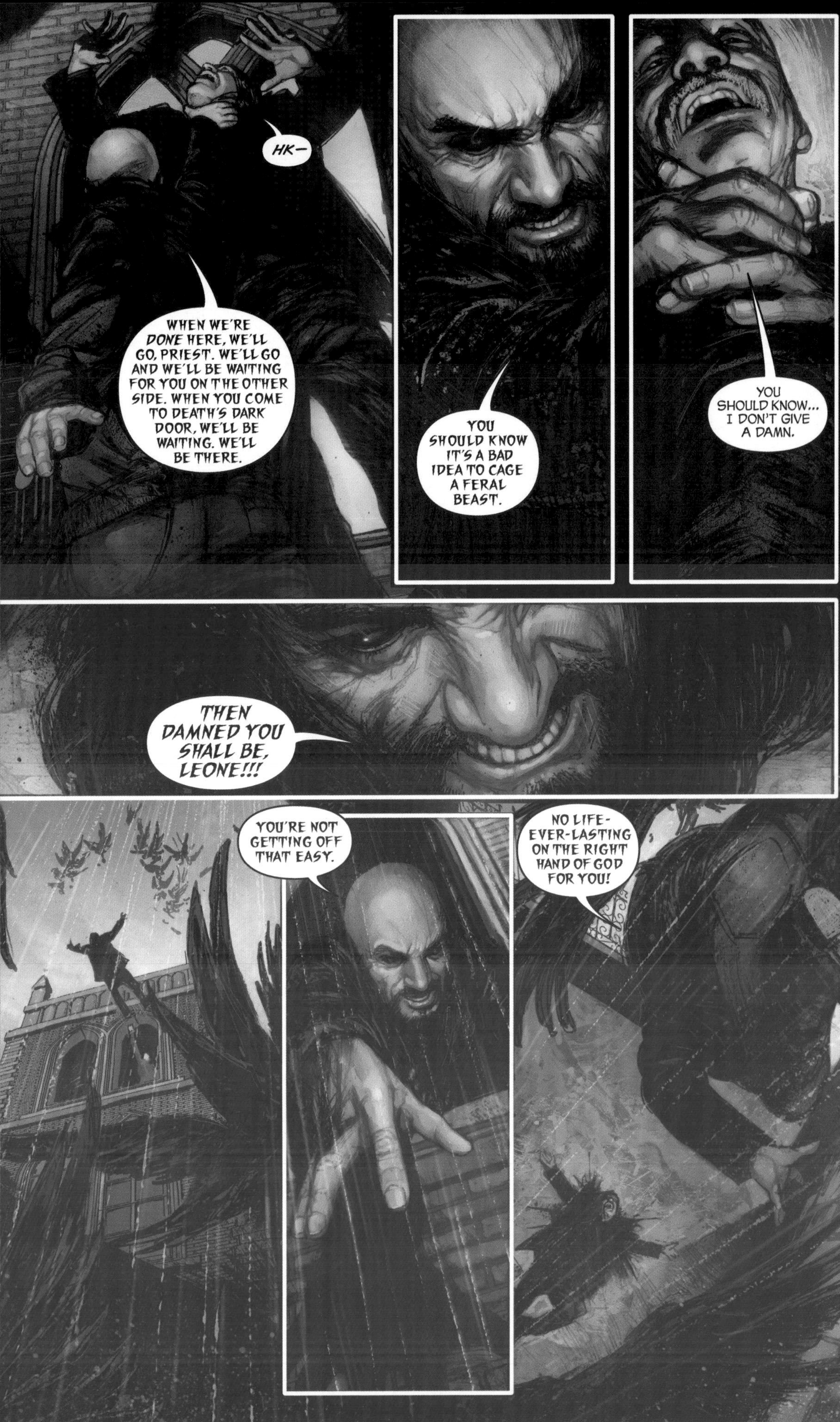
HK—
WHEN WE'RE DONE HERE, WE'LL GO, PRIEST. WE'LL GO AND WE'LL BE WAITING FOR YOU ON THE OTHER SIDE. WHEN YOU COME TO DEATH'S DARK DOOR, WE'LL BE WAITING. WE'LL BE THERE.
YOU SHOULD KNOW IT'S A BAD IDEA TO CAGE A FERAL BEAST.
YOU SHOULD KNOW... I DON'T GIVE A DAMN.
THEN DAMNED YOU SHALL BE, LEONE!!!
YOU'RE NOT GETTING OFF THAT EASY.
NO LIFE-EVER-LASTING ON THE RIGHT HAND OF GOD FOR YOU!

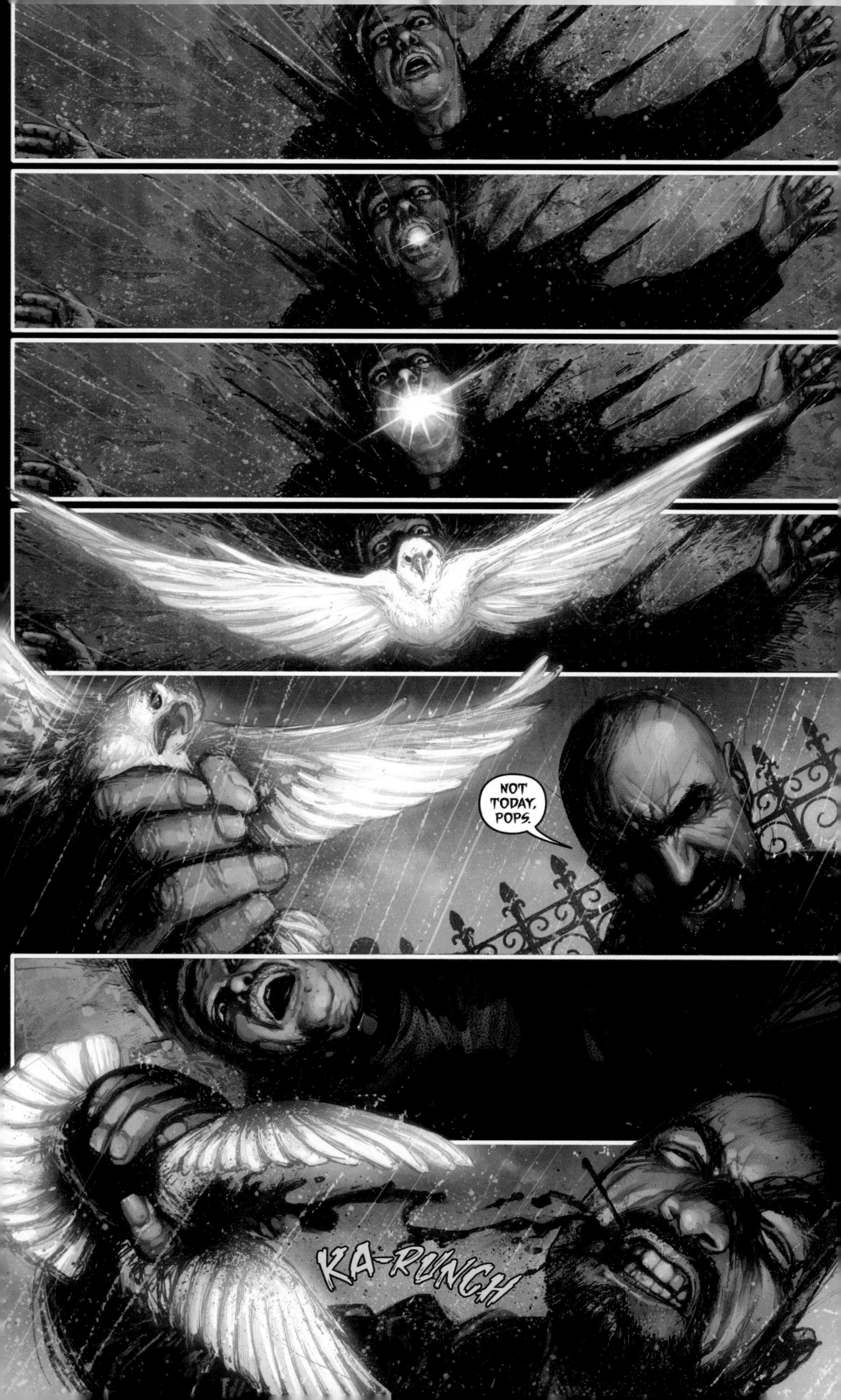
NOT TODAY, POPS.
KA-RUNCH

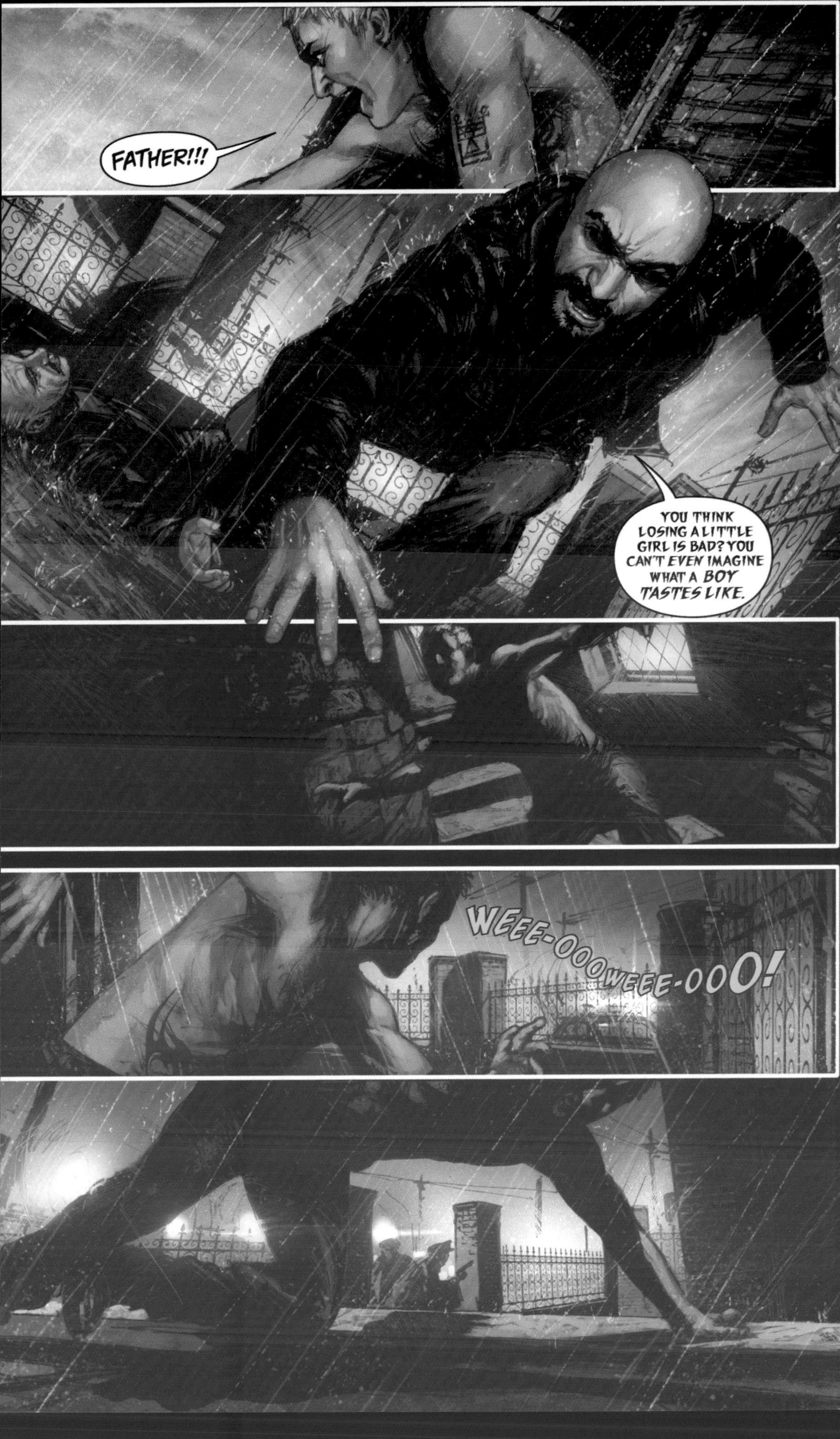
FATHER!!!
YOU THINK LOSING A LITTLE GIRL IS BAD? YOU CAN'T EVEN IMAGINE WHAT A BOY TASTES LIKE.
WEEE-OOOWEEE-OOO!

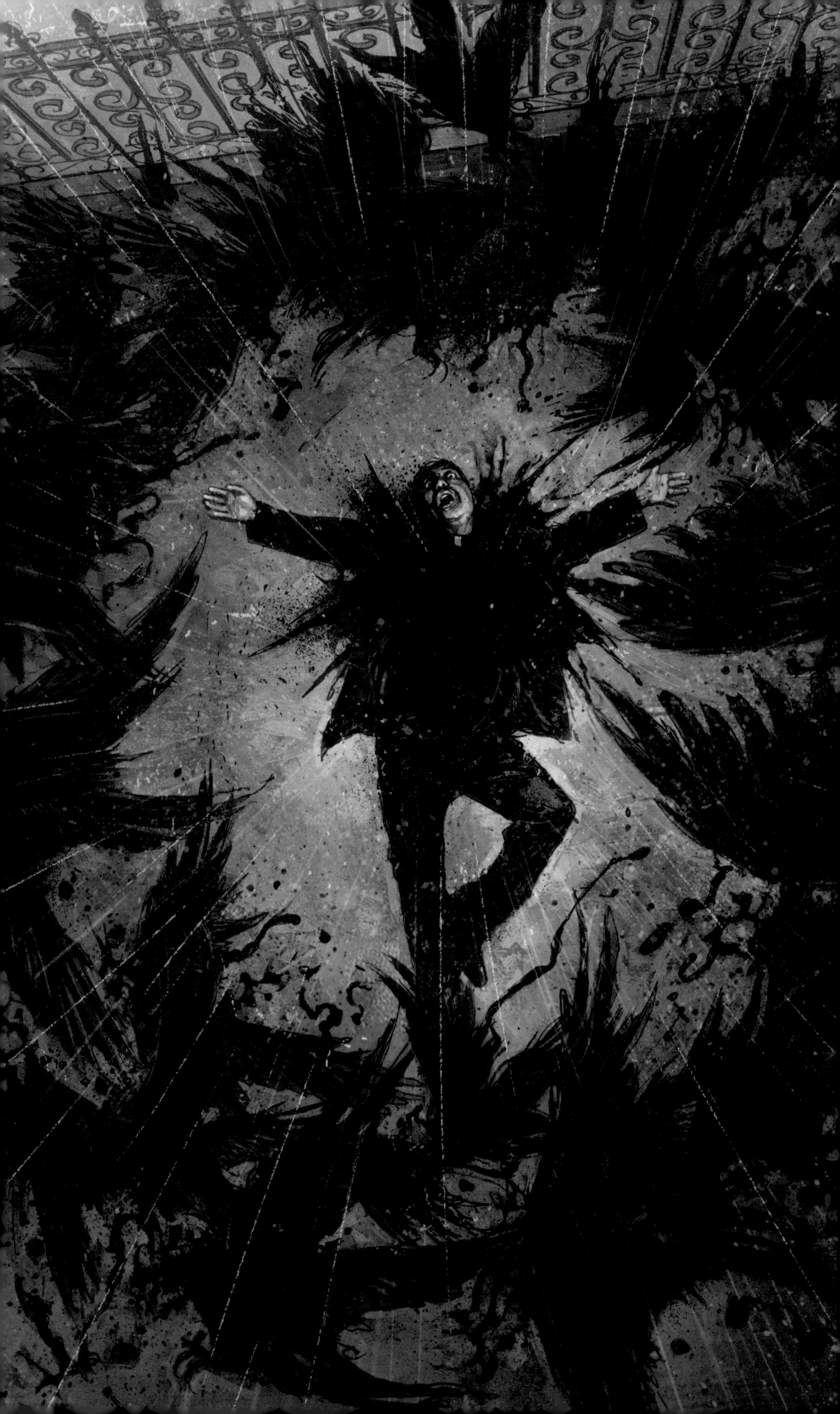

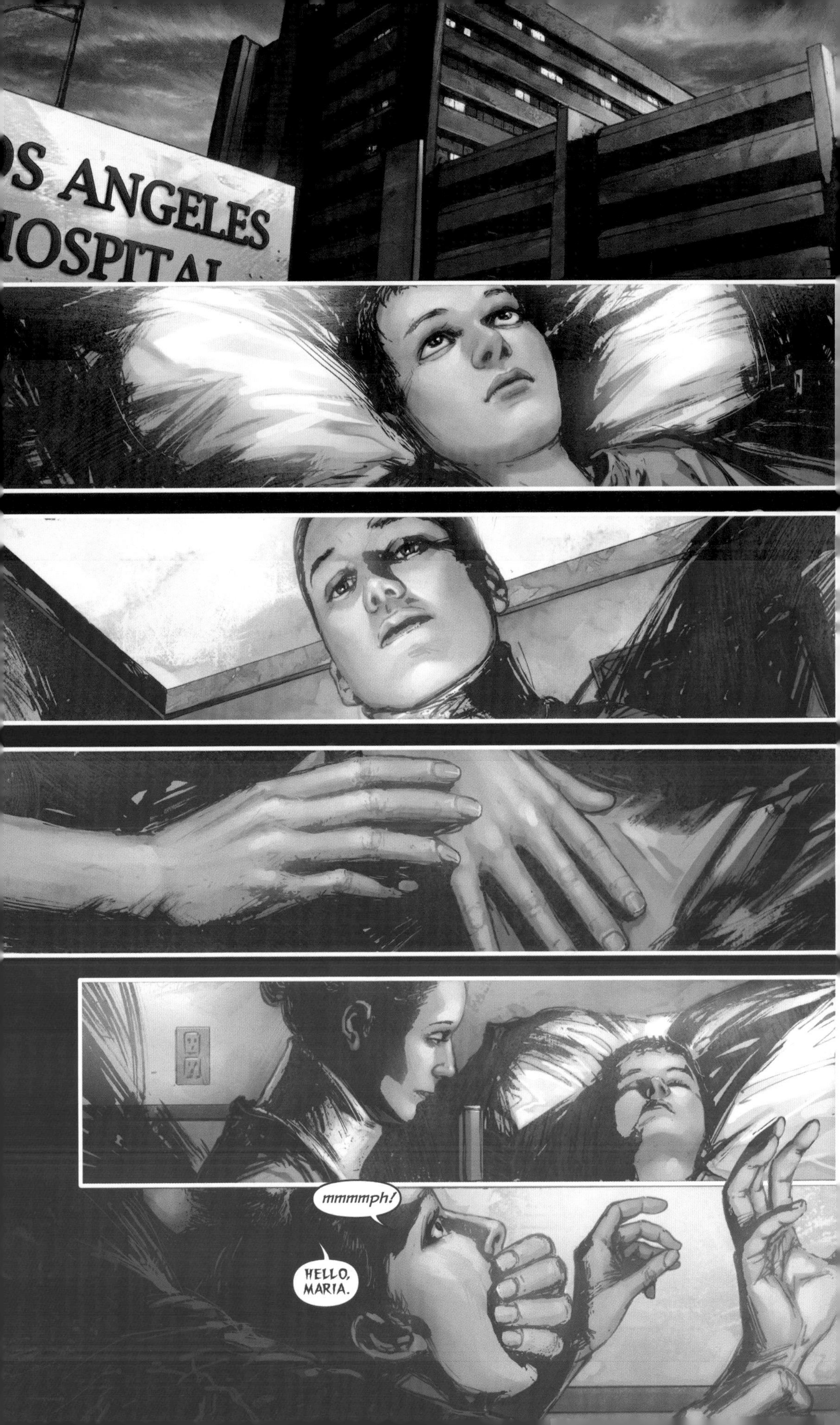
OS ANGELES
HOSPITAL
mmmmph!
HELLO, MARIA.

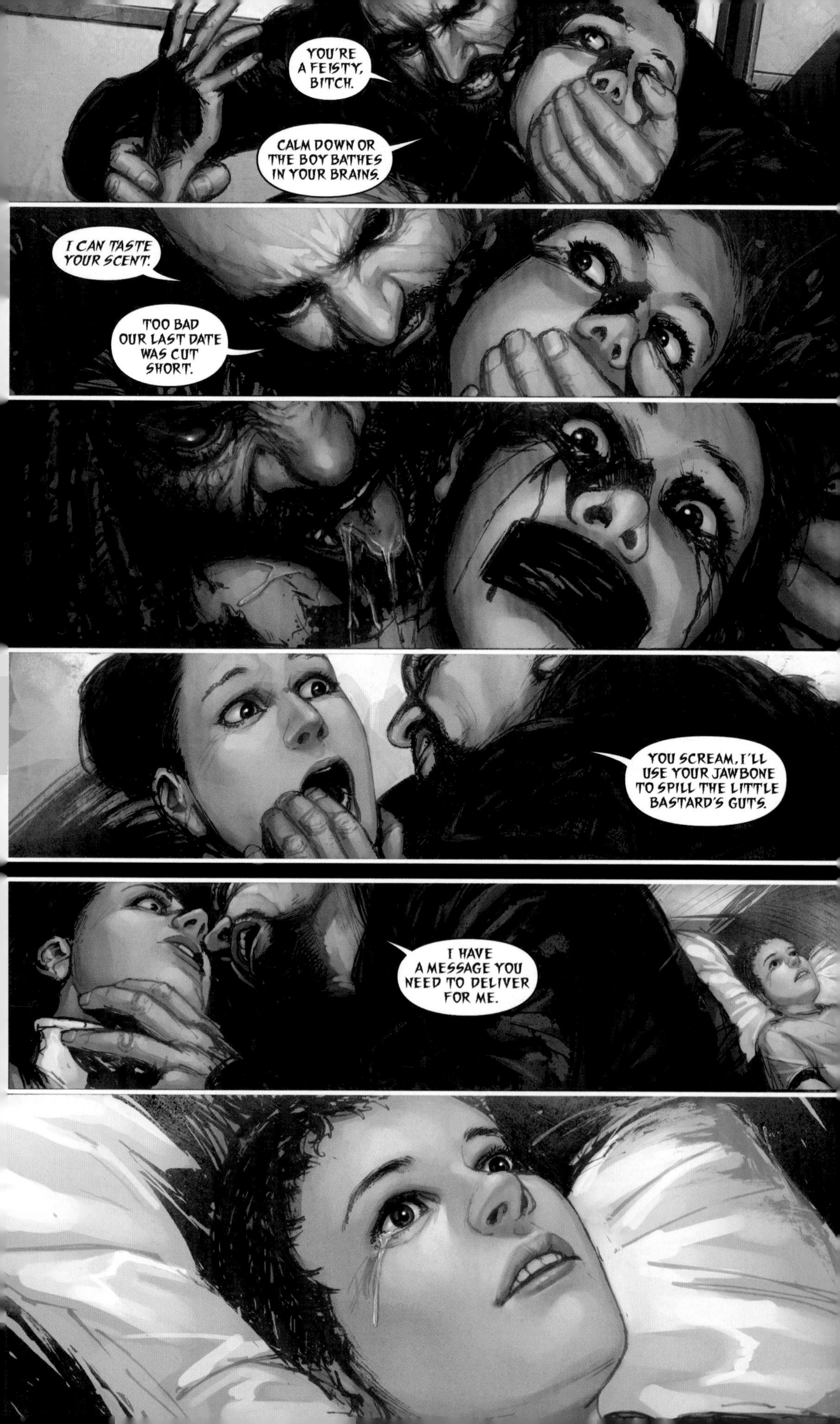
YOU'RE A FEISTY, BITCH.
CALM DOWN OR THE BOY BATHES IN YOUR BRAINS.
I CAN TASTE YOUR SCENT.
TOO BAD OUR LAST DATE WAS CUT SHORT.
YOU SCREAM, I'LL USE YOUR JAWBONE TO SPILL THE LITTLE BASTARD'S GUTS.
I HAVE A MESSAGE YOU NEED TO DELIVER FOR ME.

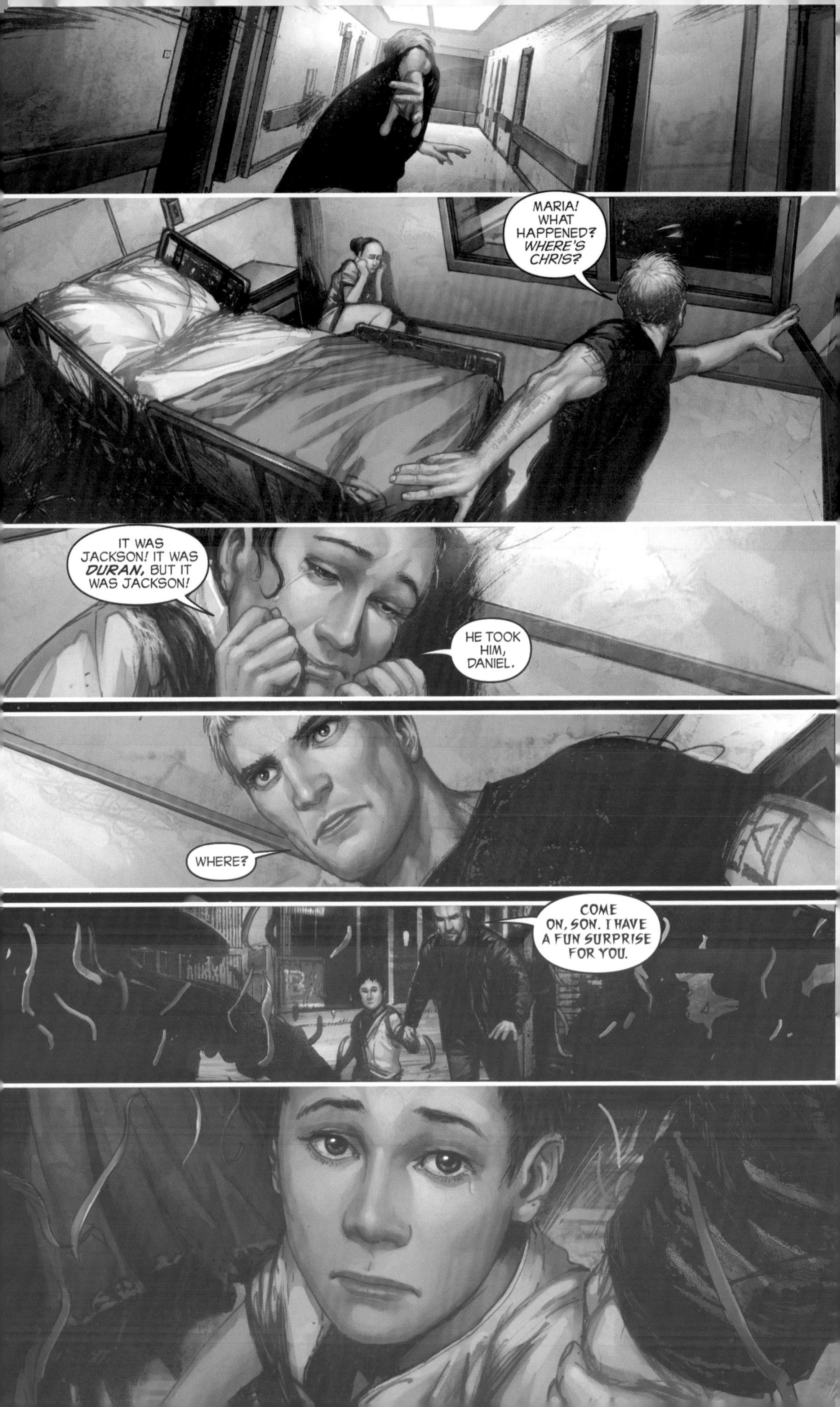
MARIA! WHAT HAPPENED? WHERE'S CHRIS?
IT WAS JACKSON! IT WAS DURAN, BUT IT WAS JACKSON!
HE TOOK HIM, DANIEL.
WHERE?
COME ON, SON. I HAVE A FUN SURPRISE FOR YOU.

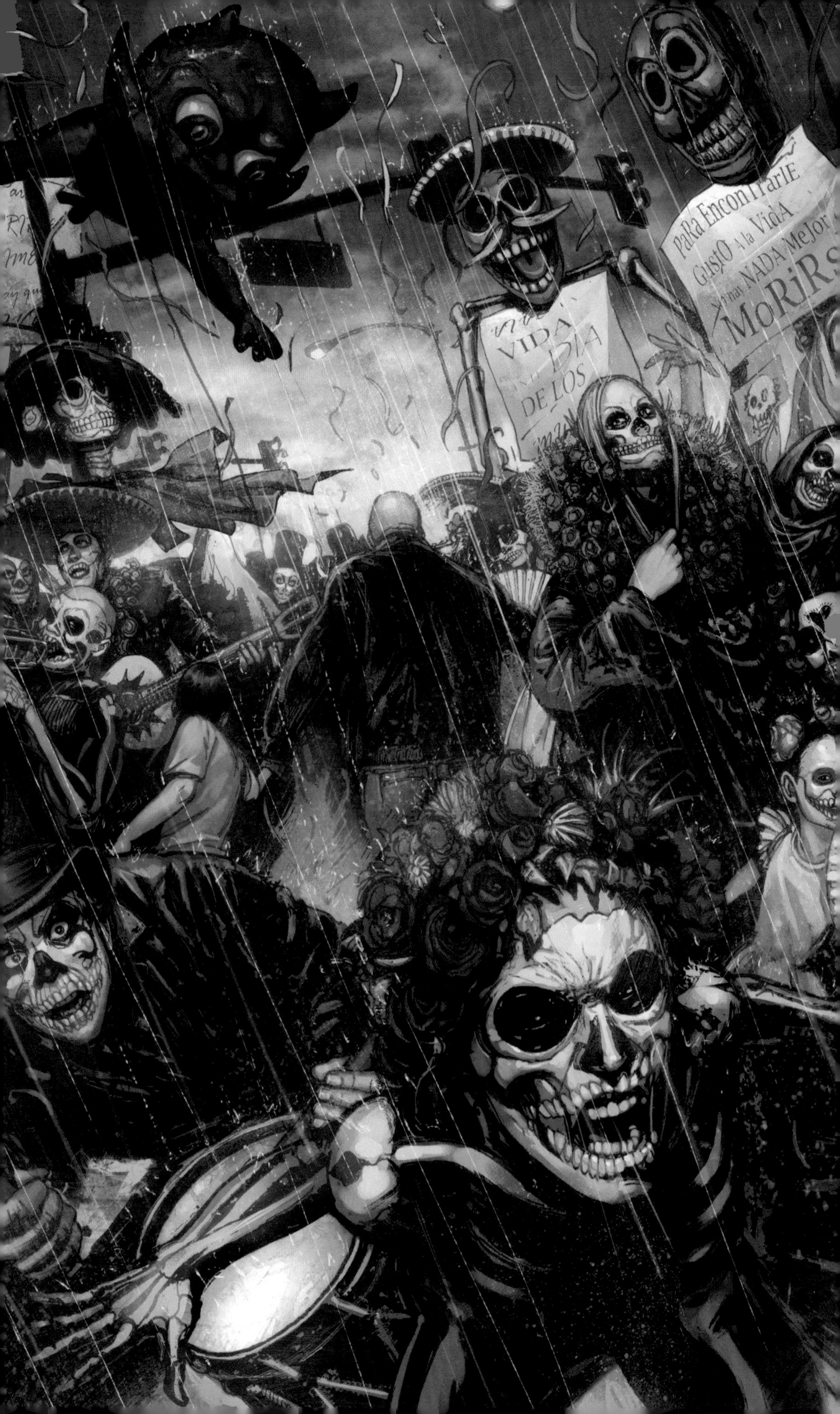
PaRa EnconTrarlE
GustO a la VidA
NADA MeJor
MoRiRs
VIDA
DIA
DE LOS

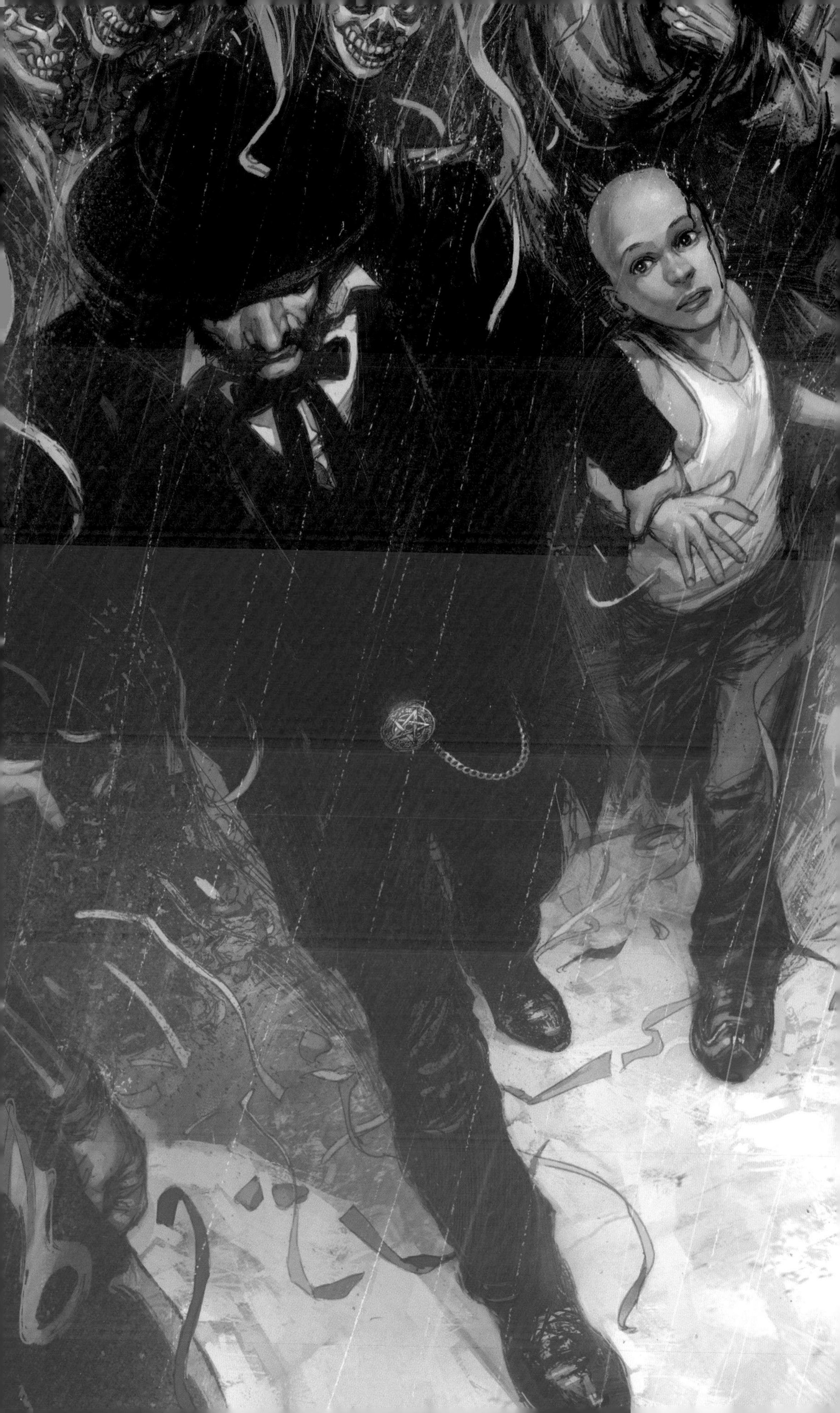

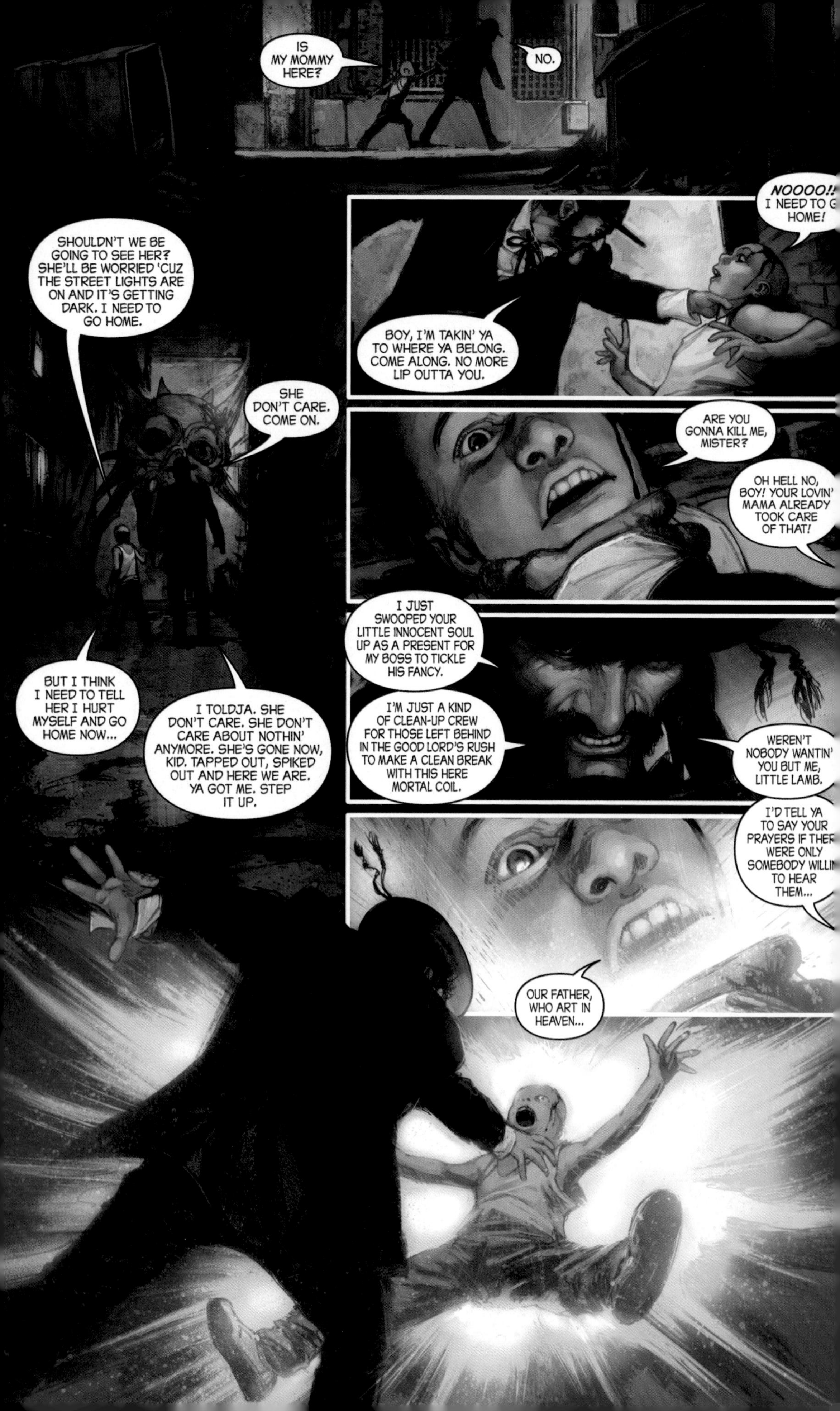
IS MY MOMMY HERE?
NO.
SHOULDN'T WE BE GOING TO SEE HER? SHE'LL BE WORRIED 'CUZ THE STREET LIGHTS ARE ON AND IT'S GETTING DARK. I NEED TO GO HOME.
SHE DON'T CARE. COME ON.
BUT I THINK I NEED TO TELL HER I HURT MYSELF AND GO HOME NOW...
I TOLDJA. SHE DON'T CARE. SHE DON'T CARE ABOUT NOTHIN' ANYMORE. SHE'S GONE NOW, KID. TAPPED OUT, SPIKED OUT AND HERE WE ARE. YA GOT ME. STEP IT UP.
NOOOO!! I NEED TO G HOME!
BOY, I'M TAKIN' YA TO WHERE YA BELONG. COME ALONG. NO MORE LIP OUTTA YOU.
ARE YOU GONNA KILL ME, MISTER?
OH HELL NO, BOY! YOUR LOVIN' MAMA ALREADY TOOK CARE OF THAT!
I JUST SWOOPED YOUR LITTLE INNOCENT SOUL UP AS A PRESENT FOR MY BOSS TO TICKLE HIS FANCY.
I'M JUST A KIND OF CLEAN-UP CREW FOR THOSE LEFT BEHIND IN THE GOOD LORD'S RUSH TO MAKE A CLEAN BREAK WITH THIS HERE MORTAL COIL.
WEREN'T NOBODY WANTIN' YOU BUT ME, LITTLE LAMB.
I'D TELL YA TO SAY YOUR PRAYERS IF THER WERE ONLY SOMEBODY WILLIN TO HEAR THEM...
OUR FATHER, WHO ART IN HEAVEN...

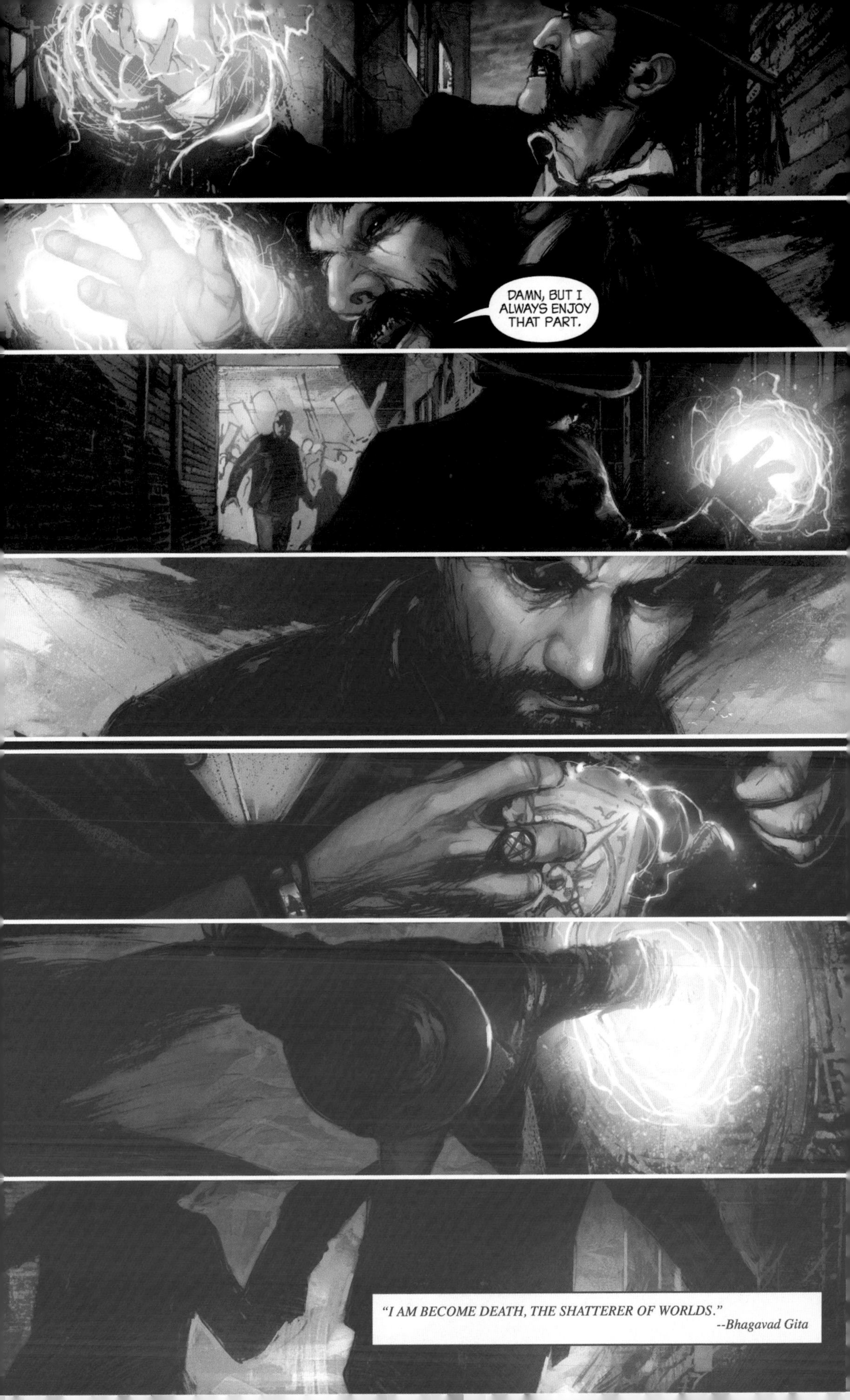
DAMN, BUT I ALWAYS ENJOY THAT PART.
"I AM BECOME DEATH, THE SHATTERER OF WORLDS."
--Bhagavad Gita

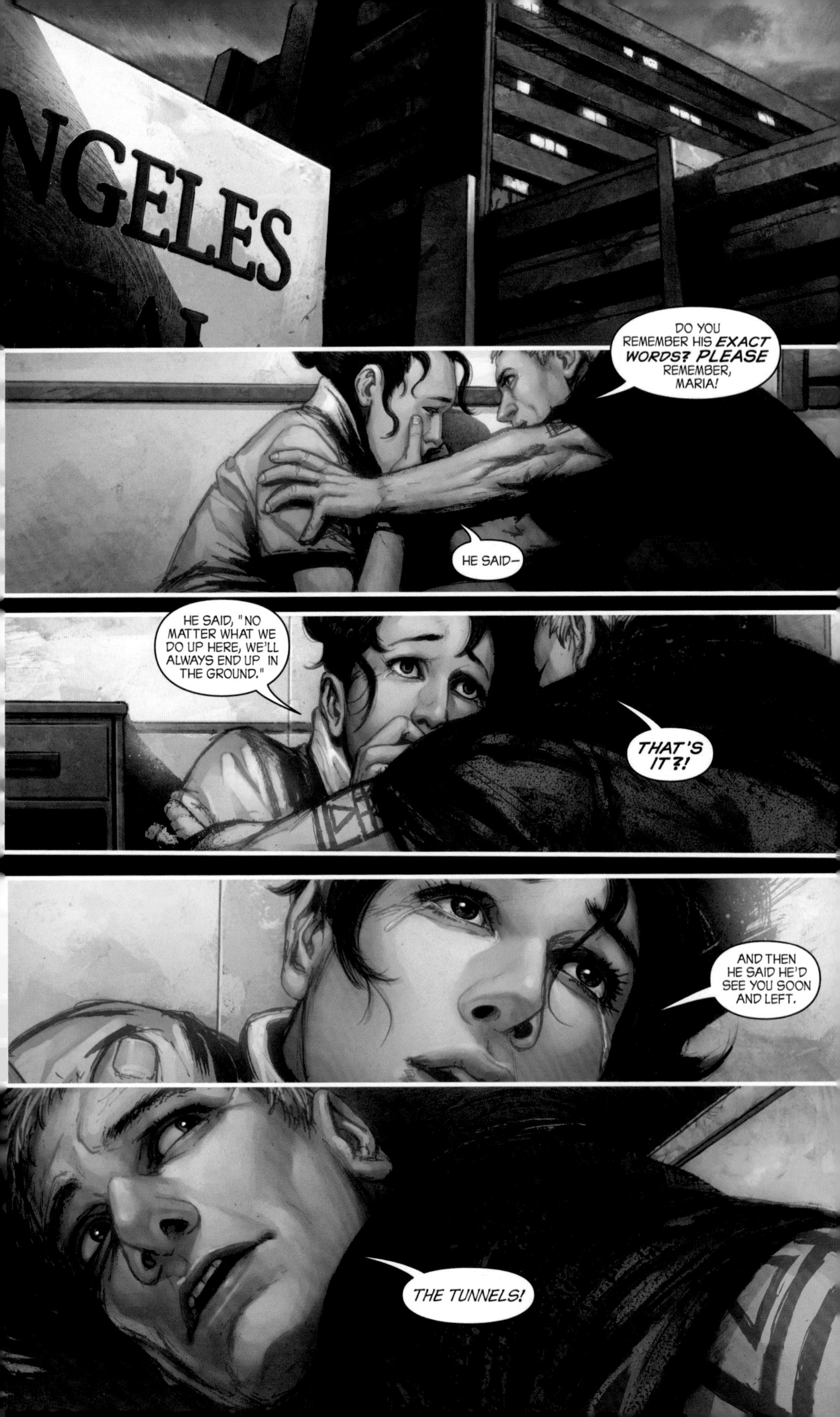
NGELES
DO YOU REMEMBER HIS EXACT WORDS? PLEASE REMEMBER, MARIA!
HE SAID—
HE SAID, "NO MATTER WHAT WE DO UP HERE, WE'LL ALWAYS END UP IN THE GROUND."
THAT'S IT?!
AND THEN HE SAID HE'D SEE YOU SOON AND LEFT.
THE TUNNELS!

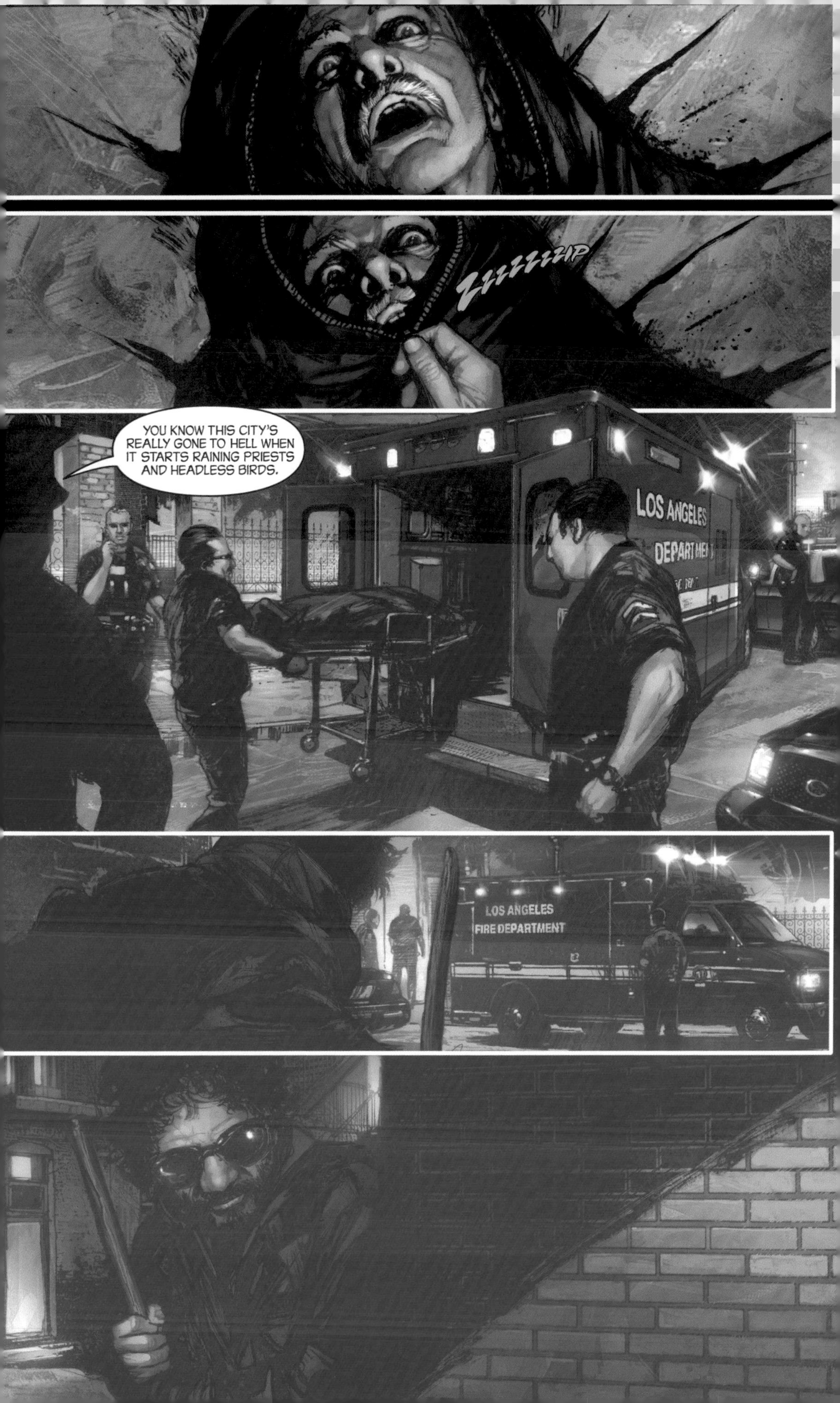
ZZZZZZZIP
YOU KNOW THIS CITY'S REALLY GONE TO HELL WHEN IT STARTS RAINING PRIESTS AND HEADLESS BIRDS.
LOS ANGELES
LOS ANGELES
FIRE DEPARTMENT

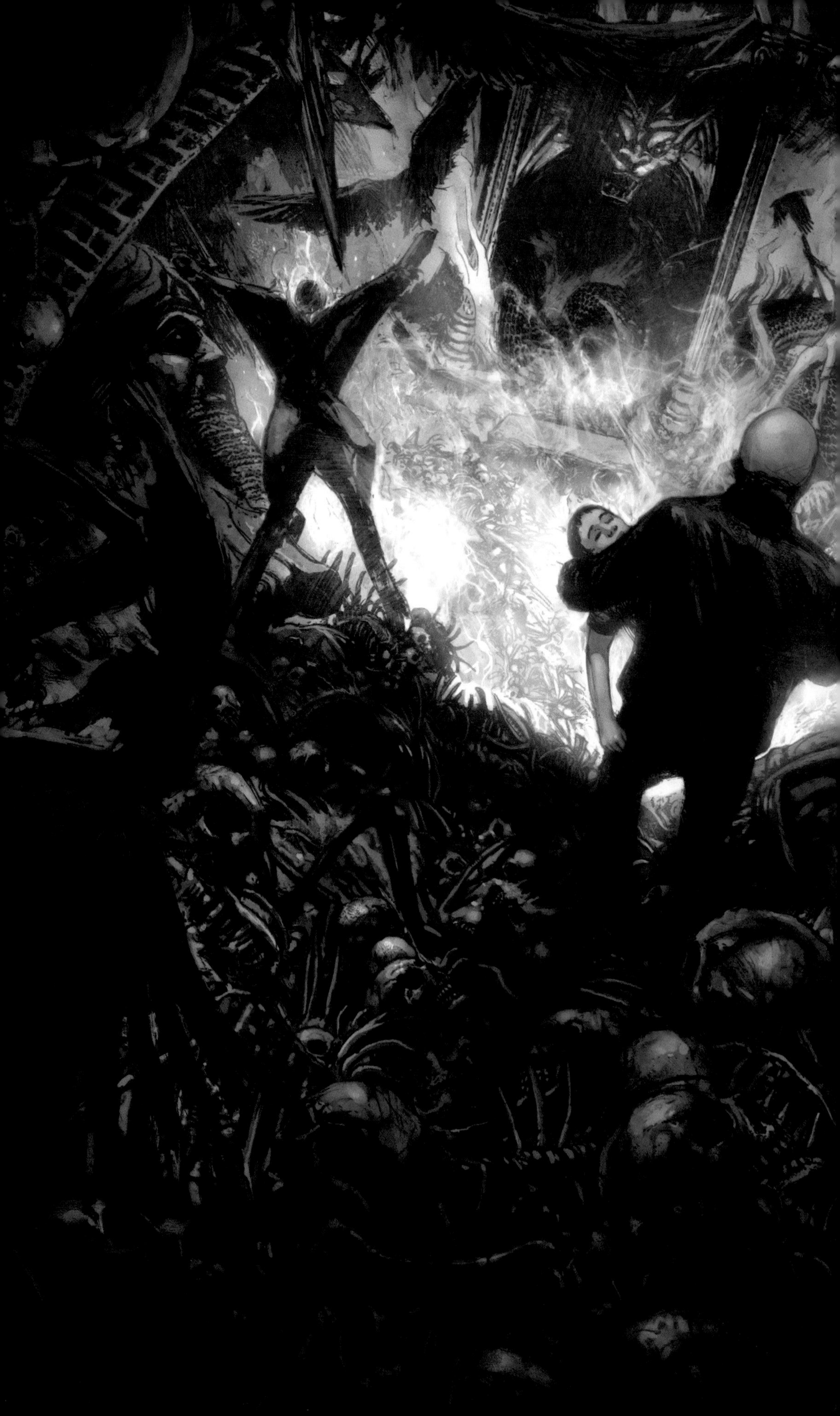

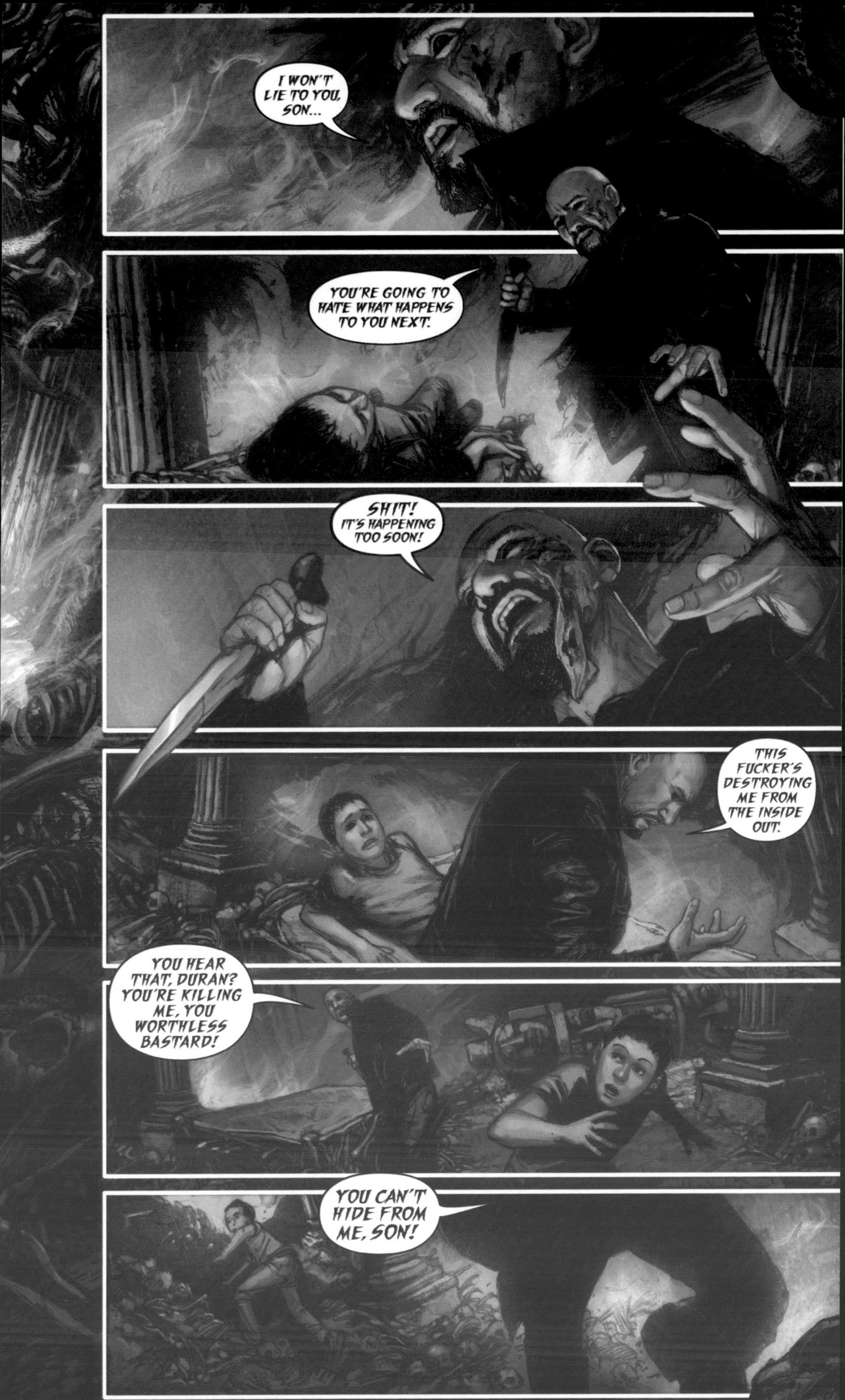
I WON'T LIE TO YOU, SON...
YOU'RE GOING TO HATE WHAT HAPPENS TO YOU NEXT.
SHIT! IT'S HAPPENING TOO SOON!
THIS FUCKER'S DESTROYING ME FROM THE INSIDE OUT.
YOU HEAR THAT, DURAN? YOU'RE KILLING ME, YOU WORTHLESS BASTARD!
YOU CAN'T HIDE FROM ME, SON!

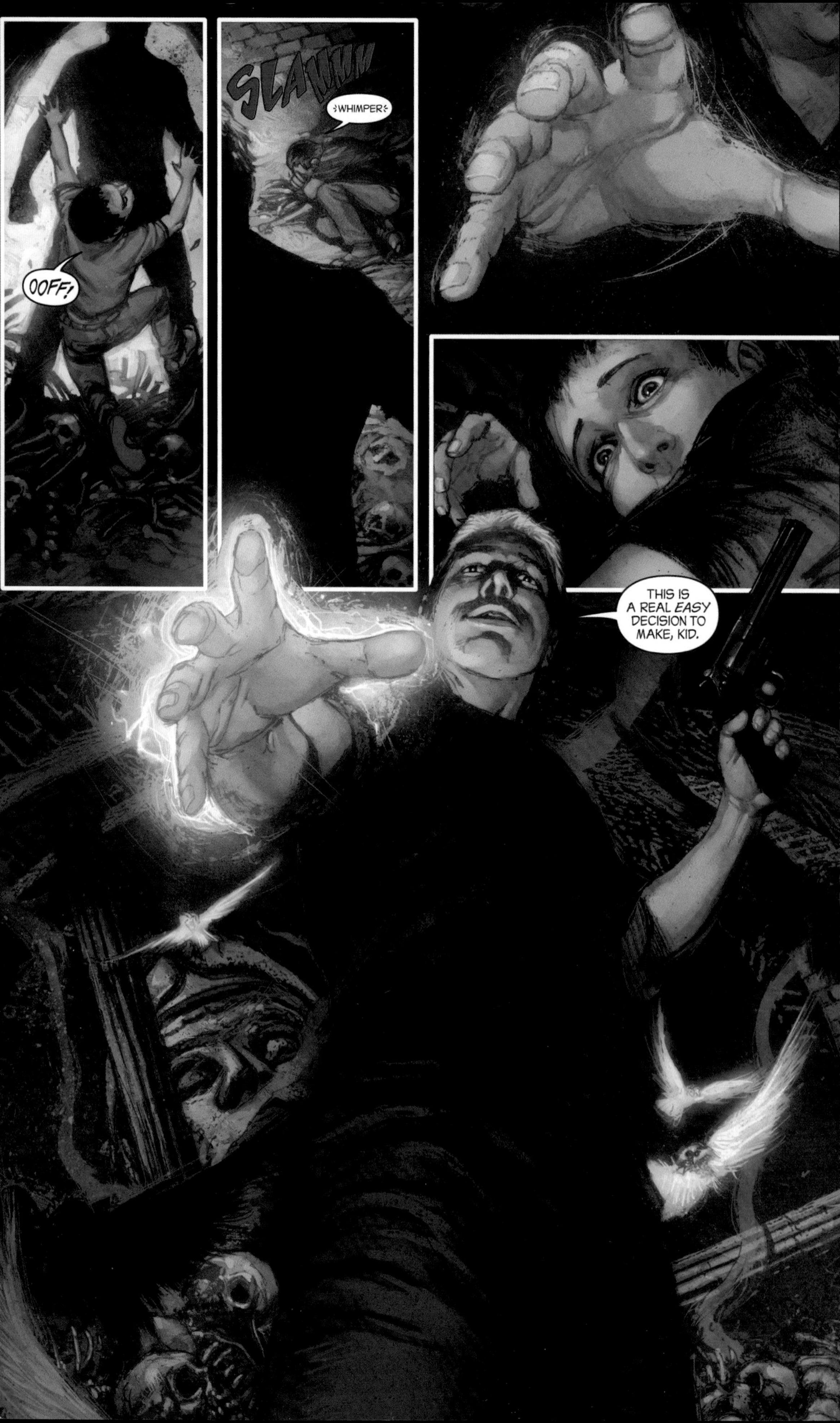
OOFF!
SLAMMM
WHIMPER
THIS IS A REAL EASY DECISION TO MAKE, KID.

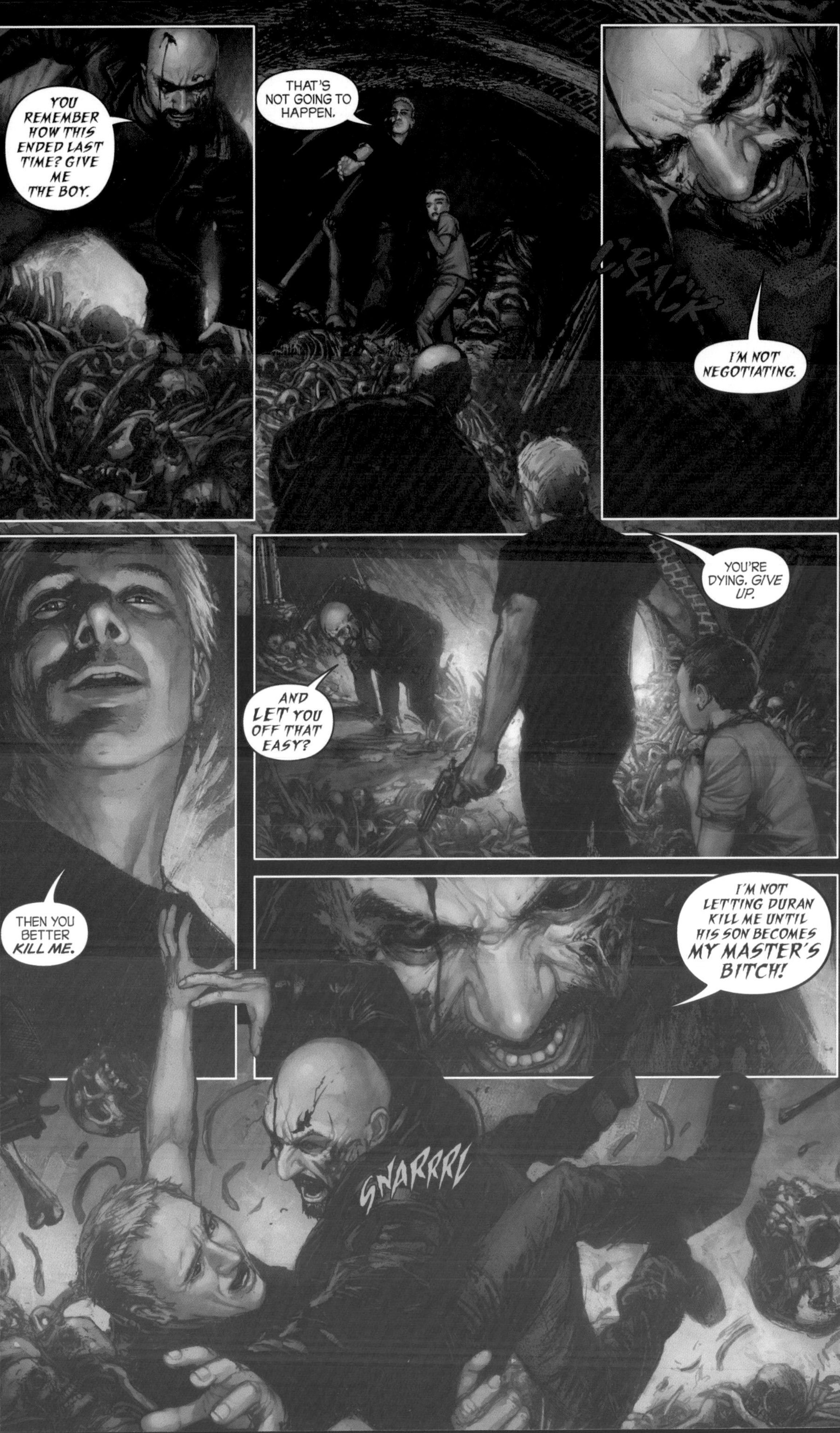
YOU REMEMBER HOW THIS ENDED LAST TIME? GIVE ME THE BOY.
THAT'S NOT GOING TO HAPPEN.
I'M NOT NEGOTIATING.
YOU'RE DYING. GIVE UP.
AND LET YOU OFF THAT EASY?
THEN YOU BETTER KILL ME.
I'M NOT LETTING DURAN KILL ME UNTIL HIS SON BECOMES MY MASTER'S BITCH!
SNARRRL

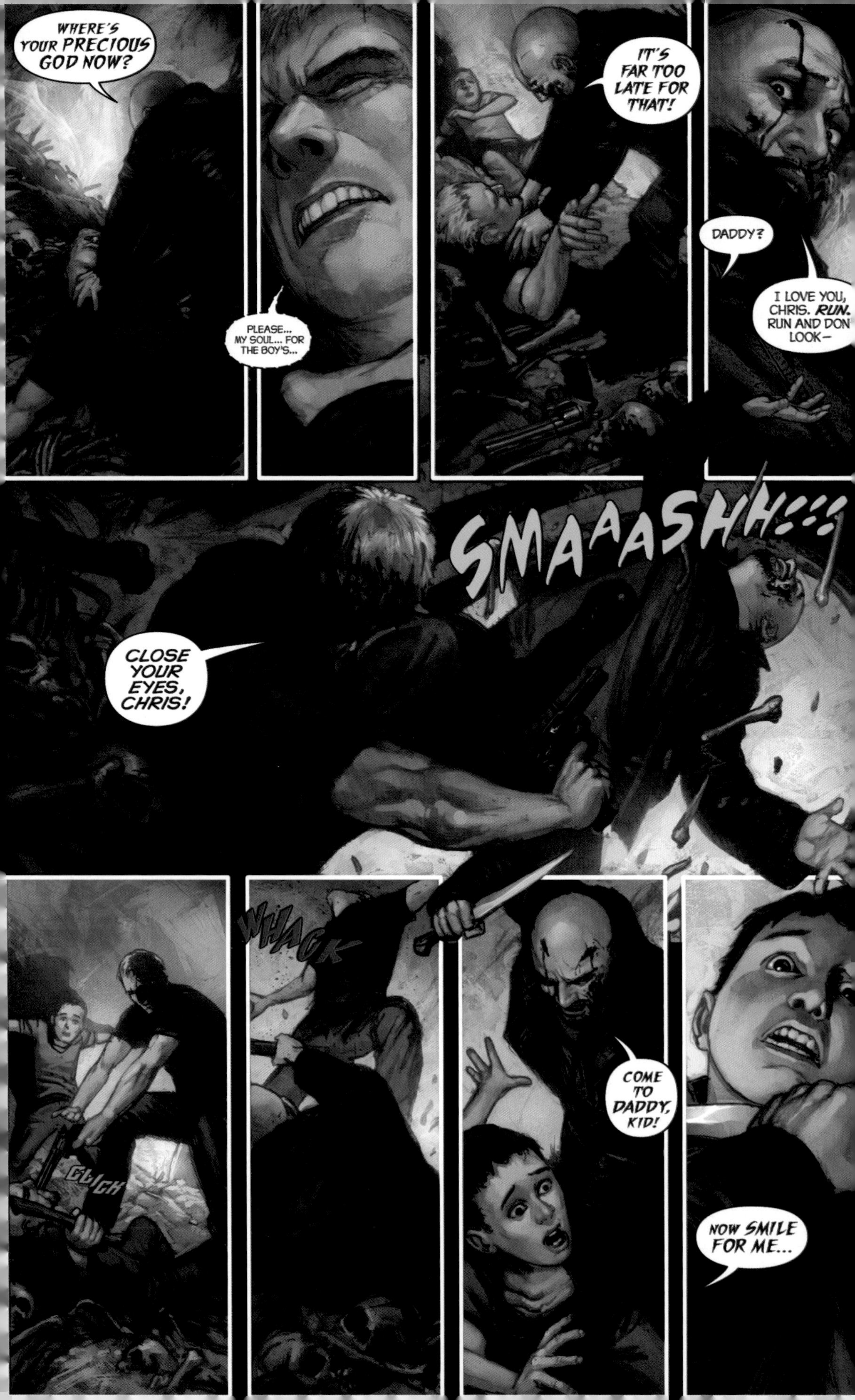
WHERE'S YOUR PRECIOUS GOD NOW?
PLEASE... MY SOUL... FOR THE BOY'S...
IT'S FAR TOO LATE FOR THAT!
DADDY?
I LOVE YOU, CHRIS. RUN. RUN AND DON'T LOOK—
SMAAASHH!!!
CLOSE YOUR EYES, CHRIS!
CLICK
WHACK
COME TO DADDY, KID!
NOW SMILE FOR ME...

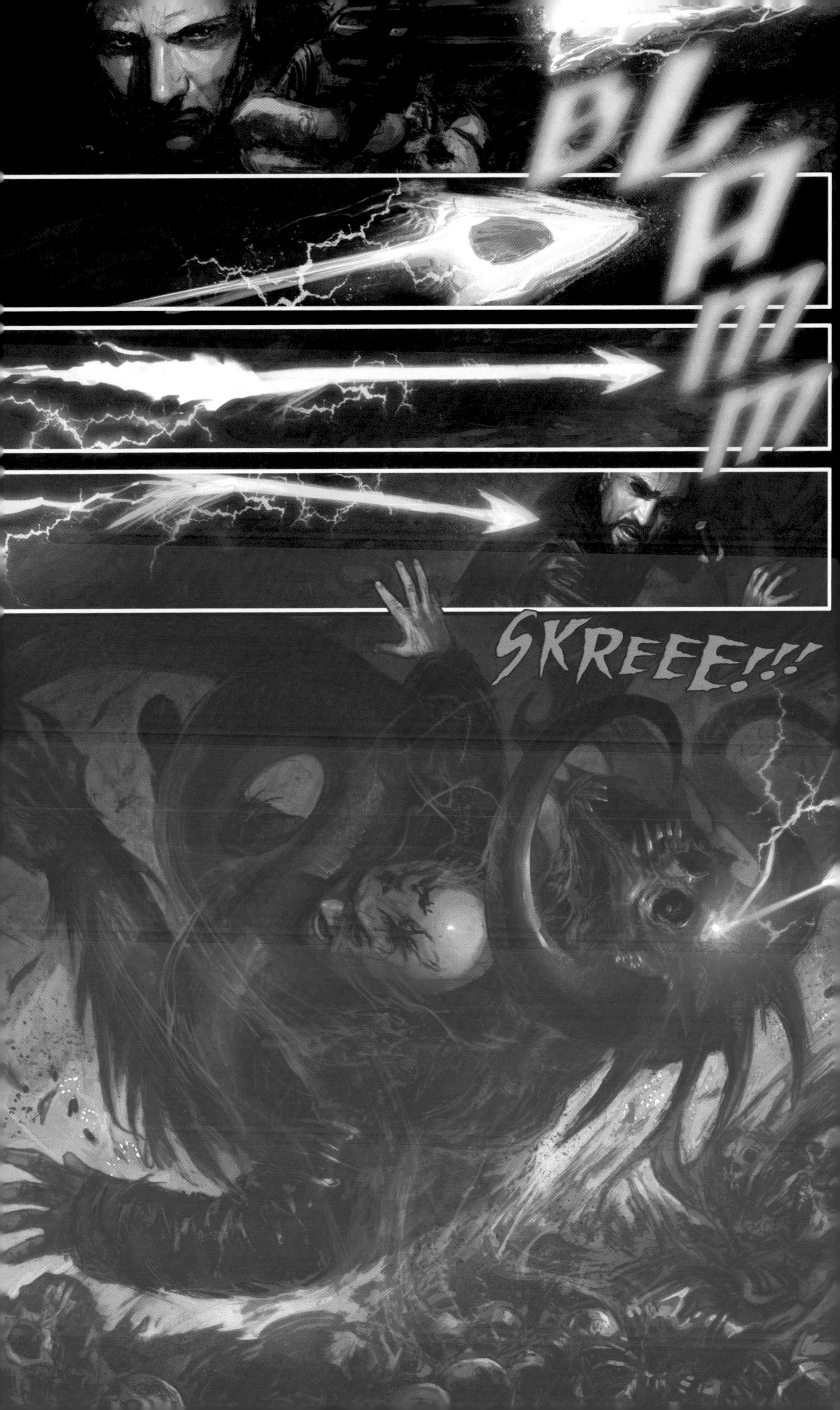
BLAMMM
SKREEE!!!

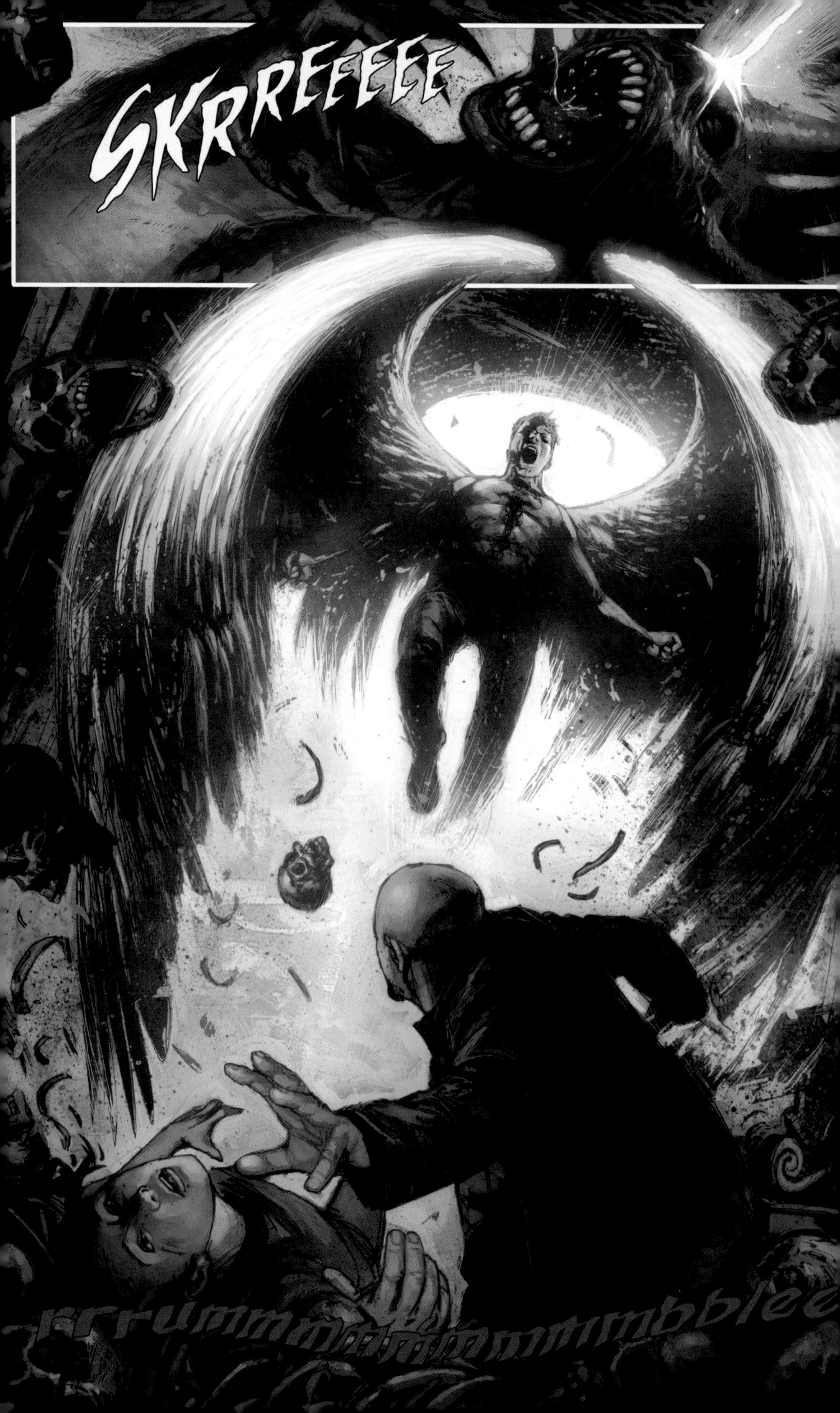
SKRREEEEE
rrrummmmmmmmmmmmmbblee

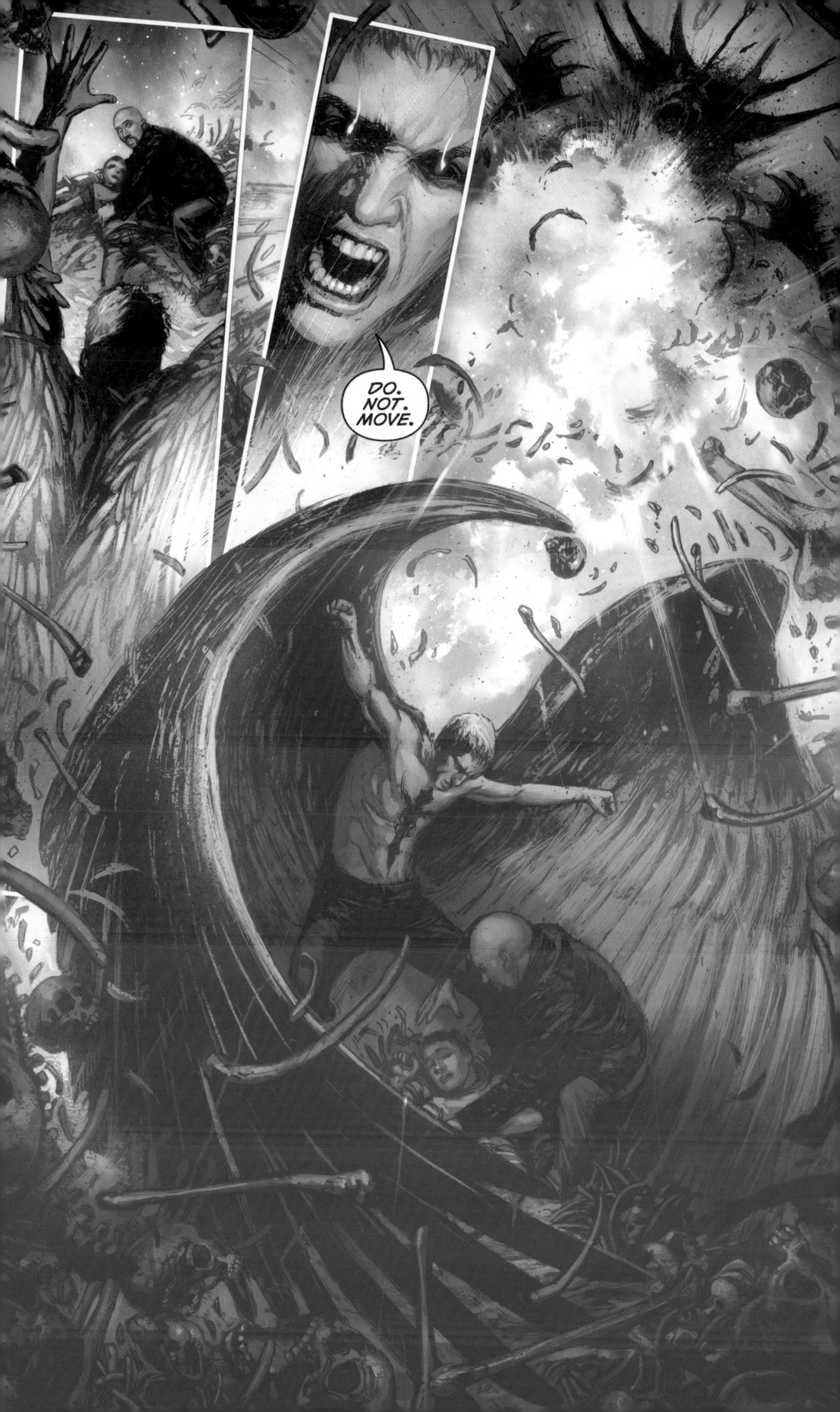
DO. NOT. MOVE.

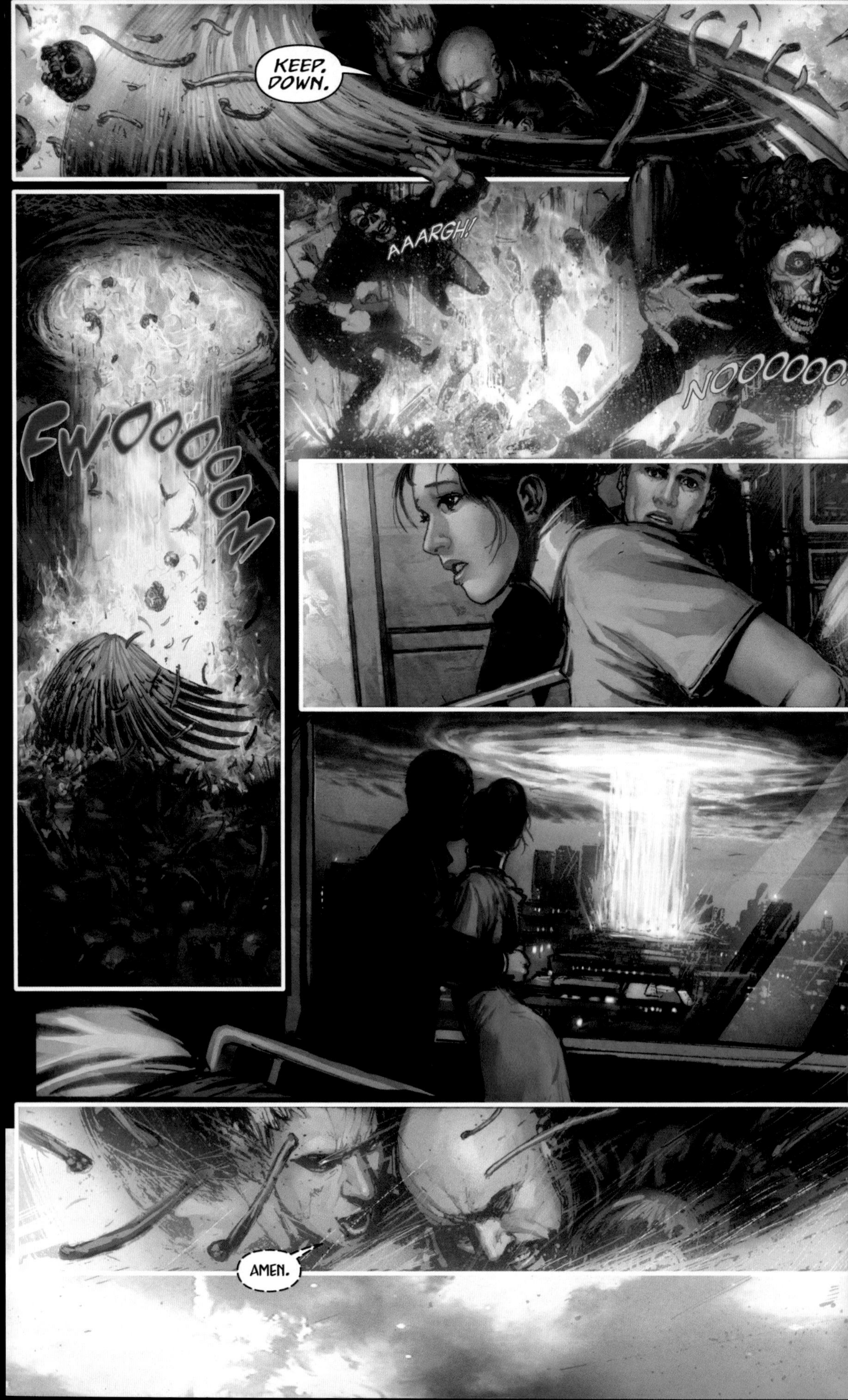
KEEP. DOWN.
AAARGH!
NOOOOOO!
FWOOOOOM
AMEN.

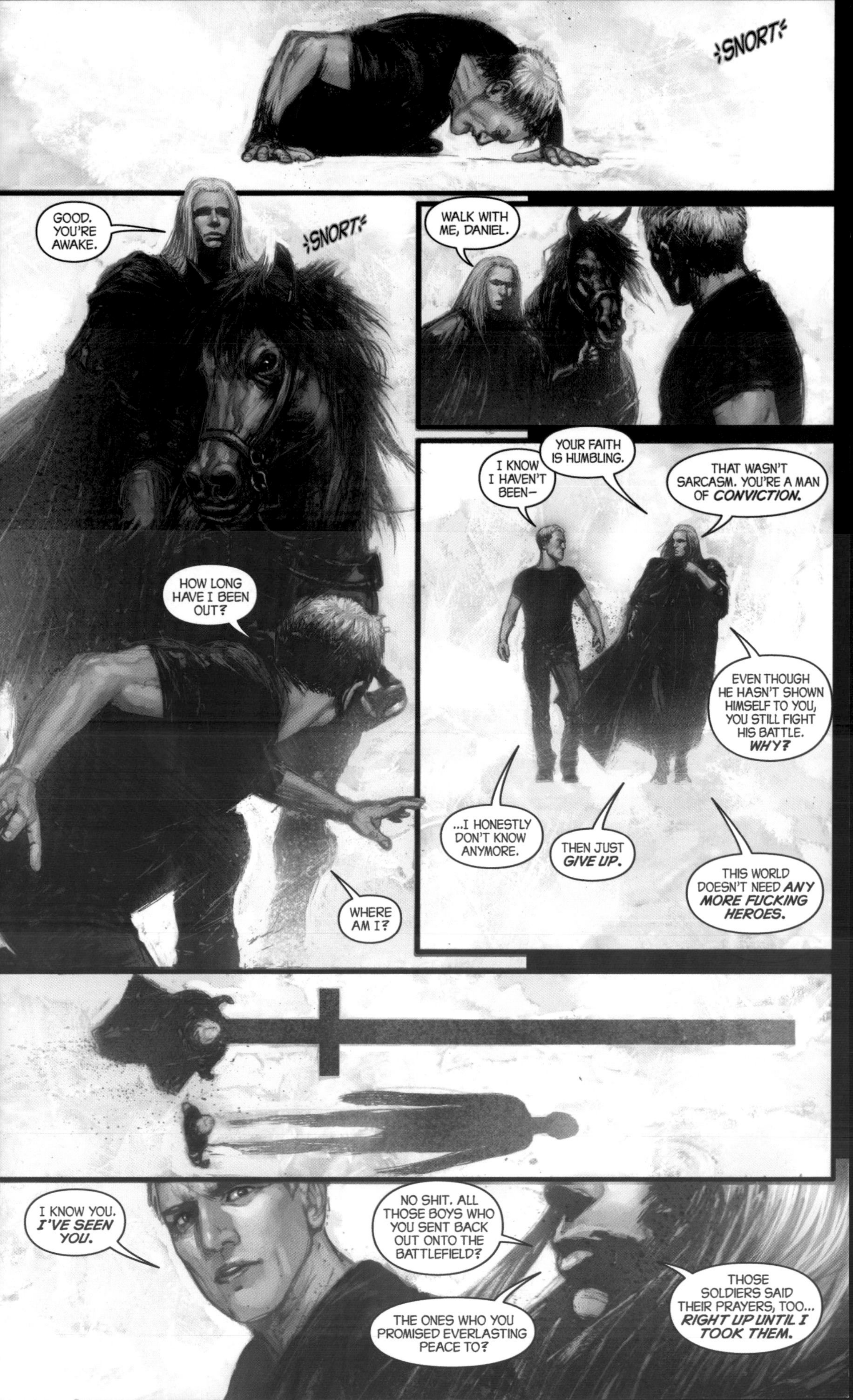
SNORT
GOOD. YOU'RE AWAKE.
SNORT
HOW LONG HAVE I BEEN OUT?
WHERE AM I?
WALK WITH ME, DANIEL.
I KNOW I HAVEN'T BEEN—
YOUR FAITH IS HUMBLING.
THAT WASN'T SARCASM. YOU'RE A MAN OF CONVICTION.
EVEN THOUGH HE HASN'T SHOWN HIMSELF TO YOU, YOU STILL FIGHT HIS BATTLE. WHY?
...I HONESTLY DON'T KNOW ANYMORE.
THEN JUST GIVE UP.
THIS WORLD DOESN'T NEED ANY MORE FUCKING HEROES.
I KNOW YOU. I'VE SEEN YOU.
NO SHIT. ALL THOSE BOYS WHO YOU SENT BACK OUT ONTO THE BATTLEFIELD?
THE ONES WHO YOU PROMISED EVERLASTING PEACE TO?
THOSE SOLDIERS SAID THEIR PRAYERS, TOO... RIGHT UP UNTIL I TOOK THEM.

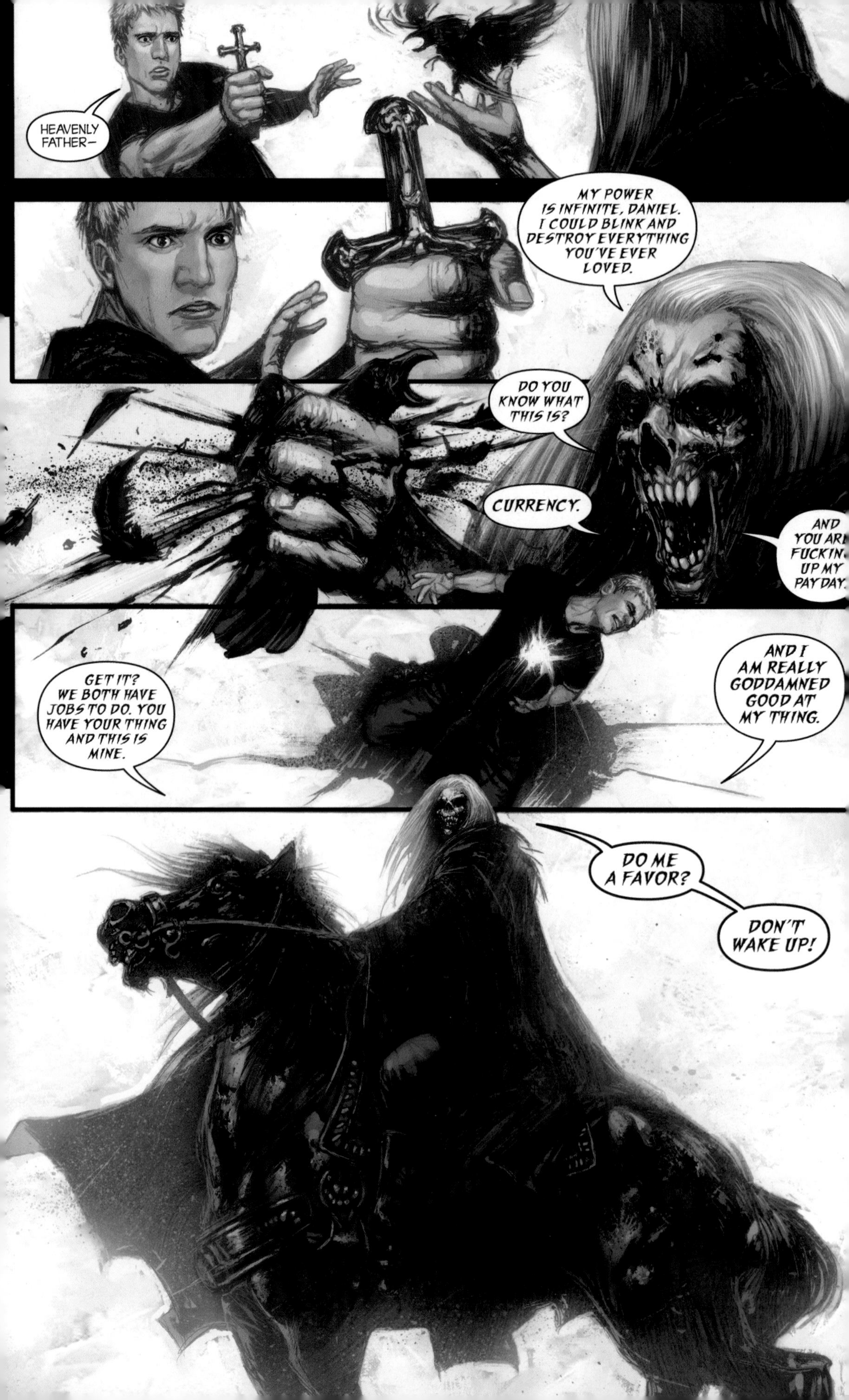
HEAVENLY FATHER—
MY POWER IS INFINITE, DANIEL. I COULD BLINK AND DESTROY EVERYTHING YOU'VE EVER LOVED.
DO YOU KNOW WHAT THIS IS?
CURRENCY.
AND YOU ARE FUCKIN UP MY PAY DAY.
GET IT? WE BOTH HAVE JOBS TO DO. YOU HAVE YOUR THING AND THIS IS MINE.
AND I AM REALLY GODDAMNED GOOD AT MY THING.
DO ME A FAVOR?
DON'T WAKE UP!

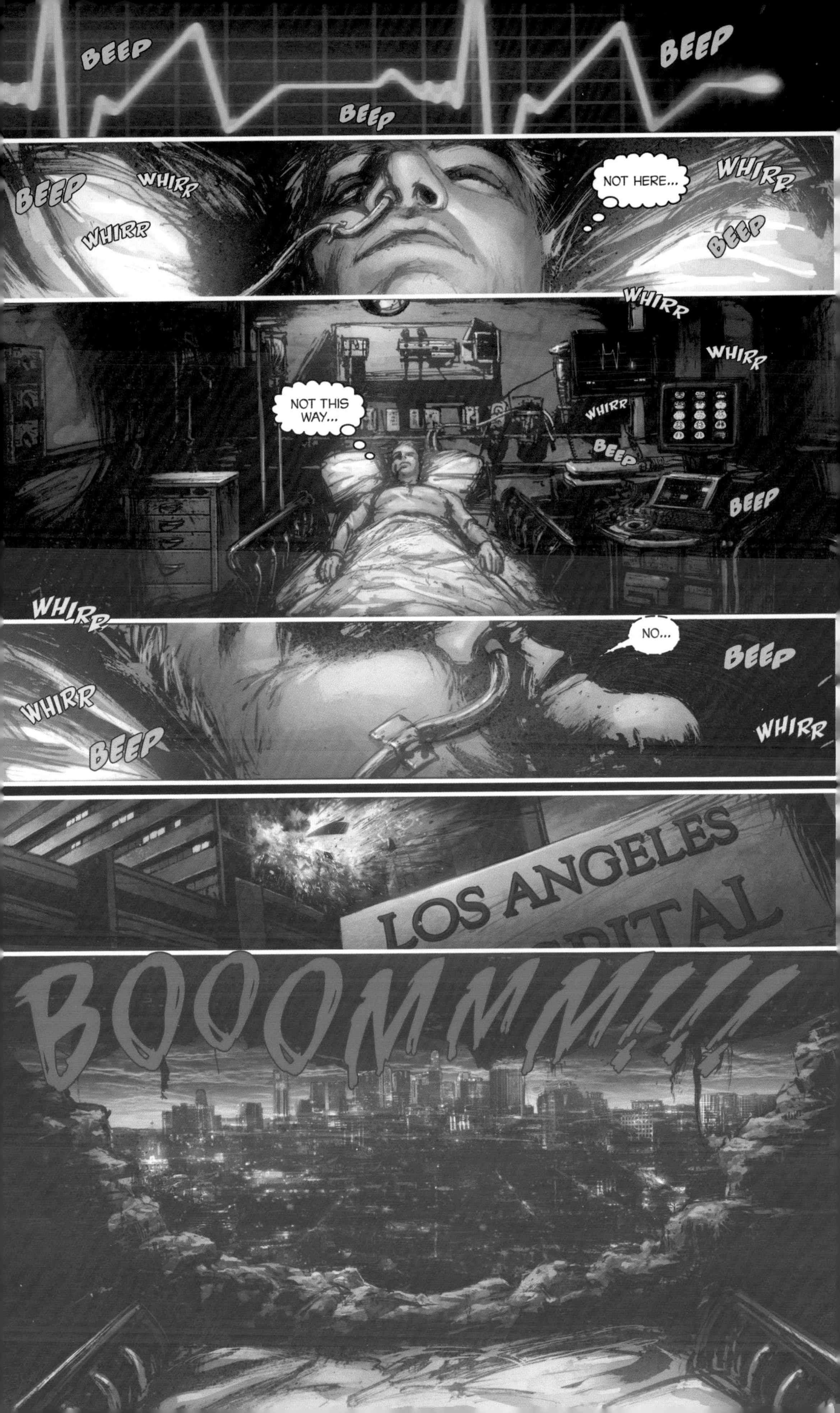

BEEP
BEEP
BEEP
BEEP
WHIRR
WHIRR
NOT HERE...
WHIRR
BEEP
WHIRR
WHIRR
NOT THIS WAY...
WHIRR
BEEP
BEEP
WHIRR
NO...
BEEP
WHIRR
BEEP
WHIRR
LOS ANGELES
BOOOMMM!!

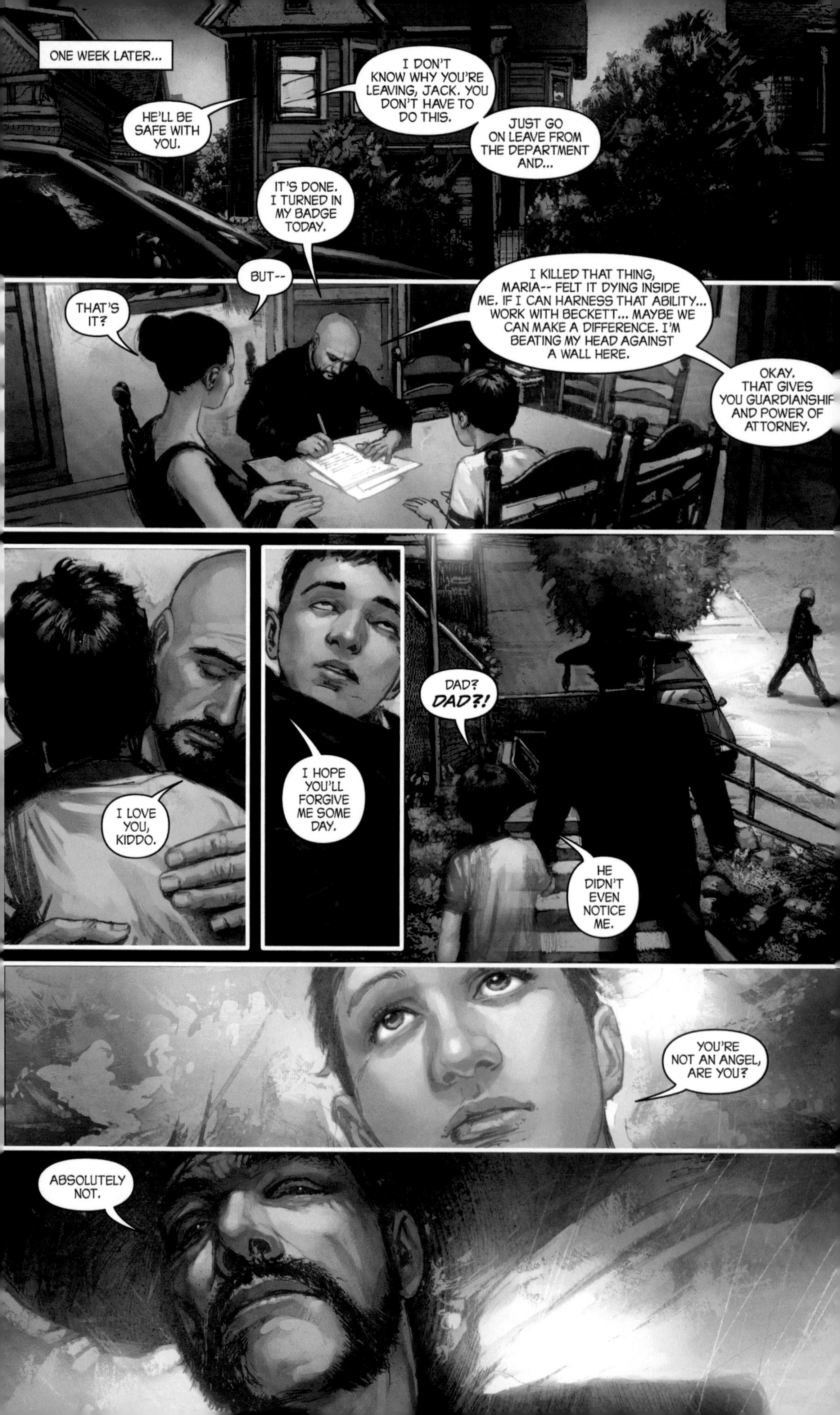
ONE WEEK LATER...
HE'LL BE SAFE WITH YOU.
I DON'T KNOW WHY YOU'RE LEAVING, JACK. YOU DON'T HAVE TO DO THIS.
JUST GO ON LEAVE FROM THE DEPARTMENT AND...
IT'S DONE. I TURNED IN MY BADGE TODAY.
BUT--
THAT'S IT?
I KILLED THAT THING, MARIA-- FELT IT DYING INSIDE ME. IF I CAN HARNESS THAT ABILITY... WORK WITH BECKETT... MAYBE WE CAN MAKE A DIFFERENCE. I'M BEATING MY HEAD AGAINST A WALL HERE.
OKAY. THAT GIVES YOU GUARDIANSHIP AND POWER OF ATTORNEY.
I LOVE YOU, KIDDO.
I HOPE YOU'LL FORGIVE ME SOME DAY.
DAD? DAD?!
HE DIDN'T EVEN NOTICE ME.
YOU'RE NOT AN ANGEL, ARE YOU?
ABSOLUTELY NOT.

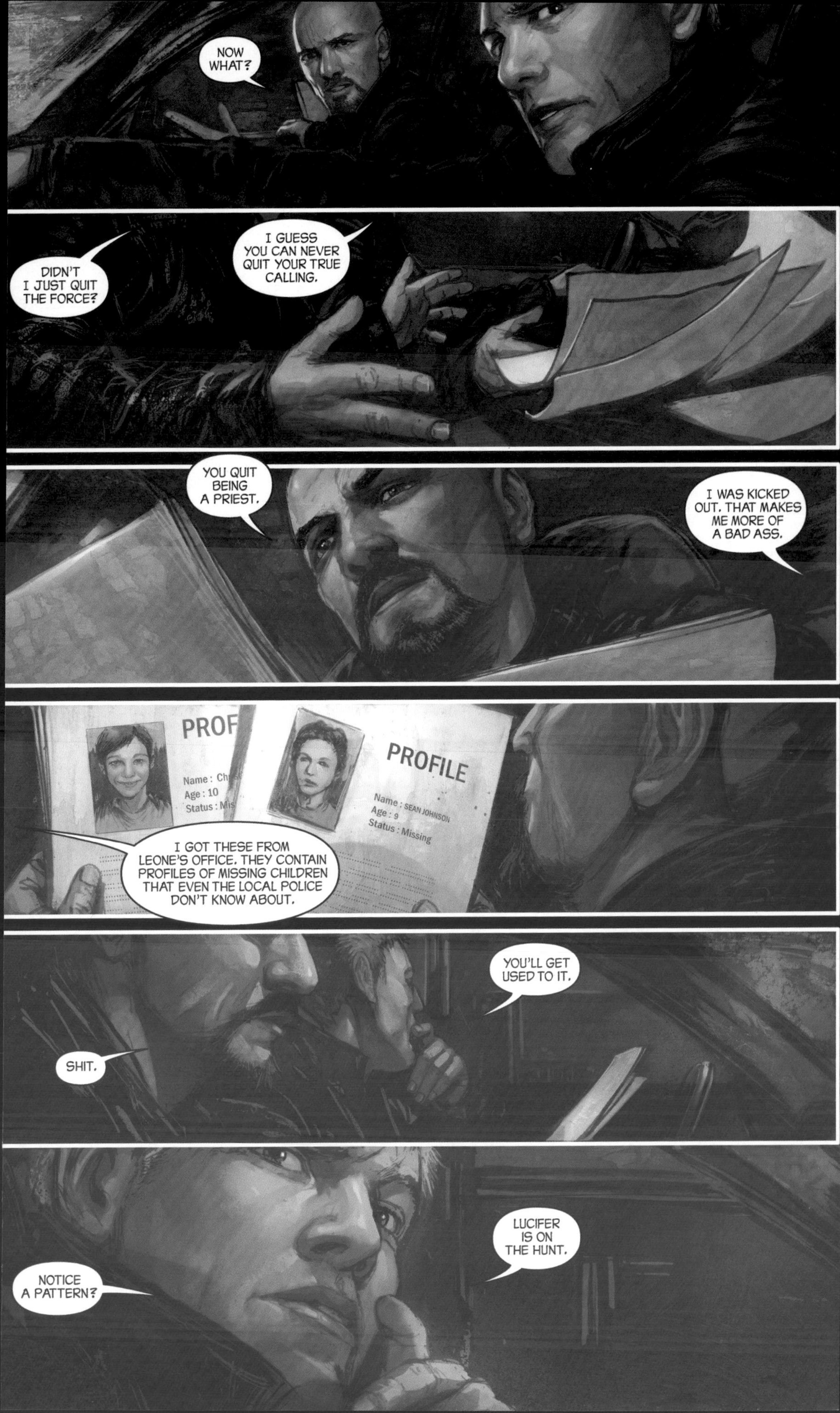
NOW WHAT?
DIDN'T I JUST QUIT THE FORCE?
I GUESS YOU CAN NEVER QUIT YOUR TRUE CALLING.
YOU QUIT BEING A PRIEST.
I WAS KICKED OUT. THAT MAKES ME MORE OF A BAD ASS.
PROFILE
Name : SEAN JOHNSON
Age : 9
Status : Missing
I GOT THESE FROM LEONE'S OFFICE. THEY CONTAIN PROFILES OF MISSING CHILDREN THAT EVEN THE LOCAL POLICE DON'T KNOW ABOUT.
SHIT.
YOU'LL GET USED TO IT.
NOTICE A PATTERN?
LUCIFER IS ON THE HUNT.

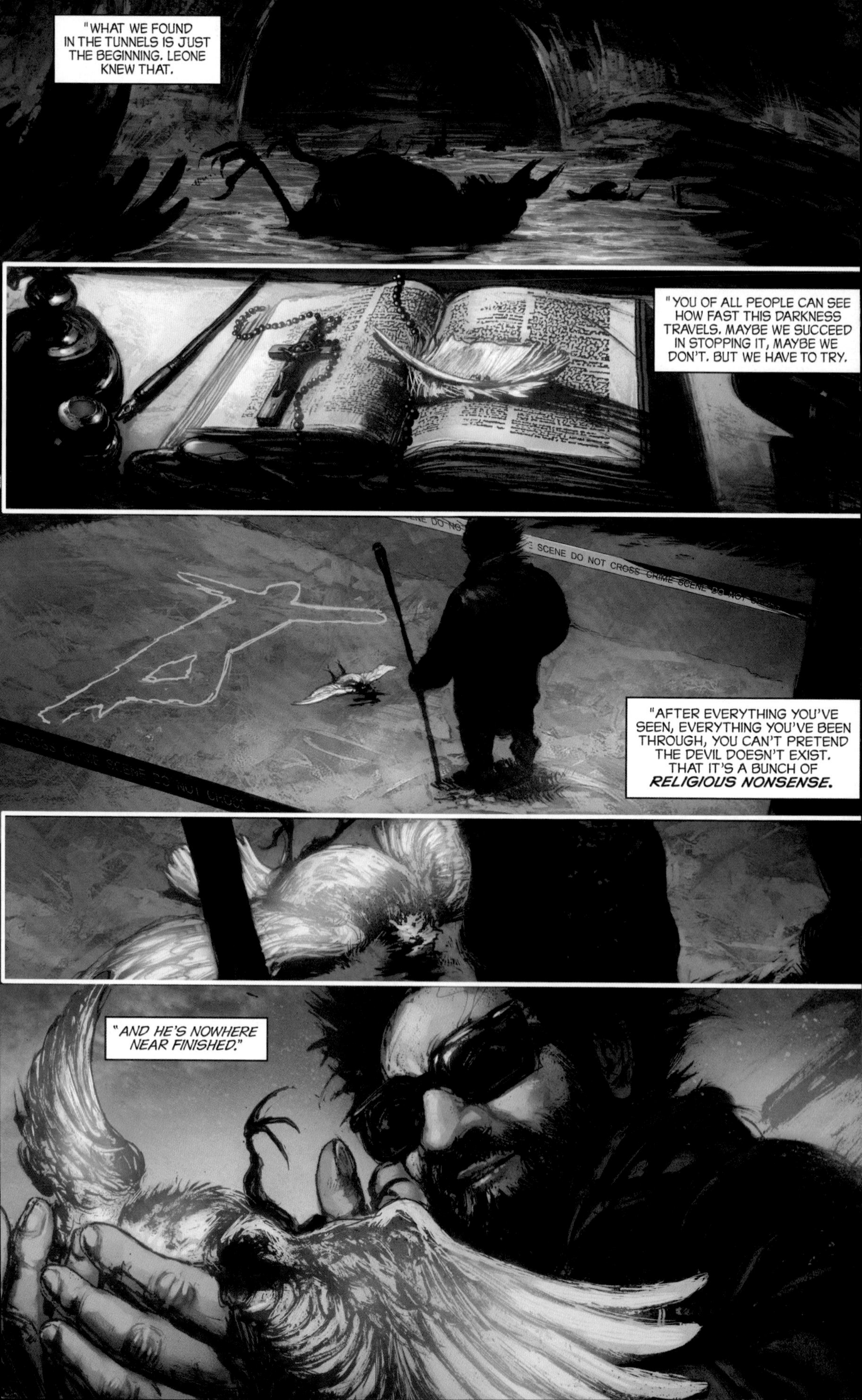
"WHAT WE FOUND IN THE TUNNELS IS JUST THE BEGINNING. LEONE KNEW THAT.
"YOU OF ALL PEOPLE CAN SEE HOW FAST THIS DARKNESS TRAVELS. MAYBE WE SUCCEED IN STOPPING IT, MAYBE WE DON'T. BUT WE HAVE TO TRY.
SCENE DO NOT CROSS CRIME SCENE
"AFTER EVERYTHING YOU'VE SEEN, EVERYTHING YOU'VE BEEN THROUGH, YOU CAN'T PRETEND THE DEVIL DOESN'T EXIST. THAT IT'S A BUNCH OF *RELIGIOUS NONSENSE*.
"*AND HE'S NOWHERE NEAR FINISHED.*"

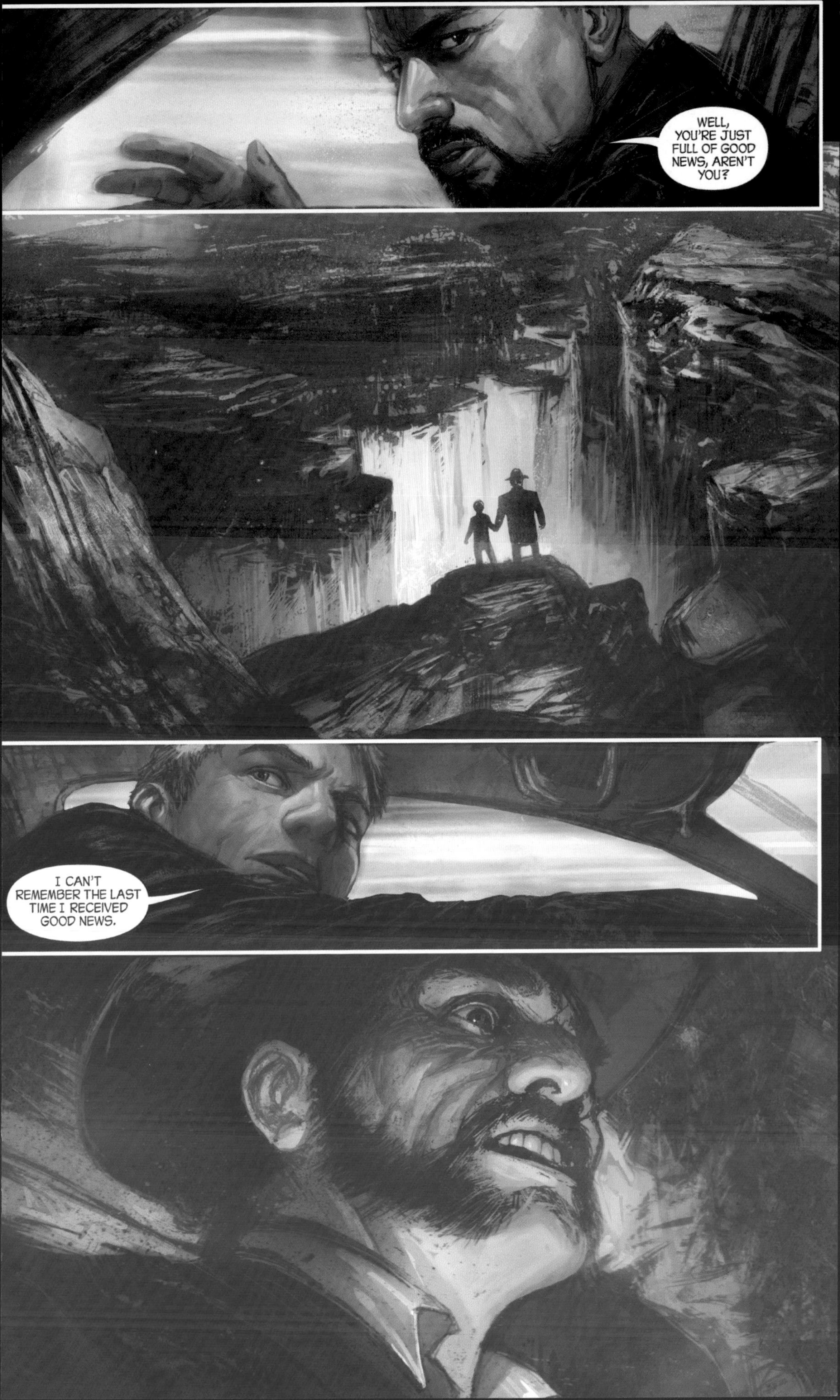
WELL, YOU'RE JUST FULL OF GOOD NEWS, AREN'T YOU?
I CAN'T REMEMBER THE LAST TIME I RECEIVED GOOD NEWS.

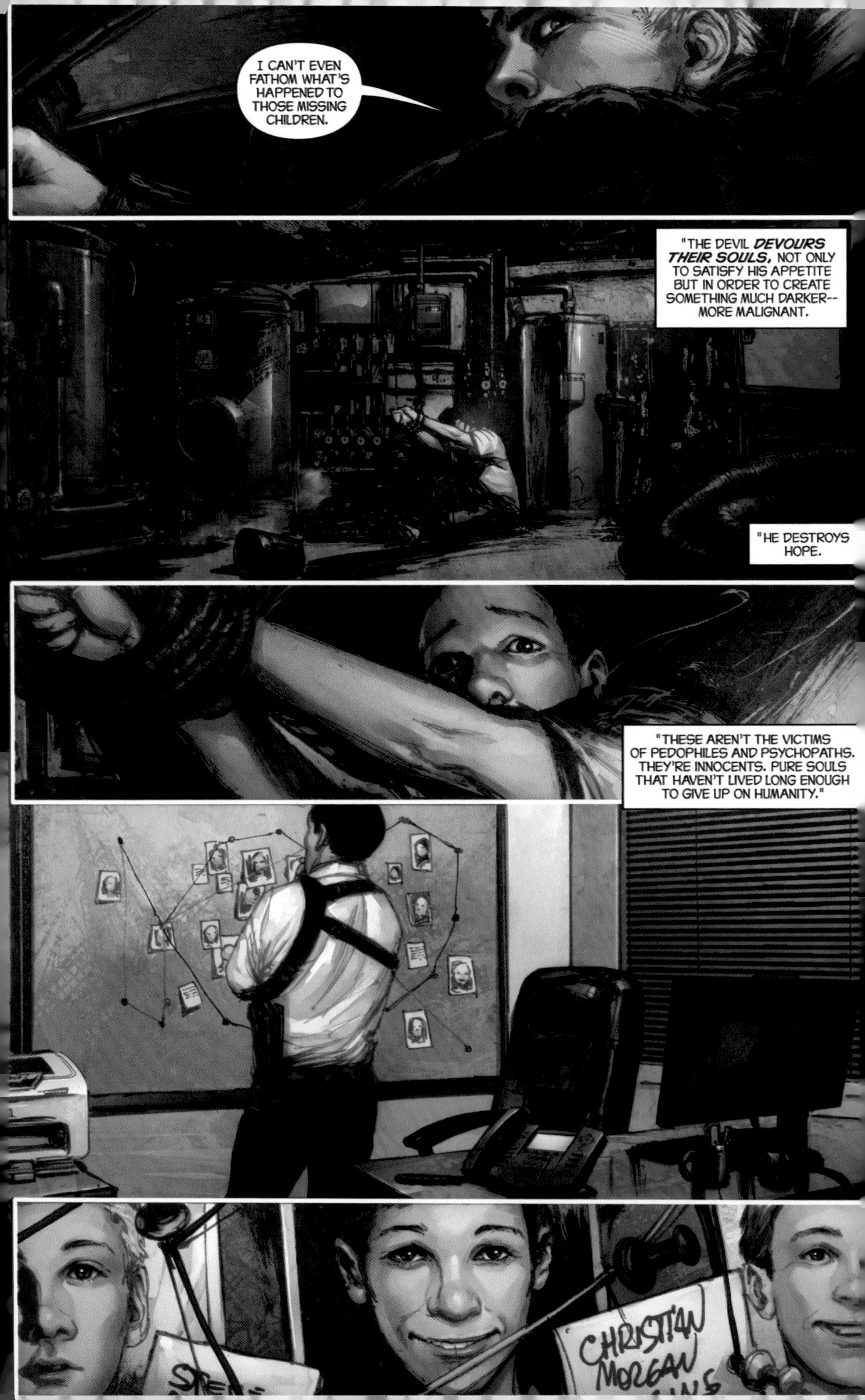
I CAN'T EVEN FATHOM WHAT'S HAPPENED TO THOSE MISSING CHILDREN.
"THE DEVIL *DEVOURS THEIR SOULS,* NOT ONLY TO SATISFY HIS APPETITE BUT IN ORDER TO CREATE SOMETHING MUCH DARKER-- MORE MALIGNANT.
"HE DESTROYS HOPE.
"THESE AREN'T THE VICTIMS OF PEDOPHILES AND PSYCHOPATHS. THEY'RE INNOCENTS. PURE SOULS THAT HAVEN'T LIVED LONG ENOUGH TO GIVE UP ON HUMANITY."
CHRISTIAN MORGAN

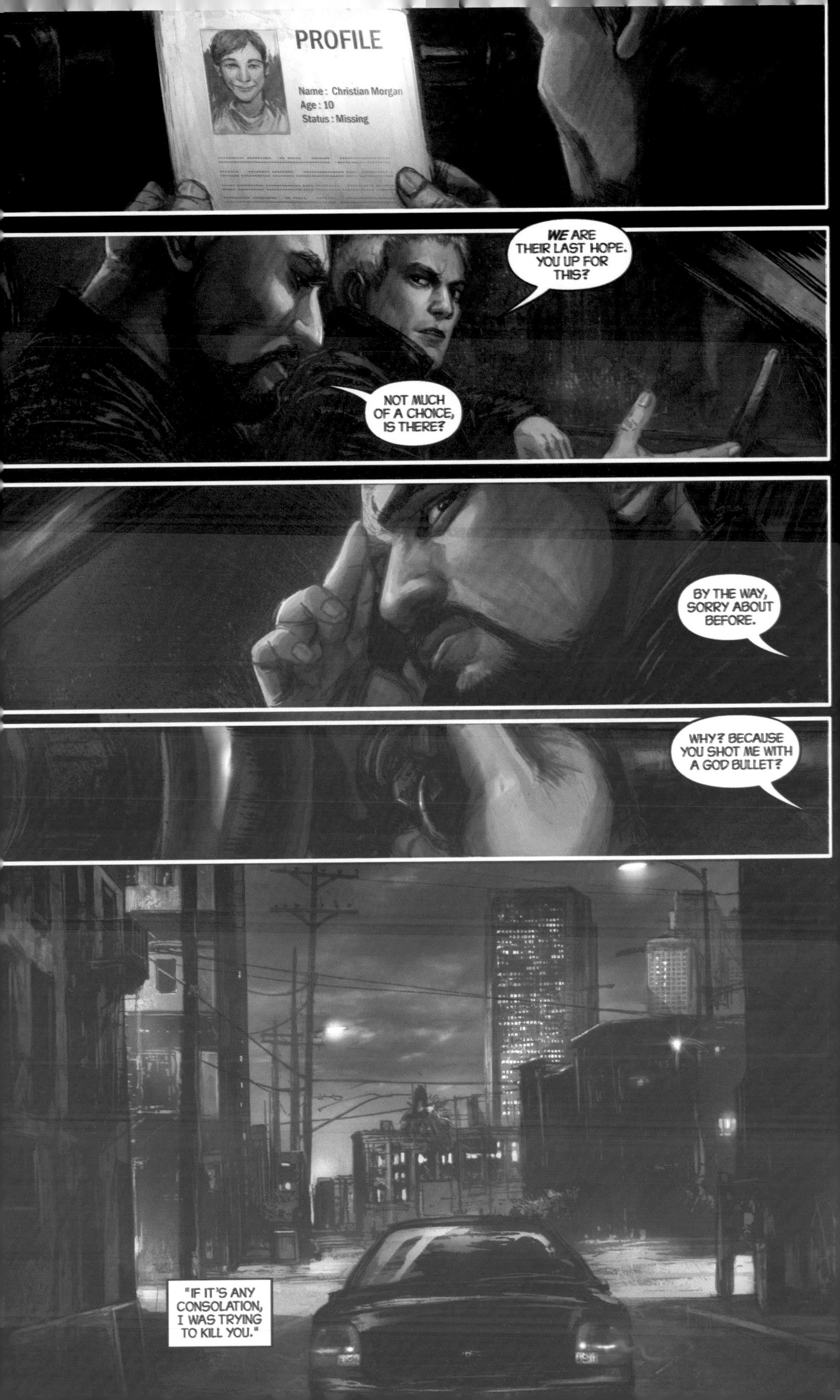
PROFILE
Name : Christian Morgan
Age : 10
Status : Missing
WE ARE THEIR LAST HOPE. YOU UP FOR THIS?
NOT MUCH OF A CHOICE, IS THERE?
BY THE WAY, SORRY ABOUT BEFORE.
WHY? BECAUSE YOU SHOT ME WITH A GOD BULLET?
"IF IT'S ANY CONSOLATION, I WAS TRYING TO KILL YOU."

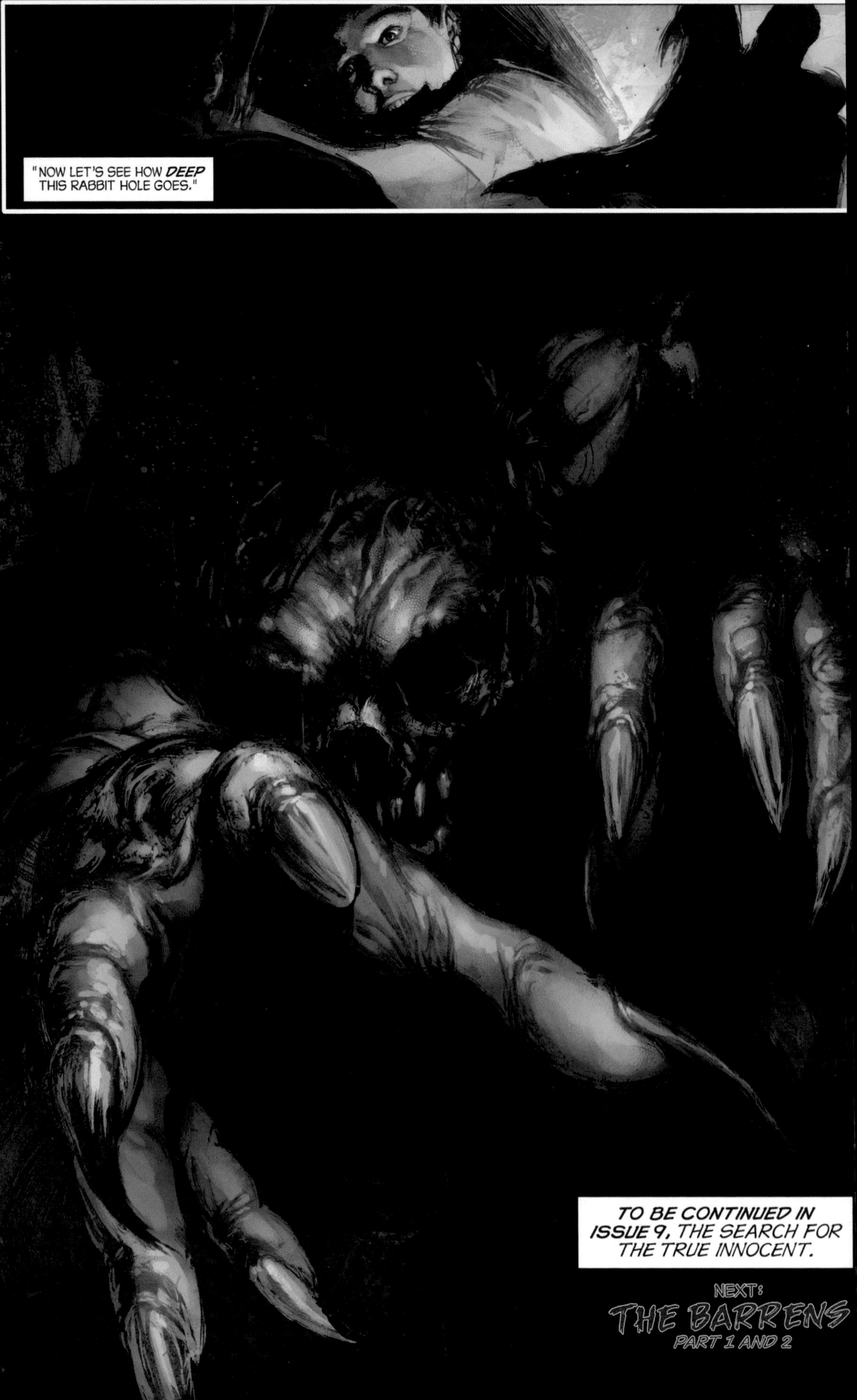
"NOW LET'S SEE HOW *DEEP* THIS RABBIT HOLE GOES."
TO BE CONTINUED IN ISSUE 9, THE SEARCH FOR THE TRUE INNOCENT.
NEXT: THE BARRENS PART 1 AND 2

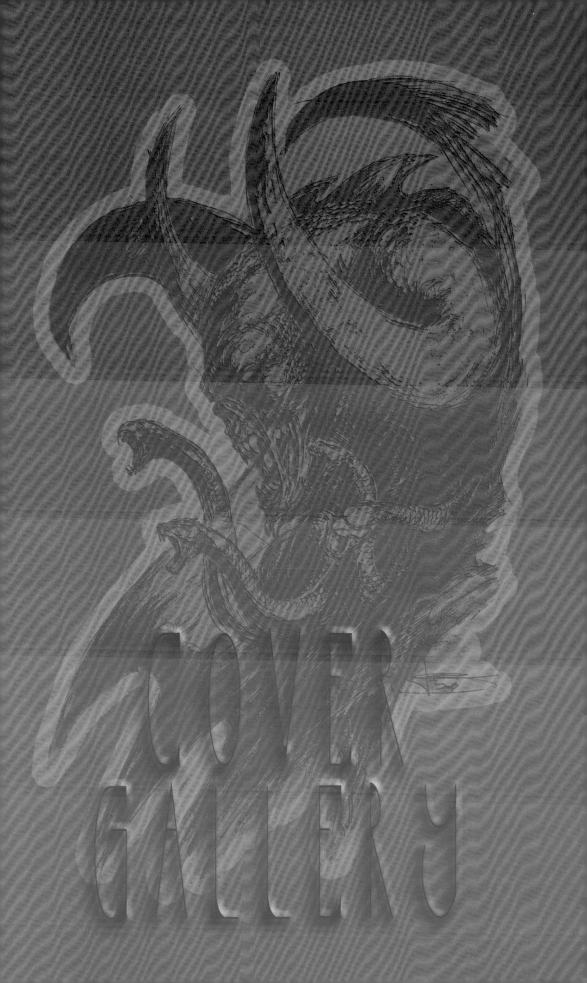

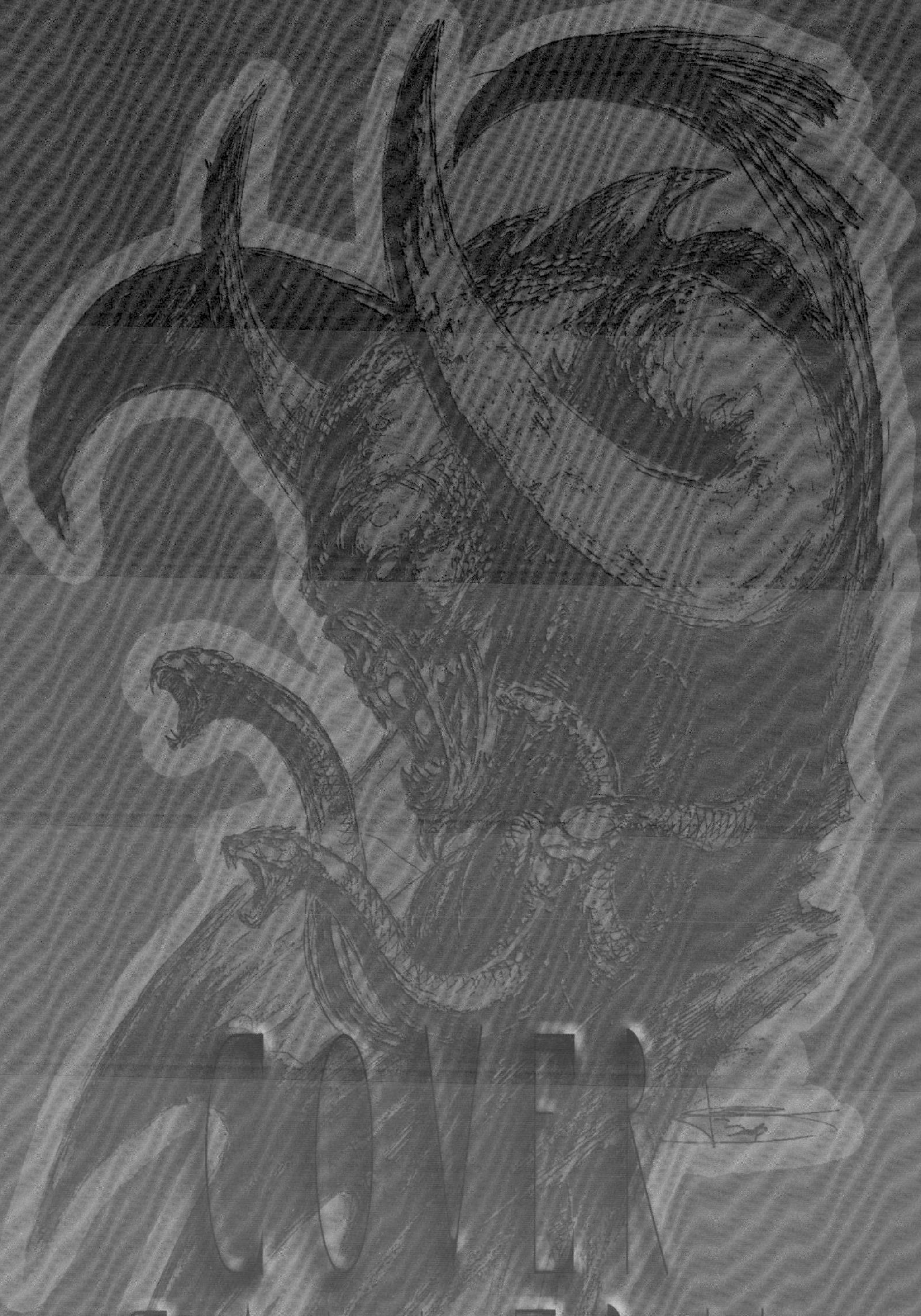
COVER
GALLERY

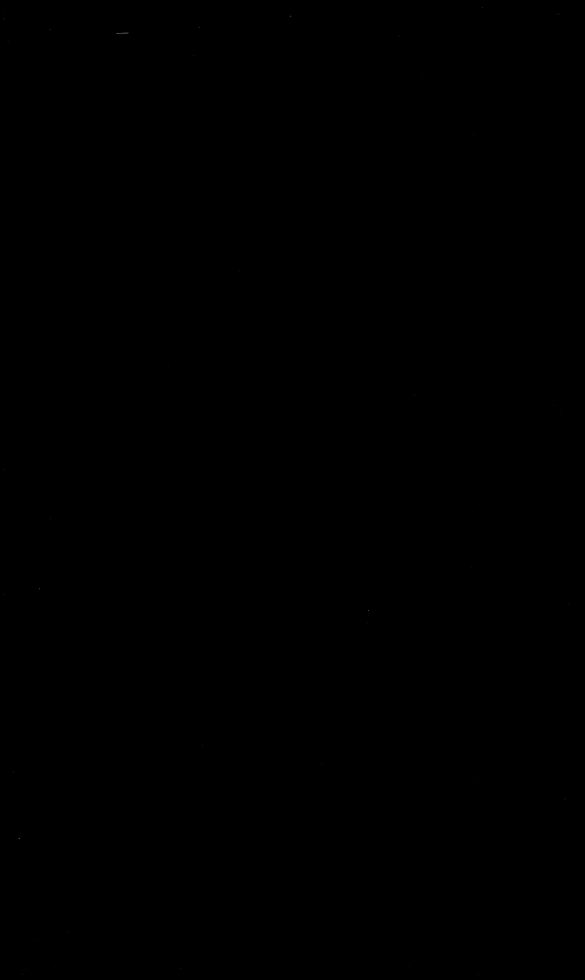

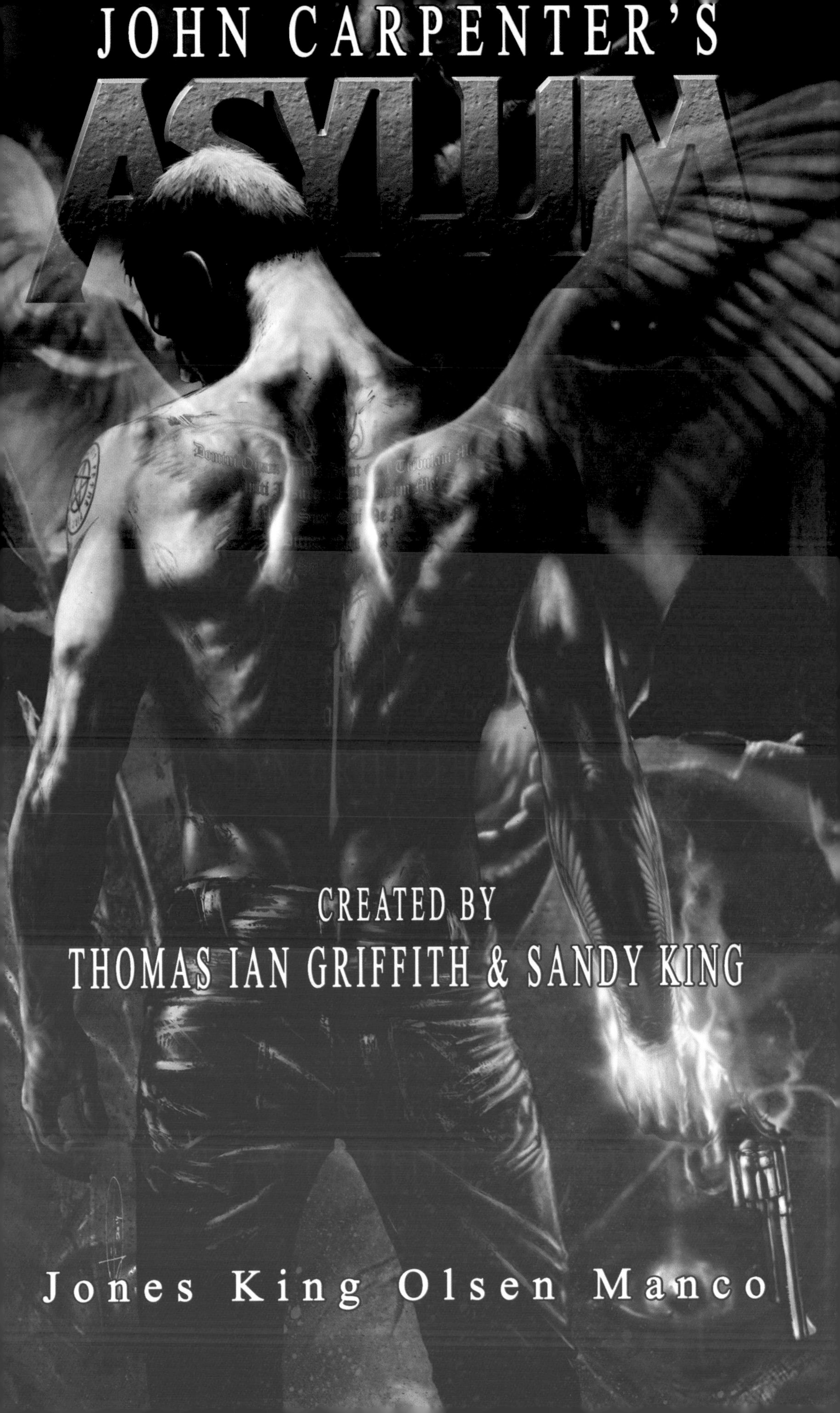
JOHN CARPENTER'S
ASYLUM
CREATED BY
THOMAS IAN GRIFFITH & SANDY KING
Jones King Olsen Manco

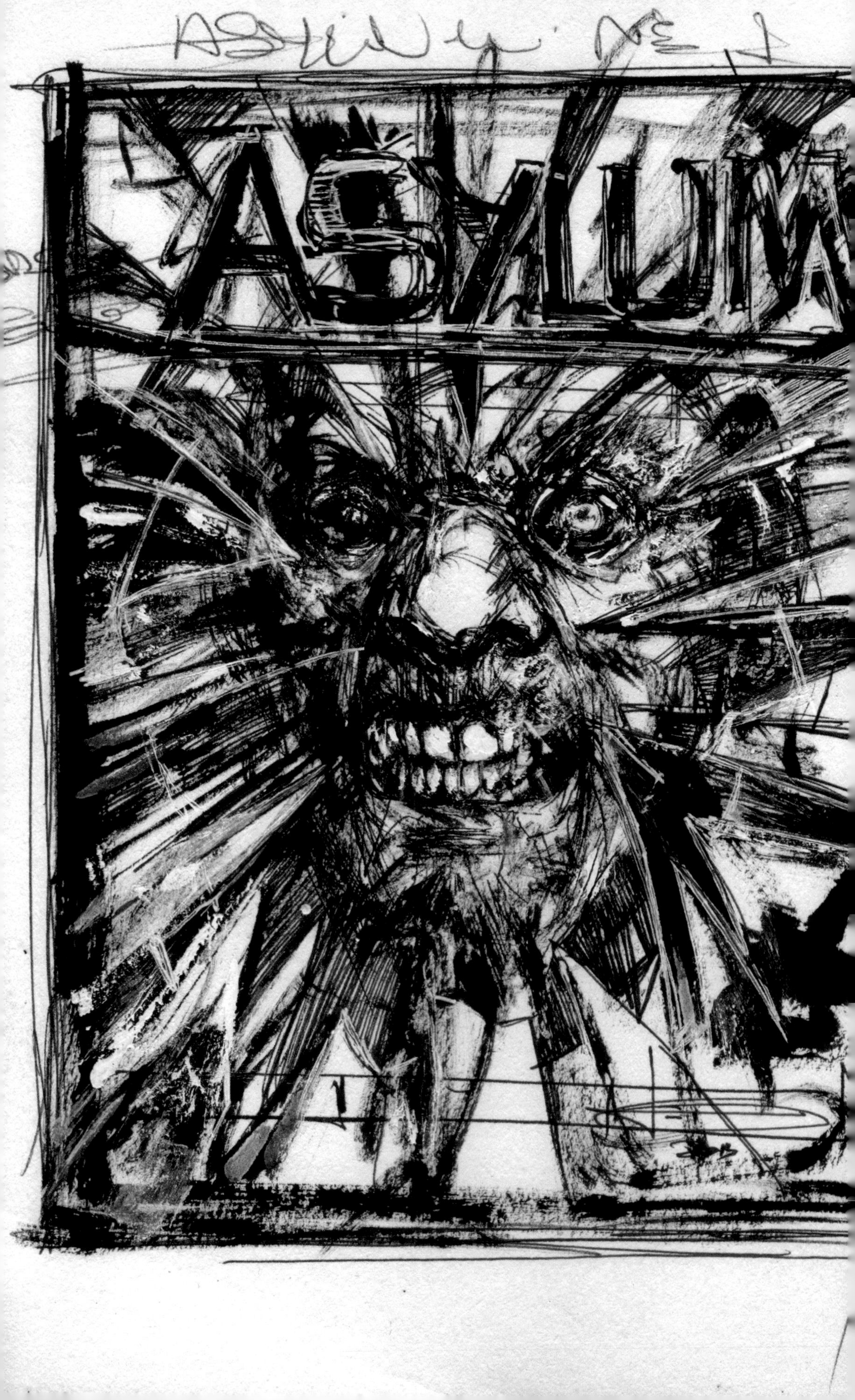

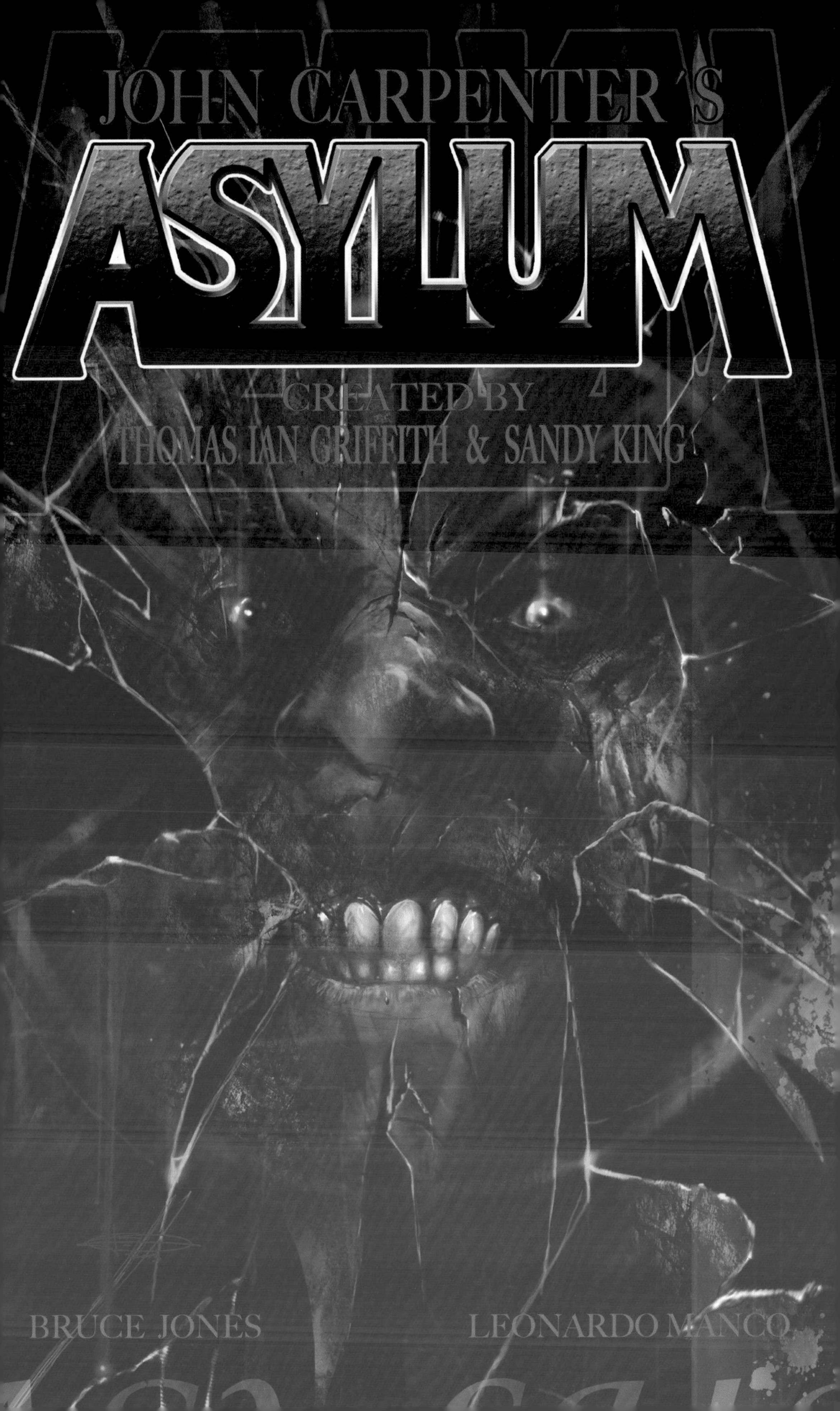
JOHN CARPENTER'S
ASYLUM
CREATED BY
THOMAS IAN GRIFFITH & SANDY KING
BRUCE JONES
LEONARDO MANCO

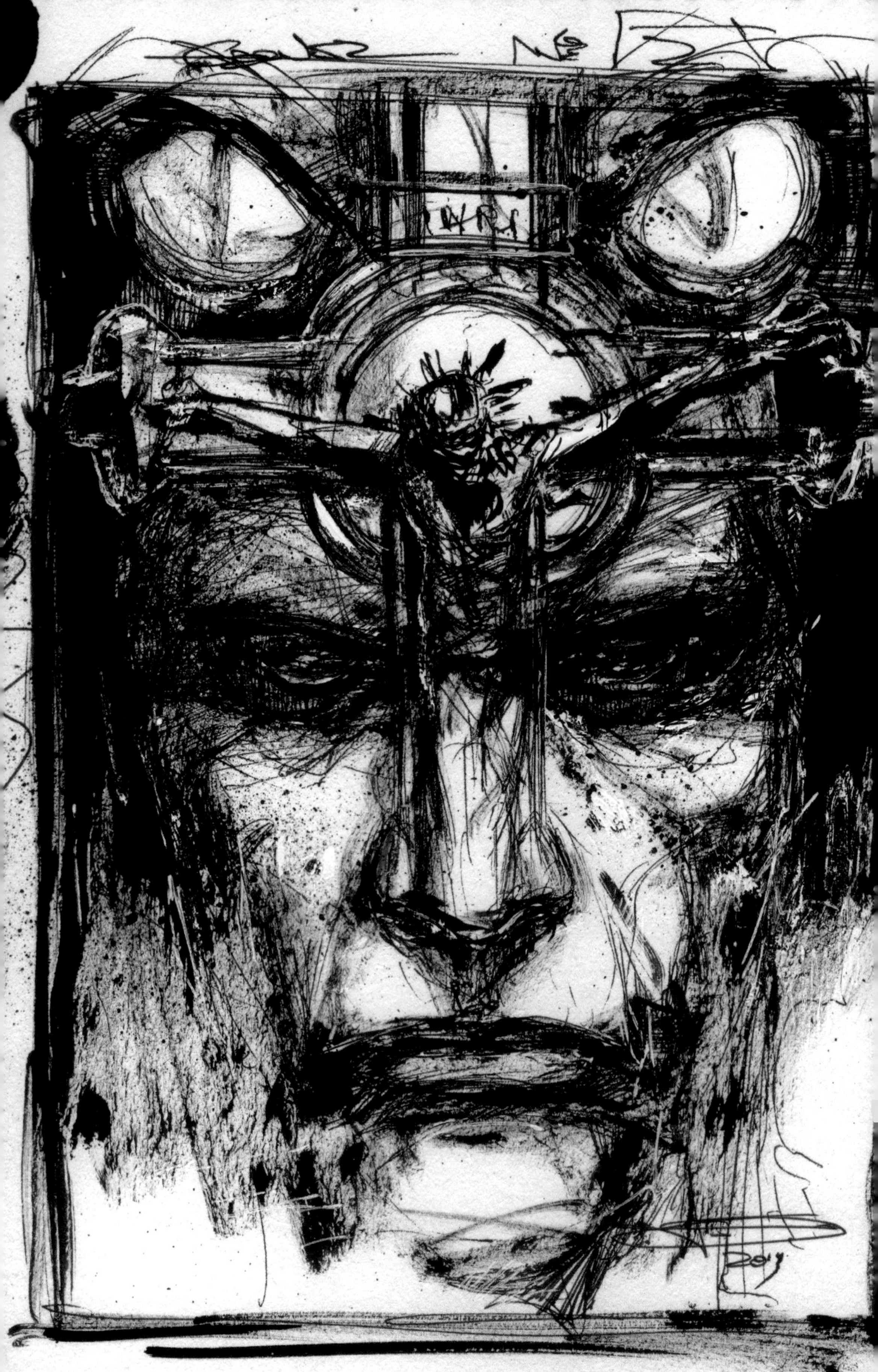

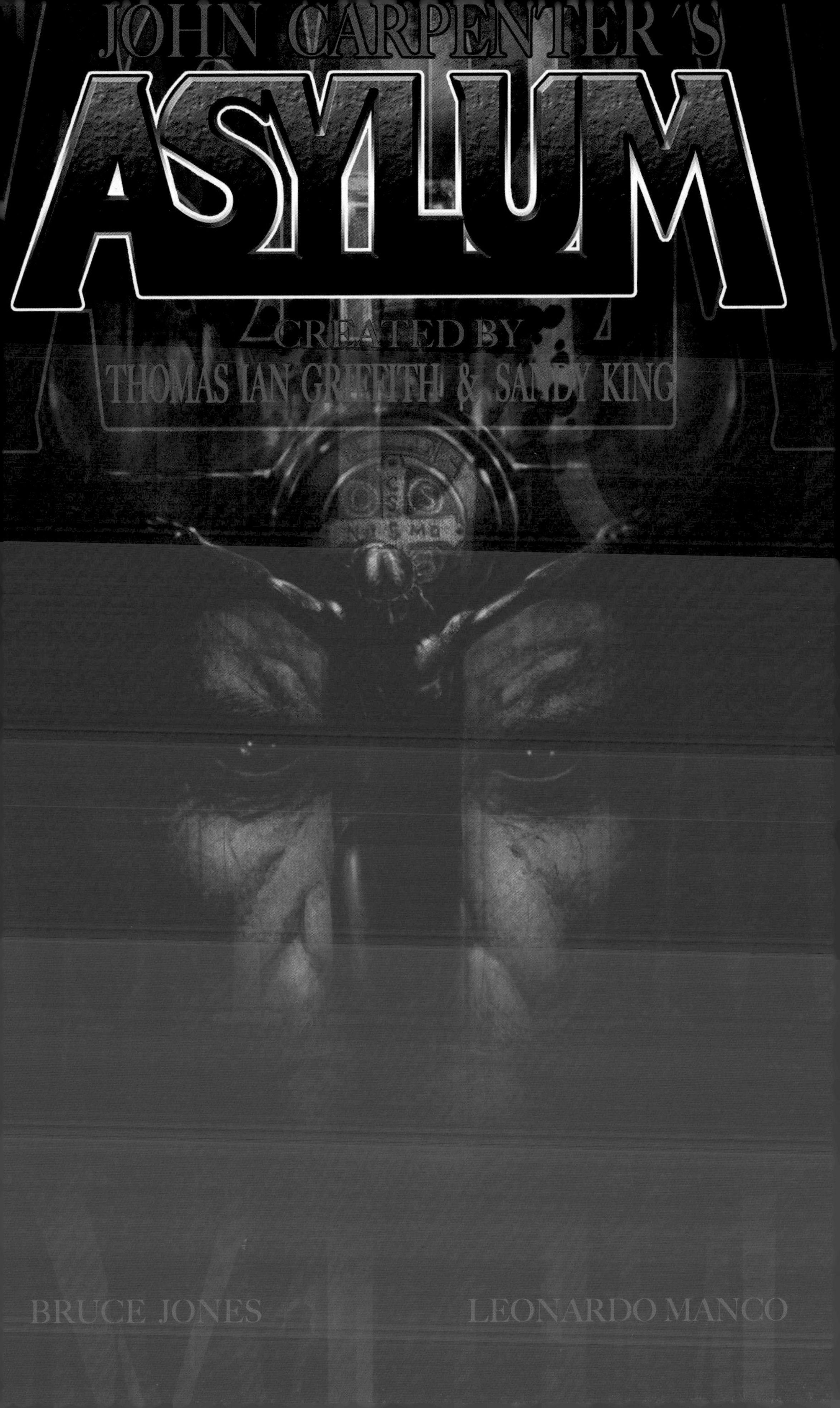
JOHN CARPENTER'S
ASYLUM
CREATED BY
THOMAS IAN GRIFFITH & SANDY KING
BRUCE JONES
LEONARDO MANCO

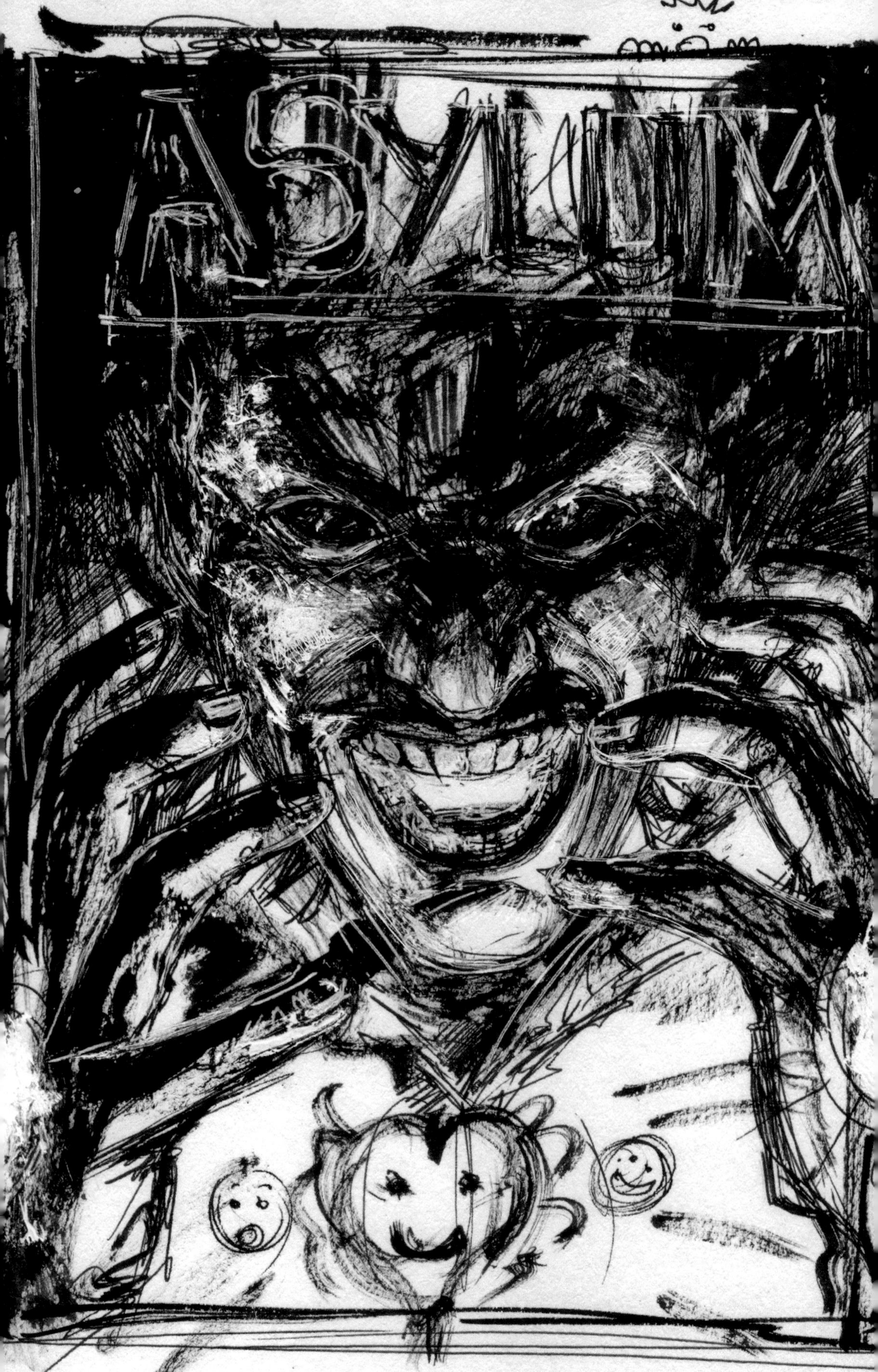
ASYLUM

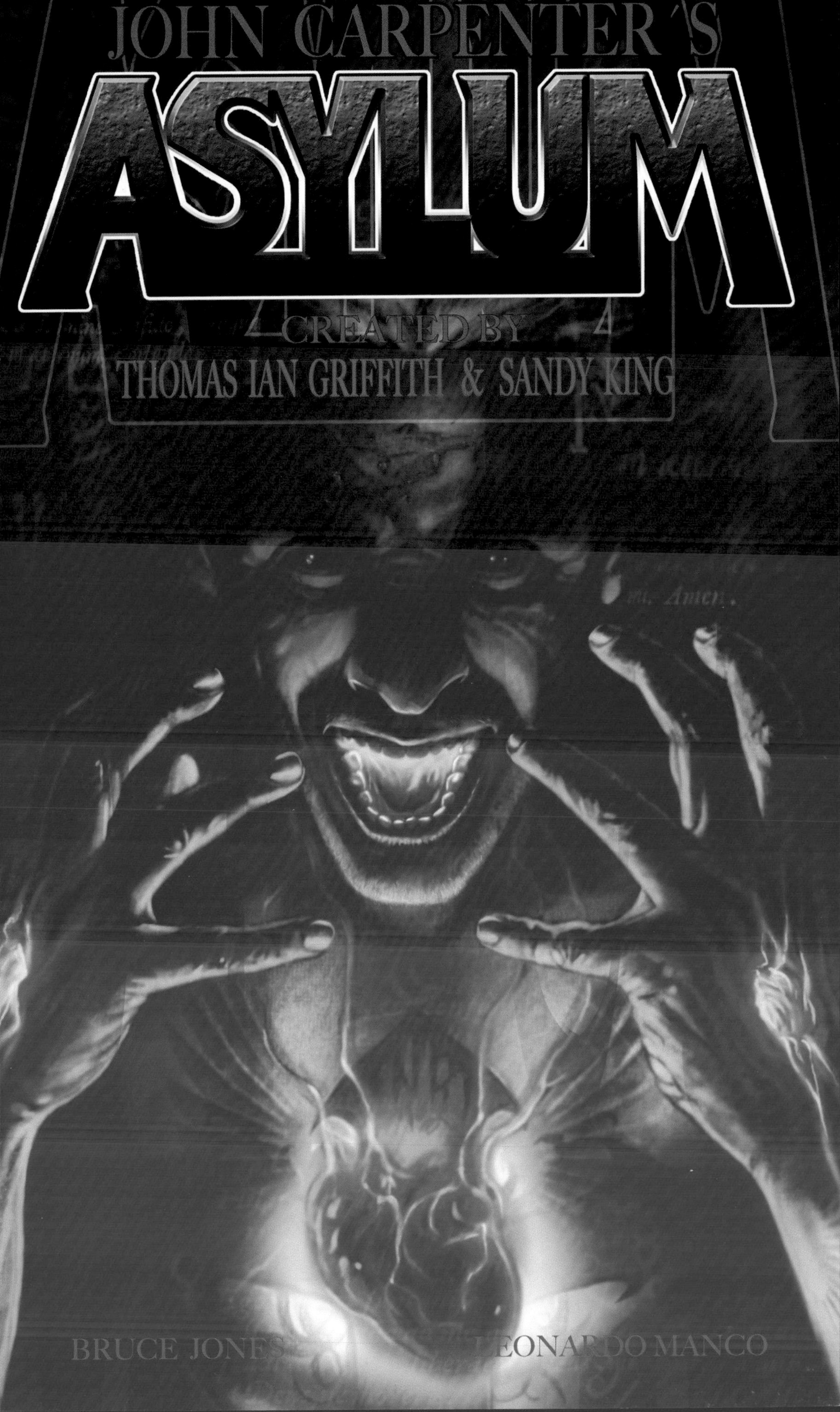
JOHN CARPENTER´S
ASYLUM
CREATED BY
THOMAS IAN GRIFFITH & SANDY KING
BRUCE JONES
LEONARDO MANCO

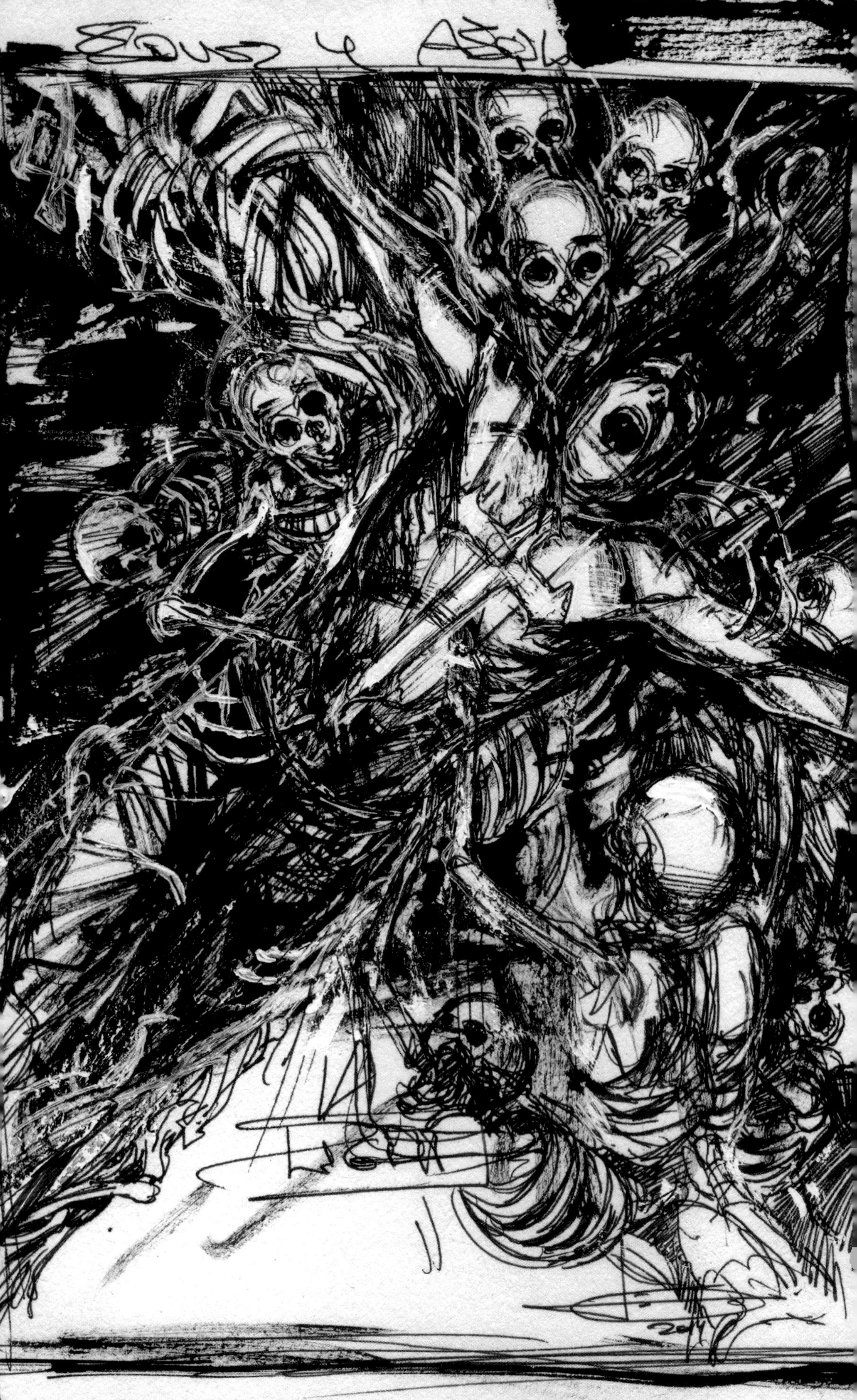

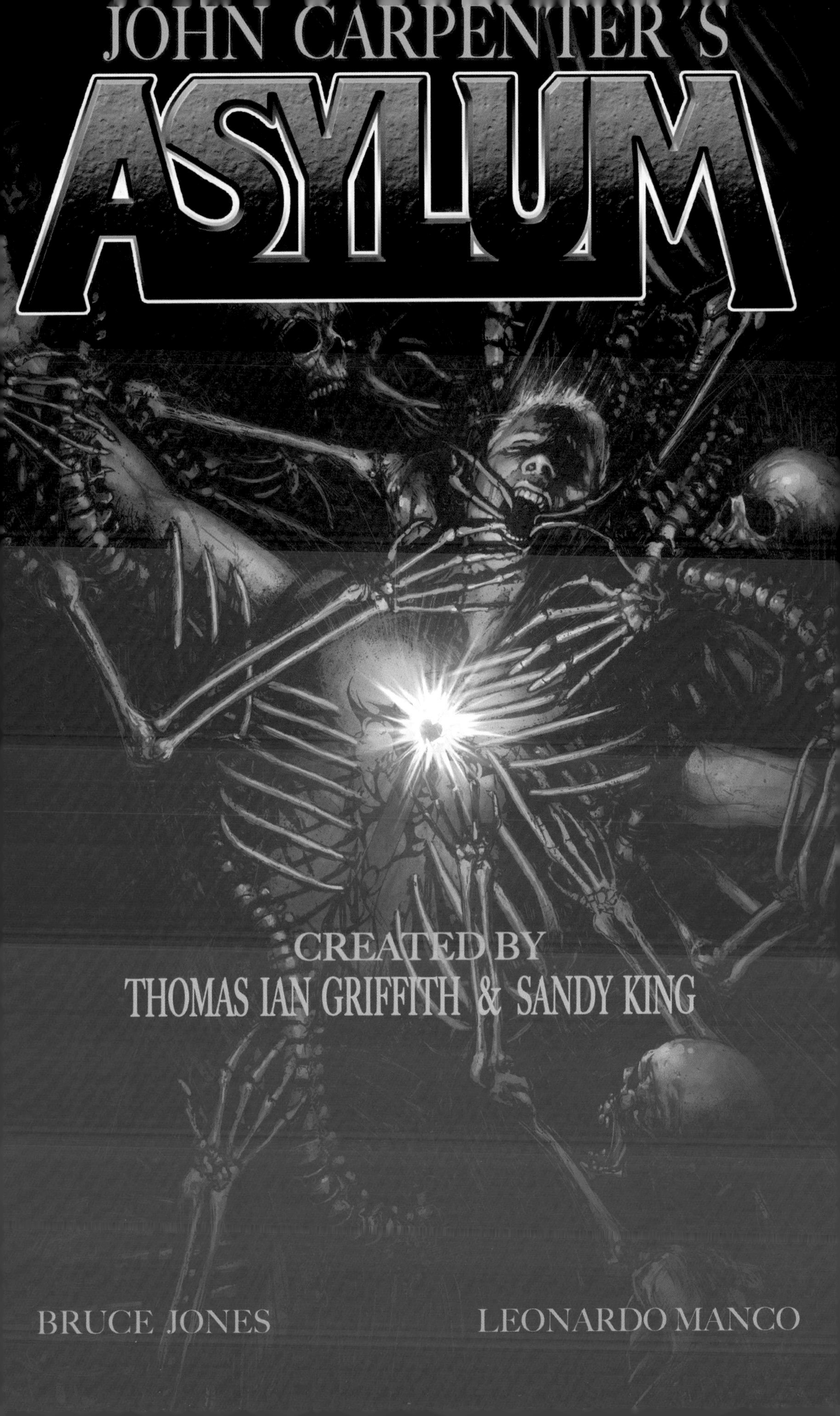
JOHN CARPENTER'S
ASYLUM
CREATED BY
THOMAS IAN GRIFFITH & SANDY KING
BRUCE JONES
LEONARDO MANCO

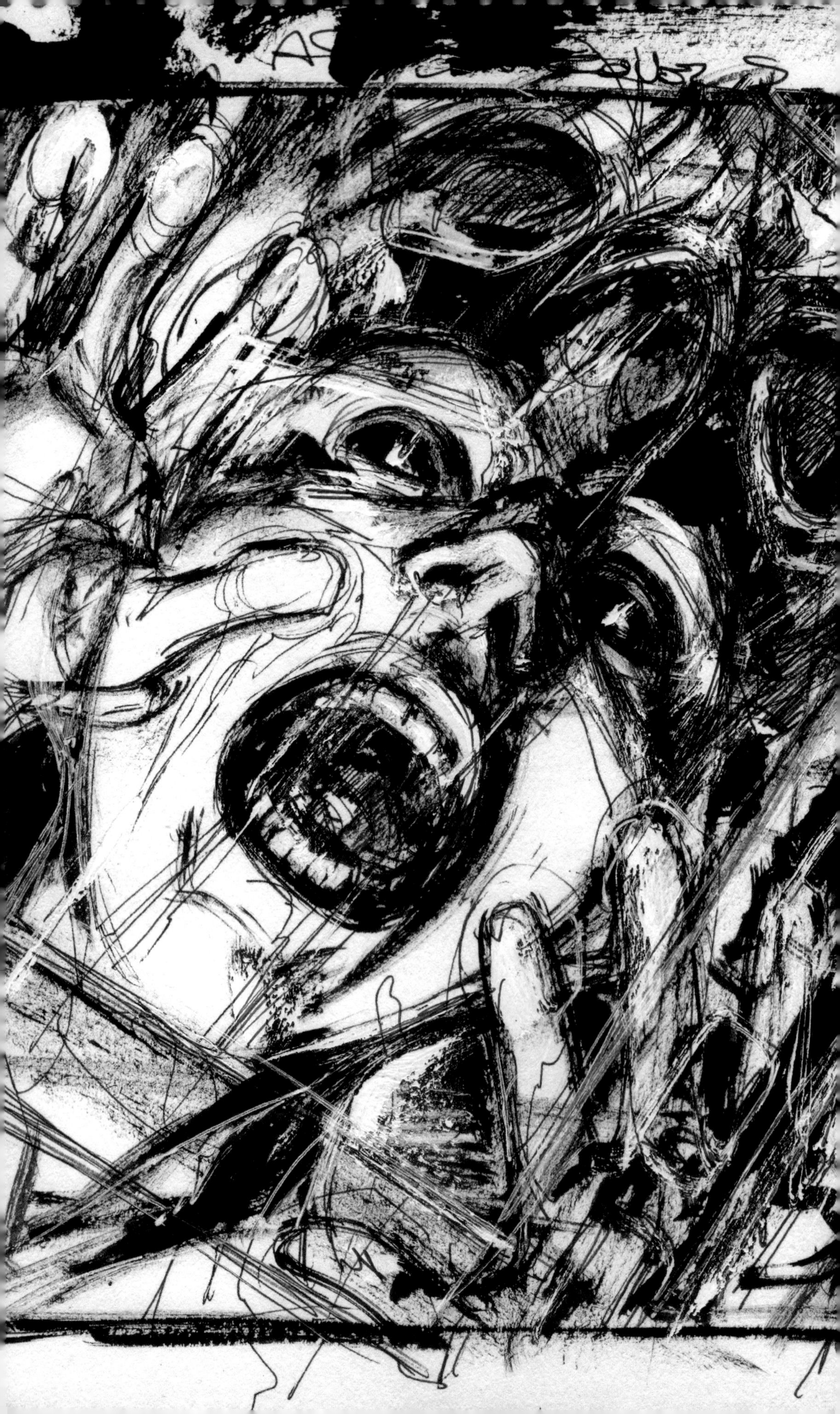

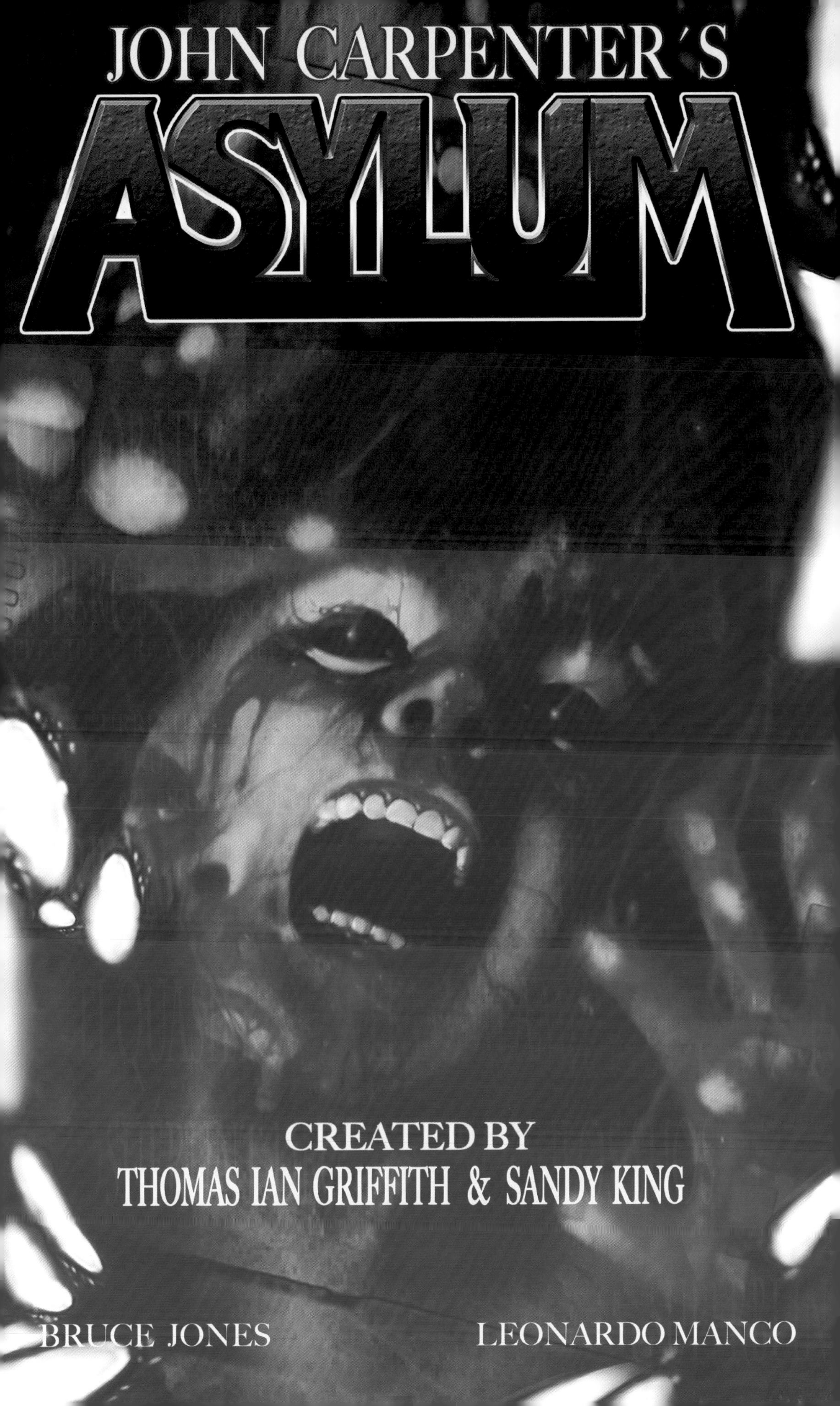
JOHN CARPENTER'S
ASYLUM
CREATED BY
THOMAS IAN GRIFFITH & SANDY KING
BRUCE JONES
LEONARDO MANCO

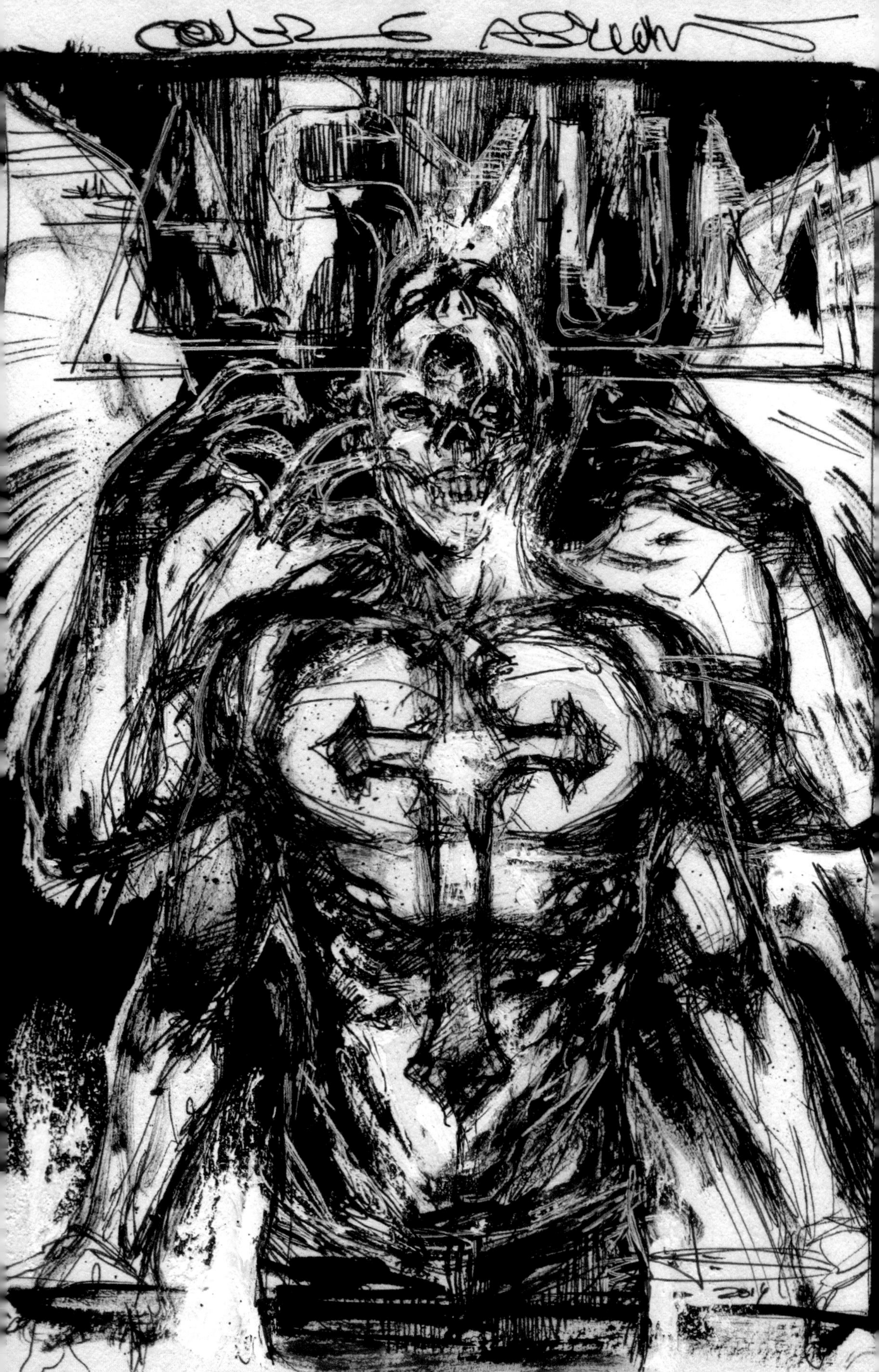

JOHN CARPENTER'S ASYLUM

CREATED BY
...MAS IAN GRIFFITH & SANDY KING

...OLSEN & KING   LEONARDO MAN...

SKETCHBOOK

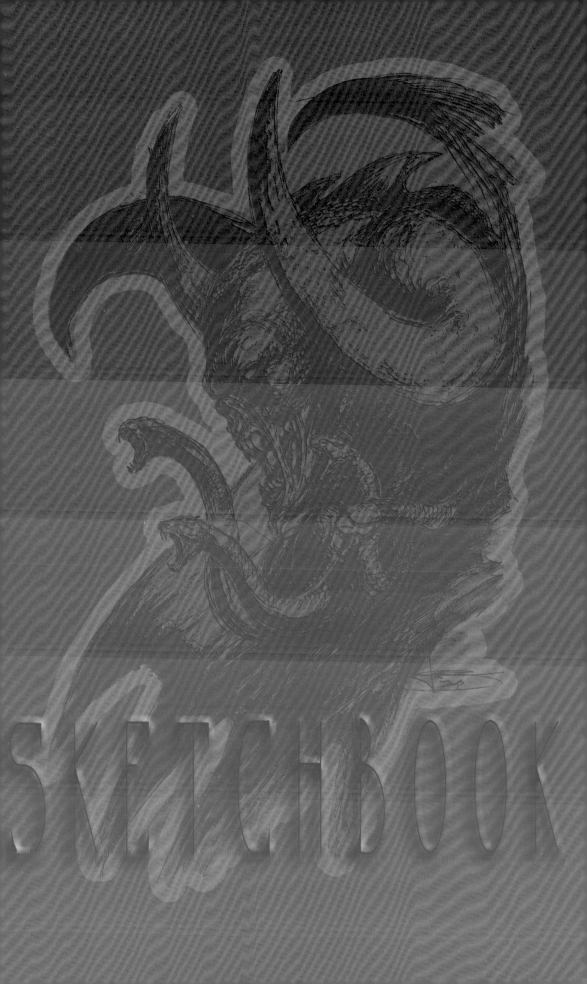

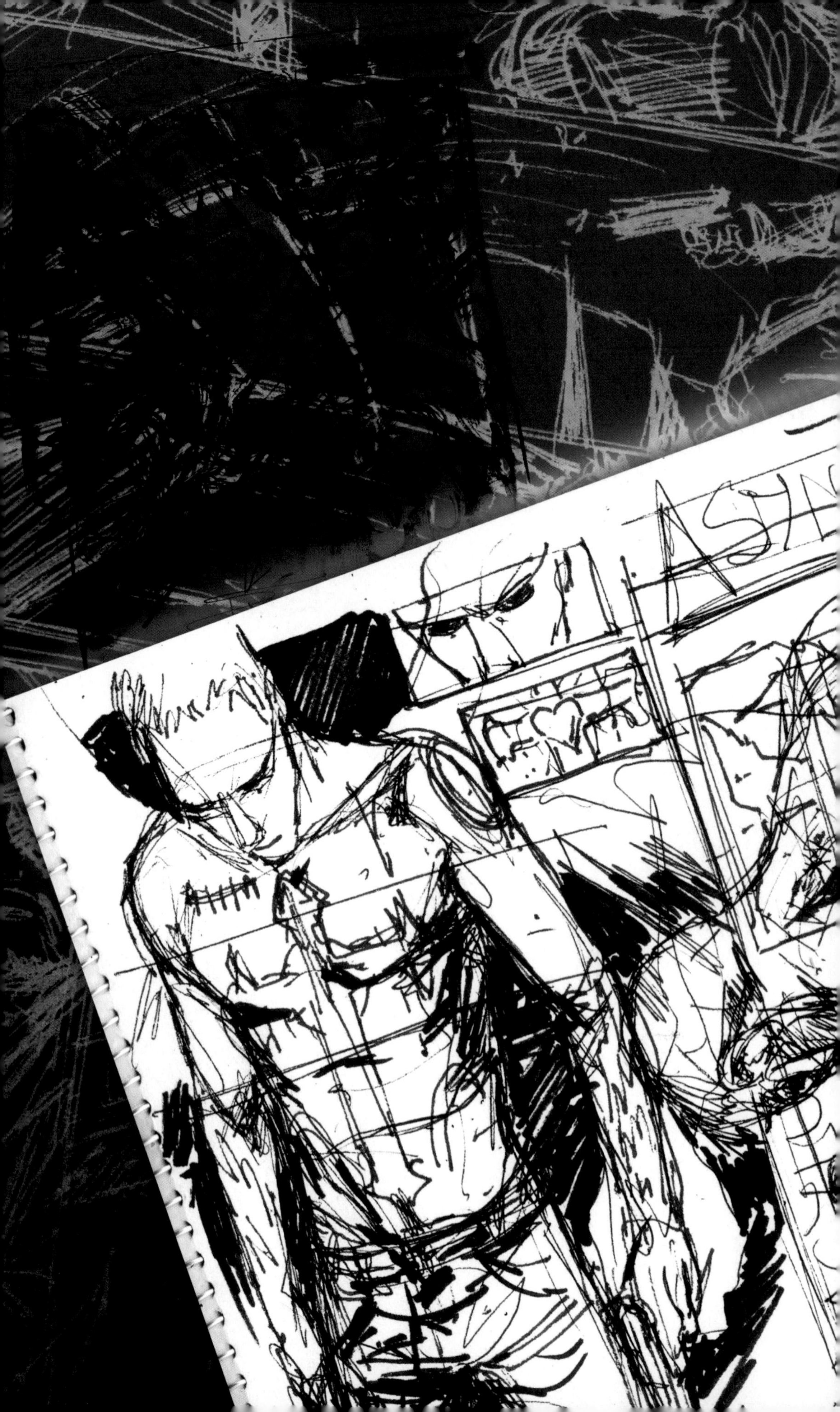

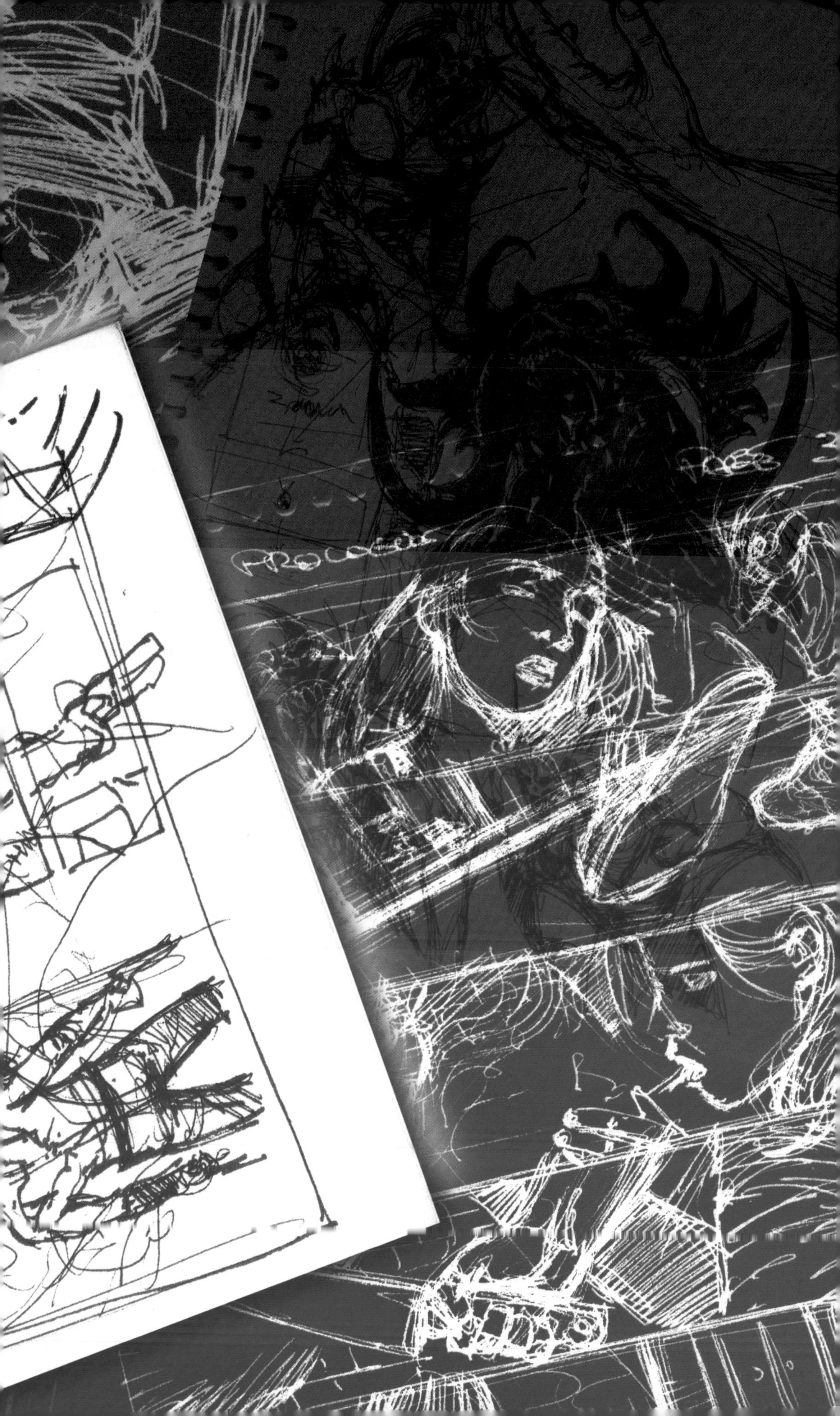

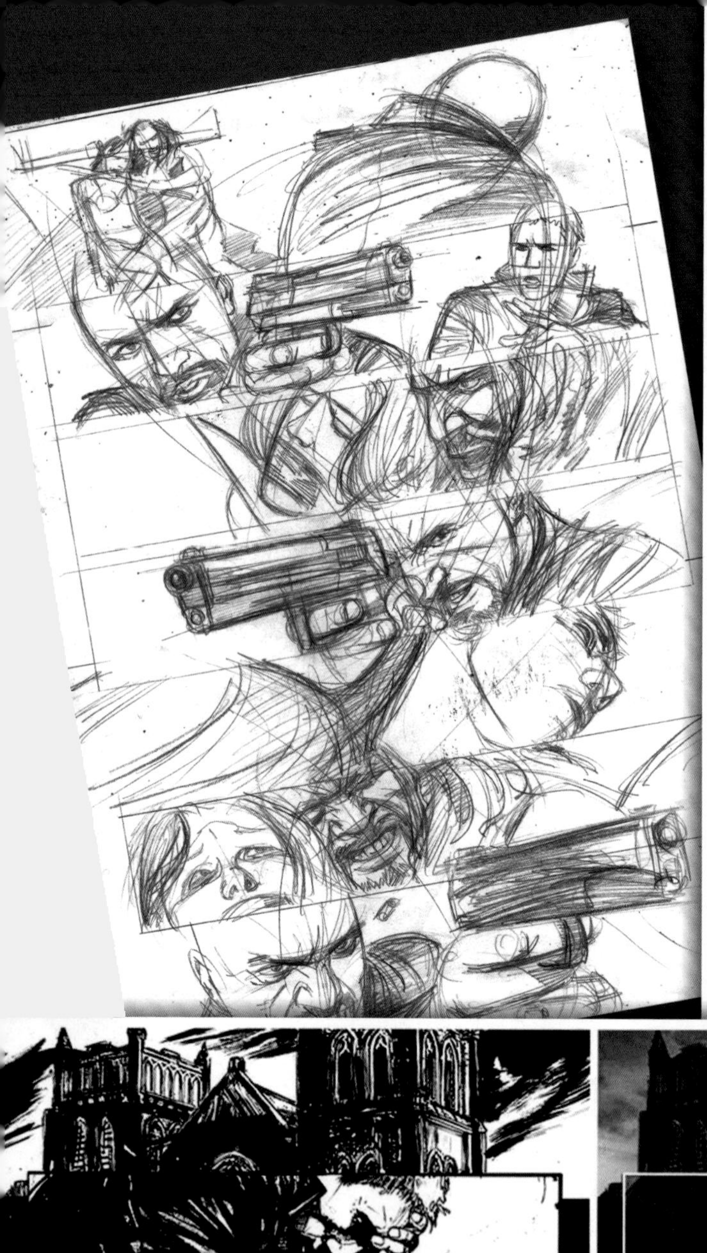

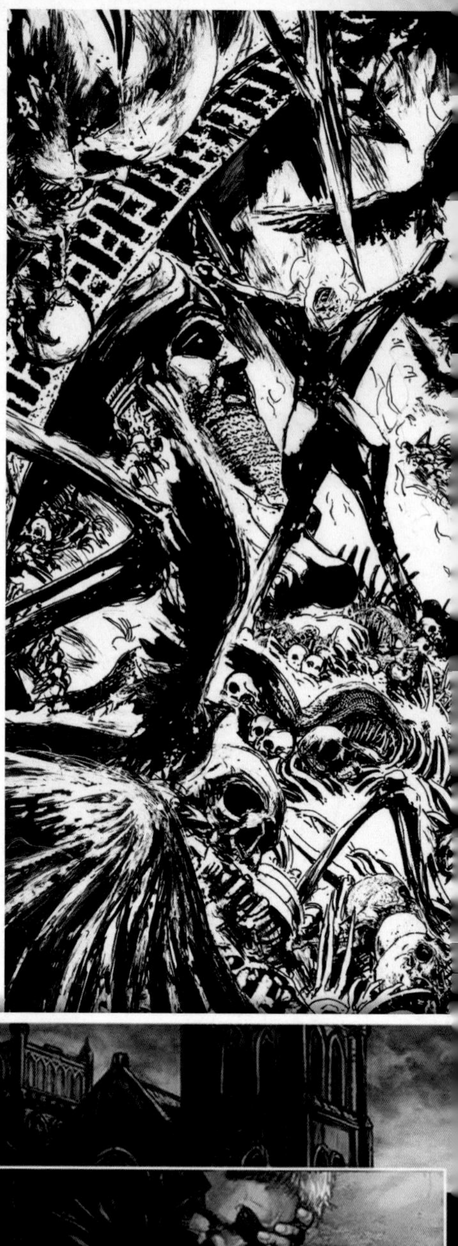

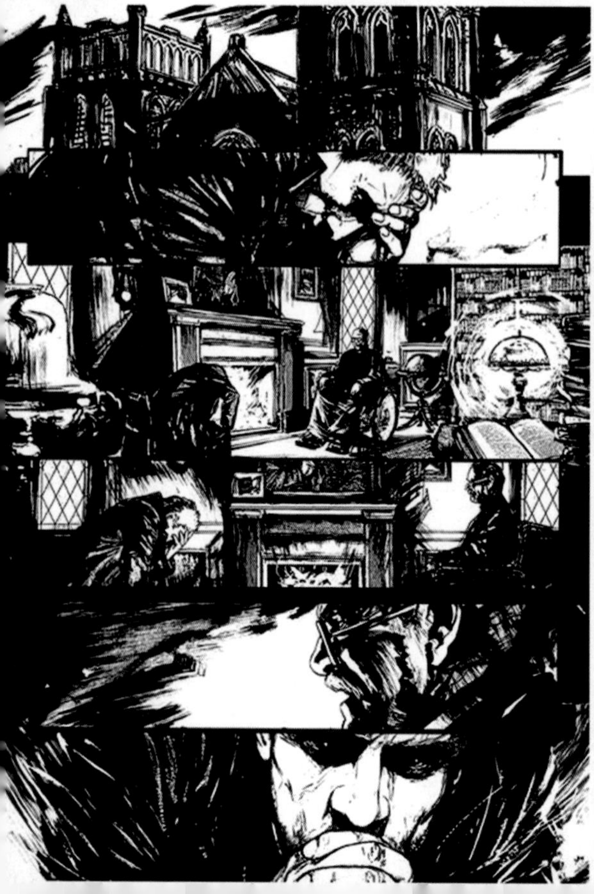

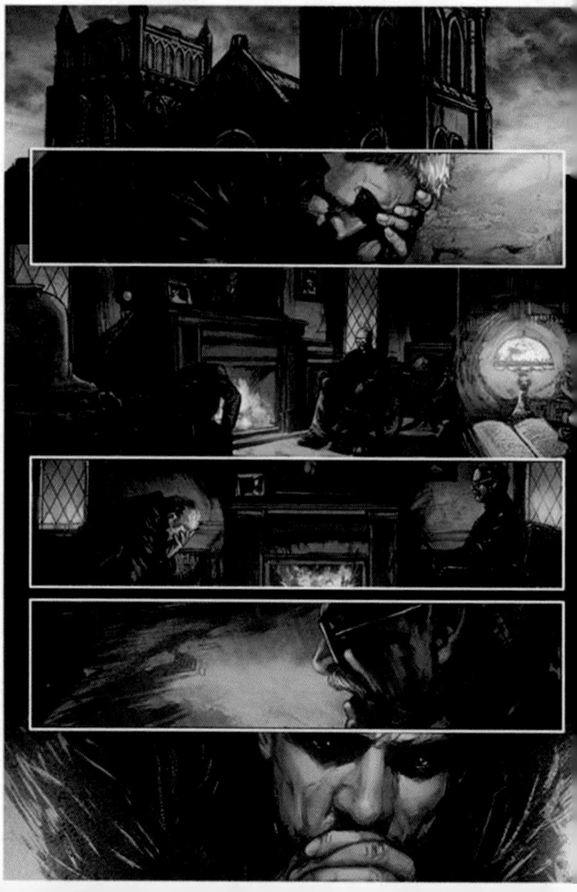

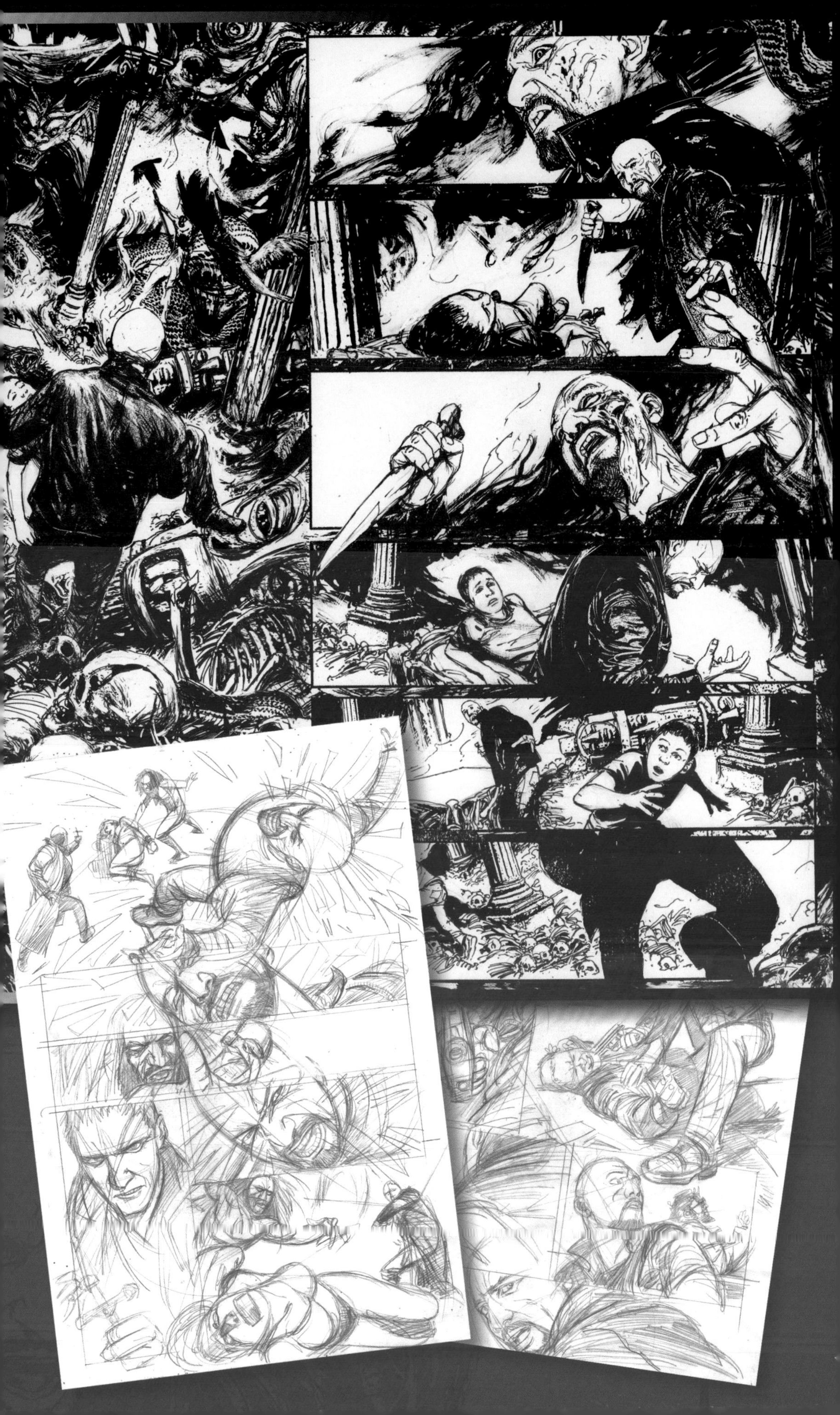

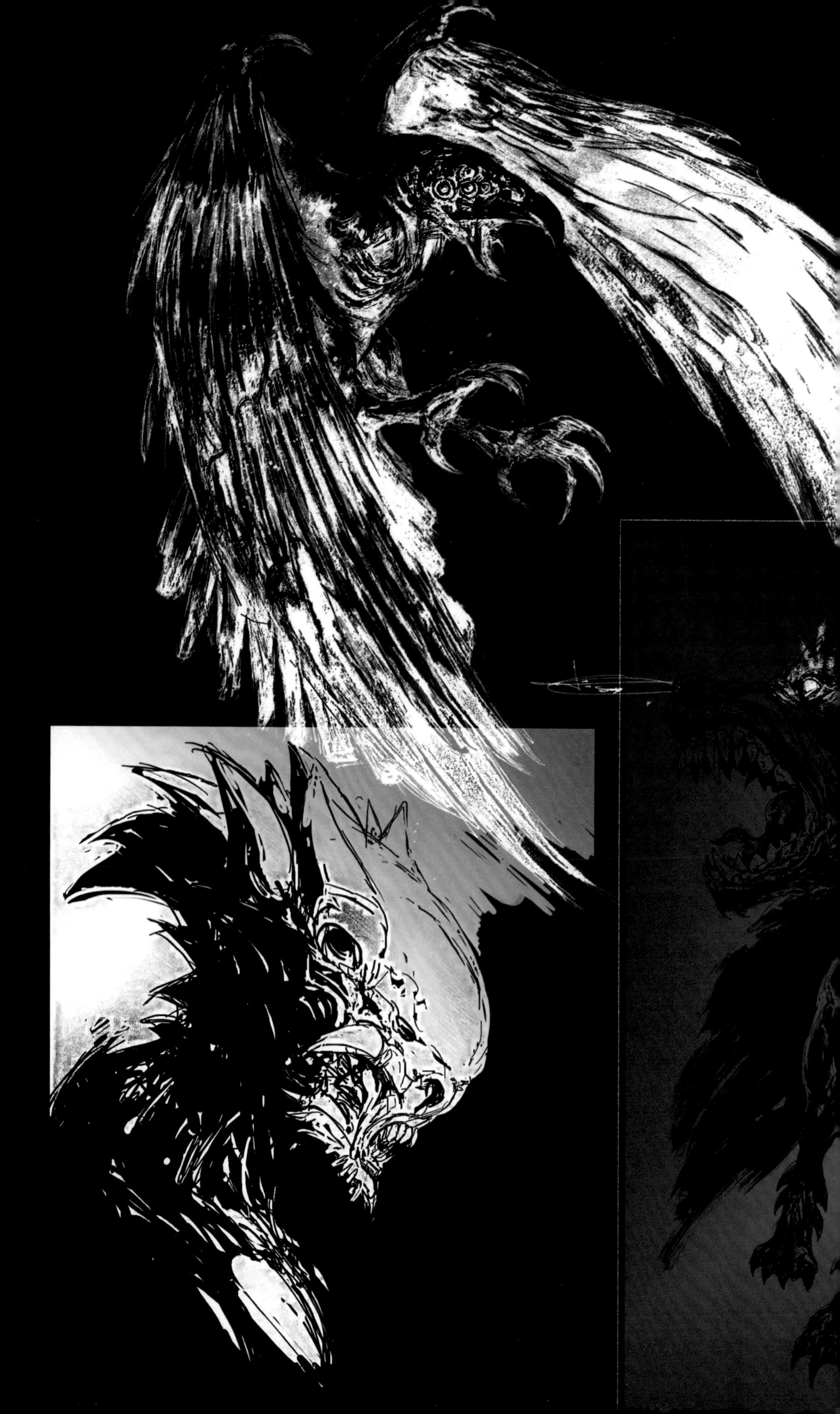

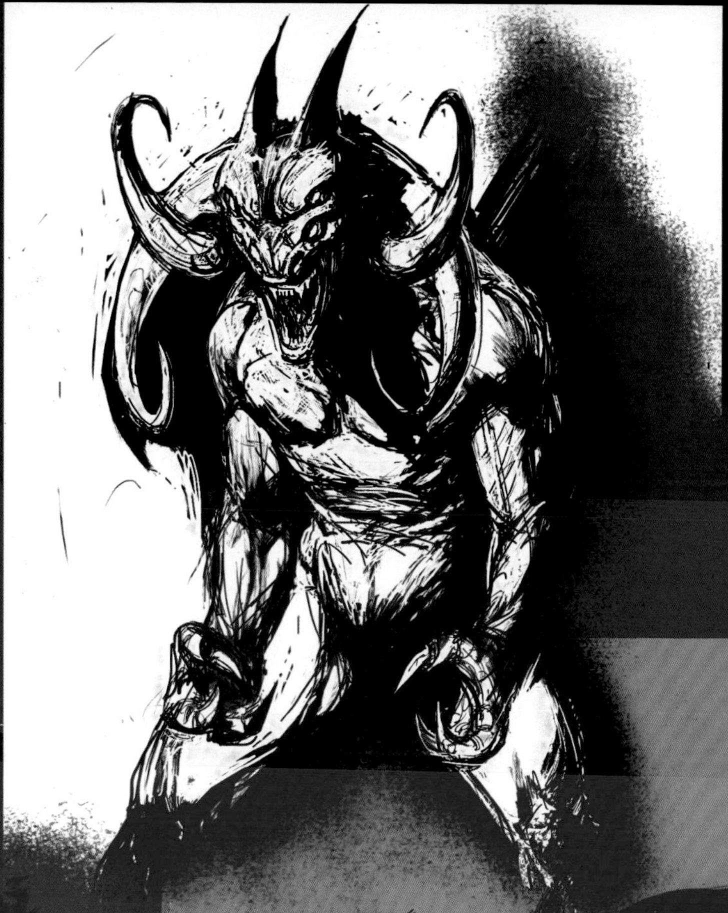

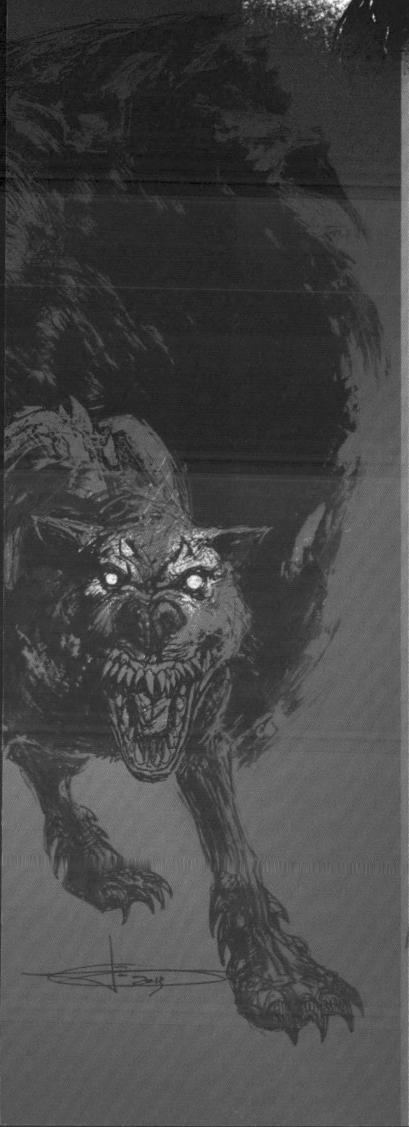

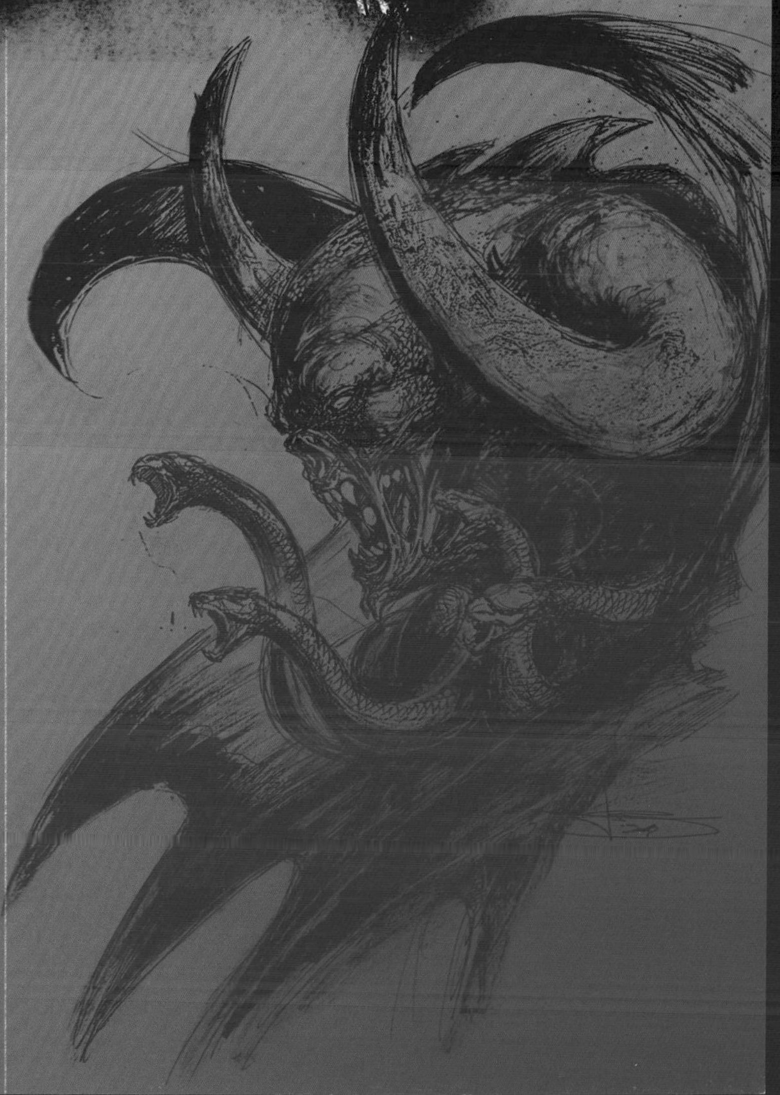

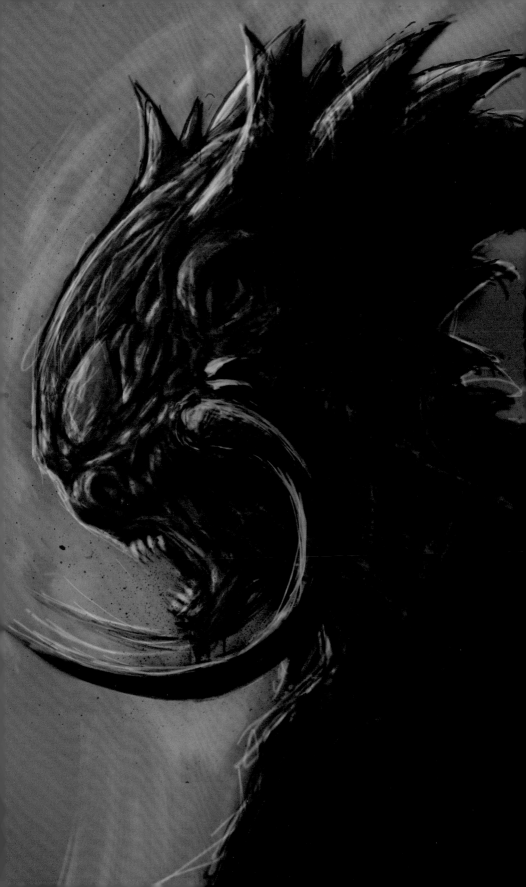

CHARACTER
SKETCHES

BECKETT

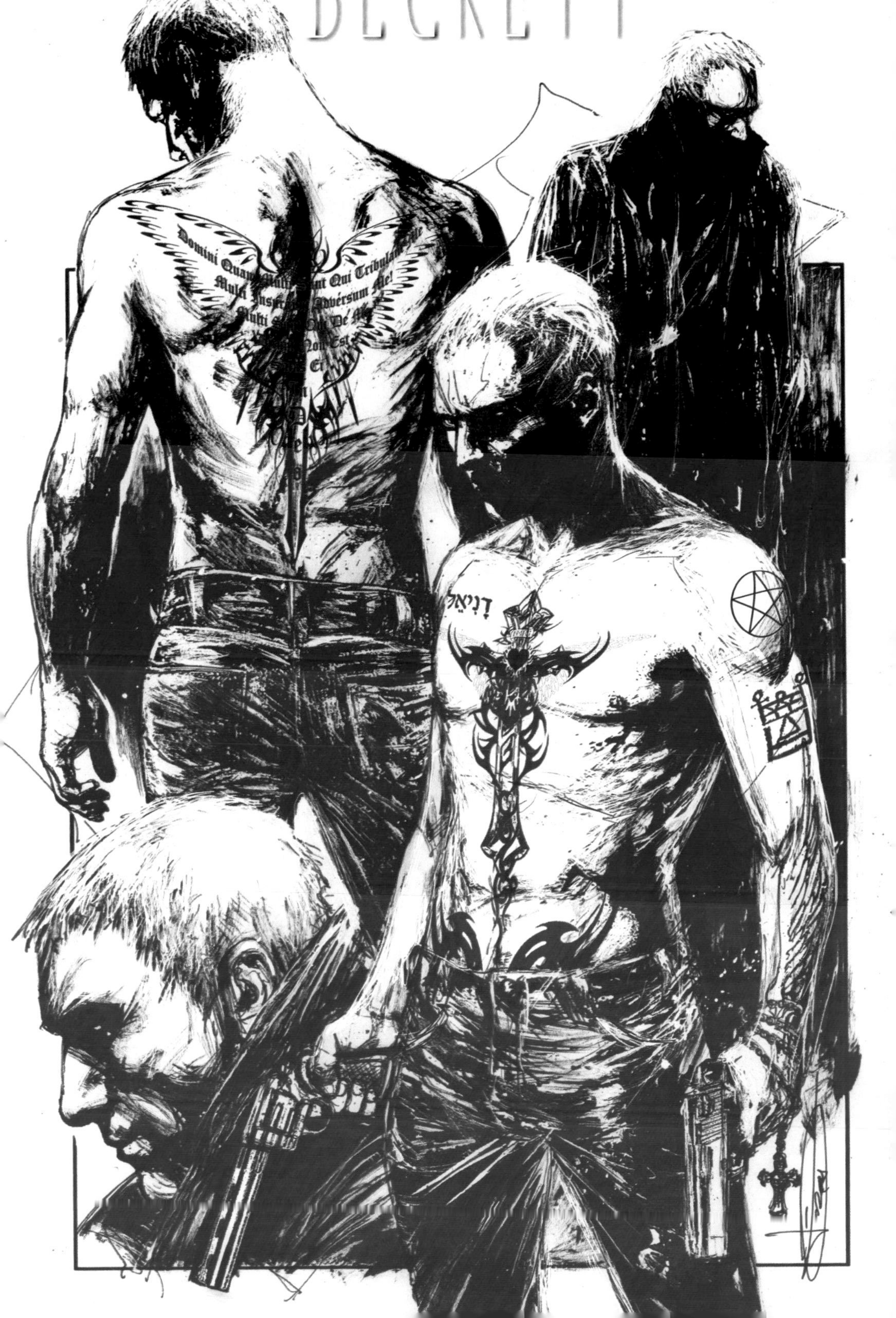

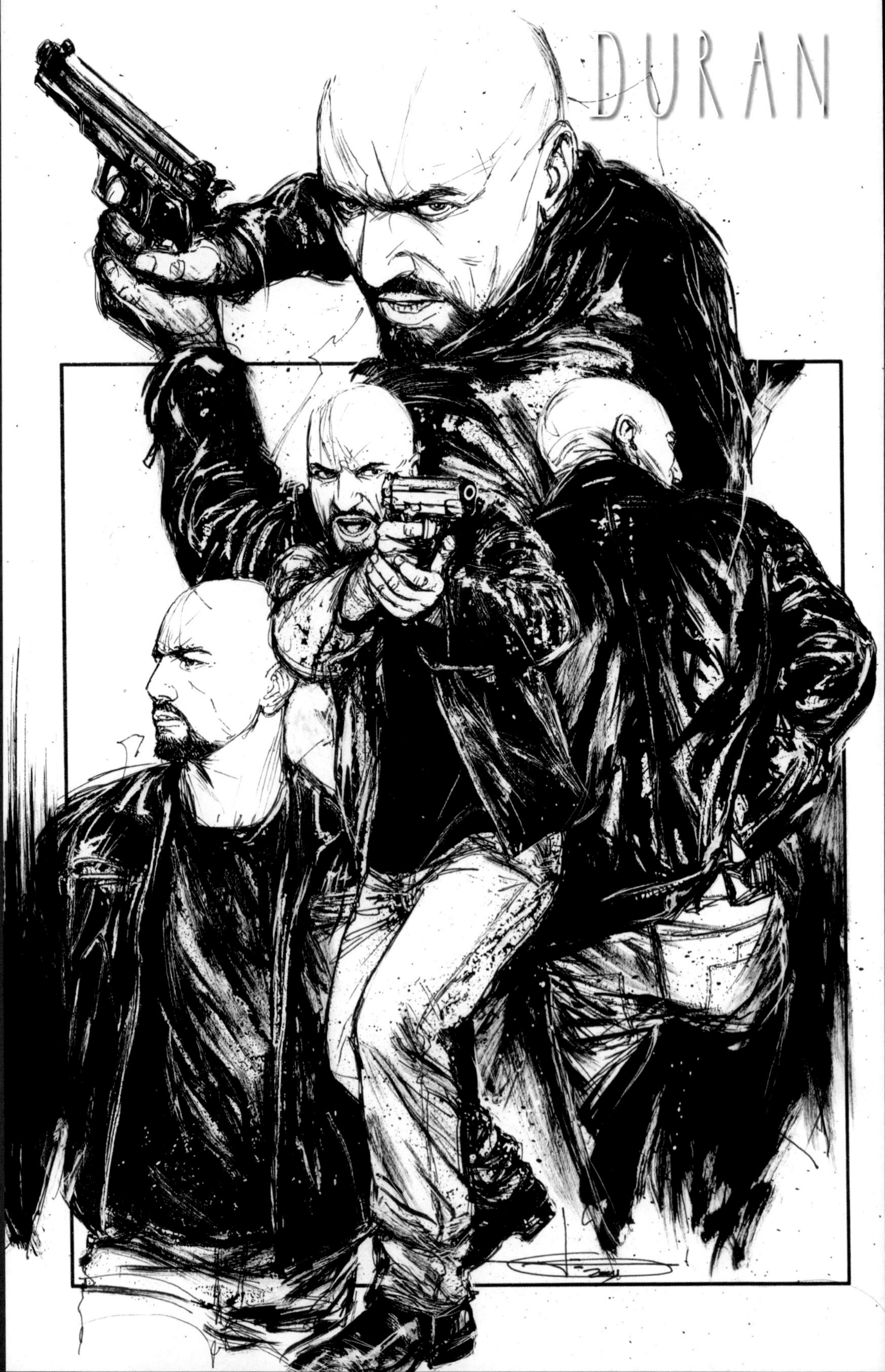
DURAN

FTH LEONE

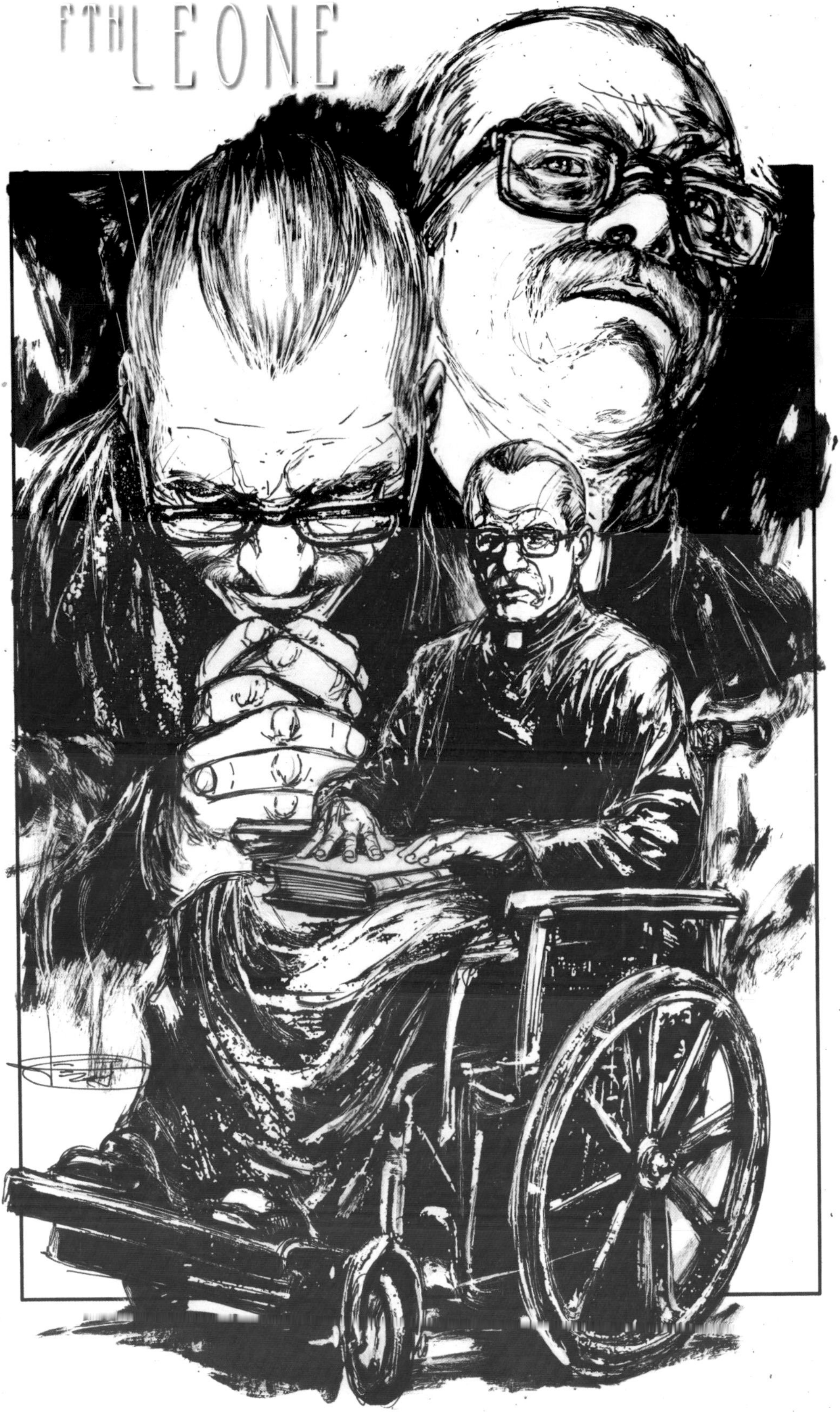

KING LEO

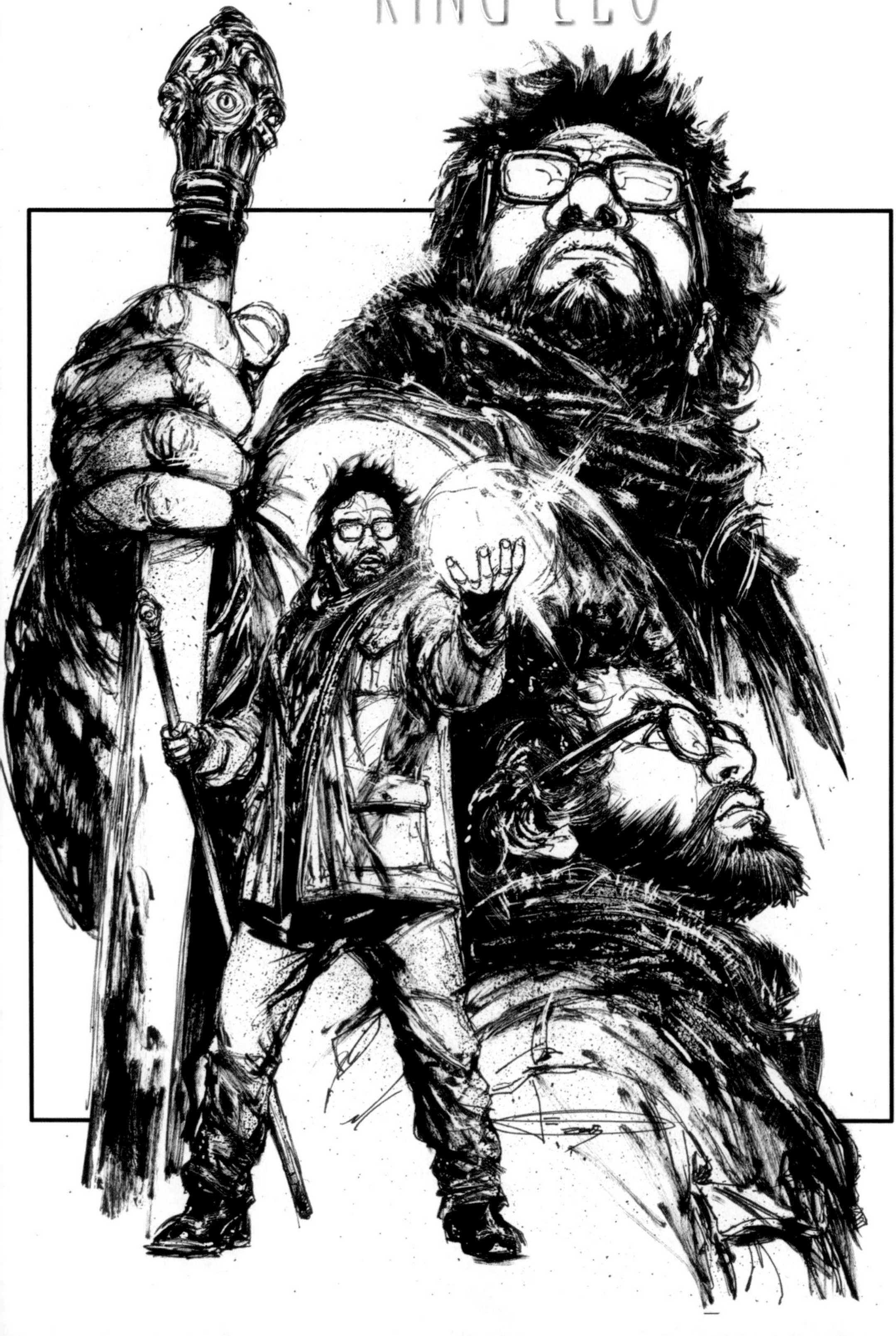

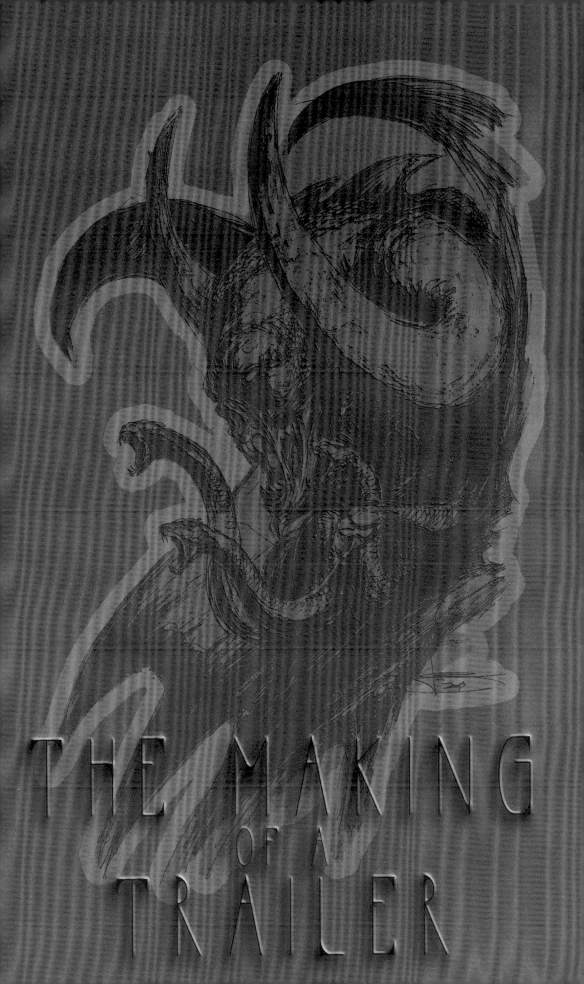

THE MAKING
OF A
TRAILER

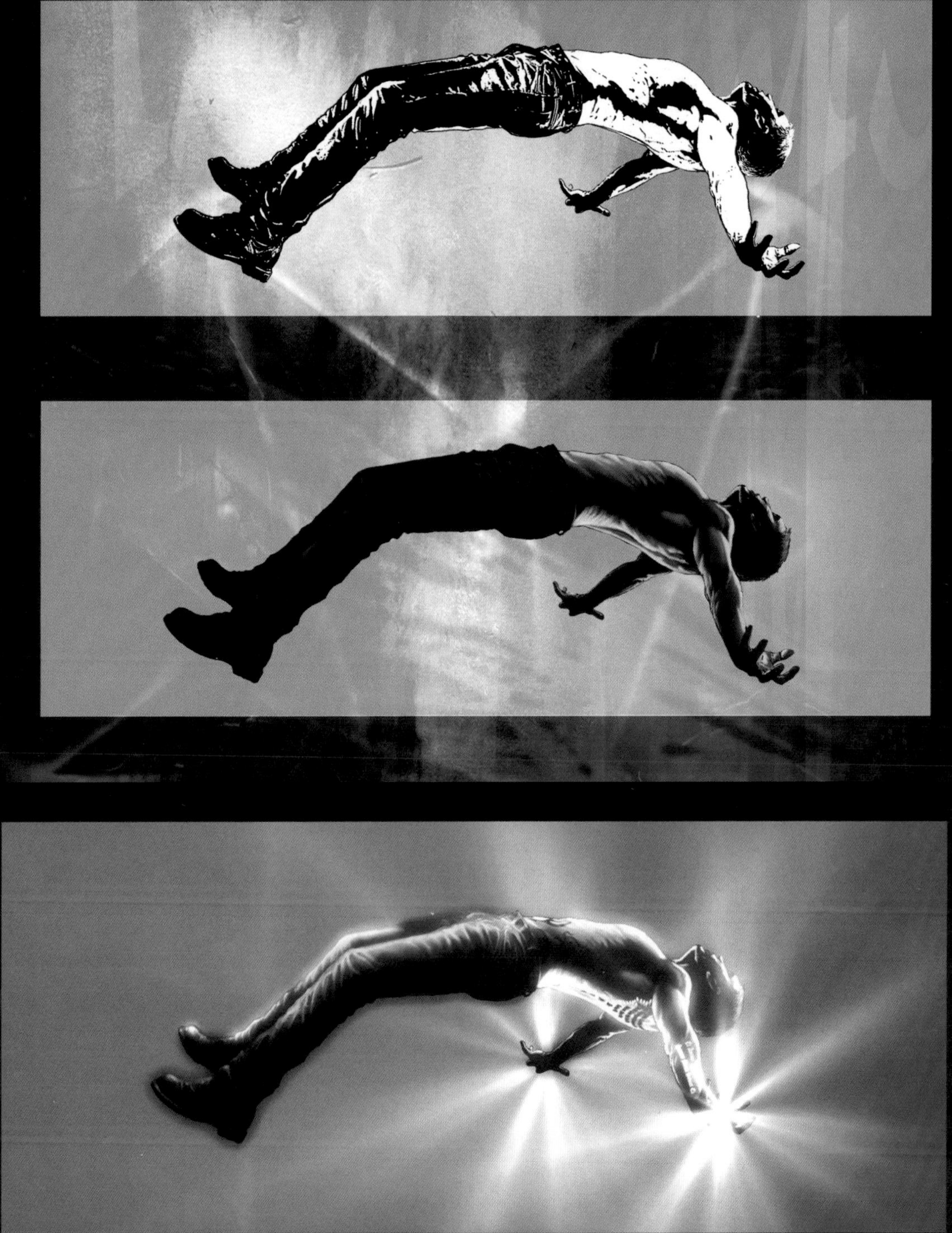

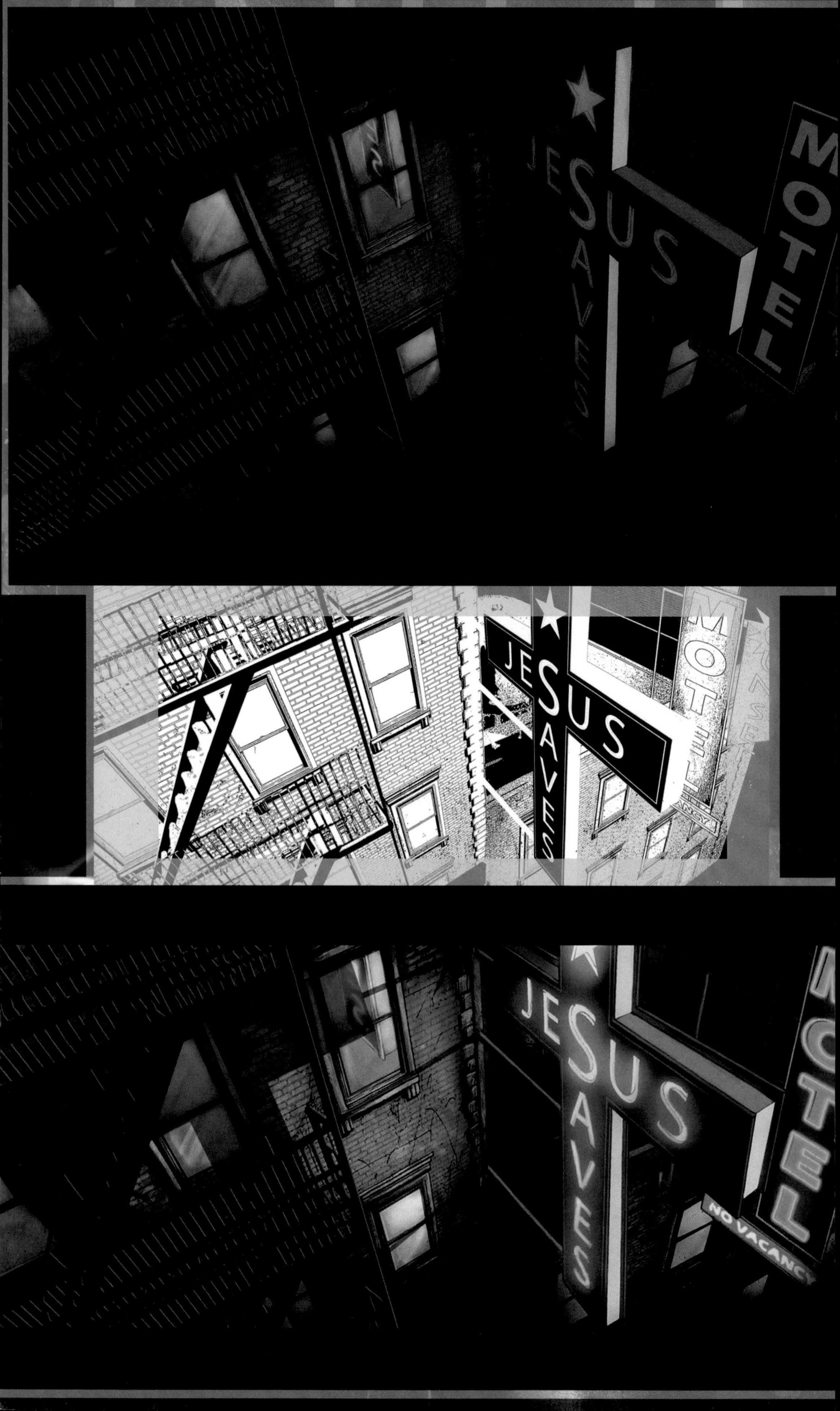
JESUS
SAVES
MOTEL

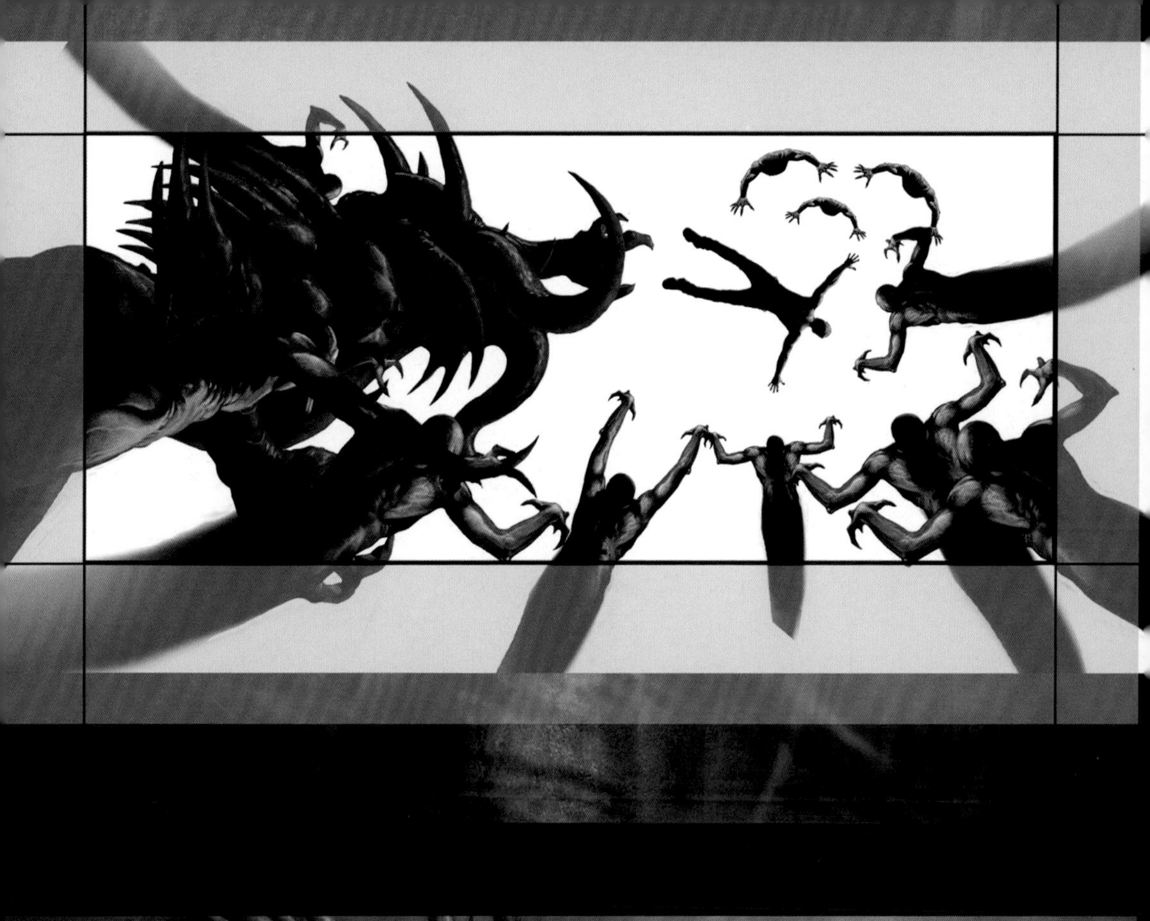

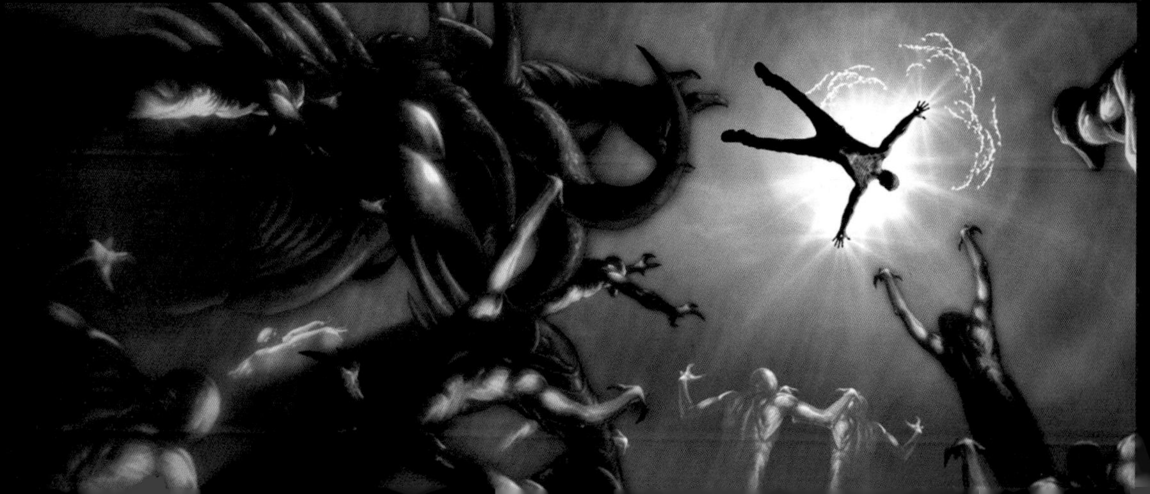

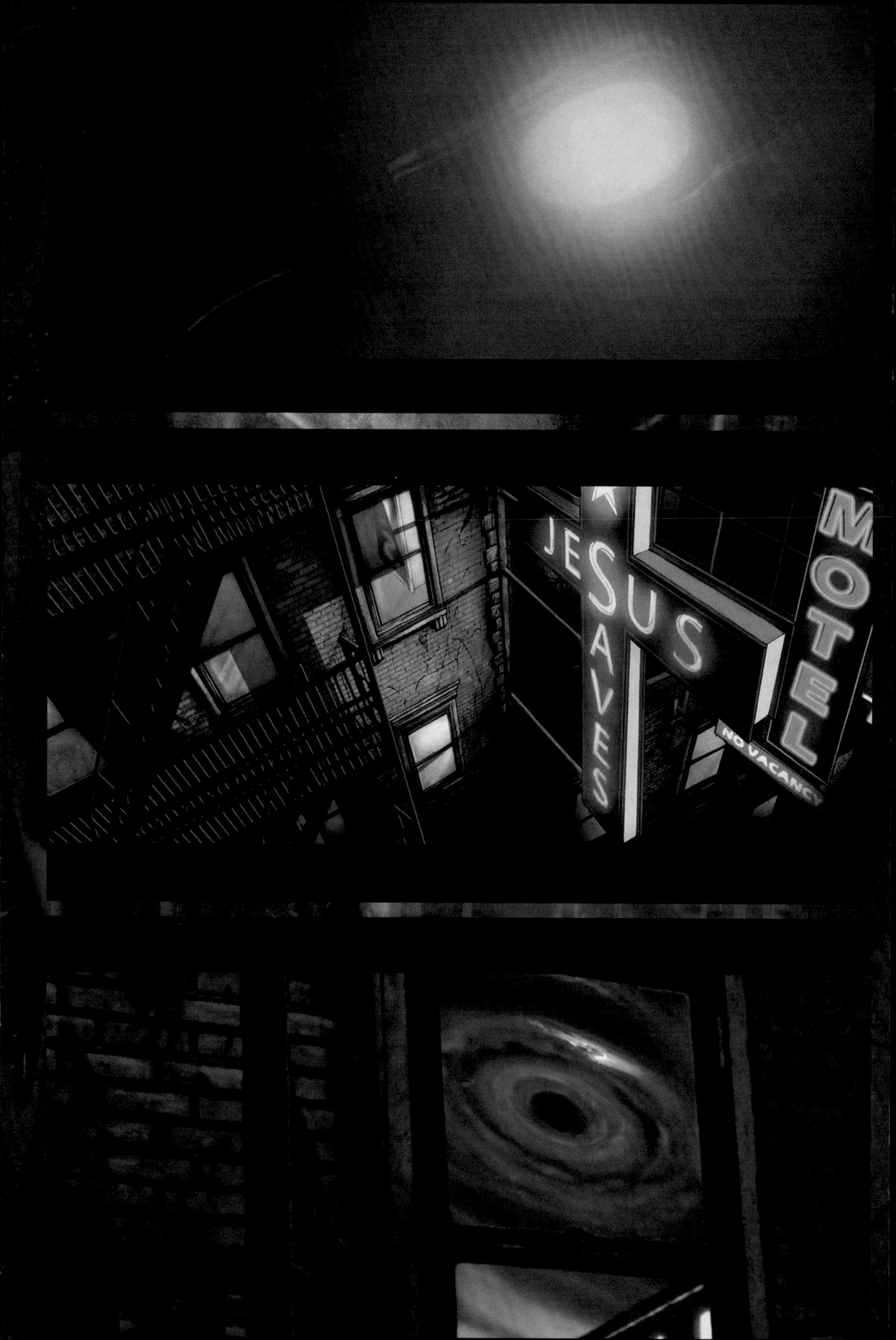
JESUS
SAVES
MOTEL
NO VACANC

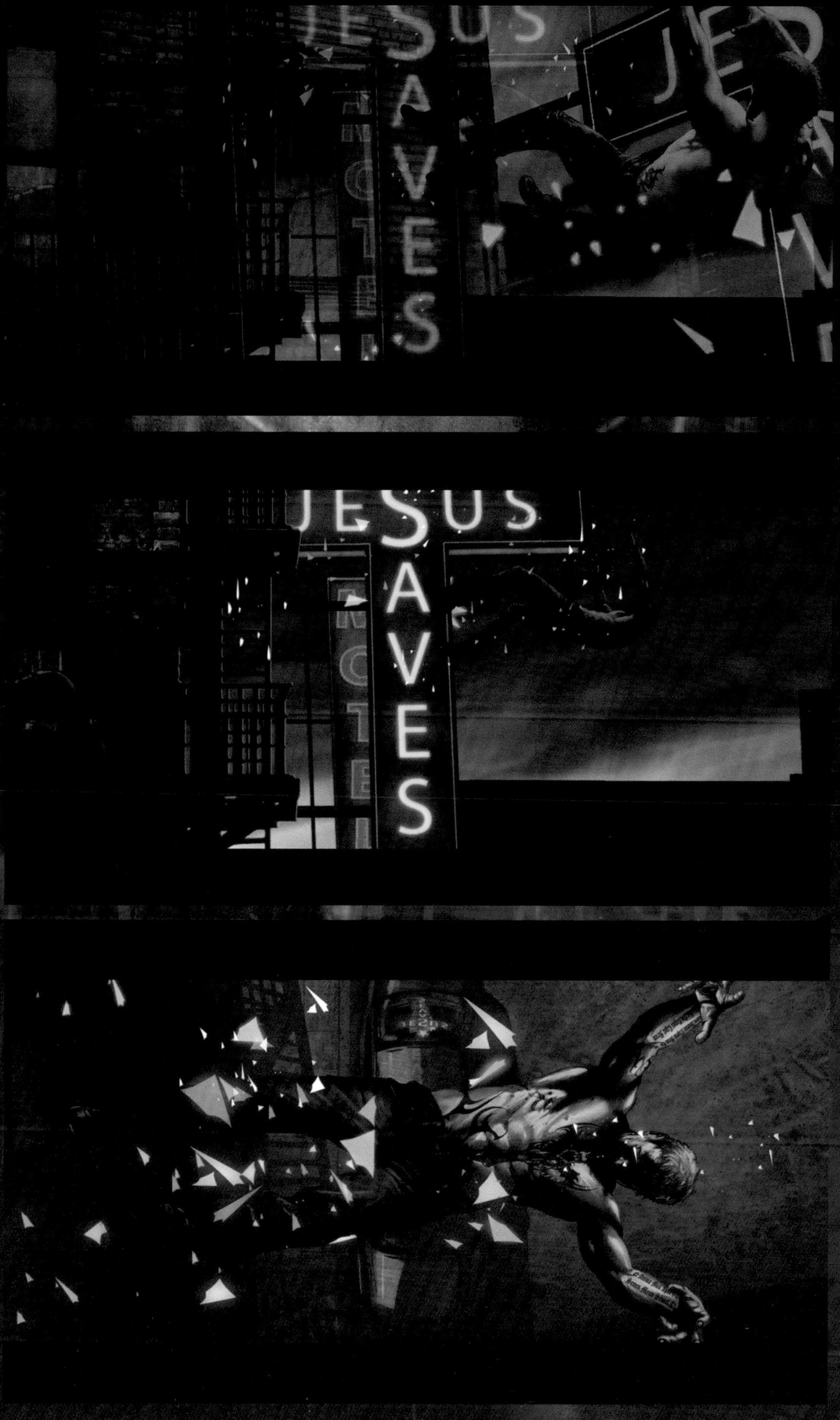
JESUS
SAVES
JESUS
SAVES

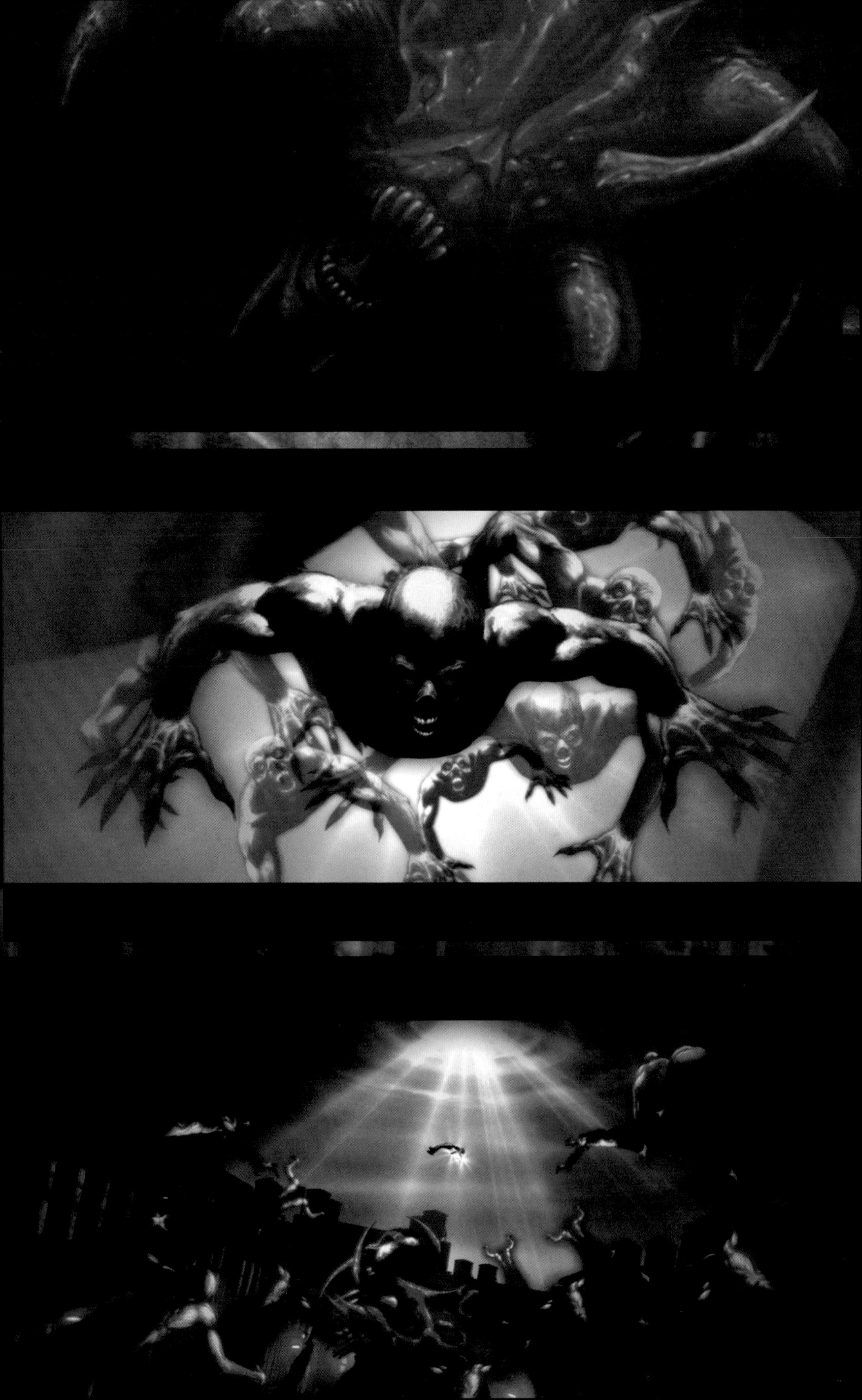

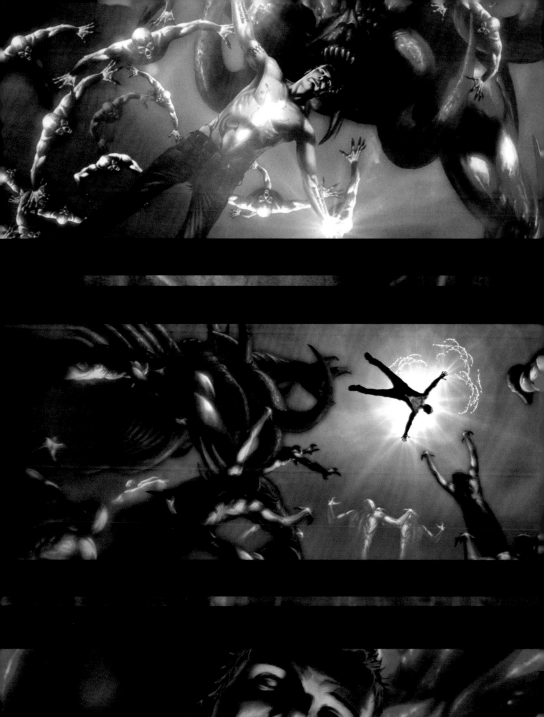

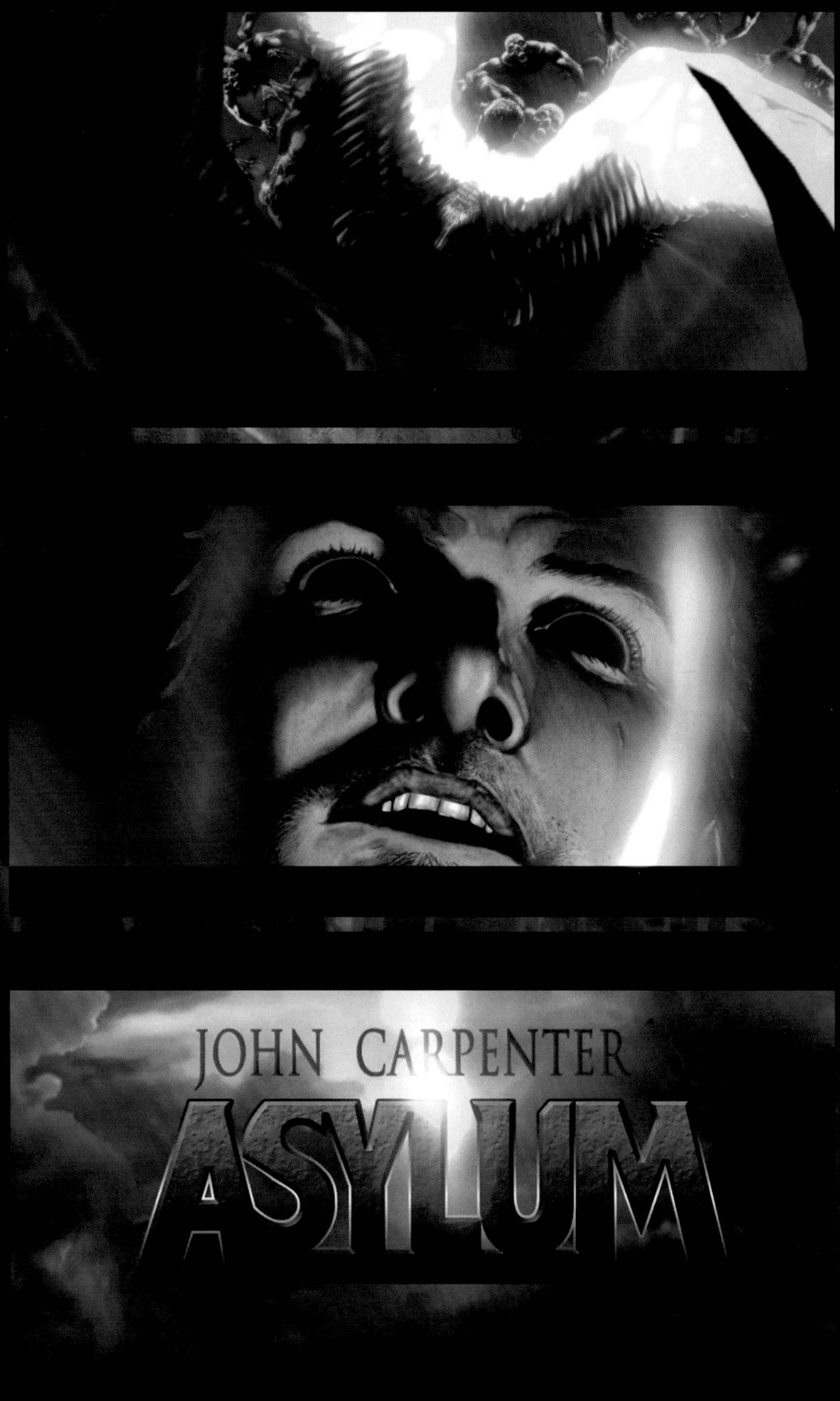
JOHN CARPENTER
ASYLUM

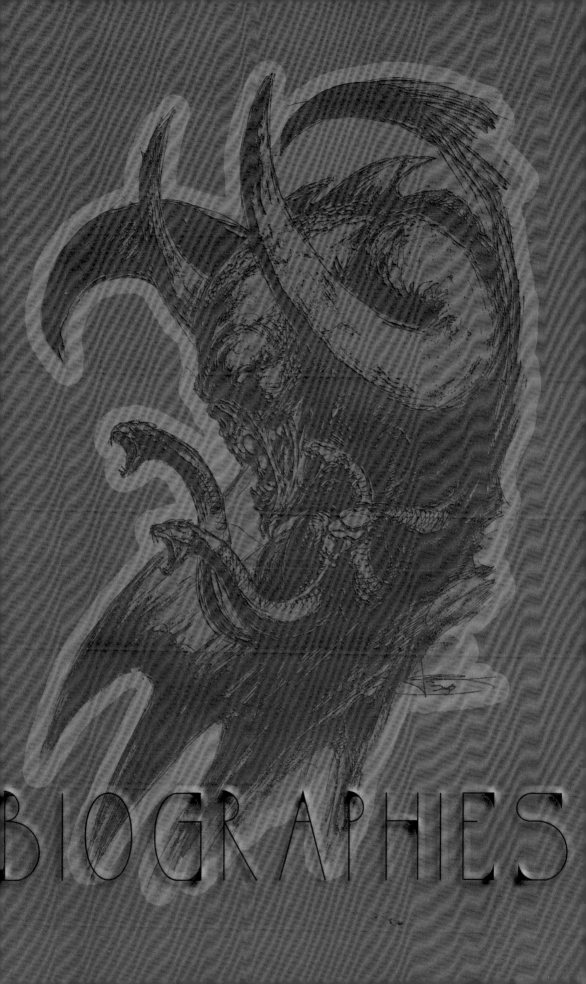

BIOGRAPHIES

John Carpenter

Co-Creator

Director…writer…composer…and now. comic book creator. From the man who brought you **Halloween. The Thing** and **Escape From New York** comes a new comic book. **John Carpenter's Asylum**.

Carpenter's breakthrough film was **Halloween.** the seminal horror movie. that made Michael Myers the best known boogey man in modern times. It was the most profitable independent movie of its day and launched the genre of the teen slasher film.

His movie. **The Thing.** remains a space alien classic which opened new frontiers in creature effects and suspense. while **Escape From New York** introduced the world to the iconic character of Snake Plissken. who along with **They Live's** John Nada. epitomizes American cool.

With this step into the comic book world. John Carpenter brings it all to the serial world he's loved since childhood. Supernatural horror with that twist of fate that only flawed mankind can provide.

Artist, writer, film producer and president of Storm King Productions.

With a background in art, photography and animation, Sandy King's filmmaking career has included working with John Cassavetes, Francis Ford Coppola, Michael Mann, Walter Hill, John Hughs and John Carpenter.

She has produced films ranging from public service announcements on Hunger Awareness to a documentary on astronaut/teacher Christa McAuliffe, and major theatrical hits like John Carpenter's Vampires. From working underwater with sharks in the Bahamas to converting 55 acres of New Mexican desert into the vast red planet of Mars, new challenges interest and excite her. The world of comic books is no exception. It allows her to bring her art and story telling experience to a new discipline with an expanded group of collaborators.

King also was a writer on the Harvey Award-nominated anthology comic, Womanthology: Space.

She is married to director, John Carpenter and lives in Hollywood, California.

THOMAS IAN GRIFFITH   Co-creator

Thomas Ian Griffith began his career as an actor on Broadway and in regional theatre. He moved to Los Angeles where he starred in numerous TV and feature films, including "John Carpenter's Vampires", where he had the privilege of working with John Carpenter. His desire to continue to work with the horror master led to the creation of "Asylum". As a writer, Griffith has several feature films to his credit and is a staff writer on the television series, "Grimm". He currently resides in Los Angeles with his wife, actress Mary Page Keller.

BRUCE JONES   Writer

BRUCE JONES started his career as an illustrator after attending the Fine Arts program at KU in Lawrence. He published artwork in several men's magazines as well as Warren's EERIE and CREEPY before becoming a full-time writer with the famous Bernie Wrightson illustrated story, JENIFER, which was made into an hour-long episode of MASTERS OF HORROR for Showtime.
Bruce went on to write KA-ZAR THE SAVAGE and CONAN before his company, Bruce Jones Associates, went to Pacific Comics in the 80's to produce the now iconic TWISTED TALES, ALIEN WORLDS, and SOMERSET HOLMES. He also wrote and drew several stories for artist and publisher Richard Corben while pursuing a career as a screenwriter and a novelist in Hollywood. He was staff writer along with April Campbell Jones, his partner, for a season on THE HITCHHIKER for HBO.
In the early 2000's he was the writer for the popular Marvel comic book, THE HULK, taking it to new heights of popularity. After the success of THE HULK he spent some time as DC comics, writing, among other things, NIGHTWING, BATMAN, and numerous other DC Universe characters.
Bruce Jones is also the author of twelve novels including (under the pseudonym Bruce Elliot) the bestselling STILL LIFE, plus numerous screenplays, teleplays and graphic novels, including ARENA, which he wrote and illustrated for Marvel. Jones won the Upcoming Author of the Year award from the Bertelsman Book Club. Recently he has gotten into ebook publishing with Bruce Jones Associates, Inc. as packager, and has penned four new books in that format, including SHIMMER, THE DEADENDERS, THE TARN, and his second collection of short stories, SOMETHING WAITS.
He lives with his wife, novelist and screenwriter April Campbell Jones, and their dogs Pete and Lily. The Joneses spend their time in the ethers between Los Angeles and the Midwest

.

TRENT OLSEN

Having grown up surrounded by the film industry, Trent Olsen opted for the writerly life. Although a departure from screenwriting, Trent excitedly dove headlong into his primary life passion… comic books. Influenced and inspired by his 30,000 book collection, Trent happily tackles the world of John Carpenter's Asylum with sick glee – gladly referring to himself as a "writer of wrongs." This is his first comic credit and most certainly not his

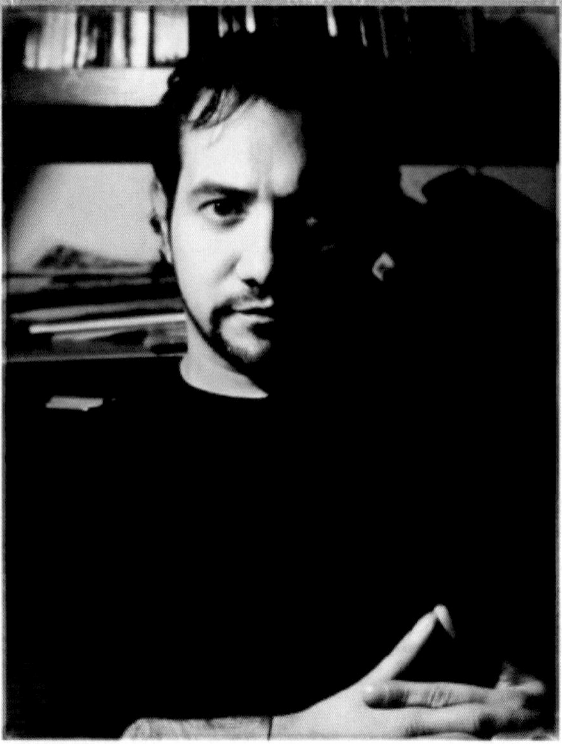

LEONARDO MANCO   Comic book Artist

Appearing at his first ever European convention, Leonardo Manco is an Argentine comic book artist, who has a somewhat unique dark and gritty style. Perhaps best known for his work on Vertigo's Hellblazer title, he first started out in mainstream comics back in the mid 1990's, doing most of his work for Marvel and DC. His run on Hellblazer was a long one, and many consider him to have been 'THE HELLBLAZER ARTIST'. He practically illustrated all of Mike Carey's long run, and stuck with the book through Denise Mina's and Andy Diggle's runs. Books that he has worked on include: Marvel Doom, Deathlok, War Machine, Otherworld War, Druid, Werewolf by Night, Hellstrom, etc. DC/Vertigo: Hellblazer, Batman Gotham Knights, All Star Western, etc.

BOOM: 28 Days Later, Hellraiser, etc.

COVERS: Lots of covers for varous titles. At the moment, Leo is producing the visually stunning artwork for the Storm King Comics adaption of John Carpenter's Asylum.

JANICE CHIANG   Letterer

Janice Chiang is a traditional and digital letter artist. All of her digital fonts were created by Janice based on her hand lettering styles. She began in the early '70's at Neal Adams Continuity Studios, taught hand lettering skills by her mentor Larry Hama and Ralph Reese and learned production values at the Marvel Bullpen. Her reentry to the industry in 1980 marked a productive period of output which included work with Marvel, DC Comics,First Comics, Tundra, Harvey Comics, Acclaim Comics, Disney Adventures, Dark Horse Comics, and other major comic publishers.

Titles Chiang has been associated with include Transformers, Visionaries, Rom, Conan the Barbarian (1982–1990), Alpha Flight(1987–1994),Iron Man (1987–1990), Ghost Rider vol. 2 (1990–1996), What If? (1990–1995), Spider-Girl, and Impulse (1999–2002).

Outside of the superhero genre, Chiang has worked on manga titles for CMX/Wildstorm, Del Rey, and TokyoPop. Presently, she is working on the English translated The Smurfs graphic novels and other Peyot series, hand lettering the Spider-Man series published byKing Features.

A recent graphic Chiang lettered is THE SHADOW HERO byGene Luen Yang and Sonny Liew which debuted in third place on the NYTimes best seller list. Chiang lives upstate New York with her husband, Danny Louie.

KINSUN LOH   Colorist

Malaysian born artist, Kinsun Loh, has colored books for Top Cow, DC, and Image comics. He teamed up with Leonardo Manco on the book **Driver for the Dead** and has worked as a digital artist within the video game industry.

Afterword

Writing is a solitary process but the creation of a comic book, much like the making of a movie, is a collaborative effort.

The click of the computer keys still echoes through the darkness, yet around the globe, our colleagues labor virtually side by side with us and we feel their collective spirit.   Inspiration hits in the Hollywood Hills and starts its travels across the page in the form of an idea which moves to Buenos Aires, Argentina via Skype and a conversation with artist, Leo Manco. More ideas flow and a story becomes substance as story beats become sketches. Sketches become finished panels and pages.

The comic book is being born.

As the pictures give life to the story, the words are refined to match the power of the images. A new dynamic emerges on the page. In Malaysia, at the hands of Kinsun Loh, colors burst forth, refined, finalized. In New York, Janice Chiang, the letter artist, completes the process bringing full life to the page, giving it its voice, its words.

Page after page the dance continues.

This is our first comic book. We come from movies—from writing, production, post-production. The process is similar, but the art form itself is totally different. Make no mistake about it: Comics are an art form. Along with movies, blues and rock and roll, they are a uniquely American art form.

First and foremost, cinema and comics are storytelling. We are privileged to tell our stories in both of these great American traditions.

John Carpenter and Sandy King